D1590789

# LISTENING TO STANLEY KUBRICK

## The Music in His Films

Christine Lee Gengaro

THE SCARECROW PRESS, INC.
*Lanham • Toronto • Plymouth, UK*
2013

Published by Scarecrow Press, Inc.
A wholly owned subsidiary of The Rowman & Littlefield Publishing Group, Inc.
4501 Forbes Boulevard, Suite 200, Lanham, Maryland 20706
www.rowman.com

10 Thornbury Road, Plymouth PL6 7PP, United Kingdom

British Library Cataloguing in Publication Information Available

**Library of Congress Cataloging-in-Publication Data**

Gengaro, Christine Lee.
   Listening to Stanley Kubrick : the music in his films / Christine Lee Gengaro.
      p. cm.
   Includes bibliographical references and index.
   ISBN 978-0-8108-8564-6 (cloth : alk. paper) — ISBN 978-0-8108-8565-3
(ebook)
   1. Kubrick, Stanley—Criticism and interpretation. 2. Motion picture
music—History and criticism. I. Title.
   ML2075.G46 2013
   781.5'42—dc23
                                                                2012027850

# Contents

Acknowledgments   v

Introduction   vii

1. Early Projects: Shorts and Early Features   1

2. Love Themes, Leitmotifs, and Pop Music:
*Spartacus, Lolita, Dr. Strangelove,* and *Full Metal Jacket*   33

3. The Music of the Spheres: *2001: A Space Odyssey*   69

4. "It Was Lovely Music That Came to My Aid":
*A Clockwork Orange*   103

5. "I Was Lucky Enough to Have Superb Material to
Work With": *Barry Lyndon*   147

6. Midnight, the Stars, and You: *The Shining*   179

7. Kubrick's Final Word: *Eyes Wide Shut*   219

Appendix A: Films and Their Source Material   257

Appendix B: Film Synopses   259

Appendix C: Soundtracks and Track Lists   267

Bibliography   287

Index   297

About the Author   305

# Acknowledgments

THIS BOOK COULD NOT HAVE BEEN WRITTEN without the help and coopera-
tion of many parties. Several archives and libraries were kind enough to
allow me access to their collections. These include the Margaret Herrick
Library Department of Special Collections, which houses archives for
the Academy of Motion Pictures of Arts and Sciences, and the American
Heritage Center at the University of Wyoming. I offer special thanks to
the Stanley Kubrick Film Archive, LLC, Warner Bros., and University of
the Arts London for permission to use their materials. I am grateful also
to the Anthony Burgess Foundation and Burgess experts all over world for
allowing me a forum for my work on *A Clockwork Orange*.

Special thanks must be given to Jan Harlan, who offered time and
expertise in conjunction with this project. Gerald Fried shared his recol-
lections with me and kindly gave his permission for the use of his scores
for Kubrick's early films. Jocelyn Pook granted me an interview and generously answered any and all questions about her participation in *Eyes Wide
Shut*. Friend and colleague Jon Burlingame deserves special thanks for immediately and unfailingly lending me his unique expertise in film music.
His liner notes to the 2007 Intrada CD of Alex North's lost score were
particularly helpful in the completion of chapter 3, and his own interview
with Jocelyn Pook enhanced the final chapter. These wonderful people are
in no way responsible for any inaccuracies in the book that may remain.

I am indebted to far too many friends to name, but I wish to recognize a few. Mike deHilster and Dr. Vanessa Rogers read through many
versions of this manuscript and offered suggestions for its improvement.
Fellow musicologist and film music specialist Katherine McQuiston has

generously shared her time and her expertise on the subject of Kubrick and music. I would also like to give special thanks to Helen Moulinous and Daniel Stent, Andrea Moore, David Aguilar, Cael Marcus Edwards, and Thomas Witwer for their helpful comments. Finally, I must thank my mother, Geri, my father, Frank, and my sister, Michelle, for their unceasing love and support. Special recognition must go to my father for supplying me with classical music and soundtrack LPs in my formative years, for sharing his musical expertise on doo-wop for chapter 7, and for giving me my first copy of *A Clockwork Orange*, thereby starting this whole thing.

# *Introduction*

MUSIC IN FILM IS POWERFUL. It enhances emotion, signals danger, accompanies epiphany, and depicts movement. It forms the aural element of an invented world, contributing to its authenticity and its vitality. Those directors who truly understand the power of music will create films that use it wisely and well. Stanley Kubrick is one of a handful of directors whose musical choices over the course of his career demonstrated a keen understanding of what music could bring to a film, and through almost fifty years and more than a dozen film projects, Kubrick's musical sensibilities developed and became finely tuned. The music in his films displays insight, inventiveness, and vision. Furthermore, Kubrick's musical choices have affected the world outside of his films, influencing cultural consumption of certain pieces of classical music. It seems appropriate then to compile a guide detailing the music in Kubrick's films, both the traditional scores and the preexistent music chosen for the later films. Kubrick's musical journey has often been overshadowed by other aspects of his work—his films' visual look, his meticulous, near-obsessive work habits, his unwillingness to travel or appear in public—but music is a very important element of Kubrick's art, one that needs analysis if it is to be truly appreciated.

Kubrick's use of music is certainly one of the things that have made his films legendary, and we must wonder where his affinity for music originated. Indeed, we wonder what combination of influences created all aspects of Kubrick's filmmaking genius. Many biographers and Kubrick scholars have spent much time and many pages searching Kubrick's past for clues to his greatness, for indicators in his childhood and young adulthood that would signal the development of a genuinely singular talent. Each book (including this one) dutifully explains similar aspects of Kubrick's origin story. Stanley Kubrick was born in the Bronx in 1928. As a boy, he didn't care much for school. He loved playing chess, and he had an eye for photography. All biographies mention his supportive parents Jacques and Gertrude, and his little sister, Barbara. Special mention is usually made of the strong intellectual relationship Kubrick had with his father, a doctor. It was his father who both introduced him to chess and gave him his first camera. Kubrick's parents allowed Stanley the academic freedom to pursue his own projects, and they trusted him enough to let him learn on his own. One of these passions, photography, started Kubrick on a career path while he was still a teenager.

Another of Kubrick's early passions, chess, might have sent him down a different path. He was a good player, hustling games for money as a young man, but he quickly discovered that chess hustler is not a good career, although his skill at the game seems to many to be one of those important indicators of Kubrick's future success. Interviewer Michel Ciment stated that Kubrick's passion for chess taught him the art of strategy, which helped his storytelling. When asked if chess influenced his filmmaking, Kubrick spoke of the connection between chess and decision making, especially in the way it allows one to avoid the impulsive decision and deliberate the alternatives patiently. No one would argue that Stanley Kubrick wasn't deliberate in his decision making in his films. As he got older, and his films got further and further apart, this deliberation was quite long indeed.

Music too was a part of Kubrick's formative years, although less important to him than chess or photography. He was the drummer for his high school jazz band, and he was a great lover of all genres of music, even film scores. One score in particular stands out as a great influence, and indeed Kubrick's admiration of this score has been mentioned by a number of biographers. According to childhood friend Alex Singer, Kubrick was so taken with the music of *Alexander Nevksy* that after seeing the film as a young man, he purchased the soundtrack album. Showing a tendency toward obsession that would come to be associated with him, he played the record so much and so often that his sister apparently broke it out of frustration.[1] The power of this film score certainly affected him, and the film itself was a landmark.

*Alexander Nevsky* (1938) was directed by Sergei Eisenstein[2] and scored by Sergei Prokofiev.[3] It was Eisenstein's first sound film, and unlike the director's previous, more experimental films, it had a traditional narrative structure. Eisenstein and Prokofiev collaborated in a unique way. Whereas in most films, the editing is completed before the composer finishes his work, and the music is cut to the edits made by the director, with *Alexander Nevsky*, Eisenstein and Prokofiev were both involved in the editing process. Eisenstein could make cuts that would accommodate Prokofiev's music or ask for the composer to alter the music for a particular shot. The result is a musical score that effectively evokes the emotions and actions on-screen, but also retains an organic sense of structure that translates well to the concert setting.[4]

Although the scores for Kubrick's first films were produced in the traditional way—after footage was shot and edited, a composer produced new music for the film—the model of Eisenstein and Prokofiev must have stayed in his mind. Kubrick was always very respectful of the music he used in his projects, even—and especially—when that music was not originally intended for his films.

Although chess must have taught Kubrick how to plan things out, photography must have informed the visual look of his films, and love of music allowed Kubrick to develop a sense of respect for the art form, there is no single detail about Kubrick's life that would indicate that he would become a legendary filmmaker. The early biographical details aren't unimportant, yet the role they play in his genius has likely been overstated. Kubrick grew and changed as an artist throughout his life. Each film was a learning experience, and his ideas about how to make films changed as he matured. Since this is a book about the music in Kubrick's films, the films will be our primary source material. The first chapters will explore the music in Kubrick's films up to 1968, while the later chapters explore the films that required more preexistent cues and little to no original music.

The music in Kubrick's films has been given some attention in recent years. In 2002, Gerrit Bodde produced a book in German called *Die Musik in den Filmen von Stanley Kubrick*. In it, Bodde describes what he believes are the two main functions of music in Kubrick's films: informative and interpretive.[5] German composer Bernd Schultheis has made a documentary about the music in Kubrick's films, noting a few recurring musical tropes in these works. Among these tropes are the use of waltzes, marches, electronic music, liturgical music, and fanfares.[6] These sources begin to scratch the surface of what is a fascinating aspect of Kubrick's work, and this book, and others to come, will build on that foundation.

## NOTES

1. Vincent LoBrutto, *Stanley Kubrick: A Biography* (New York: Da Capo Press, 1997), 56.

2. Eisenstein is often associated with the idea of montage in films, specifically with the creation of meaning through the juxtaposition of multiple images. Eisenstein was assisted by fellow director Dmitri Vasilyev in order to make sure the film stayed within the Soviet standards for filmmaking.

3. Prokofiev had been a child prodigy and, interestingly, like Kubrick, a master at chess. He composed his first opera at the age of nine and attempted to compose a symphony at eleven. Early in his career he was fascinated with new music and, again like Kubrick, found the formal aspects of education quite uninteresting. His first public works caused controversy because of their forward-looking harmonies and their use of dissonance.

4. Alexander Walker, *Stanley Kubrick Directs*, expanded ed. (New York: Harcourt Brace Jovanovich, 1972), 13. The most famous cue from the film is the one that accompanies that Battle on the Ice between the Russians of Novgorod and the Teutonic Knights.

5. Bodde names four subheadings under the "Informative" heading: constructive, cumulative, doubling, and delimiting. Under "Interpretive," he lists five functions: stimulating, descriptive, contrapuntal, expressive, and substituting. Gerrit Bodde, *Musik in den Filmen von Stanley Kubrick* (Osnabrück: Der Andere Verlag, 2002), 16.

6. These ideas were collected in an essay for the Kubrick Exhibition that began at the Deutsches Filmmuseum. Bernd Schultheis, "Expanse of Possibilities: Stanley Kubrick's Soundtracks in Notes," *Stanley Kubrick Catalogue*, 2nd ed. (Frankfurt am Main: Deutsches Filmmuseum, 2007), 266–279.

# Chapter One

―――――――――――○―――――――――――

# Early Projects
## Shorts and Early Features

## THE SHORTS

WHEN STANLEY KUBRICK HIT HIS EARLY TWENTIES, he had already been working for *Look* magazine for a few years. He sold a photo to them when he was still in high school and, following that, produced feature photo essays for the magazine with titles like, "Dixieland Jazz Is 'Hot' Again," "Montgomery Clift . . . Glamour Boy in Baggy Pants," and "Kids at a Ball-Game."[1] He was moderately successful with these essays, but after working for the magazine for a while, he began to become interested in filmmaking. In an article about Kubrick called "Quiz Kid," in the photography review the *Camera* from 1949, the interviewer notes, "Stan is also very serious about cinematography, and is about to start filming a sound production written and financed by himself and several friends."[2] It seems as though this might refer to Kubrick's first short film, a newsreel project suggested by high school friend, and later successful television director, Alex Singer.

Newsreels, which had been very popular before television, were a dying species as the fifties approached, but still, series like Time Inc.'s *The March of Time* and Pathé News produced shorts for movie theaters until 1951 and 1956, respectively.[3] Kubrick's subject for his first short film was boxing. He had done a feature for *Look* magazine called "Prizefighter" in 1949, and he used both the subject and the idea for that feature—a day in the life of middleweight Walter Cartier—as the basis for the film, which he called *Day of the Fight*.[4] It appeared as part of RKO-Pathé's "This Is America" series, a collection of newsreels that were patriotic features

1

rather than hard news. Another entry in this series was *Sailors All* from 1943, which featured the United States Coast Guard,[5] and "They Fly with the Fleet" from 1951, which follows a cadet in the aviation branch of the United States Navy.[6]

Kubrick handled many of the details of the production including writing, producing, cinematography, and editing, although his work was uncredited for some of these on the title cards. Singer recalled, "He did that sports short as if he were doing *War and Peace*. He was meticulous with everything."[7] Part of the filmmaking process was figuring out what to do about the musical score. Kubrick had a friend from the old neighborhood—a guy he used to play baseball games with when the two were teenagers—who studied music at Juilliard. Kubrick decided to ask his old pal Gerald Fried to write the music for his very first film. Fried hadn't written any scores, but he was willing to try it. The two young men watched lots of films in preparation, discussing the various functions of music in film, but most of their learning came "on the job."

### Synopsis and Score Description for *Day of the Fight*

*Day of the Fight* begins with an exposition about the popularity of boxing. The narration was done by Douglas Edwards, the first television news anchor for CBS. Kubrick had originally considered Montgomery Clift for the narration since they had met on a photo shoot for *Look*, but ultimately chose Edwards for the job.[8] Although this is a feature story, the narration has a seriousness that borders on parody. Because Kubrick had studied newsreels like *The March of Time* so closely, the attitude of the production has a whiff of propaganda about it:

> What is the fascination? What does the fan look for? Competitive sport? Scientific skill? Partly. But mostly he seeks action. Toe to toe body contact. Physical violence. The triumph of force over force. The primitive, vicarious, visceral thrill of seeing one animal overcome another.

Kubrick biographer Vincent LoBrutto senses a hint of film noir in the words and cadences of Edwards's voiceover: "The narration is crisp and lean, like that of a forties detective novel. . . .The text poses as documentary fact, but it is filled with noir poetry."[9] LoBrutto goes on to talk about the noir-ish lighting, the use of shadows, the kinds of visual aspects of filming that Kubrick would revisit in *The Killing* and *Killer's Kiss*, although at the beginning of the film and at the very end, the music does not support the noir angle. The central musical cue for the film came to be called, on later compilations, "March of the Gloved Gladiators." True to its name, it is a lively, brass-heavy fanfare. Just as Kubrick had studied *The March of Time* and other news films to mimic their visual and narrative structure, Fried must have studied the shorts to absorb the musical language of the newsreels. He was also inspired by a distant fanfare in an orchestral work from turn-of-the-century French composer Claude Debussy.[10] The main theme of the cue is this fanfare, played by woodwinds and brass. This line is the flute part, easily heard, while the rest of the orchestra fills it out with harmony:

Example 1.1.   March of the Gloved Gladiators. Main theme.

Unfortunately, this cue was replaced by a similar piece—not by Fried—when the short film went into franchise. Most existing versions of the film feature this other music. When asked about this change, Fried had no explanation: "Somebody, for some reason, replaced the original music."[11] The "Gloved Gladiators" theme exists in its entirety on two compilation albums (see appendix C), so one can still enjoy Fried's triumphant fanfare.

The uncredited driving march that accompanies the title cards continues throughout the first two minutes of the film, during Kubrick's exposition on boxing and its popularity. The segment ends with a montage of knockouts from various fights that are accompanied with rat-a-tat brass and worried tremolos. When the narrator asks, at about two minutes in, "But why do they do it? The fighters," the music changes. The underscore becomes sweeter, with a melody in the strings as Kubrick shows us from where—and from what professions—boxers come. But as we return to the gym to see these men from various walks of life train to fight, once again the music becomes more aggressive to match the rhythmic sounds of punching bags and jumping rope. There is something militaristic—even patriotic—in the music here. Once again, the music changes tone as Kubrick cuts to footage of boxing historian Nathaniel Fleischer, who is flipping through a book about boxing.[12] The smooth descending melody once again relies on the strings and the woodwinds for a sweeter sound. There is hardly a need for percussive underscore to accompany Mr. Fleischer's turning of pages. When Fleischer stops on a particular page, the narrator says, "Let's take one name out of the book at random. Say, Walter Cartier. What would his story be like?"

Now that we have reached the focal point of the story, Fried's music enters the soundtrack and reflects the change. The tone darkens considerably as Kubrick shows footage of New York City while the narrator explains that during the day of a big fight, waiting is the hardest part. Fried has the low woodwinds pulse a relentless moderate beat over which the higher woodwinds play slightly dissonant and ominous-sounding chords.[13] The low brass adds to this dark mood, which culminates as Walter and his twin brother Vincent take communion at an early mass on the day of the fight. The narrator intones: "It's important for him to get holy communion in case something should go wrong tonight." Fried's music shows hints of doubt, melancholy, and darkness. Boxing is a dangerous sport, he seems to be telling us, but of course, that is what makes it so intriguing to its audience. The tone of the *Look* feature on Cartier struck a similar mood. One caption read: "Boxing's atmosphere discourages gaiety and lightheartedness. The scenes are grim, filled with slashing blows of leather on flesh."

Kubrick found ways to bring contrast into the film, as did Fried. In an interlude, Vincent makes breakfast for Walter. The short cue is in a major key, underscoring the neutral activity of breakfast as the narrator explains that Vincent—who lives out of town—stays with Walter before big fights. Vincent, in addition to being a lawyer, is also Walter's manager. Kubrick seems to want to stress their connection, the sweetness of their relationship, and Walter's gentleness (he is later seen playing with a dog)[14] to bring a sharp contrast to the violence of Walter's day job. This gentle theme is played by the oboe (with harmony provided by the other woodwinds).

Example 1.2.   Gentle theme from Day of the Fight.

As Walter is examined by a physician, the music again takes a darker turn that continues through Walter's lunch at a steakhouse owned by a friend. According to the narrator, the time is four o'clock, and there are still six long hours to the fight. Fried's music becomes a bit more anxious, especially in the sequence where Kubrick shows Walter's "tools of [the] trade": gloves, robe, ice pack, shorts, tape. The cue at the end of this sequence gives way to tense music with a driving, percussive beat in the woodwinds and brass. The music grows to a fever pitch as the narrator explains Walter's necessary transformation as fight time approaches:

> Walter isn't concerned with the hands of the clock now, just his own hands. As he gets ready to walk out there in the arena, in front of the people, Walter is slowly becoming another man. This is the man who cannot lose, who must not lose. The hard movements of his arms and fists are different from what they were an hour ago. They belong to a fierce new person. They're part of the Arena Man: the fighting machine that the crowd outside has paid to see in fifteen minutes.

The pulse of the music at this point has gotten faster, louder, and higher in pitch. But once Walter walks out to enter the ring, Kubrick makes an interesting choice. The underscore disappears, as does the narrator, and the sound of the arena becomes the soundtrack. Because the music has been constant, the ambient noise of the fight draws the audience in. We hear the announcer on the tinny microphone (in typical announcer-speak, he introduces "Walter Car-teer"), the clang of the bell, the cheers and whistles of the crowd, and the sounds of the gloves hitting their targets. The fight becomes real, and the audience experiences it in real time. For the fight itself, Kubrick and Singer both shot from different angles—so as not to lose any footage—and Singer caught Cartier's knockout of his opponent while Kubrick was reloading.[15] As Cartier's opponent Bobby James hits the canvas, Fried's score starts again, cymbals heralding the "Gloved Gladiators" cue—which makes its first and only appearance here, and in truncated form—before the referee has even finished counting to ten. The narration returns for a brief comment to neatly tie things up, and Fried's music ends with a triumphant major chord and crash of the cymbals. Fried led the nineteen musicians well and achieved a tight score for the project. He would go on to score more newsreels for RKO, and indeed his career as a composer for film and television was quite successful thereafter. He continued to work with Stanley Kubrick, scoring the director's first four features.

After the successful completion of *Day of the Fight*, Kubrick went on to do another short for RKO called *The Flying Padre*, this time for the Screenliner series. The score for this film was written by Nathaniel Shilkret, a successful composer and instrumentalist who worked for RKO-Pathé. This short is the story of two days in the life of Father Fred Stadtmueller, a priest who commutes among his eleven parishes in New Mexico by Piper Cub airplane.

## Synopsis and Score Description for *The Flying Padre*

For the opening shot, Kubrick shows a beautiful vista and the skies over what we assume must be Harding County, New Mexico. This is accompanied by the voiceover and Shilkret's pleasant music. Because of the location of Father Stadtmueller's parishes and the population he serves, Shilkret composed a lively opening that echoes some of the Latino-inspired local music. We see footage of Father Stadtmueller flying his plane, the *Spirit of St. Joseph*, both from inside the cockpit, and from the ground. As the Flying Padre goes in for a landing, Kubrick is sure to let the audience hear the sounds of a herd of cattle that must move out of the way for Stadtmueller's descending plane. When Father Stadtmueller lands in Gallegos to perform a funeral mass, the music becomes more solemn, entering into a minor key to accompany the footage of the simple funeral procession. As Father Stadtmueller returns to his main parish in Mosquero for evening devotions, the score brightens up. The accompanying music for his actions on the altar includes heavenly chords on a harp. When a young girl visits the priest after breakfast the next morning, Shilkret features a playful melody with accents on a solo guitar, suggesting folk music. As Father Stadtmueller rushes to fly to a woman fifty miles away with a sick child, the music becomes quick and apprehensive. As he arrives, landing in a field, the music becomes grand, nearly triumphant. He prepares to take mother and child to Tucumcari where an ambulance waits. Kubrick and Shilkret build tension here, but once the plane lands in Tucumcari, we breathe a sigh of relief that Father Stadtmueller has saved the day. The final shot is taken from the ambulance as it drives away, leaving Father Stadtmueller and his plane to recede into the distance.

Unlike Douglas Edwards's narration in *Day of the Fight*, Bob Hite's narration is less stylized and more pleasant. There is no noir poetry here, and there is no darkness in either the shots or Shilkret's music. It is a businesslike affair that gets the job done, although there is little to suggest elements of Kubrick's style that we have come to expect. The music is a bit clichéd at times, even mimicking the actions on-screen with musical gestures (for example, an ascending melody accompanying the rising airplane), a practice that has come to be called, "mickey-mousing."

Kubrick's third short, *The Seafarers*, was a documentary for the Seafarers International Union, Atlantic and Gulf Coast District AFL. Because the work was produced on such a small budget, the music for the film is stock. It is an innocuous background score with the main purpose of filling in sound in between sections of narration. The film explains the benefits of joining the union, including medical benefits, insurance, and a place to socialize with other seafaring men when ashore. Will Chasan wrote the copy and Don Hollenbeck narrated the film. This short was often omitted from filmographies of Kubrick until the mid-1970s, when Gene Phillips mentioned it in a monograph about Stanley Kubrick. Phillips learned of it from Frank Tomasulo, the audio-visual director of the Seafarers International Union. When Tomasulo began the job, he asked to see all of the previous AV materials for the union and was shocked to see that "the" Stanley Kubrick was responsible for the film.[16] The film remained lost to the general public until recently, when Alexander Pietrzak bought the rights to the film from the Seafarers Union and released the short on DVD.

## FIRST FEATURES

Kubrick's first feature was *Fear and Desire*. Intending to produce the film without the financial support of a studio, Kubrick raised about $10,000 from family and friends. Before shooting began, Kubrick told an interviewer at the *New York Journal-American*, "I'm very certain we can do it for $50,000. The answer is careful planning. We have worked out every scene, every shot. There will be no writers, producers, directors or art directors to contend with. There won't be any time lost in argument or discussion. There will be only one boss—me."[17] The production ended up costing about $53,000 in the final tally. Shooting the film without synched sound—a decision Kubrick thought would save money—actually added a great deal to the cost of the film. Kubrick said of the decision, "The dubbing was a big mistake on my part; the actual shooting cost of the film was nine thousand dollars but because I didn't know what I was doing with the soundtrack it cost me another thirty thousand."[18] Investor Richard de Rochemont (whose older brother created *The March of Time* newsreel series) helped Kubrick deal with the costs of post-production, including paying part of the fees for the twenty-three musicians who played on the score. After *Fear and Desire*, de Rochemont gave Kubrick a job shooting second unit footage for a television series on Abraham Lincoln. One of the main investors in the film was Kubrick's uncle, Martin Perveler. Perveler was a wealthy man who owned a couple of drugstores in California, and he believed in Kubrick's talent. After asking for—and not getting—a multipicture deal with his nephew, Perveler settled for an associate producer credit on this single film. Kubrick chose Gerald Fried to compose the score. Fried had grand designs for the music.

> The music was supposed to mourn the world's innocence. . . .This movie
> was supposed to say everything. There were going to be no more mov-
> ies after this. So I had to be sophisticated, profound yet emphatic with
> the fate of us poor human beings. So it had to be important, profound,
> meaningful, touching, despairing but yet triumphant. I thought it was
> pretty good at the time.[19]

A review of the film in the *New York Post* said, "The musical score is considered especially important, since it runs the gamut of the film drama's
expression."[20]

*Fear and Desire* was released in theaters on 31 March 1953. Despite
Kubrick's intense work on the film, reviews were mixed. A review in the
*New York Mirror* said, "Kubrick is at his best with the camera. He shows
flashes of brilliance, then spoils the impact with repetition."[21] Pulitzer
Prize–winning poet Mark Van Doren wrote a blurb for the film that was
quoted in many ads. It read, in part, "A brilliant and unforgettable film.
Everything contributes to a total effect that is both serious and original,
and to a suspense that nothing ever breaks."[22] John McCarten of the *New
Yorker* expressed a contrary viewpoint, calling *Fear and Desire* "almost a
classic piece of malarkey."[23]

In this film, four soldiers from an unnamed army are in an unnamed
war against an unnamed enemy. The characters are of the type often
seen in war movies, the leader who guides through intellect (Lieutenant
Corby), the passionate, brave, if impetuous sergeant (Mac[24]), the young,
impressionable newbie (Private Sydney), and a character whose most pronounced feature is a southern accent (Private Fletcher). Caught behind
enemy lines, this quartet makes a plan to build a raft and float downriver
to their own territory. Their plans are complicated by the discovery of an
enemy base and by the presence of a woman who accidentally finds them.

### Synopsis and Score Description for *Fear and Desire*

The film opens with a cue called "Meditation on War." It begins with a lonely
solo line played slowly, and with much rhythmic freedom, by the bassoon:

Example 1.3.   Meditation on War.

Soon, low strings accompany the line while the title cards flash on-screen. The musical lines descend, giving the sense of things getting worse and more desperate. The title cards for Fried's name and Kubrick's name are accented with military-like brass horn calls. The music has gradually grown loud and frantic, but the score softens as the narrative begins with a voiceover:

> There is war in this forest. Not a war that has been fought, or one that will be, but any war. And the enemies who struggle here do not exist, unless we call them into being. This forest, then, and all that happens now, is outside history. Only the unchanging shapes of fear and doubt and death are from our world. These soldiers that you see keep our language and our time, but have no other country but the mind.

At the end of the voiceover, plane noise takes over from the score and blurs the line between the low rumbling of the soundtrack and the engine sound. There is no music during the exposition of the plot, as Fletcher explains the soldiers' position; all we hear in the background is distant gunfire. The characters hear rustling in the woods and find a dog with a collar. Sydney, who is gentle and kind, pets the dog, but Corby shoos the dog away. As the men head toward the river Corby warns, "Some more animals might show up," a line that is greeted with a string-heavy sting complete with pizzicato and tremolos over a woodwind chord progression. Both Kubrick and Fried are foreshadowing the appearance of the woman (she's called a "strange half-animal girl" in the advertisements, but she seems human enough, even if she doesn't understand their language or speak very much).

The sting cue continues with tremolos underscoring a cue that seems to reflect both the passing of time (there is a "tick tock" feel to the melody) and the relentless forward motion of the men:

Example 1.4.   Tick Tock Cue.

Fried's contrapuntal music continues, accompanying the overlapping voiceovers of the soldiers as we hear the thoughts of each of them. Their thoughts range from the simple "Getting hungry" to the fearful "No dying in the woods!" to the paranoid "Are they watching me?" The soldiers come upon a road. The score is silent, as are the men, as they wait to see if they can cross. Mac goes up ahead to see if the coast is clear. He signals the men over and the scene fades to black. The transition to the new scene—by the river—is accompanied by a brief musical cue.

Mac spots a small airstrip and a base some ways in the distance. They ignore it for the moment, and finish building the raft they'll take down the river after dark. An enemy plane flies overhead, forcing them into the woods, and they come upon a house where enemy soldiers are eating dinner. They decide to ambush the house and take the weapons inside. Fried's tense and fast-moving music accompanies the attack, but only as far as the door of the house. Once the soldiers enter, the music stops and, like *Day of the Fight*, the sound of the struggle is the only soundtrack. The four soldiers kill the two men in the house and take their weapons. A third enemy soldier enters a few minutes later and is shot by Mac. Worried about the noise of the gunshot, three of the men leave the house, but the lieutenant stays behind, looking at the dead men. We hear his voiceover, accompanied by low sounds in the orchestra:

> We spend our lives running our fingers down the lists and directories, looking for our real names, our permanent addresses. No man is an island? Perhaps that was true a long time ago, before the ice age. The glaciers have melted away and now we're all islands. Parts of a world made of islands only.

The next day, the men return to the river to find their raft. When a native girl sees them, Mac grabs her to keep her from screaming. They decide to tie her to a tree with their belts to prevent her from running to the enemy base and giving them away. Sydney is put in charge of watching her while the others go to check on the raft. As the other men leave him, Sydney begins to slowly unravel. He remembers the ambush to get the guns and the brutality of his fellow soldiers. In the score, the double bass plays low notes as two lines in the clarinets—one low and one high—echo each other. Soon, a bassoon joins in, as does a violin. Sydney's parody of the general—to make the girl smile—is accompanied by mocking waltz in the woodwinds. As he drifts further and further from sanity, his unstable mental state is represented in the music by ascending and descending glissandos in the trombone and violin.

The other three find the raft, which does not appear to be surrounded by the enemy. Mac looks around some more, observing the enemy general through binoculars. He begins to become obsessed with killing him. There is no musical underscore for this scene, but the music returns as the scene changes to Sydney trying to entertain the girl. His efforts become more desperate and cloying. He tells her a story about a magician,[25] and the music reflects what she must see in him—growing insanity—although she does not appear as frightened as one might expect. The meter and rhythm of the music suggest a courtly dance, but the dissonance of the harmonies tells us that something is wrong with this courtship.

Sydney brings the girl water, cupped in his hand, and as she drinks, the soundtrack features a sinister-sounding arpeggio in the strings:

Example 1.5.    Sydney Gives the Girl Water.

She finally smiles, perhaps understanding that he might untie her if she returns his affection. He embraces her desperately, finally untying her hands so that she can embrace him as well. All the while the music grows faster and more disjointed. Finally free, she runs away, and Sydney shoots her.

When Mac returns and asks what happened to the girl, Sydney lies that she is resting. When Mac realizes she is dead, Sydney says, inexplicably, "It wasn't my fault. The magician did it. Honest!" Sydney points toward the river and shivers, "It's blood, Mac. Cold. Cold." Sydney runs away, laughing maniacally, leaving the three remaining men to decide what to do. The next scene change is smoothed by Fried's music, which is dark and foreboding, with a driving rhythm. The cue stops as Corby, Mac, and Fletcher discuss the plan for the evening. Mac wants to kill the enemy general. His anger at the general (in his thoughts, he calls him a "cocky little king") is so great that he's willing to sacrifice himself so the others will have an opportunity to kill him and escape in an enemy plane. Corby finally relents, and the scene ends.

The music starts up again as Corby and Fletcher leave Mac. The score here is ominous, as the soldiers say their goodbyes at the river's edge. As Mac rows down the river by himself, the opening line from the "Meditation on War" cue begins, but instead of a single bassoon playing, the strings play the theme. The passage seems to underline Mac's utter aloneness as he floats downstream, but "it's better," he says. "It's better to roll up your life into one night and one man and one gun. It hurts too much to keep hurting everyone else in every direction. And to be hurt. With all the separate hates exploding day after day." Fried made a note at this point in the score: "meditative NOT SENTIMENTAL."

Example 1.6.   Mac's Meditation.

At the enemy base, Fried's score buzzes with dissonance and frantic pizzicato lines. The general, whose head is resting on his folded arms, lifts his head into the light at the sound of a knock on the door, and the music stops. The general is played by Kenneth Harp, the same actor who plays Lt. Corby, and the general's aide is Steve Coit, the actor who plays Fletcher. Kubrick has, with this bit of stunt casting, reminded us that soldiers on opposite sides are not all that different. They fear the same things, wonder about the same things, think the same things. The dog that Sydney petted so affectionately in the forest belongs to the general.

Kubrick cuts between the two scenes—the men waiting to kill the general, and Mac floating down the river—and the music is low, but determined. Mac thinks, "No one is going to cry for me later or cheer for me now." And the volume of the music becomes louder as Corby and Fletcher approach the general. The music's insistence grows as Kubrick cuts from Mac on the river to the general to Fletcher and Corby, all moving toward their destinies. The opening line from the "Meditation on War" cue appears again in the lowest instruments in the orchestra. As thoughts and dialogue and movement cease, Fried's music shows the tension; the militaristic cadences and the rhythmic repetition of the brass all grow loud as we wait for the denouement. As Mac draws the enemy to the river with the sound of gunfire, the music stops. All we hear are gunfire, footsteps, and crickets. Once Mac is hit, the enemy guns are soon silenced. The only sound is Mac struggling a bit in the water. Then, there is the quick crash of glass as Corby and Fletcher shoot the general and his aide through the window. The general, wounded but not dead, drags himself across the floor. The general croaks out, "I surrender," but Corby kills him anyway. The two soldiers steal the enemy plane and take off into the night. The music begins again as Mac floats down the river, wounded and dying. Fried's score features high string tremolos accompanied by arpeggios in the woodwinds. Sydney appears in the mist and asks Mac if he can ride on the raft.

Safe in their own territory, Corby and Fletcher go down to the river to watch for the raft. They hear singing, and Sydney appears in the mist on the raft with Mac, who is dead. Sydney is warbling bits of this sea tune in an off-key voice:

> Full fathom five thy father lies;
> Of his bones are coral made;
> Those are pearls that were his eyes;
> Nothing of him that doth fade
> But doth suffer a sea-change
> Into something rich and strange.
> Sea-nymphs hourly ring his knell:
> Hark! Now I hear them,—Ding-dong bell.[26]

It is Ariel's song in Shakespeare's *The Tempest*, the words of which Sydney recited to the girl before he went mad. The use of this rather disturbing song at the end instead of original underscore foreshadows the folk song used at end of *Paths of Glory*, although the affect of the two songs is entirely different. (In the latter film, the "Faithful Hussar" actually brings a feeling of hope or at least humanity.) In the middle of Sydney's off-key tune, Fried's score shudders to life, reaches a loud climax, and then dies away slow with a final gong.[27]

*Fear and Desire* wasn't a spectacular film, but it was a start for Kubrick. He envisioned greater things, not only for himself, but for his collaborators from the old neighborhood, Gerald Fried and screenwriter Howard O. Sackler (with whom Kubrick attended high school). "We have ambitious future plans, in a small way," Kubrick said in an interview, "We will make a 'Love Story of New York,' shooting all around the town."[28] Working with a skeleton crew and doing much of the work himself suited Kubrick. After filming and releasing *Fear and Desire*, Kubrick explained that he wanted to remain independent so that he might "control all the parts of a production—and share in the profits."[29] In the end, *Fear and Desire* wasn't very profitable, and Kubrick did not feel satisfied with it. Years later, he reportedly acquired many, but not all, prints of the film, intending to keep them away from public view. In 1994, Film Forum in New York City showed *Fear and Desire* to the public for the first time in four decades. Kubrick tried to block the showing, but the copyright on the film had lapsed, and Kubrick could do nothing to stop it. Through a publicist at Warner Bros., Kubrick warned that the film wasn't very good, calling it "a bumbling amateur film exercise." The result of this statement was that even more people wanted to see it. Kubrick said, "It's not a film I remember with any pride, except for the fact that it was finished."[30] Since Kubrick didn't go to film school, *Fear and Desire* served as something like his senior thesis film. There are few senior thesis films of sufficient quality to become commercial releases.

## Synopsis and Score Description for *Killer's Kiss*

Stanley Kubrick's next film, *Killer's Kiss* (1955), opens with a sound effect rather than a musical cue. It's an interesting choice that intrigues the viewer. The sound is that of a train. Think of the sound of the whistle signaling a train's imminent departure, or a steam train slowly chuffing along, gaining speed. These are evocative sounds. They can bring to mind lonely travel, lovers being separated or reunited, or even hopeful change. In *Killer's Kiss*, the dark mood of the film makes the train sound feel like the expression of the characters' yearning. German composer Bernd Schultheis calls it, "a motif for longing,"[31] and throughout the film, we hear train whistles, boat horns, and clanging bells. For almost the first two minutes of the first scene, the only thing we hear while the credits flash on-screen are the ambient sounds of a train station: trains, bells, announcements. The audience is faced with some questions: Who is this man waiting for in the train station? And will whomever he's waiting for show up? Anyone who's seen *Casablanca* knows that train stations are great sources of tension because the characters must work against the rigid timetable, and that watching someone wait—even if you don't know who or what it's for—builds suspense. It turns out that Kubrick started the story with the ending—or almost the ending. The story that will follow has already happened over the previous few days. So before we find out if someone's going to leave this poor guy at the train station, we go back in time to where the story began. It starts with the protagonist's voiceover:

> It's crazy how you can get yourself in a mess sometimes, and not even be able to think about it with any sense. And yet not be able to think about anything else. You get so you're no good for anything or anybody. Maybe it begins by taking life too serious. Anyway, I think that's the way it began for me. Just before my fight with Rodriguez, three days ago.

Gerald Fried's first cue accompanies a shot of the poster advertising the fight. This musical cue isn't as triumphant as the opening music from *Day of the Fight*, but it retains a fanfare-like quality, although it's played in the low brass:

Example 1.7.   Davey's Fanfare.

While Fried's music plays, some posters for the fight are shown hanging in shop windows, but one is shown torn and hanging on a wall, while another sits in a puddle on the ground. The fighter in the picture is our main character, Davey Gordon. Unlike *Day of the Fight*'s Walter Cartier, Davey's future isn't so bright. As the narrator in Kubrick's documentary pointed out, being a boxer won't necessarily make you rich. Some men are able to eke out a living doing it, but most boxers struggle or hold down other jobs. The music turns dissonant as Davey examines his face in the mirror in his room. This is an echo of Walter Cartier looking at his own face before the fight, and the narrator of *Day of the Fight* intoning that a fighter must wonder what his face will look like in the morning.

It is the day of the fight for Davey, and he waits impatiently, puttering around his apartment. Across the way is his neighbor, Gloria. When she appears, the love theme of the film appears with her. It is a song called "Once," written by Norman Gimbel and Arden Clar.[32] Throughout the course of the film, we will hear this song numerous times, played both by an orchestra and a band. In each version, different instruments play the main theme as a soloist. The different versions of the song have different characteristics based on where they are heard and which instruments are playing. In the version where the violin is the soloist, Fried has written "Molto shmalzando" into the score, a humorous directive aimed at making this iteration of the tune the most romantic and overly emotional of all. The first time we hear the tune, the melody begins in the oboe. The second part of the melody, we'll call it part B, is led by the flute. When the A section returns, the horn plays solo. Finally, the rest of the orchestra joins in. The song continues until Davey gets on the subway and Gloria gets into a car with her boss, Vince Rapallo (played by Frank Silvera, who played Mac in *Fear and Desire*). Once Davey is on the train, he opens a letter from his Uncle George and the music shifts to a less romantic, simpler tune:

Example 1.8.   Davey Reads the Letter.

It's an apt musical cue as it accompanies the letter, which speaks about Uncle George and Aunt Grace's simple life on the farm. The theme seems to be musically related to Davey's fanfare of the opening, both in terms of time signature and rhythmic gestures.

We hear the noise of the arena, as Davey gets ready for his fight, and then we cut to the dance club where Gloria works. The men and women in the club are dancing to a record (sourced on-screen), which is actually the swing band version of "Once." The saxophone is in the lead with two trumpets, two trombones, piano, and bass to back it up. Fried writes over the saxophone solo: "with much jazz embellishment." We see Gloria getting ready to work, changing her clothes, and then we cut to the arena, where Davey's manager is applying Vaseline to Davey's face and chest. Back at the dance club, "Once" is still playing, and Vince turns on the television to see Davey's fight. The noise from the television covers the tune somewhat. Vince interrupts one of Gloria's dances (and has the unsatisfied customer removed by his goons) so that she can watch her neighbor's match.

As in *Day of the Fight*, there is no music to accompany the fight itself. Kubrick uses similar camera angles as he did on his first short, but also allows the camera to take on Davey's perspective at one point. When he is knocked down, the camera thuds to the ground and "looks up" at the lights on the ceiling. After the fight, Vince kisses Gloria to the sound of some rhythmic Latin jazz. The scene fades to black and the sound of the music becomes absorbed into ambient city noise as Gloria walks home some undetermined time later. Fried's use of Latin jazz to represent Rapallo stems from, among other things, Fried's feeling that Latin rhythms are exciting and consequently build suspense.[33]

Davey sits alone in the silent dark of his apartment. When Gloria returns and turns her lights on, Davey watches her, the band version of "Once" playing in the background. Gloria is getting ready for bed. The song continues while Davey takes a phone call from Uncle George and plays until he turns off his light and goes to bed. Dissonant music accompanies his dreams, but he is woken up by a woman's scream. He rushes to the window to find Gloria struggling with Vince. Although Davey runs to help her, Vince escapes to the sound of Latin jazz music, the same song we heard before. There is no apparent source for this music, it just appears when Vince comes out of Gloria's door, and it fades away as Vince walks out of the scene. Gloria tells Davey what happened, in flashback: Vince knocks on Gloria's door, the Latin jazz already playing before he walks in. He apologizes for what happened earlier (we don't find out exactly what he's done, but we can assume), but Gloria doesn't want to hear it. She tells him to get out and threatens to scream if he doesn't. When he won't let her go, she does scream. Vince's music ends with the flashback. Davey offers to sit with her while she sleeps. The orchestral version of "Once" plays as Davey looks around her apartment. The song ends as the scene fades to black.

Davey explains in a voiceover that he locked her door and went home, returning the next morning. Davey and Gloria are then seen eating breakfast and talking while the band version of "Once" plays under the voiceover. As the dialogue comes to the foreground, the song stops abruptly at the end of a phrase. Gloria tells Davey the story of her sister, Iris, a ballet dancer, and a new musical cue accompanies Iris's dance.[34] The music transforms into "Once" for a moment and then returns to the dance cue. At the end of Iris' story, "Once" returns. A brief interlude—in which we revisit Davey in the train station, still waiting—features the sound of the station, but then we return to the courtship and to "Once." The scene ends with Davey having professed his love for Gloria. They agree to go to Seattle to Davey's uncle's farm.

A new scene begins with Vince at the dance club, and his signature music is playing. Receiving word that Gloria is coming by to pick up her final paycheck, Vince is upset and throws an empty glass at the wall, effectively ending the scene and the musical cue. Back at the gym, Davey calls to ask his manager for the money from his last fight. Davey and his manager agree to meet in front of the dance hall. The scene changes to an evening in the city, with two Shriners dancing down the street, one of them playing "O Susanna" on the harmonica. As Gloria enters the dance hall, a slower version of "Once" plays, this time with a very jazzy piano in the lead. As Gloria crosses the dance floor, the melody is taken up by the trombone. Gloria's departure is accompanied by "Once" in the saxophone. Vince's music takes over as he sends his goons down to kill Davey. They accidentally kill Davey's manager instead, and Vince's music continues through the attack and afterward, as Davey and Gloria head home.

"Once" begins again as Davey packs, the melody in the violin. It fades away as Davey goes to Gloria's apartment. Discovering she's not there, Vince's music starts up again, and Davey hears noise across the way. The police are looking for him in conjunction with the death of his manager. Davey goes back to the dance hall in order to follow Vince and hopefully find Gloria. No music accompanies this. Eventually, Davey pulls a gun on Vince, and Vince admits that the goons are holding Gloria captive in a loft. The loft is by the river, and the sounds of ship horns are heard, reminding us of Davey and Gloria's impending journey, if only they can be together. The goons attack Davey and take his gun, and Gloria tells Vince she will go with him. Vince's music starts up, but stops when Davey escapes through the window. As Davey runs away to find Vince again, Fried provides an atmospheric cue with percussive sounds that mingle with the sounds of boats on the waterfront. After being chased across rooftops, Davey goes into a loft full of mannequins. Fried's cue "Murder 'mongst the Mannikins" begins to play. (On the original score sheets, Fried called this cue "Mannikin Weirdo #1.") The spooky string glissandi bring to mind other atonal twentieth-century works from the classical tradition, and the tremolos add tension. Fried characterized the cue as an "eerie theme scored for high strings and muted brass, with an insistent undercurrent of drums."[35] The music, which has been growing louder and more insistent, stops when Vince grabs an ax off the wall. The only sound then is their struggle among the mannequins and the wail of a police siren. The sound of Vince's scream as Davey stabs him with a hook dissolves into one of the train whistles.

Davey is waiting for Gloria, from whom he was separated in the aftermath of Vince's death. Among all the sounds of the station, a lone violin plays the "Once" theme. Davey picks up his suitcases and begins to walk to his train. But then Gloria runs toward him, kissing him, and the words "The End" show up on the screen, as just a short phrase from Fried's first cue (the boxing fanfare) plays to end the film. Even though they are never heard in the film, there are lyrics written by Norman Gimbel.

In March of 1947, Kubrick had done a feature in *Look* about Aqueduct Race Track. True to form, he focused more on spectators than the horses. In the pictures we see men in hats and overcoats, trackside, studying the racing form. Kubrick snapped a standing crowd multiple times, watching them follow the horses as they went by. He found a middle-aged woman, looking on intently, finger on her nose, racing form in her hand, a beaded oval purse hanging from her arm. In the aftermath of the races, Kubrick caught the men sweeping up the garbage of racing forms and losing tickets. In his collection of Kubrick's photos for *Look*, Rainer Crone said of the feature, "Kubrick's portrayal of a day at the track reveals a keen sense of individual pathos as well as the potential for mass hysteria that a public event on this scale could generate."[36]

Kubrick chose the racetrack as the setting for his next film, *The Killing* (1956). This high-tension crime caper was based on a novel called *Clean Break* by Lionel White. Johnny Clay (Sterling Hayden) devises a plot to steal two million dollars from a racetrack. To do this he assembles a team who will split the money after the heist. Johnny plans to take his share of the money and marry his girlfriend, Fay (Colleen Gray). His team consists of a betting teller, a cop, a sharp-shooter, the bartender at the track, and a wrestler. The men successfully steal the money, but the plan goes awry when the teller's scheming wife (who found out about the plan from her callow husband) enlists her lover, Val, to steal the money after the heist is complete. Everyone ends up dead except for Johnny, who tries to take the money and escape with Fay. Fate intervenes, and the money ends up literally scattered to the winds.

### Synopsis and Score Description for *The Killing*

The score for *The Killing* overall has something in common with *Killer's Kiss*, namely the use of semi-improvised popular music to represent a shady character. As mentioned above, in *Killer's Kiss*, Latin jazz accompanies the appearances of the villain, Vince Rapallo. In *The Killing*, jazz and swing represent the scheming wife, Sherry Peatty, and her lover Val. One of Fried's cues for the film is called "Val's Mambo." Bernd Schultheis suggested that in both films, jazz represents the element of conspiracy.[37] In *Killer's Kiss* and *The Killing*, it's unclear how much of this music is actually heard by the characters, although fluctuations in volume suggest that the music may be playing perhaps on a radio in the background or behind a closed door.

There are many more musical cues in this film than in the previous, especially because there isn't a signature tune like "Once" to make up the bulk of the score. There is a main musical theme of *The Killing*, and it is what Gerald Fried called his trademark: "a rhythmic clash of confrontation. I had half the orchestra playing a four figure. The other half of the orchestra played a three figure." So over a steady four pattern in the bass drum and timpani, the strings and brass have their rhythmic clash. In this simplified version of the theme, the first violins are on the treble staff, and the trombones are on the bass staff.

Example 1.9.   The Killing opening credits.

Example 1.9.   (*continued*)

The sonic discord between the three and the four patterns builds tension, and that, says Fried, "is what Stanley loved about that movie, you know. It had people on the edge of their chair from the beginning of the movie to the end."[38] Once the initial conflict of the opening theme resolves somewhat, the snare drum provides cadences under the woodwinds, who play a low repetitive melody. Muted brass horn calls with the snare rolls create a pseudo-militaristic sound. While the credits play on-screen, horses and their jockeys ride to the starting gate. As they pause, waiting for the start of the race, Fried ends the musical cue on a dissonant chord. The bell rings, the gate opens, and the horses run out. For a moment, we hear only the announcer and the sound of the horses running, but then those sounds fade into the background as a voiceover starts:

> At exactly 3:45 on that Saturday afternoon in the last week of September, Marvin Unger was perhaps the only one among the hundred thousand people at the track who felt no thrill at the running of the fifth race. He was totally disinterested in horse racing, and held a life-long contempt for gambling. . . .

The man on-screen, Unger, will turn out to be a peripheral character in the story, although he does set the plot into motion. Low underscore, a fragment of the original theme, accompanies Unger giving both the betting teller and the bartender secret written messages about a clandestine meeting. Then we cut to patrolman Randy Kennan meeting a loan shark at a bar. Jazz piano provides the soundtrack for this meeting. Kennan can't pay his debts, but promises that he'll be flush with cash soon. The scene ends, and the jazz piano stops. The next scene takes place with Johnny Clay, "perhaps the most important thread in the unfinished fabric," the voiceover explains. Upon his appearance, the main theme re-appears in a slower, more pensive version as he explains to Fay who will make up the team for the heist. The music softens as Fay and Johnny talk about the last five years they've been apart during Johnny's incarceration. The same slow version of the opening theme moves upward into the string section and the high woodwinds. Played this way, the cue takes on the character of a love theme, albeit a dark and pensive one.

Example 1.10.   Johnny's Theme.

The tension returns when the track bartender, Mike O'Reilly, visits the bedside of his sick wife. As he pulls out the note Unger slipped him at the track, there's a driving theme accented by dissonant stopped brass mocking the racing fanfare.

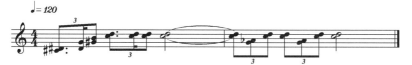

Example 1.11.   Mock Racing.

When the teller, George Peatty, returns home to his wife, Sherry, we hear a jazzy song playing in the background. The music continues as Sherry goes to see Val, her lover, and plays as the scene fades to black. When we rejoin Sherry and Val, the jazz music is replaced by ominous underscore when Sherry mentions that George is going to be part of a heist at the racetrack. The cue Fried called "George, That's How" begins with a repeating figure in the low strings:

Example 1.12.   "George, That's How."

Fried added short gestures in the horns, trumpets, piano, and percussion that enhance the tension of the cue. Sherry initially plans to take George's share of the money, but Val thinks he might be able to steal it all.

At the meet-up with Johnny, George, Mike, Kennan, and Unger, there is no underscore as the men discuss the plan. But when they hear a noise, Fried's score reflects their suspicion with a high pizzicato note. The music, sinister and questioning, continues as the boys accuse George of telling his wife about the plan. Later, when George and Sherry are both home, the music again is the improvised jazz that seems to be Sherry's signature. The music swells as the scene—with George and Sherry kissing—fades to black. Kubrick and Fried forgo underscore in the ensuing two scenes: Johnny asks the wrestler, Maurice, to provide a distraction at the track and Johnny hires the sharp-shooter, Nikki.

After meeting with Nikki, Johnny drives to a motel and asks for a room for the week. Ominous dissonant chords with snare rolls play as Johnny puts a bag in the drawer and locks the room. In the next scene, Sherry walks out of her bedroom to find George drinking coffee in the kitchen. Her actions are accompanied by a meandering line in the clarinet:

Example 1.13.   Sherry Gets Up.

Once the music stops, the only sound is the ticking of a clock, echoing George's nervousness. He is anxious, Sherry correctly guesses, because it is the day of the heist.

At the track, Fried's dissonant fanfare in the muted brass plays as we see Red Lightning, the horse favored to win the race. Johnny talks to Unger before he leaves for the track. Under their discussion is a version of the main theme, which gradually becomes tenser, louder, higher, and more elaborately orchestrated. The cue continues through the next scene as Johnny makes arrangements with the man at the motel. By the time Johnny stashes a shotgun in a box of flowers, the theme is bellowing in the brass section. Instead of continuing the gradual crescendo, Fried occasionally pulls back, giving us momentary respite from the heavy tension, but never quite breaking it either. The score does not stop; it just recedes into the lower parts of the orchestra, under the dialogue. Fried manages to keep the audience anxious, without having the score unduly intrude on the action. The underscore only disappears when Kubrick cuts to the first race.

Unger shows up at the track—unexpectedly—and Fried's score re-appears with a driving rhythm and tremolos in the winds. Rising four-note figures, played by different instruments, accompany patrolman Kennan's drive to the track. When he stops the police car under the open window—from which Johnny will throw the stolen cash—the brass plays a final dissonant fanfare and briefly falls silent. Similar music, drawing upon elements of the original main theme, appears under scenes in which Maurice takes his place at the track to start his diversion and as Nikki drives to the track.

After Nikki shoots Red Lightning, we jump backward in time a few hours. Johnny is on his way to the track. The racing fanfare plays, as do some new elements in the high strings. Fried includes the rising four-note figures as well. The result is a relentlessly forward-moving cue, one that continues to grow in both tension and complexity. Johnny's preparations for the robbery (putting on a mask, getting the gun) and the immediate aftermath, are accompanied by snare rolls, but the actual robbery is unaccompanied by the score. The brass play loudly as Johnny makes his escape from the track.

When Kennan, O'Reilly, and Peatty meet up afterward, they listen to the radio and jazz music begins to play after a news bulletin about the heist. It plays as Val enters, looking for the money. George shoots Val, setting off a shootout after which only George is left alive, although wounded. Meanwhile, Johnny retrieves the duffle bag full of cash from the motel, the score more dissonant and driving than ever. Johnny sees George stumble out of the apartment, wounded, so he drives away, intending to keep the money. As Johnny stashes the loot in an old suitcase, the opening musical conflict of three versus four appears. The jazz music re-appears as George returns home to find Sherry waiting for Val and packing her suitcase. George shoots her and then dies himself.

The rising figures in the orchestra play under the establishing shot of the airport. Due to airline rules, Johnny and Fay are forced to check the bag full of money, instead of carrying it in the cabin. As they wait outside to board their plane, a runaway dog causes Johnny's suitcase to fall off a luggage cart. The money spills out and is blown away by the turbines of the surrounding planes. Johnny and Fay nervously return to the airport while the three versus four conflict music of the opening plays. This time, the tempo is a bit slower, almost halting, as Fay and Johnny realize they are going to be caught. They try to get a taxi but cannot, and two plain-clothes policemen draw their guns and advance on Johnny as "The End" appears on-screen.

This score is Fried's densest score yet. There is a cue for nearly every scene. True to form, Kubrick and Fried chose to provide music for the tensest parts of the narrative, but left it out during the race, the actual robbery, and Maurice's diversion (which is basically a wrestling match). Composer Bernd Schultheis observed that the score "is built in modules and can therefore easily be adjusted to the dramatic needs and cutting sequences. It outlines the action superficially and sometimes, to increase the tension, grows beyond the confines of the images."[39] Fried's cues, constructed in multiple sections, allowed him flexibility to use bits and pieces throughout the film in order to suit whatever each scene required.

## Synopsis and Score Description for *Paths of Glory*

The final collaboration between Kubrick and Fried was *Paths of Glory*. What Kubrick does with the sound and music in this film represents what some may see as a turning point in his development. The sound aspect of this film is extremely important. As in other Kubrick films, there are moments where there is no musical underscore at all, and in those moments the sounds take center stage. The sound of gunfire, of artillery, of footsteps: these are the sounds of war. But there are also moments of music and their scarcity speaks volumes of meaning. The opening credits are accompanied by an orchestral version of *La Marseillaise*.[40] Fried has added some snare rolls to this version of the anthem to give it a distinctive military flavor. The song is not allowed to resolve as it was written, but instead ends on dissonant chords that give the listener the sense that something isn't quite right.

When the film begins, a voiceover explains some historical background on World War I, but underneath this voiceover, Fried has taken the opening phrases of *La Marseillaise* and altered them to form dissonant, distorted versions of the original music, wordlessly commenting on the nature of this conflict.

French General Broulard (Adolphe Menjou) asks fellow general Mireau (George Macready) if his troops can take a position called the German Ant Hill. Mireau first argues this is impossible until Broulard dangles the possibility of a promotion in front of him. Mireau agrees to try it. He asks Colonel Dax (Kirk Douglas) to engage his men in this battle. Dax believes that it will be a difficult assignment, if it is possible at all, but follows orders, bravely leading his men. When the men cannot advance, Mireau claims the men are cowards and orders that the soldiers be urged on by friendly fire. The order is refused and the surviving men retreat. Mireau, angry at the outcome, demands that one hundred men die in front of a firing squad for cowardice. Broulard convinces him that three men will do. Colonel Dax—who was a civilian lawyer before the war—defends the three men in court, although he is not allowed to enter much evidence in their defense. Despite Dax's efforts and the testimony of the men, the three soldiers are killed by the firing squad.

For most of the film, if there is music at all, it is percussive in nature. Gerald Fried's longest cue in the film underscores the scene of the night patrol. Lieutenant Roget, who spends most of his time drunk, takes two men with him on patrol and sends one ahead to scout. When the man does not return, Roget becomes anxious and wants to leave. Assuming the scout is dead, and fearing enemy fire, Roget throws a grenade that ends up killing his own man. There are a few important musical gestures in this segment. One features steady hits on a bass drum. A second is a four-note motif intended for a dampened timpani, although Fried said that he ended up changing the instrumentation to a tuned tom-tom because he was not able to find a timpani in Munich—where the score was recorded—that could play the highest note in the motif.

Example 1.14.    The timpani of the Night Patrol.

This motif grows in intensity, as the last note—the high A—becomes three notes, then more. The third motif is a tick tock cue very similar to the one heard in *Fear and Desire*, this time played by a timpani.

Example 1.15.    Night Patrol Tick Tock.

On the soundtrack to the film, the resemblance to the earlier cue is not as obvious, but on a compilation album of themes from Kubrick's films (made by the Prague Philharmonic), the similarity is eerie. There is something elemental about this cue and the one from *Fear and Desire* that for

Fried must have symbolized the fear of war, a fear that encroaches relentlessly upon one's sanity.

As the men on the night patrol grow more anxious, the timpani part
changes slightly and also becomes twice as fast. A fourth musical element
of the scene are rolls on the snare drum (there are actually two snares,
one with snares on and one with them off), which are added to the cue,
while the percussion of weapons—guns, grenades, and explosions—seamlessly becomes part of the texture. Corporal Paris, the third man in the
night patrol, continues looking for the missing man after Roget retreats.
The cue ends with a shot of the dead body of the missing member of the
night patrol. The startling discovery is accompanied by a jarring roll on a
hanging cymbal. The cue is very effective, although the Prague recording
reveals unheard instruments and musical gestures that one can easily miss
in the film.

In *Paths of Glory*, scenes with dialogue, in particular, are given no
underscore, although there are two exceptions. At the beginning of the
film, General Mireau walks through the trench, stopping to ask different
soldiers if they are "ready to kill more Germans." While he walks, rolls
on the snare drum accompany his movements. When he stops to speak,
the drum stops as well. And then there is the scene of the conversation
between Colonel Dax and Major General Broulard. Dax has come to
Broulard's house to plead once again for the lives of his men. While they
speak, waltzes from a party at Broulard's house are heard softly in the
background. Here the Johann Strauss waltz *Künsterleben* ("Artist's Life"),
from 1867, forms a stark contrast between the cruel percussion of the
battlefield and the opulent surroundings of the commanding officers. We
see General Broulard dancing at his party while we know that the men are
sleeping in the trenches, cold, filthy, and scared. Kubrick does not explicitly make this comparison by cutting between the two scenes, but it is not
a far stretch to realize how different the life of a solider is as opposed to
the life of the general.

The execution scene features the bass and snare drum, playing an
unceasing cadence that begins as the condemned men walk to the execution and continues through to the priest's final blessing. It stops just before
Lieutenant Roget calls "Ready, aim, fire!" There is one more important
musical moment in the film, and it is an extremely powerful and emotional
one. It was an invention of the screenwriters (although there was some
disagreement about who should take credit for the final decision). After
the execution, Colonel Dax returns to the men and finds them in a café,
watching some entertainment. A young German woman is there, her face

wet with tears, humiliated and scared as the host asks her to sing. She begins singing "The Faithful Hussar." The German folk song, likely dating from the early nineteenth century, speaks of a faithful soldier who travels only to return home when he hears that the woman he loves is sick. There are two musical phrases in the tune. The first phrase consists of the pick-up measure (the first measure is not a complete three beats), three full measures, and the first note of the fourth measure. The first two lines of each verse are sung to this phrase. The second phrase is actually made up of a repeated smaller phrase (starting in the middle of m. 4 and repeating in the middle of m. 8); the last two lines of the verse are meant to be repeated in this second phrase.

Example 1.16.   The Faithful Hussar (tune only).

Traditionally, there are many verses to the song, but the character sings only the following three (and then repeats the first two):[41]

Es war einmal ein treuer Husar,
Der liebt' sein Mädchen ein ganzes Jahr,
Ein ganzes Jahr und noch viel mehr,
Die Liebe nahm kein Ende mehr.

There once was a faithful Hussar
He loved his girl for a whole year,
For a whole year and much more,
His love had no end.

Und als man ihm die botschaft bracht
Dass sein herzliebchen am sterben lag
Da liess er all sein hab und gut
Und eilte seinem herzliebchen zu

And when he heard the message
That his heart's love was dying,
He left all of his belongings
And hurried to his darling.

Ach bitte Mutter bring' ein Licht,
Mein Liebchen stirbt, ich seh' es nicht,
Das war fürwahr ein treuer Husar,
Der liebt' sein Mädchen ein ganzes Jahr.

Oh please, Mother, bring a light
My love dies, I see it not,
This was indeed a faithful Hussar
Who loved his girl for a whole year.

The young woman sings (she is billed as Susanne Christian, but she was Christiane Harlan, who was to become Kubrick's third wife), and at first the men are shouting and catcalling and it is difficult to hear her. As she continues, however, the men become quiet and begin to listen. They do not know the words to the song, but they seem to know the tune, and soon they are singing along with her. Tears fall down the faces of some of the men who are watching, matching the tears of the woman.

Outside the café, Dax listens to them, his face softening for the first time in the film. It is as if music, particularly melody, is the humanity that the men have forgotten out on the battlefield. As they share the music, singing the melody in unison, they momentarily cease to be soldiers, and the line between French and German is blurred. Kubrick and Fried have made these final moments of the narrative especially powerful because they have withheld melody for the majority of the film. Besides *La Marseillaise* at the opening credits and the diegetic waltz of General Broulard's party, the only musical elements we have heard are drum rolls and the percussive cues of the night patrol scene. We the viewers—and these characters—have been starved for melody and starved for humanity. Kubrick gives us both in this final moment, and it is all the more sweet because we have been deprived of them. An orchestrated version of "The Faithful Hussar" accompanies the credits. In his book about the music of Kubrick's films, Gerrit Bodde says this about the music in *Paths of Glory*:

> We can assume that Kubrick wanted to create this interpretation of the film: France's power and glory (as shown in the main title theme) has a high price, which is paid by the soldiers. This is shown through the cinematic action, in the disconsolate mood of the soldiers' celebration, and through the end titles).[42]

The choice of a mostly percussion score was made by both Kubrick and Fried, who said: "Now Stanley had a kind of harsh, bleak vision of life, and taking the tonality out of the music, having an all-percussion score would be just a natural." After viewing the film in recent years, Fried almost seemed to regret the decision from a humanitarian point of view: "By taking away the tonality of the music, it was as if I had abandoned them, and I took away their humanity. I stranded them out there with no underscoring except bleak percussion. And I felt terrible."[43]

After this, Kubrick didn't jump directly into using preexistent music; he still had *Spartacus* and *Lolita* ahead of him, but perhaps he was beginning to see the possibilities in using other sources for his scores. Kubrick and Fried would never work together again, but remained friends. It's unlikely that Fried would have worked with Kubrick again, even if he had been asked. In recent years, Fried described the difficulty of his collaboration with the director:

He liked the first score, it was very effective and it did the job. Second score he began to get more ideas about music and then he became more demanding about certain things, and by the third score, we were already arguing. The fourth and fifth score, there were knockdown battles. But by that time, he had developed a taste and a style and he was a hard guy to argue with. . . . At the beginning, it was easy, I went my own way, but by . . . *Paths of Glory*, I had to justify every note.[44]

Furthermore, Kubrick and Fried were philosophically opposed on the issue of preexistent music in film. Fried believed that classical music took the viewer out of the film experience, especially if the music was well known. In addition to that, he has said: "[Preexistent music] doesn't support the picture because it wasn't written for the picture."[45] Kubrick, on the other hand, believed that preexistent music was a viable source for scores, especially because he saw the quality of that music overshadowing that of newly written scores:

However good our best film composers may be, they are not a Beethoven, a Mozart, or a Brahms. Why use music which is less good when there is such a multitude of great orchestral music available from the past and from our own time? . . . With a little more care and thought these *temporary* tracks can become the final score.[46]

Gerald Fried went on to a very successful career writing scores for both television and films. His philosophy of scoring, and his ability to work quickly, made him ideally suited for the job. Fried describes the highlights of his career as the score for the iconic television mini-series *Roots* (Quincy Jones began the score, writing a portion of it before Fried was brought in to complete the work), his work on the Kubrick films, and his work for the original *Star Trek* television show. One of his cues for that particular program, fight music for a battle in which Kirk and Spock must fight to the death (in an episode called "Amok Time"),[47] has entered popular culture as definitive dramatic (perhaps melodramatic) fight music.[48] In 2012, Fried was still composing, working on a musical (for which he wrote the script, music, and book), and living in New Mexico.

## NOTES

1. "Kids at a Ball-Game," *Look,* October 16, 1945; "Dixieland Jazz Is 'Hot' Again," *Look,* June 6, 1950; "Montgomery Clift . . . Glamour Boy in Baggy Pants,"

*Look,* July 19, 1949. A collection of these clippings is housed at the Stanley Kubrick Archive at the University of the Arts London.

2. Mildred Stagg, "Quiz Kid," *The Camera,* December 6, 1949, 152.

3. Raymond Fielding, *The March of Time: 1935–1951* (New York: Oxford University Press, 1978), 63.

4. Kubrick had also done another day-in-the-life piece in *Look* on boxer Rocky Graziano in its February 14, 1950, issue.

5. United States Coast Guard website, http://www.uscg.mil/history/img/Sailors_All_Poster.jpg.

6. "This Is America: They Fly with the Fleet," *Internet Movie Database,* http://www.imdb.com/title/tt0346020/.

7. Quoted in John Baxter, *Stanley Kubrick: A Biography* (New York: Carroll and Graf, 1997), 37.

8. Vincent LoBrutto, *Stanley Kubrick: A Biography* (New York: Da Capo Press, 1997), 68.

9. LoBrutto, *Stanley Kubrick,* 64.

10. LoBrutto, *Stanley Kubrick,* 67.

11. Email to the author, 5 April 2012.

12. Fleischer was editor in chief of *Ring Magazine* from 1929 to 1972.

13. Fried himself was a woodwind player (oboe), and much of his film music relies on the woodwinds to carry melody.

14. Kubrick apparently gave Cartier the dog, hoping to add a "human interest" element. LoBrutto, *Stanley Kubrick,* 61.

15. Kubrick later discussed having to do reshoots because Cartier knocked Bobby James out too quickly.

16. "The Seafarers," *Internet Movie Database,* http://www.imdb.com/title/tt0045130/synopsis.

17. From the Associated Press: "A 22-Year-Old Producer Makes Real Films for Fun and Profit," *New York Journal-American,* December 27, 1950.

18. Interview with Joseph Gelmis, "The Film Director as Superstar," *The Kubrick Site,* http://www.visual-memory.co.uk/amk/doc/0069.html.

19. LoBrutto, *Stanley Kubrick,* 80–81.

20. Review of *Fear and Desire, New York Post,* March 9, 1953.

21. Frank Quinn, *New York Mirror,* no date, clipping.

22. Letter from Mark van Doren to Stanley Kubrick, Stanley Kubrick Archive, University of the Arts London.

23. John McCarten, Review of *Fear and Desire, New Yorker,* April 11, 1953, 128, http://archives.newyorker.com/?i=1953-04-11#folio=128.

24. The character's name is later revealed to be MacClellan, perhaps a reference to Civil War general George McClellan, who was a brilliant man but a poor judge of his abilities on the battlefield. He was removed from his command by Lincoln because he twice missed the opportunity to not only end the Civil War but win it.

25. The magician Sydney refers to is Prospero, from Shakespeare's *The Tempest*. In this play, Prospero and his daughter Miranda are exiled on a remote island. Prospero uses his magic to create a storm that will bring his brother Antonio, who has usurped the throne from Prospero, to the island, along with Antonio's allies.

26. William Shakespeare, *The Tempest*, act 1, sc. 2.

27. In pieces like Richard Strauss's tone poem *Death and Transfiguration*, the gong symbolizes the moment of death. In his *Treatise on Instrumentation*, Hector Berlioz states, "The gong or tamtam is used only in compositions of a mournful character or in dramatic scenes of the utmost horror." Hector Berlioz and Richard Strauss, *Treatise on Instrumentation,* trans. Theodore Front (New York: Dover Publications, 1991), 395.

28. Irene Thirer, "Screen View," *New York Post*, March 27, 1953, 58.

29. Samuel L. Singer, "24-Year-Old Is 'Factotum' of New Film," *Philadelphia Inquirer*, Sunday Morning, July 26, 1953, 16.

30. Interview with Joseph Gelmis, "The Film Director as Superstar," *The Kubrick Site*, http://www.visual-memory.co.uk/amk/doc/0069.html.

31. Bernd Schultheis, "Expanse of Possibilities: Stanley Kubrick's Soundtracks in Notes," *Stanley Kubrick Catalogue*, 2nd ed. (Frankfurt am Main: Deutsches Filmmuseum, 2007), 267.

32. Copyright 1954, King's Crown Music.

33. Gene D. Phillips and Rodney Hill, "Gerald Fried," in *Encyclopedia of Stanley Kubrick* (New York: Checkmark Books, 2002), 125.

34. Iris was played by Ruth Sobotka, Kubrick's wife at the time. She was a professional dancer.

35. Quoted in Phillips and Hill, *Encyclopedia of Stanley Kubrick*, 126.

36. Rainer Crone, *Stanley Kubrick Drama and Shadows: Photographs 1945–1950* (London: Phaidon, 2005), 132.

37. Schultheis, "Expanse of Possibilities," 267.

38. "Interview with Gerald Fried," *Archive of American Television*, http://emmytvlegends.org/interviews/people/gerald-fried.

39. Schultheis, "Expanse of Possibilities," 267.

40. In some versions of the film, *La Marseillaise* was replaced by a percussion track. Because it was viewed as being a negative portrayal of the French military, the film stirred up controversy in France and some of its allied countries.

41. Translation mine.

42. Gerrit Bodde, *Die Musik in den Filmen von Stanley Kubrick* (Osnabrück: Der Andere Verlag, 2002), 37. Translation mine.

43. "Interview with Gerald Fried," *Archive of American Television*.

44. "Interview with Gerald Fried," *Archive of American Television*.

45. Quoted in Caryl Flinn, *Strains of Utopia: Gender, Nostalgia, and Hollywood Film Music* (Princeton, NJ: Princeton University Press, 1992), 37.

46. Michel Ciment, *Kubrick: The Definitive Edition*, trans. Gilbert Adair (New York: Faber and Faber, 1999), 177.

47. In this episode of *Star Trek*, which is the first episode of season two, Spock must return to his home planet of Vulcan to marry his berothed, T'Pring. In love with another man, she chooses kal-if-fee, a fight to the death between Spock and—instead of her lover—Captain Kirk. Fried scored the whole episode, but his battle music is the most famous portion.

48. The music has been in many instances but is notable in the film *The Cable Guy* (1996) and the television show *Futurama*. In both cases, the music was associated with battles.

# Chapter Two

═══════════○═══════════

# Love Themes, Leitmotifs, and Pop Music

## Spartacus, Lolita, Dr. Strangelove, *and* Full Metal Jacket

THE FOUR FILMS COVERED IN THIS CHAPTER encompass a number of different scoring techniques. The score for *Spartacus* (1960) was written by a single composer in response to the narrative of the film and the requests of the director. *Lolita* (1962) combines newly written underscore with orchestral arrangements of a preexistent tune as the musical centerpiece. *Dr. Strangelove* (1964) features two preexistent popular tunes used in ironic contexts and varied orchestrations of a military song. *Full Metal Jacket* (1987)—made more than two decades later than *Dr. Strangelove*—uses a similar template of minimal new underscore and the ironic use of preexistent tunes. In the intervening years between *Dr. Strangelove* and *Full Metal Jacket*, Kubrick changed the way he scored his films, using a new paradigm of preexistent and contemporary art music. *2001: A Space Odyssey*, *A Clockwork Orange*, *Barry Lyndon*, *The Shining*, and indeed his last film, *Eyes Wide Shut*, were part of this new paradigm. Each of these films will be discussed at length in the following chapters.

After the artistic, if not financial, triumph of *Paths of Glory*, Kubrick and his producing partner, James Harris, were looking for a new project. Marlon Brando was interested in working with Kubrick on a western loosely based on the life of Billy the Kid. It was while Kubrick worked on Brando's screenplay for the western that Vladimir Nabokov's novel *Lolita* was published in the U.S. Although Kubrick and Harris were both excited about adapting the novel for the screen, Kubrick was committed to the Billy the Kid project, so while he worked on that, Harris attempted to buy the rights to *Lolita*. Kubrick and Brando were both strong creative personalities, and their collaboration was difficult. There are conflicting reports of exactly how Kubrick left the film, later called *One-Eyed Jacks*, but in the end, Kubrick moved on and Brando directed the film himself.

Meanwhile, Kirk Douglas was preparing to bring *Spartacus* to the screen. Douglas, both producer and star, encountered plenty of problems on the way, everything from a similar competing project (*The Gladiators*) to an unusable screenplay to a difficult hunt for a leading lady. The studio funding the film, Universal, wanted Anthony Mann to direct even though Douglas had misgivings. Mann was known for his westerns, and it was his talent for filming outside that Universal felt would serve him well on *Spartacus*. Mann directed the opening section, in which Romans choose slaves for their gladiator schools, but in the sections that followed, Kirk Douglas found that he wasn't satisfied with Mann's work. Douglas fired Mann and suggested Kubrick (with whom he had recently made *Paths of Glory*) for the job. One weekend after Mann's last day, Kubrick began directing *Spartacus*. He reportedly filmed a scene on Monday and then spent the rest of the week rehearsing with the actors.[1]

## SPARTACUS

Some scholars have omitted *Spartacus* from discourse of Kubrick's work since it was not a project he developed himself. James Naremore has said of the film that it "has very few moments when one can sense [Kubrick's] directorial personality."[2] Kubrick distanced himself from the film as well, painting himself as someone at odds with the material. In one of his lengthy interviews with Michel Ciment, Kubrick said of *Spartacus*, "I was up against a pretty dumb script which was rarely faithful to what is known about Spartacus."[3] Kubrick fought for changes in the script, although he wasn't satisfied with reactions to his input. In a 1973 interview, Kubrick said: "When Kirk offered me the job of directing *Spartacus*, I thought that I might be able to make something of it if the script could be changed. But my experience proved that if it is not explicitly stated in the contract that your decisions will be respected, there's a very good chance that they won't be."[4]

One aspect of the filmmaking in which Kubrick had more of a say was the music. Kirk Douglas had engaged Alex North to write the score in pre-production, and North worked on it over the course of filming, which was an especially long time. Usually, film composers are given perhaps three months to complete a score, but according to North biographer

Sanya Henderson, Douglas allowed North more than a year to complete the music. This not only allowed North to research ancient Roman music, but also gave him the opportunity to work out the themes in great detail and collaborate with Kubrick. [5]

When production on *Spartacus* began, North was an up-and-coming composer. Previous to his work on *Spartacus*, North had written some uncredited stock music, music for television, like the theme for the Playhouse 90 anthology television series, and some film scores. Among them were the score to *Death of a Salesman* (1951) and *A Streetcar Named Desire* (1951), both for director Elia Kazan.[6] He also wrote the scores for the westerns *The Wonderful Country* (1959), starring Robert Mitchum, and *The King and Four Queens* (1956) starring Clark Gable.[7] After *Spartacus*, North began to write for more high-profile pictures, including another epic, *Cleopatra* (1963), *The Misfits* (1961) with Marilyn Monroe, and *The Agony and the Ecstasy* (1965).

Because the production time was so long, Kubrick interacted with North over the course of filming. Alex North's biographer describes their connection as "a deep, mutual understanding."[8] To aid Kubrick during production, North reportedly arranged a temporary track of his music using two pianos and two percussion instruments.[9] This allowed Kubrick to get a sense of the musical score as it was being written. In addition, Kubrick encouraged North to listen to Prokofiev's score to *Alexander Nevsky*, and within that recommendation, there was the unspoken understanding that brass passages would accompany ceremony and violence, while strings would underscore love scenes.[10]

Kubrick provided to Alex North a list of places where he thought there should be music, and he described to North what he thought should be there. Under the heading of "Reel IX and Reel XI," for example, Kubrick lists the following events in the film with corresponding musical ideas:[11]

Reel IX
Empty arena – NIGHT        LOVE THEME
DRABA HANGING             BROODING THEME
KITCHEN—GLADIATORS ENTER—MUSIC OUT
LS ESCAPING UPHILL—HEROIC THEME

Reel XI
GLABRUS—NO MUSIC
OYSTERS AND SNAILS—EXOTIC, SHIMMERING MUSIC

In addition to these musical guidelines, six months later, Kubrick made a list of "musical sweeteners," which are musical additions to cues that have already been written (for example, an additional musical line added to a recorded cue). Once again, they're organized by reel. Reel 7, for example, needed three sweeteners:

1. Sweetener after Kirk's fall in Draba fight.
2. Sweetener for night brooding sequence.
3. New music cue for breakout starting with Kirk's lunge at Marcellus.[12]

Music played an important role on set. Both Kubrick and Douglas knew that directors of silent movies would play appropriately emotional music for the actors to help them get into character or to set the mood. In *Spartacus*, Kubrick decided to use the technique for scenes that were shot without sound (sound to be added later), and it proved to be very effective.[13] This is the first time it's mentioned that Kubrick used music on set to inspire the actors, but it would not be the last.

North was excited about the challenge of the project. It was certainly a bigger film than anything he had worked on before, a multimillion-dollar epic, and North wanted to do his very best. In addition to researching ancient music, North investigated different kinds of instruments to use on the score. The subject matter of the film, and the skill of the players in the orchestra, gave North free rein to experiment with both "exotic ethnic instruments, and various unusual combinations of instrumental groups within a large symphonic orchestra."[14]

North's score for *Spartacus* was massive. The film itself was more than three hours long, and North's music was present for more than two-thirds of the screen time. Norman Kagan reasoned that the film valued action over dialogue. This leaves much of the dramatic weight on the physical characteristics of the actors—their facial expressions and bodily movements—and on the music.[15] The official cue sheet for the film has more than seventy musical cues over twenty-six reels.[16] In her biography of Alex North, Sanya Henderson provides a detailed analysis of the score to *Spartacus*, outlining a number of musical phrases that take on meaning and are repeated throughout the film. The technique is the use of what are called leitmotifs.

The concept of the leitmotif was born in the Romantic period in music (roughly corresponding with the nineteenth century). Any music that has no text, but aims to relate a narrative or some nonmusical idea is called programmatic. A number of composers in the Romantic period began assigning extra-musical meaning to their compositions and specifically to musical phrases. In 1830, French composer Hector Berlioz wrote a pro-grammatic, five-movement symphony about a man who falls in love with a woman. The object of affection was musically represented by the *idée fixe*, a melody that would appear whenever the main character encountered her or even thought of her in the course of the narrative. Opera composers of the late Classical and early Romantic periods would use what are called "reminiscence motifs," musical melodies that represented characters, emotions, or events and could create connections among them within the drama. The reminiscence motifs often appeared unchanged and were not often used extensively throughout an entire work.

German opera composer Richard Wagner, however, extensively used leitmotifs. Although Wagner himself did not use the term, it is most closely associated with his operas. A leitmotif in a Wagner opera could represent something abstract like love, or something concrete, like a sword. Leitmotifs included everything from characters to emotions, and Wagner's use of them was all-encompassing; one opera might contain dozens and dozens of leitmotifs.[17] In contrast to reminiscence motifs, leitmotifs may form a system that can reach over multiple works. In Wagner's Ring Cycle, a set of four operas that tells a single complex nar-rative, the composer uses leitmotifs that retain their meaning throughout all four operas. There is a web of leitmotifs shared among these works that is both complicated and subtle. The orchestral appearance of many leitmotifs in a single scene might musically paint an intricate picture of what is going on in the story.

Leitmotifs emerge in the orchestra, rather than in the sung parts, and they often reveal the true thoughts or feelings of the characters onstage. They might reveal subtext that is different from what was being sung. The fact that these musical ideas conveyed ideas beyond the words made them ideally suited for film. Leitmotifs might easily lead the audience into as-sociations or emotions to help the narrative move forward.

Leitmotifs in film can refer to emotions or objects, but often musical themes are there to identify specific characters. Many of the early film composers used the technique, and indeed the idea of what film music scholar Mervyn Cooke calls "codified scoring practices based on the eco-nomic variation of recognizable themes according to dramatic context" had been in place since the 1920s.[18] Although leitmotifs were used by com-posers like Max Steiner and Erich Korngold, their use was by no means universally praised and accepted. Outspoken critics of film music like Theodor Adorno and Hans Eisler, for example, deplored the use of these

musical signals, which, they complained, were rather simplistic and repetitive and not at all creative. They also argued that a film score provided
an inadequate amount of music in which to explore a musical leitmotif; its
meaning could never be developed beyond the very rudimentary recognition of a character or emotion. Film scores must serve the visual narrative
and therefore have cuts and interruptions that don't allow the composer
the necessary continuity to explore the themes.[19]

Despite the complaints of Adorno, Eisler, and others, the leitmotif
technique has survived into the present day. Perhaps the most successful
film composer of the late twentieth and early twenty-first century who
used the leitmotif technique is John Williams. Like Wagner before him,
Williams extended a system of leitmotifs beyond a single work. Williams'
scores to the six films of the *Star Wars* series and his scores to the first
three *Harry Potter* films each use a system of musical gestures that develop
throughout, while retaining the same basic meaning in all of the movies.

North's use of the leitmotif technique in *Spartacus* was particularly
effective, since it allowed the audience to recognize—within North's
wall-to-wall score—certain important musical gestures. The character of
Spartacus has a theme, as do the slaves. Spartacus's love interest, Varinia,
also has her own theme. North not only wrote different melodies for these
themes but chose different instrumentation based on the context of the
scene. The orchestra at North's disposal had almost ninety pieces, including some unusual instruments North thought would enhance the sound
of the cues.[20] He was also aware of the emotional associations of certain
instrumentation.

> I tried for a deliberately cold and barbaric quality, avoiding strings un-
> til the thirteenth reel, when the love story begins to blossom between
> Kirk Douglas and Jean Simmons. . . . I relied on combinations of brass,
> woodwinds and some quite unusual and exotic percussion—for instance,
> I underscored a party scene with Novachord, vibes, marimba, boo-bams,
> crotales, fixed piano, harp, lute, guitar, sleigh bells (various pitches) and
> Chinese tree bell.[21]

North clearly equates the strings with love, but in contrast Bernd Schultheis, composer and Kubrick scholar, believes that the use of strings—not
just in *Spartacus* but across Kubrick's oeuvre—represents loneliness
or solitude. He uses as an example the scene in which Roman senator
Crassus attempts to seduce Varinia. The instrumentation of the cue is
solo violin (emphasizing Varinia's aloneness without Spartacus) accompanied by other string instruments and ondioline, an electronic keyboard

instrument. Varinia refuses the advances of Crassus, refuses to love him. Varinia's theme—a symbol of the love between Varinia and Spartacus—emerges as almost an echo in her memory and plays against a theme associated with Crassus. Schultheis explains that the combination of leitmotifs shows "Varinia's faithfulness towards Spartacus and her steadfastness."[22]

## Synopsis and Score Description for *Spartacus*

*Spartacus* begins with an overture of triumphant music.[23] Like the overtures to many operas, it is, in fact, derived from cues within the main work. Despite the ending of the film, which involves the crucifixion and death of the title character, the music here betrays none of the troubles ahead. It is straightforward and lively, with a parade-like atmosphere. Spartacus's theme is a fanfare. After the overture, the triumphant music continues through the main titles. Drum cadences on the snare proliferate in the main title, suggesting the martial music of soldiers or of training. For the visuals, Kubrick has chosen stills of a statuary, but mostly small details: hands, the very tips of swords, a pair of lips, Latin inscriptions in stone. As the musical cue grows louder and more frantic, Kubrick switches to the images of faces in sculpture. He fades them in and out, while the cue crescendos to a fever pitch. As the music bubbles over, the last face begins to splinter and crumble, a symbol of the fall of Rome. One musical cue that is absent from the overture and the main titles is the theme that represents Varinia and the relationship between her and Spartacus.

As the voiceover explains that Rome is "fatally stricken with a disease called human slavery," North has chosen instrumentation for the cue that seems to echo the work of the slaves: metallic percussion sounds and the plucking of the harp (along with low brass), which mimic the pick and axe work of the slaves in the mines. The melody is in a minor key. After Batiatus chooses Spartacus as one of his gladiators, they travel to Capua accompanied by a modal melody.[24] No music accompanies Batiatus's speech to the slaves, their branding, or the beginning of the training by Marcellus.

The next musical cue appears after Batiatus and Marcellus choose a female companion for Spartacus. Varinia is sent to Spartacus and when she enters his cell, the cue begins when Spartacus first sees her. As Henderson explains, the cue's "basic motif is a simple broken triad which changes the mood between minor and major during the course of the music cue."[25] The theme is played at first by a solo oboe. The choice of this particular instrument might have had many meanings for North. The oboe, a double reed, has a thin timbre, perhaps illustrating Varinia's loneliness. The cue is easily recognizable by the initial leap of a fifth, and then the drop of a third. The final note of the first three lands on the downbeat, anchoring the gesture. As Spartacus looks at her in wonder, the theme is taken up by the oboe d'amore, a lower instrument in the same family that has a slightly warmer sound. When Spartacus tells her he's never had a woman, the cue changes to the major mode, and Varinia turns to face him, removing her tunic. The conclusion of the theme is interrupted by the jeers and laughter of Marcellus and Batiatus. The cue continues after Spartacus tells them to go away and gives Varinia back her tunic.

Kubrick then juxtaposes scenes of Spartacus and the gladiators training—accompanied by North's loud and raucous music—and scenes in which Spartacus and Varinia steal glances at each other. In the scene in which Marcellus is showing areas of attack by painting Spartacus's body with different colors, we hear an echo of Varinia's theme. Here, the leitmotif shows us that underneath all the training, Spartacus is still thinking of her. And in this scene, she does appear, drawing Spartacus's attention away from training. Marcellus notices this and he forces Spartacus to look at her. In the next scene, Spartacus is in his cell and the women are being offered to the gladiators. His door opens and Varinia enters, accompanied by a fragment of her cue (the major version) played on the violin, but Marcellus takes her away, leaving Spartacus alone in his cell. To emphasize Spartacus's loneliness, North gives us just the opening triad of Varinia's theme in the oboe (and in the minor version).

At a meal, Spartacus and the other gladiators sit and wait for food. The music tells us that Spartacus is thinking of Varinia, but North has transformed the theme somewhat, as if her feelings are transforming. It's clear that Spartacus feels strongly for her, but we're not certain how she feels about him. It's in this scene that Varinia's expression seems to change. Spartacus's genuine concern for her is causing her to fall in love with him. The soft and gentle quality of this theme is followed immediately by the dissonant and rhythmically complex training music. Back in the kitchen, Varinia pours Spartacus water and the loving theme returns. They briefly touch hands and exchange a cautious smile.

The entrance of Crassus, essentially the film's villain, is heralded by a cue heavily orchestrated with brass and percussion. Henderson characterizes it as "pompous," and indeed Crassus fits the description.[26] A scene follows in which Crassus and his friends impose upon Batiatus to arrange two pairs of gladiators to fight to the death, and while this action goes on, soft music can be heard in the background. It is low in the mix because it was likely meant to represent music being played in Batiatus's house, for his guests. Again, North uses a modal melody, this time for music that is supposed to be contemporary within the narrative. Since Varinia is serving them, it is fitting that the opening leap of the fifth from her cue is echoed in the music. This sourced music—although the source remains unseen—continues in the next scene. Crassus arranges to buy Varinia, and consequently this music becomes significant for their interactions. This theme will appear again, when the two are reunited at Crassus's house toward the end of the film.

Slow, serious music plays as Spartacus and fellow gladiator Draba wait their turn to fight. As the fight between Crixus and Galino comes to a close—with Galino's death—the music surges to a crescendo. Drums and cymbals accompany the entrance of Spartacus and Draba to the arena. North scored the music for the opening of the actual fight with percussion, harp, and woodwinds. The theme is complex and integrates snare rolls with the previous music North associated with the slaves. After the fight, in which Draba does not kill Spartacus, whom he has bested, the music takes a brief pause. It returns as the gladiators file back to their quarters and pass Draba's corpse, which is hanging upside down as a warning to the others (Draba had attacked Crassus and his friends rather than kill Spartacus; Crassus stabbed him). The musical cue here is appropriately called "Brooding,"[27] as Kubrick treats us to close-ups of individual characters, each seeming pensive.

The music that accompanies the gladiators' rebellion has low, fast-moving notes played by the strings. Once most of the gladiators begin to escape, there is more percussion and brass. Within this cue, the fanfare associated with Spartacus can be heard. As the slaves run from the compound, the music becomes triumphant, and this music bleeds over into the title card that announces we are now in Rome. The scenes in the Senate are unscored; music might have been too much for these dialogue-heavy scenes. The next cue was written for Crassus's arrival at his home.[28] It is a short cue, similar in spirit to the cue that heralded the character's first appearance. A scene of the slaves burning houses and looting is accompanied by drums.

Spartacus returns to the abandoned gladiator school. As he enters his old cell, we hear Varinia's theme. Spartacus then goes out to see the other slaves, who are watching two older men, patricians, fight for their enjoyment. Unwilling to watch such a spectacle, Spartacus puts forth the idea that the slaves should travel to the coast and escape the country by sea. Their journey is accompanied by North's triumphant music from the overture. At one point, a group of escaped slaves meets up with Spartacus's group, and one of them is Varinia; her theme appears just as Spartacus realizes she's there. North combines her music with the music of the gladiators, almost as if Spartacus's feelings are torn between his duty to his men and his desire to be with Varinia. Varinia's theme takes over when Spartacus lets the men go on without him to reunite with Varinia. As they travel on horseback across a ridge in front of an orange sky, Varinia's theme is played by the trumpets, no longer relegated to a quiet solo. Varinia and Spartacus are free and in love, and the music is suitably joyful as they ride away.

The next musical cue is the one that Kubrick described as "exotic shimmering music," and it accompanies the scene between Crassus and his young Sicilian slave, Antoninus. This scene was cut from the film because of its suggestion of Crassus's bisexuality.[29] Crassus, who is being washed by Antoninus in a large bathtub, attempts to seduce Antoninus by engaging him in a metaphorical discussion about oysters and snails. In the intervening years since *Spartacus* was released in 1960, the dialogue track was lost, so the scene was re-dubbed in 1991 for the restored edition of the film. Tony Curtis, who had portrayed Antoninus in the film, dubbed in Antoninus's lines, while Anthony Hopkins—who knew and worked with Laurence Olivier—provided Crassus's dialogue (Olivier died in 1989). North achieved a shimmering effect in the score by using innovative instrumentation. Henderson lists the instruments in this cue as: vibraphone, marimba, crotales, tuned bongos, Novachord, guitar, piano, harp, lute, and Chinese bells.[30]

The following scene shows Spartacus on horseback touring his camp. This music has as shifting metrical pulse, which seems to propel it forward. It is a buoyant cue, full of hope and promise. The scene shows many aspects of the camp, the men standing guard over the valley, the escaped slaves training and learning to fight (using some of the same techniques used at the gladiator school), Varinia bathing the children of the camp, and the introduction of new recruits, including Antoninus, who has escaped from Crassus. The merry music of the camp is contrasted in the next scene with the music of the Roman garrison (led by Glabrus). Instead of shifting meters, Glabrus's music is a relentless military call for trumpets. The difference in the musical cues for Spartacus's group and the Roman army echoes the variable quality of the former and the trained precision of the latter. When we return to the camp some unknown time later, the operation of day-to-day life seems to be going even more smoothly. The music, now a steady meter, shows that this group is also growing in precision. The montage shows training exercises featuring a fitter, faster group of "soldiers." They perform difficult maneuvers on horseback. Kubrick shows individuals riding up to gourds (attached to sticks) and slashing through them. North accents the action by providing a cymbal hit for each gourd's "decapitation."

The mood softens as Antoninus provides a show around the campfire. There is quiet music, suggesting that it is sourced on-screen. There is a man with what appears to be a lyre, but the music does not match up with his movements. Someone in the crowd asks Antoninus for a song, and the guitar and the oboe d'amore play a soft melody as he recites a poem about returning home. Spartacus and Varinia leave the campfire, while in the distance the music plays, and Antoninus teaches the song to the others. Spartacus and Varinia have a conversation about his desire to learn about the world. North has given this cue, effectively a love theme for the two characters, to the strings. It is exceedingly warm, gentle, and intimate and includes Varinia's theme as the scene fades to black.

As Spartacus's army prepares for battle with the garrison, North provides a fast-moving cue for brass and percussion. The cue is louder for scenes of the men riding on horseback but continues more quietly under dialogue. The scene shifts to the burning of the Roman camp. The music is complex with dissonant accents that seem to echo the rising flames. A final drumroll completes the cue as the defeated Glabrus is questioned by Spartacus. Spartacus gives a short but rousing speech and sends Glabrus away to deliver the message to Rome that the slaves will not stop until they have their freedom. Under his speech, there is a soft but determined melody that is loudly taken up by the orchestra once Spartacus commands his men to put Glabrus on a horse. A musical intermission follows that continues the fast music of battle.

When we rejoin the former slaves, who are on the march south to Brundisium, North gives us the opening theme of the overture, including Spartacus's fanfare. Kubrick's talent for choreographing large-scale outdoor scenes is enhanced by North's expansive musical score. Kubrick scholar Norman Kagan describes the visual and the musical aspect of these scenes of marching and of battle as "a ponderous ballet of power. There is martial music, no speech."[31] Although the march is long and Kubrick shows us a montage of scenes in which the former slaves walk unceasingly over large areas, marching in the rain and snow, the spirit of the musical cue does not lose its brightness. North and Kubrick do provide one sad scene, in which a couple must bury their infant, who has died on the journey, and North's music is simple and folklike, a mandolin, violin, and bells. In the background of this scene, the people still walk.

Spartacus's group establishes a camp and North provides lively music for the montage of the activities there. Spartacus consults with his men over a map of Italy, Antoninus and another man spar, a woman milks a goat. Later, Varinia floats in a small pond and Spartacus sees her there. The music of this scene provides a respite from the military music of the camp and the march. Varinia's theme is prominent here. When she tells Spartacus that she's pregnant with his child, her cue switches to the major mode. He kisses her and soon we are back to a brief scene of marching and to North's driving music.

The slaves' triumphant entrance into the city of Metapontum is accompanied by ecstatic music in the orchestra. Back in Rome, members of the Senate sit in a bath and share details about the battles with Spartacus's army. Two musicians stroll about the bath playing music. One is playing a meandering modal melody on what is perhaps an aulos, a Greek woodwind instrument similar to the modern oboe. The other man is playing a small plucked harp (perhaps meant to be a lyre or kithara).[32] In his research of ancient music, North would have discovered that the Romans often adopted the instruments of other cultures including those of the Greeks, the Etruscans, and the Egyptians.

When we return to Spartacus's group, they have reached the sea. They make camp and celebrate, dancing to folklike music featuring tambourines. While this cue plays softly in the background, Tigranes, the pirate, tells Spartacus that Crassus has paid the fleet of pirate ships (on which Spartacus and the slaves were to escape Italy) to leave Brundisium. Spartacus and the slaves are trapped between two advancing armies at the southern tip of the country. Crassus has forced Spartacus and his army to turn back and march on Rome. The underscore begins to stir as Spartacus thinks. He commands Antoninus to tell the trumpeters to play. North responds with appropriate calls for the brass, as Spartacus tells the news to his people. Kubrick intercuts scenes from Spartacus's speech with scenes from Rome in which Crassus takes over the commander of Rome's army. When the armies set forth, North urges them on with cues drawing upon related earlier themes. The cue is in three parts, with Spartacus's theme at the center and the music of the Roman army on either side of it, hemming it in. By constructing the cue in this fashion, North musically illustrates the position of the slave army.[33]

Gentle, pastoral music accompanies Spartacus's walk through the camp at night. He sees people of all ages and sizes. He sees soldiers, and he sees families. The opening gesture of Varinia's theme makes an appearance as Spartacus looks at a young boy, perhaps thinking of the son he hopes for. He and Varinia talk in their tent, and when he asks her to tell their son about him, should he not survive, the strings play her theme.

As the slave army waits for the battle with the army of Rome, North provides percussive hits, which work with Kubrick's editing. For each hit, we see a different part of the army, the front line on horseback, the varied faces of the army standing and waiting, the commanders. As he did at the end of *Paths of Glory*, Kubrick humanizes the army, in this case showing old fighting next to young, women alongside men. This is a force of individuals. An ominous low hum accompanies the shot of the faceless Roman army opposite. Trumpet calls tear through the tension, and the advancing Roman army provides rhythm with their formation marching. North's music begins in earnest when Spartacus has his men roll flaming logs toward the Roman army. The cue is relentless, as is the fighting. When the battle is over, the echo of Varinia's theme is heard, as are eerie voices as the camera surveys the dead. A baby cries.

In the famous scene in which the prisoners are told that they must identify Spartacus, North begins with low notes that eventually rise up. The motion of the music mimics each of the men rising up and identifying themselves as Spartacus. The surviving prisoners march to North's drum cadences and low brass. Varinia has been taken to Crassus's house. In the scene, Crassus attempts to encourage Varinia to feel affection for him. The music in this scene is at times reminiscent of the seduction scene between Crassus and Antoninus, while at times it sounds similar to the chamber music playing when Crassus first saw Varinia at the gladiator school. There are also shadowy references to Varinia's music, as if a memory. Fragments of the slave theme also appear. Here, the leitmotifs provide a layer of subtext, adding meaning to words spoken on-screen.

A low but determined theme appears as the underscore to a conversation between Spartacus and Antoninus. They are the final two prisoners who are waiting to be crucified. The music gives a sense of purpose, and a feeling that the spirit of rebellion is not dead, but still present, as long as they live. Crassus rides out to see them, asking Antoninus if the other man is indeed Spartacus. While he waits for an answer, North's score becomes tense, finally breaking as Crassus yells and slaps Spartacus across the face. Spartacus, in turn, spits at Crassus. The orchestra provides accents for both the slap and the spit. Crassus forces Antoninus and Spartacus to fight to the death. The victor is to be crucified. The music for their fight begins in the low strings. It is a combination of the slave theme and

Varinia's theme. After Spartacus kills Antoninus to save him from a slow death on the cross, Crassus taunts him by telling him that Varinia and the child live in his house. This dialogue is accompanied of course by the shimmering ondioline version of her theme.

Varinia, however, will escape to freedom. On her way out of the city with Batiatus—using documents given to them by Gracchus—Varinia sees Spartacus dying on the cross. She shows him his son (who was born during the battle and whom he has not yet seen), and her theme turns to the major mode. Spartacus can say nothing, and she must leave him. The film and cue end with a fragment of Spartacus's theme and the victorious entrance music heard at Metapontum, but it is Varinia's theme that plays over the credits, accenting the bittersweet ending. Spartacus must die, but Varinia and their son live on in freedom.

There is a lot of music in *Spartacus*. Some types of scenes, like those in the Senate, have no underscore, while battle and training scenes have much more score than dialogue. The overall mood is one of triumph and determination, with some melancholy melodies. The story of *Spartacus* had political resonance in 1960, especially in light of the Hollywood blacklist[34] and the nascent civil rights movement, and this was an aspect of the film that was very important to both Kirk Douglas and Alex North. Art and politics share a bond, and even Spartacus understands this when he tells Antoninus—who wants desperately to fight—that he should teach the escaped slaves a song. "There's a time for fighting and there's a time for singing," says Spartacus. The film depicts a struggle—ultimately lost by the protagonist, but one that will continue. The triumphs and defeats are both present in the score. In his book *Reel Music*, Roger Hickman draws a distinction between Alex North's score for *Spartacus* and the scores for other epics, like Miklós Rósza's music for *Ben-Hur*, noting that the mood of *Spartacus* is more pessimistic than that of the other epics:

> Brass fanfares still dominate, but North includes prominent low brass instruments in addition to trumpets, a thicker texture, syncopated rhythms, and dissonances. Although this sound has often been equated with the decadence of Rome, it seems rather to suggest its brutality and cruel power. Historically, Rome was about to enter its most dominant era. The music leaves us with the feeling that while Rome, perhaps standing for America, is building its mighty Empire, it is also planting the seeds of its decay.[35]

By the time Kubrick made *Spartacus* he had made a crime caper, a noir-ish love story, and two war movies, one small in scale, one quite a bit larger. In *Paths of Glory*, we can see Kubrick's skill in filming battle scenes, while *Spartacus* showed off "Kubrick's talent for spectacle."[36] About a decade later, Kubrick planned to film another epic—this one about Napoleon—that would have rivaled *Spartacus* in many ways. Kubrick's Napoleon project never made it to the screen, and consequently *Spartacus* remains the only epic on Kubrick's resume.

The music for *Spartacus* is also epic in scope, lush and orchestral, filled with many different musical themes. Kubrick's collaboration with North resulted in a finished product that works well for the film, and the film's expansive budget allowed North to experiment with modal melodies and many different kinds of instruments. Kubrick had very little say in the script because it was already a finished product by the time he arrived; but the film score, which is normally created later in the production process, allowed him a creative outlet for his opinions and ideas. Although the circumstances of Kubrick's work on *Spartacus* were unique, the idea of Kubrick as perfectionist was already in the public imagination about him. He was already known to take control of many aspects of filmmaking even though *Spartacus* was only his fifth feature. In 1960, an article stated, "[Kubrick's] preoccupation with detail has by now become almost legendary."[37] He was thirty-two years old.

## LOLITA

Kubrick's next project, a screen adaptation of Vladimir Nabokov's novel *Lolita*, courted controversy from the very beginning. The novel, which was considered by some to be pornographic and was later hailed as a classic, dealt with a subject thought so delicate and difficult to film; the tagline says it all: "How did they ever make a movie of *Lolita*?" Not only was the subject matter problematic, Kubrick encountered difficulties in adapting this novel to screenplay form. Kubrick had originally engaged Calder Willingham, with whom he had worked on *Paths of Glory*, to write the screenplay, but that partnership did not work out.

Kubrick then engaged the assistance of Vladimir Nabokov, the author of the novel. Nabokov had never written a screenplay before and had at first turned down the opportunity to do the adaptation. When he finally agreed, he started with Kubrick's rough outline of the first part of the novel. Over a few months, Nabokov states that the two men met about every two weeks; but after a while, "outlines ceased altogether, criticism and advice got briefer and briefer, and by midsummer I did not feel quite sure whether Kubrick was serenely accepting whatever I did or silently rejecting everything."[38]

When Nabokov finally delivered his screenplay to Kubrick, it was four hundred pages long, and Kubrick explained that such a screenplay could not be filmed. His producing partner at the time, James Harris, said, "You couldn't make it. You couldn't *lift* it."[39] Nabokov took suggestions from Kubrick, deleting some scenes, devising new ones, and generally shortening the script. When the revised script arrived Nabokov reports that it was deemed "fine" by Kubrick.[40] But, if the film itself is any evidence, the revision did not satisfy Kubrick. He asked for no more changes, but ended up changing much of the script himself. Perhaps Kubrick felt unable to articulate what he wanted, or perhaps he did not quite *know* what he wanted.

Nabokov received a screen credit for his work, but when he saw *Lolita*, he realized that "only ragged odds and ends of [his] script had been used."[41] Nabokov published his screenplay of *Lolita* as a "vivacious variant" of the novel, which might have been of interest to his readers, complete with a foreword discussing the collaborative process.[42] It is indeed enlightening to see what Nabokov made of the experience (and how few of Nabokov's scenes made it into the movie), but Kubrick was concerned that Nabokov's published screenplay might give the impression that the film *Lolita* had "spoiled a work of art."[43]

In correspondence between Kubrick and Nabokov, there were also indications that Nabokov wanted to be more involved in the adaptation process, seeking to interview possible actors for the film. Nabokov's input on the film, however, was severely limited. At one point, Nabokov's wife, Vera, wrote to Kubrick in the hopes that their son could sing for the soundtrack.[44] Perhaps she (and her husband) had hoped that Nelson Riddle would set to music the lyrics of a song Nabokov had included in the pages of his screenplay. During the road trip after Humbert picks up Lolita at camp, they stop in a coffee shop and Lolita asks for a dime to play the jukebox. "Oh," she says, "they have my song." These are the words:

> Lolita, Lolita, Lolita!
> For ever tonight we must part:
> Because separation is sweeter
> Than clasping a ghost to one's heart.
>
> Because it's a maddening summer,
> Because the whole night is in bloom
> Because you're in love with a strummer
> Who brings his guitar to your room.

You know he's a clown and a cheater,
You know I am tender and true—
But *he* is now singing, Lolita,
The songs I've been making for you![45]

Kubrick did not use this song, nor did he ask Dmitri Nabokov (who was a successful opera singer), to take part in the music of the film.

Finding an appropriate musical score for *Lolita* had its difficulties, although Kubrick settled on a score that included aspects of both popular and traditional film scoring styles. Kubrick biographer Vincent LoBrutto described the score as "appropriately schizophrenic," utilizing a lush orchestral style for melodrama and featuring stretches with no musical underscore. Some of the music takes on a satirical irony, especially in the scenes in Charlotte Haze's house.[46]

James Harris, Kubrick's producing partner, suggested they use, as the love theme of the film, a song written by James's brother Bob Harris.[47] Kubrick agreed and then set about hiring Bernard Herrmann to complete the score, using the love theme as a centerpiece, as Gerald Fried had done with the song "Once" in *Killer's Kiss*. Whatever interest Herrmann might have had in the project vanished when Kubrick told him about Bob Harris's tune. Herrmann, who was vocal in his disapproval of using popular music in film scores, refused to take the job.[48] Instead, Kubrick hired composer and arranger Nelson Riddle. Kubrick was aware of Riddle's work on Frank Sinatra's albums *In the Wee Small Hours* and *Only the Lonely*,[49] but Riddle had also done some work in film, notably *Ocean's Eleven* (1960). Kubrick must have reasoned that Riddle wouldn't object to using arrangements of the preexistent theme for the film, and of course Riddle handled the job with aplomb. Riddle even brought in orchestrator Gil Grau, with whom he had worked on many projects, to help.

The collaboration between Nelson Riddle and Stanley Kubrick worked smoothly, with Riddle willing to make concessions to serve the needs of the film, willing even to change a theme from a minor key to a major key at the producers' request. Harris and Kubrick were concerned that the mood of the music, if too dark, might make Humbert seem even more distasteful and sinister. As Riddle biographer Peter Levinson states, "they believed any form of dissonance in the music would make Humbert Humbert appear too lascivious to the audience."[50] The mood of the score, both in the love theme and the pop elements, seems more ironic than serious, and the film has a great deal of wry humor in it, as did Nabokov's novel.

*Lolita* was one of Riddle's first film projects, but his work in film and television often took a backseat to his work as an arranger. For eleven years (1950–1961), he acted as "house arranger" for Capitol Records and worked with more than twenty artists in this capacity,[51] preparing arrangements for singers like Nat "King" Cole, Frank Sinatra, and Judy Garland.[52] He continued to create such arrangements into the 1980s (having particular success with Linda Ronstadt), while working on the occasional television special or film score when time permitted. He was nominated for a number of Academy Awards and took home the statue in 1975 for his adapted score to *The Great Gatsby*.[53] A complete discography of his work in film and television is available on his official website.[54]

## Synopsis and Score Description for *Lolita*

At the opening of the film, we see a young girl's feet and hear a lushly orchestrated version of Bob Harris's love theme. While hands reach out to paint the toenails the theme is played by "piano and strings in a warmly romantic vein with more than a hint of the Rachmaninov used throughout *Brief Encounter*."[55] The choice of the visual for the opening is suggestive of the intimacy between Humbert and Lolita without being obvious. It also implies transformation and artifice and Humbert's active role in Lolita's transformation from child to "nymphet."[56] The music begins low in the orchestra and gradually moves up through an arpeggio—that travels seamlessly through the orchestra—until it blossoms into the theme, played on piano with string accompaniment. Lolita's foot rests gently on Humbert's hand—which wears a wedding ring. As we reach the end of the credit sequence, the music swells on Nabokov's card and on James Harris's as well. Kubrick's card arrives just as the music resolves on its final cadence, and Humbert begins to paint the last toenail.

The credits and song end, and Humbert drives down a foggy road to Clare Quilty's house. Upon entering, Quilty's theme begins, a dissonant yet carousel-like tune on the organ and dulcimer (with tense strings in the background), to which Humbert adds a harp glissando (he sees a harp in the room and runs his fingers along it). The mansion is odd and disorienting to Humbert, who stumbles around in the mess, knocking over discarded bottles and glasses. The music, which is without a central home pitch, seems to represent both the disarray of the house and Humbert's confusion. At Humbert's call, Quilty appears from under a sheet. When asked if he is Quilty, he responds, "No, I'm Spartacus." This is obviously an ad lib from the brilliant Peter Sellers, who plays Quilty. Perhaps because of Peter Sellers, or because Kubrick wanted to make Quilty's involvement in the narrative more obvious in the film, Quilty's role is much expanded from his part in the novel. James Mason's Humbert Humbert is grief stricken, and confused enough to play a brief game of Ping-Pong with Quilty before pulling a gun. The underscore fades out and disappears for the rest of this scene, except for Quilty's brief stint at the piano, in which he plays the opening of Chopin's Polonaise op. 40, no. 1 ("Military"). He claims to have recently written the piece and suggests that Humbert help him come up with lyrics for it so that they might share in the profits if the song makes it to the hit parade. After suggesting some insipid lyrics about the moon being blue, Quilty throws a bottle at Humbert and attempts to run up the stairs.

Humbert shoots Quilty, at first in the leg but then fatally, after Quilty hides behind a painting. This has the practical purpose of saving the audience from seeing Quilty's death (and certainly must have pleased the ratings board), but also allows Humbert to attack the artifice, to shoot the artificial image of Quilty who fooled and eluded him in the previous years.

The title card "Four Years Earlier" and the subsequent shot of a plane flying over New York are accompanied by jaunty traveling music. Once Humbert arrives in Ramsdale, New Hampshire, at the home of Charlotte Haze, the music disappears. The next cue features a pop song that was written by Riddle and Harris called "Lolita Ya-Ya." This song, in various versions, forms the main theme for the first part of the narrative. Charlotte Haze has been trying to charm her potential lodger while showing him around the house. She seems to be oblivious to his discomfort and distaste for her, but he politely asks for her phone number (so that he might "think it over") and reluctantly agrees to see the garden. It is there that Humbert and the audience first see Lolita. She is iconic in her bikini, large sun hat, and sunglasses. She sits on a blanket, reading a book, and when Humbert sees her, he seems entranced by her young beauty. "Lolita Ya-Ya" is sourced from the transistor radio that sits on the blanket beside her. Charlotte asks her to turn down the music, which she does, allowing Humbert and Charlotte to talk about the rent. Pulling off her sunglasses (not the heart-shaped glasses from the movie poster, but ones in a more cat-eye shape), Lolita wordlessly regards Humbert and Charlotte for the rest of the scene. This is the song that plays as Humbert begins his subtle seduction of Lolita.

"Lolita Ya-Ya" was recorded as a single, featuring Sue Lyon, the actress who played Lolita, on vocals. The catchy bubble gum pop song was likely meant as ironic counterpoint to Humbert's high-class taste in art and literature.[57] In Riddle's biography, Levinson explains that the song "perfectly captured the humor of Humbert's lust for the teenybopper" but also provided satirical commentary on the insipid simplicity of contemporary popular music.[58] Despite the irony, "Lolita Ya-Ya" enjoyed some success as a single. *Cash Box* (a competitor to *Billboard* magazine) gave "Lolita Ya-Ya" a B+ calling it a "cute item from the upcoming 'Lolita' flick. . . . [It] is presented with an enjoyable sprightly rock-a-cha touch by the full ork and chanting chorus. Catchy cut." Lyon also sang the B side of that 45 rpm record, "Turn Off the Moon," which was composed by Harris with lyrics by Al Stillman (Stillman wrote lyrics for many hit songs, including "Chances Are," made famous by Johnny Mathis). *Cash Box* gave it a B.[59] The absurdity of the song might strike the older viewer—its only lyrics are "ya ya wo wo ya ya"—but this quality magnifies the improbability of Humbert's having happened upon a house in Ramsdale in which a nymphet lives.[60] Although it is not discussed or addressed in the film, the Humbert of the novel offers an explanation from his past as an excuse for his love of nymphets. He is not attracted to nymphets *because of* Lolita; she is merely the quintessential example of the elusive nymphet he first saw in his young love, Annabel Leigh.[61] Nabokov took pains to include information about Annabel in the screenplay, using a few precious pages to describe the relationship between young Humbert and Annabel.[62]

A brief scene follows in which we see a sequence from the horror film *The Curse of Frankenstein* (1957) in which the monster tears off the bandages on his face, revealing the deformed visage underneath. (Perhaps Humbert is a monster in a mask?) Charlotte and Lolita flank Humbert in the front seat of the car at the drive-in. Each woman grabs one of Humbert's hands during a scary moment, Humbert's hand wriggling out of Charlotte's grip to comfort Lolita. The moment turns even more awkward as Charlotte reaches out for Humbert and accidentally grabs Lolita's hand instead. The film cue has its own music, which comes to a neat end at the close of the scene. The music for the clip was likely written by Riddle, although it matches very closely with James Bernard's score from the original film. Riddle's cue has louder stings and is in general more dynamic, a quality that helps suggest what is happening on the movie screen, since we are watching Charlotte, Lolita, and Humbert for most of the scene. "Lolita Ya-Ya" next appears a minute later as Charlotte and Humbert play chess. Lolita kisses Humbert goodnight, and Charlotte seems to like playing house with him. The song continues through the next scene as Lolita is hula-hooping, Humbert surreptitiously peering over his book at her.

When the ersatz family of Charlotte, Humbert, and Lolita attends the summer dance, the music is sourced on-screen with a live band. Lolita dances with a boy named Kenny to Nelson Riddle's song "There's

No You." Charlotte tells Humbert that Lolita and Kenny might begin going steady that evening, to Humbert's dismay. Charlotte's friends Jean and John Farlow arrive and say hello. The band's next song is a more up-tempo number called on the soundtrack "Quilty's Caper." Charlotte spots Quilty dancing with a sour-faced dark haired woman and cuts in. Despite having had a brief fling with Charlotte, Quilty must be reminded who she is, but then remembers that she has a daughter with a "lovely, lyrical, lilting name." In his screenplay, Nabokov describes Quilty as "a tremendously successful phony."[63] Quilty, Charlotte reminds us, is an artist. He is able to see pretense, because pretense and artifice are the currency of the artist.[64]

After her awkward exchange with Quilty, Charlotte, who has conspired with the Farlows to get Lolita out of the house for the evening, attempts to get Humbert alone. Riddle's song "Put Your Dreams Away" plays in the background as Charlotte convinces Humbert to return home without Lolita, who has been invited to the Farlows'. At the Haze house, Charlotte turns on some music, a cue on the soundtrack called "Shelly Winters Cha Cha," so that she might dance with Humbert. (Nabokov had specifically mentioned a cha-cha in his screenplay; it is one of the few details that Kubrick retained.) Her attempts to seduce him are made in earnest but seem ridiculous, especially in the presence of the music. The final "cha cha cha" of the song happens just as Lolita arrives back unexpectedly. This spoils Charlotte's plan, and she and Lolita argue. When Lolita finally goes to bed, Humbert quickly decides to go to bed as well, to Charlotte's bitter disappointment.

For a scene in which Humbert and Charlotte eat dinner, and in which she explains that Lolita will be attending camp for the rest of the summer, Riddle has provided subtle and quiet "Music to Eat By." The following morning, Lolita, who is about to leave for camp, runs into Humbert's arms to the surging music of the love theme. This is its first appearance since the opening credits. It continues after her departure (she tells him, "Don't forget me," just as she runs off) as Humbert goes into Lolita's room and sits on her bed. The maid delivers a note from Charlotte, which Humbert reads aloud. It is her confession of love for him. He laughs at it, and the music is again the ironic counterpoint; the love theme does not play for Humbert and Charlotte. It is meant for Humbert and Lolita. He will do anything to be with Lolita, even marry her mother. In the next scene, some time has passed and Charlotte and Humbert have already returned from their honeymoon. On this particular morning, they argue, and Charlotte reads Humbert's diary, in which he has detailed his feelings about Lolita.

He tries to calm Charlotte down with a drink, with Riddle's subtle ominous underscore underneath. The cue is called, appropriately, "The Last
Martini," because the phone rings, informing Humbert that Charlotte,
who has run out of the house, has been hit by a car and killed.

As Humbert lounges in the bathtub with a drink some time later,
"Lolita Ya-Ya" re-appears. It plays through the scene as the Farlows come
to offer their condolences. They are very upset, and become even more
so when they see a loaded gun (which had belonged to Charlotte) in the
bathroom. Thinking he is contemplating suicide, they tell him he must
go on for Lolita's sake. The music, going through various, ever-higher
modulations, glosses over the funeral and brings us right to the moment
in which Humbert picks up Lolita from Camp Climax. It fades out for a
moment, to allow the dialogue between Humbert and Charlie (with whom
Lolita confesses to have been "revoltingly unfaithful"), but begins again
soon, and continues playing as they drive in the car as if the song were on
the radio. The atmosphere remains light because Humbert tells Lolita only
that Charlotte isn't well, not that she has died.

When the scene changes, Quilty's theme appears briefly, as does
Quilty himself. Bernd Schultheis suggests that his theme "creates an
atmosphere known from crime stories."[65] Quilty speaks to the manager
of the Enchanted Hunters Hotel, Mr. Swine, but walks off when Lolita
and Humbert enter to the strains of "Lolita Ya-Ya." Quilty recognizes
Lolita and listens to the conversation between Humbert and Mr. Swine.
The song continues as they go to their room with its single bed. Humbert
explains that they may have to share lodgings while they travel and then
leaves her alone in the room and goes downstairs for a drink. Music, a
jaunty little upbeat number, which sounds like it's coming from a room
off the lobby, continues under a scene in which Humbert has a conversation with Quilty. Quilty, who keeps his face averted, tells Humbert he's a
policeman and elicits details about Humbert and Lolita's travels.

The scenes in the hotel room following the meeting with Quilty un-
fold with no underscore. There is a comical interlude in which Humbert
and a bellhop try to put up a cot in the room without waking Lolita. In
the morning, Lolita asks Humbert if he'd like to play a game. Not being
sure what she means, he plays dumb until she explains (she whispers in
his ear). In the car later that day, presumably after the physical relationship between Lolita and Humbert has begun, he tells her that Charlotte
has died. The news is not accompanied by any music. But when Humbert
comforts her and tells her they will go to Beardsley College and live there,
a quiet version of the love theme plays, the melody in the high woodwinds.

A brief musical cue provides the transition from the road to Beardsley in Ohio. Humbert tells us in voiceover that "six months have passed" and that Lolita is now attending a good school. In Lolita's bedroom, Humbert is at the foot of the bed, painting her toenails (an echo of the opening of the film, although there is no music this time). They argue about her friends and her after-school activities. The next cue appears in the next scene; it is the brief opening of Quilty's theme as Humbert arrives home to find Dr. Zempf (Quilty in disguise) waiting there for him. During the course of the scene, in which Dr. Zempf convinces Humbert to let Lolita participate in the school play, there is no underscore.

The next scene takes place at Lolita's school, at the performance of Quilty's play "The Hunted Enchanters" (a reversal of the name of the hotel, the Enchanted Hunters Hotel, where Quilty by chance met up with Humbert). Again, there is another bit of Quilty's theme, as we see him, undisguised, exchanging a glance with Lolita before her last entrance onstage. The end of the play and the ensuing argument between Lolita and Humbert has no underscore.

A lively cue transitions from Beardsley to the road, as Lolita and Humbert take off on a trip. The cue becomes more sinister and minor as Humbert's voiceover reveals that they are being followed. The music becomes tense as Humbert sees Lolita talking to a person in a strange car. The music is in a minor key, with pizzicato strings and tremolos. Gerrit Bodde describes the cue as "bumpy," suddenly changing pace from the lively music of the road trip.[66]

Lolita becomes ill and Humbert takes her to a hospital. Humbert, who soon falls ill himself, receives a mysterious phone call (from Quilty), which prompts Quilty to pick her up from the hospital in the night. Upon finding out that she has left earlier in the evening with an uncle, Humbert becomes belligerent. The love theme appears low in the orchestra, creeping up, as Humbert realizes that he has lost Lolita. As he leaves the hospital, dejected, the music gains prominence, the piano solo taking over. The cue ends on an unresolved cadence, as if to reflect that things are up in the air.

A few years have passed, and Lolita—now married and pregnant—types up a letter to Humbert, asking for money. The next scene begins with a determined cue for muted brass, percussion, and string tremolos, which accompanies exteriors of the car driving to Lolita's house. When he parks, Humbert takes a gun out of the glove compartment. It is a tense, repetitive cue, echoing Humbert's sense of purpose. Humbert presses Lolita for answers about how and why she disappeared, and a slow, dreamy version of the love theme accompanies her explanation about her affair with Quilty. The music ends as Lolita's husband, Dick, comes in from the backyard. But the love theme begins again when Humbert asks Lolita to come with him. She refuses, and as he runs from the house, the theme surges louder on the soundtrack, and suddenly we see the misty foggy road from the opening of the film. The cue, which becomes thornier and more dissonant as Humbert walks through the mess of Quilty's house, ends as Humbert calls out for Quilty. The dissonant version of the cue continues over the epilogue, which states that Humbert died in prison awaiting trial. The theme ends in a minor key, reflecting the tragic ending. The epilogue says nothing about what happens to Lolita. In the film, we must imagine that she and Dick have paid off their debts (with the money Humbert provided) and moved to Alaska. In the novel, however, we are told in the foreword by the fictional John Ray, Jr., Ph.D., that Humbert dies awaiting trial and that Lolita died giving birth to a stillborn child just a few months after Humbert's visit.

The soundtrack to *Lolita* performs a number of dramatic tasks. The two recurring musical ideas—"Lolita Ya-Ya" and the love theme—illustrate the natures of the two protagonists. "Lolita Ya-Ya" is the musical representation of Lolita the character—at least as she is at the beginning of the film. It is simple, repetitive, and there's not much to it. However, it can also be viewed as a symbol of her youth, her girlhood. Tellingly, it pauses just as Charlie enters at Camp Climax; he is the young man to whom Lolita has lost her virginity. If "Lolita Ya-Ya" is a symbol of her purity, it retreats when Charlie appears. Once the physical relationship is consummated between Humbert and Lolita, the song is not heard again, because Lolita's girlhood is gone. By contrast, Bob Harris's love theme is Humbert's *idealization* of Lolita. It is the sound of a grand love story written in the stars. It is Humbert's fantasy, and as he sees this fantasy crumble and his last hope gone, the love theme collapses into dissonance.

Kubrick understood the power of music to elicit emotion from the audience, and he also knew that music could help his actors. Just as he played music for Woody Strode and Kirk Douglas on the set of *Spartacus* (and would later play Stravinsky's *Rite of Spring* for the young actor in *The Shining*), Kubrick also played music on set for Sue Lyon in *Lolita*. A blurb in the *Journal-American* explains that the director played Sinatra albums during rehearsals to help Lyon get into the proper emotional mood for certain scenes.[67]

The soundtrack to *Lolita* offered Kubrick his first opportunity to financially capitalize on the music from a film. Bob Harris's "Love Theme for

Lolita" entered the charts in a couple of versions, and it was such a hit that the *New York Post* reported that legendary classical pianist Van Cliburn was going to record a piano version of it: his first "popular" recording.[68] At some press screenings (and even some public premieres) paper disks of songs from the soundtrack were given to attendees. An ad for the film in a Philadelphia paper touted, "To the first 500 patrons, souvenir recordings of the smash hit 'Lolita Ya-Ya.'" Kubrick's view of music in his films was changing, and *Lolita* was an important step on this musical journey.

## DR. STRANGELOVE

*Dr. Strangelove or: How I Learned to Stop Worrying and Love the Bomb* was Kubrick's next project. Adapted from a novel called *Red Alert* by Peter George, Kubrick shared screenwriting credit with him and Terry Southern. Peter Sellers contributed a lot of ad libs in the dialogue but was not given a writing credit. Because the role of Quilty was expanded in the film version of *Lolita*, and because Sellers did such an admirable job playing Quilty in multiple disguises, Columbia Pictures agreed to finance *Dr. Strangelove* if Sellers was given multiple roles. Of the four roles he was slated to play—British Captain Lionel Mandrake, U.S. President Merkin Muffley, former Nazi scientist Dr. Strangelove, and Major T. J. "King" Kong—Sellers played only the first three. Slim Pickens memorably played Kong, a character who, at the first sign of trouble, puts on his cowboy hat. Pickens had appeared in Brando's *One-Eyed Jacks*, the film project Kubrick had briefly worked on before *Spartacus*.

The film began as a serious Cold War drama; however, as Kubrick worked with the material, he began to see the comedic possibilities in the topic. He envisioned what he called a "nightmare comedy" about a paranoid general (played by Sterling Hayden, who starred in Kubrick's *The Killing*) who initiates an unprovoked attack on the Russians that cannot be recalled. To add to the comedy, the character of Dr. Strangelove was added, an over-the-top former Nazi whose right arm and leg seem to be out of his control. The music adds ironic counterpoint to the film, although *Dr. Strangelove* is not a very musical movie. There are two preexistent songs that bookend the film, and there is the recurrent musical trope of "When Johnny Comes Marching Home." Many of the scenes—especially those in the war room and at Burpelson Air Force Base—have no underscore at all. For the musical portions of the film, Kubrick hired British composer and arranger Laurie Johnson. In his career, Johnson has worked with big bands, including the Ted Heath Band and his own London Big Band, and has composed and arranged music for film, television, and the stage.

### Synopsis and Score Description for *Dr. Strangelove*

The opening credits feature footage of an air force bomber refueling in midair to an orchestral version of "Try a Little Tenderness." The romantic mood of the song against the obvious sexual reference of the long fueling tube engaging with the bomber's tank sets the satiric tone for the rest of the film. The music and the visuals bring to mind what Luis M. Garcia Mainar calls the "main ideas in the film: the connection between desire and destruction." [69] When the tube disengages, the song concludes gently, with an almost melancholic air.

At the end of the film, the efforts to recall the last B-52, piloted by Major Kong, fail, and the nuclear bomb dropped by the plane begins a chain reaction of bombs around the world, annihilating mankind. A montage of nuclear explosions appears with Vera Lynn's World War II–era song "We'll Meet Again." The lyrics, by Hughie Charles, speak of loved ones re-uniting, ostensibly after the war. Kubrick had toyed with the idea of showing the lyrics on-screen, with a bouncing ball cueing the audience when to sing. Although he ultimately decided against this, the version of the song in the film featured an informal group of voices singing along with the chorus.

The musical centerpiece of the film is the tune "When Johnny Comes Marching Home." Multiple versions of this song appear over the course of the film, during scenes inside Major Kong's bomber. There are eight such scenes, and Johnson provides a different variation of the song in each, some with full versions of the tune, some only with fragments of certain lines. The instrumentation and tempo may vary, but in each case a drum, particularly the snare, is present.

The song "When Johnny Comes Marching Home" is credited to Irish American composer and bandleader Patrick Sarsfield Gilmore. Gilmore led a Boston band as part of the 24th Massachusetts Infantry. In 1863, Gilmore claimed to have written "When Johnny Comes Marching Home," although it bears striking melodic similarity to an Irish tune, "Johnny I Hardly Knew Ye." Although it was written during the Civil War, the song became a popular wartime tune, spawning many parodies and alternate versions. [70]

In the first bomber scene, the crew receives the order of "Wing Plan R," a serious bombing mission that carries the implication that a field commander is retaliating for a surprise attack. The music begins only after the crew has confirmed the order from base. The first version features snare and trumpet and later humming male voices under Major Kong's pep talk. The next scene in the bomber begins with humming voices and drum. The humming voices complete one verse then pause for drum rolls. Then they perform another verse. Major Kong distributes the attack plans to all members of the crew so they can lock in the code prefix (that will only allow the person with the code, Hayden's General Jack D. Ripper, to call off the attack). Brass instruments play the tune, with two extra measures of drum cadences between each line of the verse, effectively making the tune last twice as long. The humming version has no such delay. In the third scene in the bomber, the crew looks at the contents of their survival kits. Playing the tune this time with the drums is a harmonica. In the fourth bomber scene, in which a missile is tracking the bomber, the tune moves into the low brass, with echoes and arpeggios in the trumpets. The music gets lost in the noise after the missiles hit the plane, but part of the tune reappears at the end of the scene as the plane regains control. In the fifth bomber scene, the drum cadence has changed somewhat, allowing for an augmented (that is, lengthened) version of the tune, although we do not get the tune in its entirety, only fragments.

In the sixth bomber scene, the trumpets are in the middle of the tune, playing the last phrase. Here, Laurie Johnson adds a downward arpeggio in the lower brass. This is the least coherent version of the tune so far. In the seventh bomber scene, the tune is heard in its entirety, played in an augmented version by the lower brass. The low brass then provide squawking accents during the tune's repetition. The arpeggios are not in time with the drum cadence. In the eighth bomber scene, the tune is played in its entirety, played by muted brass. When the crew is arming the bomb, an alternate melody appears in the muted trumpet. Then the tune is played by the French horn. As Major Kong goes down to the bomb bay, the tune continues, with drum and brass accompaniment, and then it appears in the trumpet with low brass accents. More drums have been added, ratcheting up the tension. When the bomb bay doors open, the music stops, as Major Kong drops with the bomb onto the target area.

Although *Dr. Strangelove* did not have the same potential to sell soundtracks as did *Lolita*, music still formed part of the promotion of the film. Columbia released a 45 rpm record on Colpix with the A side as "Theme from Dr. Strangelove" and B side called "Love That Bomb." The latter song, which does not appear in the film, is a comedic early-sixties doo-wop song. At about a minute and a half in length, it belongs to a genre known as the novelty record. The artist on the 45 is listed as Dr. Strangelove and the Fallouts. Colpix also planned to release a 45 of Vera Lynn's version of "We'll Meet Again" in conjunction with the film.[71] The soundtrack album for *Dr. Strangelove* is actually a compilation album of songs from Colpix soundtracks. Notable on the album is a cue from Maurice Jarre's score to *Lawrence of Arabia*. The only song from *Dr. Strangelove* on the album is the so-called "Theme from Dr. Strangelove," which is Laurie Johnson's arrangement of "When Johnny Comes Marching Home." Missing from the album are "We'll Meet Again," "Try a Little Tenderness," and the popular music that Captain Mandrake finds playing on a transistor radio (clueing him in that there is no actual nuclear emergency at hand).

Although the music in *Dr. Strangelove* is perhaps less integral than one might see in the later films like *2001*, *A Clockwork Orange*, and *The Shining*, interviewer Michel Ciment suggested that it was in *Dr. Strangelove* that Kubrick began to use "music as a cultural reference";[72] however, one could argue that this is something Kubrick did very skillfully in *Lolita*. In either case, Kubrick's relationship with the music in his films was about to change greatly with *2001*. But more than twenty years after *Dr. Strangelove*, Kubrick would revisit the same kinds of cultural musical references as he did in the 1967 "nightmare comedy." There is no Kubrick film that uses popular music as a cultural reference point more intelligently than 1987's *Full Metal Jacket*.

## FULL METAL JACKET

For his first project after the horror film *The Shining*, Kubrick once again drew upon a war story, this time set in a marine boot camp and then in Vietnam. Kubrick's source material for this film was the 1979 novel *The Short-Timers* by Gustav Hasford. Screenwriter Michael Herr, who had written the Vietnam memoir *Dispatches*, also contributed personal anecdotes to the film. Kubrick follows a platoon of marines from the beginning of their training to their deployment into a war zone. Kubrick drew primarily on popular music for the soundtrack. Additional original underscore was provided by Kubrick's daughter Vivian, writing under the pseudonym Abigail Mead. *Full Metal Jacket* was Kubrick's first film in more than a decade to eschew classical or art music as part of the score. As Kubrick discovered in *Dr. Strangelove*, popular music can be very powerful in the two main ways it creates meaning for the viewer: "Through its musical features (rhythm, melody, lyrics, etc.) and through the connotations such songs may suggest to the viewer, who is supposed to share the culture that has produced them."[73] At the time of the film's release, many of the viewers of *Full Metal Jacket* were old enough to remember both the war and the music Kubrick chose for his soundtrack.

### Synopsis and Score Description for *Full Metal Jacket*

The music for the film's opening, a country song by Johnny Wright called "Hello, Vietnam," sets the tenor of the film, much like Purcell's *Funeral Music for Queen Mary* does in *A Clockwork Orange* and the *Dies Irae* does in *The Shining*. Kubrick shows the characters getting their heads shaved at the beginning of basic training. Kubrick chose not to have the sound of the razors at all on the soundtrack, preferring instead to have the music be the only sound. Each of the character's expression is a little different from the others, some obviously upset about the loss of their hair (for some, a symbol of their individuality) and others seemingly indifferent. During the first part of the film, when the protagonist Private Joker attends boot camp at Parris Island, South Carolina, the aural landscape of the film consists of the booming voice of the senior drill instructor, played by real-life gunnery sergeant R. Lee Ermey, and orchestrated military cadences.

The very first scene of the film, after the haircuts, is the introduction of the gunnery sergeant. There is no exposition before this, and we are thrust into boot camp without any ado. The gunnery sergeant sings cadences and the platoon echoes him. After a few scenes of training, drums take over the cadence and the training continues. The drum attacks are sharp, making them sound at times more like gunshots than drums. The men of the platoon are able to move with the rhythm of the cadence, but one marine named Leonard—although he is called "Private Pyle" in reference to Gomer Pyle—cannot seem to get into the rhythm of it; he is falling behind. For scenes of Private Joker teaching Private Pyle, there are percussive cadences with distant-sounding brass. On the shooting range, sounds of gunshots overtake music on the soundtrack.

The soundtrack's first ominous cue from Mead comes when Private Pyle is beaten by the rest of his platoon. Music of this type will return when Pyle has a mental breakdown. Similar cues appear when the platoon is in Vietnam. The intimation of this repetition suggests that the war begins for this platoon when they must turn against one of their own for the good of the many. Other musical moments include the platoon singing "Happy Birthday" to Jesus at Christmas, and graduation, which features a band version of the Marine Corps Theme Song (played by the Goldman Band).

On the last night of basic training, Private Joker takes fire watch, and an ominous cue called "Leonard" plays. It features percussive sounds played at irregular intervals and an unpredictable melodic line. Underneath, there is what sounds like breathing, almost like the sound of a respirator in a hospital. The music is tense and uneasy. Joker finds Private Pyle in the head, loading the magazine for his rifle. When the gunnery sergeant comes in, the distant and indistinct melody gets louder. Pyle shoots the sergeant and then sits on a toilet and shoots himself in the mouth.

Nancy Sinatra's "These Boots Are Made for Walkin'" provides the transition from the first part of the film—ending with Private Pyle's murder-suicide—to Vietnam. It begins as a prostitute walks toward Joker. This could be her theme song, this woman with an attitude, but more likely the boots belong to these soldiers who are walking through Vietnam, who, in effect, walk "over the inhabitants of the country."[74] While the song plays, Joker haggles with the woman over her price. The song fades out to the sound of a helicopter and a change of scene. The Dixie Cups' "Chapel of Love" plays on the holiday of Tet, accompanying a scene in the barracks. In both of these scenes, the music could be playing on-screen. It's quiet under the dialogue and "Chapel of Love" fades out when the soldiers leave the barracks to fight. "Chapel of Love" seems an ironic choice since the song discusses innocent love and commitment, while on-screen a marine looks at a magazine with nude pictures. The song continues playing as the men discuss the condition of those who see battle. Some original underscore, a cue called "Ruins," follows Joker and fellow journalist Rafterman to a mass grave.

Sam the Sham and the Pharoahs' "Wooly Bully" accompanies the scene in which Joker meets up with Cowboy's platoon (Cowboy was one of Joker's friends at Parris Island). As the platoon moves through the country, again, the music seems to rise out of the sound effects of war. In this case, it is overtaken by the gunshots of battle. "Surfin' Bird" by the Trashmen accompanies images of journalists filming footage of soldiers in battle and of a helicopter being filled with wounded soldiers. As the platoon searches for a sniper in the film's denouement, Mead's musical cue "Ruins" creaks and wheezes. Again, there is no recognizable melody, only repeated sounds. Like the war itself, it is unpredictable and unsettling. A different cue, "Sniper," is more melodic and distant and plays underneath the discussion of what to do with a dying sniper, who turns out to be a young woman. She begs to be shot, the music gaining volume and intensity with her pleas. The cue quiets down at Joker's single gunshot.

At the end of the film, Private Joker and the surviving members of the squad march to the Perfume River singing their own version of the "Mickey Mouse Club" theme song as a kind of cadence. It is a song that seems at odds with the bombed out and burning landscape.[75] Joker's voiceover, however, explains the cheerfulness of the song, the elation after the near-death experience with the sniper. Joker says, "I am so happy that I am alive, in one piece. In short: I'm in a world of shit. Yes. But I am alive, and I am not afraid." The soldiers singing together is a distant echo of the end of *Paths of Glory*, but in both cases it's a restoration of the men's humanity, a shared experience that seems to pull them back from the brink of inhumanity, cruelty, and the horrors of war. Again they "are more like children, frightened and happy to be alive, than like killing machines."[76] The final credits are accompanied by the Rolling Stones' song "Paint It Black."

What is so striking about the original underscore is how seamlessly it blends with the diegetic sounds of the scenes and rises up out of nowhere, like the enemy. The cues may appear at first to be sounds on-screen, but then take on structure that reveals them to be musical. When the cues are over, they can then retreat into the background again. The utilization of musical "noise" over traditional or orchestral music suits the subject matter quite well. If, as in *Paths of Glory*, melody is humanity, Mead has captured the inhumanity of war.

The commercially available soundtrack for *Full Metal Jacket* begins with R. Lee Ermey's cadences set to a drumbeat with some help from guitar. This five-minute track was arranged by Abigail Mead (Vivian Kubrick) and Nigel Goulding and was released as a single called "Full Metal Jacket." The soundtrack contains almost all of the popular songs from the film, including "These Boots Are Made for Walkin'" and "Wooly Bully," but the Rolling Stones' "Paint It Black" does not appear on the soundtrack. Mead's cues from the film appear on the album's second half (the B side, when it was issued on vinyl) and were performed on a Fairlight Series III synthesizer. *Full Metal Jacket* was Kubrick's penultimate film, and it was his last powerful meditation on the nature of war.

## NOTES

1. Thomas M. Pryor, Hollywood Dossier, *New York Times*, February 22, 1959.
2. James Naremore, *On Kubrick* (London: British Film Institute, 2007), 17.

3. Michel Ciment, *Kubrick: The Definitive Edition*, trans. Gilbert Adair (New York: Faber and Faber, 1999), 151.

4. Interview with Gene D. Phillips, in *Stanley Kubrick Interviews*, ed. Gene D. Phillips, (Jackson: University Press of Mississippi, 2001), 145.

5. Sanya Shoilevska Henderson, *Alex North, Film Composer* (Jefferson, NC: McFarland, 1993), 62.

6. Roger Hickman, *Reel Music: Exploring 100 Years of Film Music* (New York: Norton, 2006), 200.

7. For a complete filmography of all of North's credits, see Henderson, *Alex North, Film Composer*, 219–224.

8. Henderson, *Alex North, Film Composer*, 71.

9. Henderson, *Alex North, Film Composer*, 133.

10. Gene D. Phillips and Rodney Hill, "Gerald Fried," in *Encyclopedia of Stanley Kubrick* (New York: Checkmark Books, 2002), 267.

11. "Spartacus Music Notes," revised January 21, 1960, Stanley Kubrick Archive, University of the Arts London.

12. "Music Sweeteners and New Cues," June 1, 1960, Stanley Kubrick Archive, University of the Arts London.

13. Vincent LoBrutto, *Stanley Kubrick: A Biography* (New York: Da Capo Press, 1997), 175.

14. Henderson, *Alex North, Film Composer*, 131.

15. Norman Kagan, *The Cinema of Stanley Kubrick* (New York: Holt, Rinehart and Winston, 1972), 79.

16. Henderson, *Alex North, Film Composer*, 134.

17. Ernest Newman, in his detailed text *The Wagner Operas* (Princeton, NJ: Princeton University Press, 1949), systematically lists and names every identifiable leitmotif in Wagner's ten major operas.

18. Mervyn Cooke, *A History of Film Music* (New York: Cambridge University Press, 2008), 81.

19. Theodor Adorno and Hans Eisler, *Composing for the Films* (London: Athlone Press, 1994), 4–6.

20. One of the rarest instruments was the ondioline, a touch-sensitive electronic keyboard instrument invented in 1941 by Georges Jenny. It could play many different timbres, everything from traditional instruments like the violin, trumpet, and bassoon to instruments like the ukulele, the so-called Arabian flute, and the mandolin. The ondioline also had a setting called "Theater Organ" and one called "Burlesque Effect." Pianist Jean-Jacques Perrey recorded a demonstration record for Jenny in the 1950s.

21. Quoted in Henderson, *Alex North, Film Composer*, 132. The Novachord was a synthesizer developed by Hammond (famous for their organs). Hammond unveiled the instrument at the 1939 World's Fair. It was difficult to use and fell out of favor, but its odd timbres were used in the scores for science fiction films in the 1950s.

22. Bernd Schultheis, "Expanse of Possibilities: Stanley Kubrick's Soundtracks in Notes," *Stanley Kubrick Catalogue*, 2nd ed. (Frankfurt am Main: Deutsches Filmmuseum, 2007), 268.

23. For a complete and thorough analysis of the score for *Spartacus*, please see pp. 134–158 in Henderson, *Alex North, Film Composer*.

24. Modes as we know them today are collections of notes, much like the major and minor scales used in the Western system. Historically, modes go back to ancient Greece, although the modes used today have their origins in the Catholic Church of the eighth and ninth century. There is little known about Roman music, but a modal context seems to signify ancient times to audiences.

25. Henderson, *Alex North, Film Composer*, 142.

26. Henderson, *Alex North, Film Composer*, 144.

27. Henderson, *Alex North, Film Composer*, 146.

28. Parts of Hearst Castle stood in for Crassus's home.

29. Both the Production Code Administration and the Legion of Decency suggested the film be cut.

30. Henderson, *Alex North, Film Composer*, 148–149.

31. Norman Kagan, *The Cinema of Stanley Kubrick* (New York: Holt, Rinehart and Winston, 1972), 77.

32. Sanya Henderson erroneously identifies the wind instrument as an "ancient saroussophone" [sic]. Henderson, *Alex North, Film Composer*, 152. The instrument known as the sarrusophone was invented by Pierre Louis Gautrot in the 1850s, intended as a replacement for oboe and bassoon in outdoor bands. The instruments of the sarrusophone family are akin to saxophones, and they share so much in common that Adolphe Sax sued Gautrot over the similarities in design. Jerome Roche, "Sarrusophone," in *The New Grove Dictionary of Music and Musicians*, ed. Stanley Sadie (London: Macmillan, 2001), 296–298.

33. Henderson, *Alex North, Film Composer*, 154.

34. Kirk Douglas did his part to end the blacklist, hiring Dalton Trumbo, a member of the "Hollywood Ten," as a screenwriter on *Spartacus*.

35. Roger Hickman, *Reel Music*, 272.

36. Neil Jackson, "Stanley Kubrick," in *Contemporary North American Film Directors: A Wallflower Critical Guide*, ed. Yoram Allon, Del Cullen, and Hannah Patterson, (London: Wallflower, 2000), 302.

37. Robin Nobel, "Killers, Kisses . . . and Lolita," *Films and Filming* 7, no. 3 (December 1960).

38. Vladimir Nabokov, *Lolita: A Screenplay* (New York: McGraw-Hill, 1974), xx.

39. James Harris interview with Robert Corliss, quoted in LoBrutto, *Stanley Kubrick*, 200.

40. Nabokov, *Lolita: A Screenplay*, xx.

41. Nabokov, *Lolita: A Screenplay*, xxi.

42. Nabokov, *Lolita: A Screenplay*, xx.

43. Letter to Nabokov January 17, 1966, Stanley Kubrick Archive, University of the Arts London.

44. Letter from Vera Nabokov to Harris, December 14, 1960, Stanley Kubrick Archive, University of the Arts London.

45. Nabokov, *Lolita: A Screenplay*, 127.

46. LoBrutto, *Stanley Kubrick*, 199.

47. Bob Harris is probably best known to later generations as the composer of the theme song to the Spider-Man animated television series.

48. Herrmann left Hitchcock's *Torn Curtain* over the same issue. Herrmann biographer Steve C. Smith details the situation between Hitchcock and Herrmann in the thirteenth chapter of his book *A Heart at Fire's Center: The Life and Music of Bernard Herrmann* (Berkeley: University of California Press, 1991), 267–275.

49. Peter J. Levinson, *September in the Rain: The Life of Nelson Riddle* (New York: Billboard Books, 2001), 206.

50. Levinson, *September in the Rain*, 206, and LoBrutto, *Stanley Kubrick*, 214.

51. Levinson, *September in the Rain*, 103.

52. Gene D. Phillips and Rodney Hill, "Nelson Riddle," in *Encyclopedia of Stanley Kubrick* (New York: Checkmark Books, 2002), 299.

53. Awards Database for Academy of Motion Picture Arts and Sciences. http://awardsdatabase.oscars.org/ampas_awards/BasicSearchInput.jsp.

54. Nelson Riddle: The Official Website, http://www.nelsonriddlemusic.com/nr_tv.htm.

55. Cooke, *A History of Film Music*, 441.

56. Luis M. Garcia Mainar, *Narrative and Stylistic Patterns in the Films of Stanley Kubrick* (Rochester, NY: Camden House, 1999), 56.

57. Schultheis, "Expanse of Possibilities," 268.

58. Levinson, *September in the Rain*, 206.

59. "Best Bets," *Cash Box*, April 28, 1962.

60. Gerrit Bodde, *Die Musik in den Filmen von Stanley Kubrick* (Osnabrück: Der Andere Verlag, 2002), 62.

61. An obvious reference to Edgar Allan Poe's poem "Annabel Lee," which deals with the death of a woman, the young love of the narrator.

62. Nabokov, *Lolita: A Screenplay*, 5–8.

63. Nabokov, *Lolita: A Screenplay*, 56.

64. Garcia Mainar, *Narrative and Stylistic Patterns*, 56.

65. Schultheis, "Expanse of Possibilities," 269.

66. Bodde, *Die Musik in den Filmen von Stanley Kubrick*, 61.

67. Louis Sobol, "New York Cavalcade," *Journal-American*, June 29, 1962.

68. Earl Wilson, "It Happened Last Night," *New York Post* 14 May 1962.

69. Garcia Mainar, *Narrative and Stylistic Patterns*, 54–55.

70. "When Johnny Comes Marching Home Again," Library of Congress, http://lcweb2.loc.gov/diglib/ihas/loc.natlib.ihas.200000024/default.html.

71. Letter from Marvin Cane, V.P. Columbia Pictures Screen Gems TV Music and Record Division, January 16, 1964, Stanley Kubrick Archive, University of the Arts London.

72. Ciment, *Kubrick: The Definitive Edition*, 152.

73. Garcia Mainar, *Narrative and Stylistic Patterns*, 55.

74. Garcia Mainar, *Narrative and Stylistic Patterns*, 55.

75. This is a device Kubrick had used before. The cheeriness of the song contrasts the starkness of the landscape in much the same way that the upbeat "Singin' in the Rain" contrasts the cruel violence of Alex and his gang in *A Clockwork Orange*.

76. Garcia Mainar, *Narrative and Stylistic Patterns*, 56.

# Chapter Three

———————————————————O———————————————————

# The Music of
# the Spheres
## 2001: A Space Odyssey


*2001: A Space Odyssey* WAS, IN MANY WAYS, the film that changed everything. For Stanley Kubrick, it divides his early and middle works from his mature works; for film history it is a dividing line between traditional and experimental; and for film scores it is a watershed. Both controversial and influential, *2001* was made possible because of Kubrick's growing bankability as a director. In 1964, Kubrick was coming off a string of successes, with *Spartacus*, *Lolita*, and *Dr. Strangelove*. Despite being the darkest of black comedies, *Dr. Strangelove* convinced the studio heads at MGM that Kubrick knew what he was doing. MGM expected Kubrick to deliver a traditional narrative film in about two years, for about two million dollars. In the end, the project would take four years to complete, and the price tag would soar to more than ten million dollars. It also lacked the instant popularity of some of Kubrick's successes of the previous decade. Although the stunning visuals received attention quickly, the film itself puzzled some viewers. Film critic Pauline Kael called the film "redundant," "monumentally unimaginative," and a "limp myth."[1] In fact, it was quite misunderstood when it was released. But then a couple of very surprising things happened: a revised marketing strategy changed people's expectations of the film (and therefore their experience of the film), and the soundtrack became a best seller.

In the decades since the release of *2001: A Space Odyssey*, critics have come around to the film, which is now considered a classic in the realm of science fiction, and indeed of film itself. Many viewers consider this film to be Kubrick's masterpiece, representing the peak of his ideals as a filmmaker. It is breathtakingly beautiful, with incredible special effects, and a visual language that elevated the mainstream film to an artistic level. It confused some who wanted a traditional linear narrative, but it intrigued and inspired others.

Kubrick's gamble paid off. There is no doubt that he knew it would, of course. Kubrick's belief in his choices had passed from a quirk of his youth into the territory of parody. Despite outside pressures of the studio and his collaborators—Arthur C. Clarke and Alex North among them—Kubrick showed a level of steadiness and commitment to his own ideas that remains an examplar of autonomy to auteurs, one that will not likely be duplicated.

Kubrick was autonomous, and his auteurship is taken for granted, but was Kubrick a solitary figure? Was he the proverbial lone wolf, responsible for every aspect of filmmaking? Evidence seems to support this. Even the way Kubrick scored his films from *2001* onward suggests a man who wanted so much control over all aspects of his film that he would rather use preexistent music than deal with a living composer who might disagree with him. But that is perhaps an overly simplified model of Kubrick's working procedures during the last three decades of his career. Even Wendy Carlos, with whom Kubrick collaborated on the scores for *A Clockwork Orange* and *The Shining*, calls the director a "collaborative . . . open person."[2] He appears to have listened to suggestions from many people throughout these thirty years, but in each case, made the final decision himself alone. Kubrick would likely not have claimed that he was capable of doing all of it himself; he understood that he needed collaborators. They provided options, which were what he craved, especially in cases where he was not able to articulate exactly what he wanted. This aspect of Kubrick's filmmaking as it pertains to musical scores will become clear in this and the following chapters.

## THE BIRTH OF *2001: A SPACE ODYSSEY*

There are a few musical references in the pages of the novel *2001: A Space Odyssey*. The appearance of the first monolith is accompanied by a drumming sound; Dave Bowman recalls hearing some unnamed music when he wakes up from hibernation in the Texas training center; another astronaut, Frank Poole, hears his family singing "Happy Birthday" to him during the mission; and, of course, there is HAL's "mental breakdown" to the strains of "Daisy Bell." (The latter two are the only musical directives in the script). There is also the description of music Dave Bowman listens to after he is left alone on the *Discovery One* spaceship. In the film, we assume Bowman leaves *Discovery* in the pod right after disconnecting HAL's memory, but in the book a much longer time passes. Bowman fills the silence of the empty ship with plays and poetry and then with opera. He chooses operas in Italian or German so he will not be distracted by the narrative or by the words, but finds that the presence of human voices makes him feel even more alone. Clarke then describes Bowman's reaction to Verdi's *Requiem Mass*. "The 'Dies Irae,'" Clarke says

> roaring with ominous appropriateness through the empty ship, left him completely shattered; and when the trumpets of Doomsday echoed from the heavens, he could endure no more. Thereafter, he played only instrumental music. He started with the romantic composers, but shed them one by one as their emotional outpourings became too oppressive. Sibelius, Tchaikovsky, Berlioz, lasted a few weeks, Beethoven rather longer. He finally found peace, as so many others had done, in the abstract architecture of Bach, occasionally ornamented with Mozart.[3]

Music was part of the development of this story and film at every stage. Before the cameras rolled, Carl Orff's *Carmina Burana* inspired Kubrick and Clarke, who were apparently so taken by the dramatic music that they briefly discussed commissioning the score for the film from Orff.[4] Film historian Royal S. Brown mentions that Bernard Herrmann, "the pioneer of inventive science-fiction scoring," was asked to score the film, but his fee was too high.[5] Kubrick was, at one point, listening to the music of Gustav Mahler, especially the Third Symphony, for possible inclusion in the score.[6] Kubrick did end up commissioning a score from Alex North, but did not use it, and that part of the story will be discussed in detail below.

Another musical work makes a cameo appearance in an early draft of the novel. Clarke published excerpts from some of these drafts in a book called *The Lost Worlds of 2001*, published in 1972. At one time, Clarke and Kubrick had imagined that there were other astronauts besides Bowman and Poole awake on *Discovery*. In this particular iteration of the story, another astronaut, Peter Whitehead (who is in hibernation in the final draft and identified only as "Whitehead") is in one of the pods performing some extra-vehicular activity when he experiences a malfunction that sends the pod hurtling away from the mother ship. There is no chance of rescue. One of his last requests is for Dave back on the ship to play him some music, "something cheerful," he says. He asks simply for the Beethoven's *Pastoral* Symphony.[7]

Because music was so important to the development of the story, it is not difficult to see why music is such a crucial element of the film *2001:*

*A Space Odyssey.* The film is as much an aural experience as it is a visual one. Music, while not strictly part of the narrative, is still an important part of the storytelling, and a significant part of the film-going experience, enhancing the ideas of discovery, weightlessness, loneliness, and chaos.

*2001: A Space Odyssey* was Kubrick's follow-up to *Dr. Strangelove*, a classic dark comedy that ended with nuclear annihilation. The later film, Kubrick's first foray into the genre of science fiction, allowed the director to leave Earth and its petty problems behind, traveling into a future where the Russians and Americans have backed away from the abyss of war, although theirs is a tenuous détente, with the Americans obfuscating details about the anomaly on the moon. Instead of weapons, there is technology: scheduled flights into space, an orbiting station, a base on the moon, and spaceships that can travel all the way to Jupiter. But before we can get to the cool, clean future, Kubrick takes us far back into the past, to the Dawn of Man. Music takes on narrative duty, tying the disparate threads together, although there is a great deal of silence in the film as well, emphasizing perhaps the vastness of space and the isolation of individuals.

Turning *2001* into a film was a unique experience in adaptation since Kubrick and science fiction author Arthur C. Clarke essentially cowrote a story knowing that it would become both a novel (with Clarke as the author) and a film (with Kubrick at the helm). In 1964, it was Kubrick who sought out Clarke as a collaborator on a science fiction project, and Clarke, who lived in Sri Lanka, began the process by sending some short stories to Kubrick. According to Clarke, Kubrick "wanted to make a movie about Man's relation to the universe,"[8] and one of Clarke's short stories, "The Sentinel," caught the director's attention. Written in the late 1940s for a competition (which it did not win), it was published in 1951 in the *Avon Science Fiction and Fantasy Reader* under the title "Sentinel of Eternity" (the story was later published in other collections). The kernel of "The Sentinel" that ended up most important to the plot of *2001* is the presence on the moon of an artifact left there by an alien species. The narrator of the story theorizes that the object is meant to trigger a message to the alien people who buried the object on the moon. The message might be that the human race has advanced sufficiently enough to travel into space. Whether the alien people will react to this development with a generous welcome or with a hostile attack is left untold.

In the film *2001*, at different points in the story, rectangular monoliths (not a pyramid as "The Sentinel" describes) appear. Although Kubrick is not explicit on the point, these monoliths are alien intervention. At each appearance, they urge the human race forward to a new stage in its development. The first appearance takes place back at the Dawn of Man. A barely bipedal australopithecine, Moon-Watcher (as he is named in the novel), touches the monolith (as do his tribe-mates), and soon realizes that bones can be used as weapons against a neighboring tribe, and they can also fell animal prey. This development allows for the consumption of meat, which in turn makes the animals stronger, expanding their brain capacity and the ability to control their environment. Instead of showing all of these incremental changes on-screen, Kubrick ingeniously omits these steps by cutting from Moon-Watcher's bone—flung triumphantly into the air after a kill—to an orbiting satellite.

As in "The Sentinel" story, there is an alien artifact on the moon. Clavius base detects a magnetic anomaly in the large Tycho crater (called TMA-1 for Tycho Magnetic Anomaly-1). Excavators then find under the moon soil a rectangular black monolith identical to the one seen in the Dawn of Man sequence. This time, it emits an earsplitting sound aimed at Jupiter, urging a manned spaceship to eventually follow the direction of the sound. Once there, an astronaut, Dave Bowman, encounters a third monolith, the effects of which are harder to interpret.

Clarke and Kubrick spent four years on their collaboration. They began in 1964 and undertook the daunting task of writing a story about future space exploration from the vantage point of the dawn of the space race. They had to be careful to write what could not be disproven over the ensuing years of space travel.[9] It was a complicated process; Clarke didn't just write a novel that Kubrick adapted to the screen:

> Toward the end, both novel and screenplay were being written simultaneously, with feedback in both directions. Some parts of the novel had their final revisions after we had seen the rushes based on the screenplay based on earlier versions of the novel . . . and so on.[10]

The film premiered in April of 1968 and the novel—which sold more than a million copies—appeared in July of the same year. In 1966, long after MGM expected a finished film, Kubrick was asked to put together some scenes for MGM (ostensibly to show them where their money was going). Clarke reports that this screening, which he attended, featured Felix Mendelssohn's *Midsummer Night's Dream* and Vaughn Williams's *Antarctica Suite*, the former for scenes of weightlessness and the latter for the Stargate effects and scenes on the moon.[11] Although he used neither of these pieces in the film, Kubrick used the latter work on set to create an appropriate mood for actor Kier Dullea in the filming of the Stargate sequence.[12] In the end, Kubrick ended up with only preexistent art music on the soundtrack, and it was something of a coup for director and for the studio. An extremely popular and financially successful soundtrack, it far exceeded anyone's expectations.

## CLASSICAL MUSIC IN FILM

In using preexistent art music in his film Kubrick was bucking the established practice of having a single composer write the score for his film. But, perhaps unintentionally, Kubrick's musical choices drew on an even older tradition from the early days of film, when newly written film scores were not the norm. In fact, in the silent film era, musical accompaniment was often at the discretion of individual film pianists, who were called upon to choose appropriate music for scenes and to play that music live, often without the opportunity of viewing the film ahead of time. Sometimes the "score" consisted of a list of suggested preexistent pieces to play during specified scenes in the film. These lists, called cue sheets, provided recorded timings of scenes and the intended emotional tenor of the images.

In 1924, Ernö Rapée, a conductor and virtuoso pianist, published a collection of classical and popular tunes (transcribed for keyboard) categorized into general emotions or physical actions. The collection was called *Motion Picture Moods for Pianists and Organists: A Rapid-Reference Collection of Selected Pieces.* The subtitle refers to the table of contents printed in the margin of every page listing the fifty-two moods and situations in the book. The organist could then easily switch from one mood to another.

Rapée categorized film sequences into three groups: those depicting actions, those showing psychological situations, and those whose main purpose is to provide atmosphere. For the last category, Rapée included music for accompaniment that he calls "Neutral." The pieces under this heading include Schubert's *Moments Musicaux, Albumblatt* by Grieg, and *The Lotus* by Theodora Dutton.[13] For action sequences like "Fire-Fighting," Rapée included the "Card Trio" from Bizet's *Carmen.* For "Festivals," an organist can choose the March and Procession of Bacchus from Léo Delibes's ballet *Sylvia.* For the atmospheric heading "Grotesque," the organist may play Grieg's *Tanz aus Jölster.*[14] Similar collections were published toward the end of the silent era. In truth, by the time these collections categorized the music, the sound era had just about begun. More and more, directors called upon composers to write new music for their films, and the use of preexistent music began to wane, although it never disappeared altogether.

Over the course of film's first hundred years, the dominant tradition became the single composer and the newly composed score, but other traditions emerged as well, like that of the pop score heard in films like *The Blackboard Jungle*, *Easy Rider*, and *American Graffiti*. We have also seen the emergence of scores drawing upon world music, electronic music, and the avant garde. It was Kubrick himself and *2001: A Space Odyssey* (and a few years later *A Clockwork Orange*) that thrust the preexistent classical score back into the public consciousness.

## PREEXISTENT MUSIC IN KUBRICK'S FILMS

The choices of preexistent music in film, whether handpicked by a director or in a pinch by a silent film pianist, bring additional meaning into the film experience. A director might draw upon these meanings in a narrative or referential function to enhance the experience of his or her film. Kubrick was far more interested in the sounds of works and how the sounds matched with his visual images rather than what they "meant." In an interview with the author, Kubrick's brother-in-law and sometimes executive producer, Jan Harlan, explained that Kubrick was often unaware of the extra-musical meanings of his chosen works. With the very first musical cue in *2001*, *Also Sprach Zarathustra*, it might be easy to connect the dots and assume that Kubrick chose the piece because of its extra-musical meaning, but there just isn't evidence to support this. Harlan explains that Kubrick, in searching for an appropriate cue, asked simply for "something big that comes to an end."[15]

We cannot deny, however, that whether or not Kubrick was aware of these programs, ideas, or narratives, they have still become part of the films' fabric. They may be hidden to some and obvious to others, but as we discuss the musical works Kubrick used in the films of the second half of his career, I will tell the stories and anecdotes of these works, whether Kubrick knew them or not, because regardless of Kubrick's knowledge, they exist and they affect the way the film is read, accepted, and experienced.

Kubrick's preference for classical music over original compositions for his films is an important part of his work. When asked about his penchant for using preexistent music in his scores he said, "Unless you want a pop score, I don't see any reason not to avail yourself of the great orchestral music of the past and present."[16] After *Paths of Glory* (1957), scored by

Gerald Fried, and *Spartacus* (1960), scored by Alex North, Kubrick began to experiment with scores that used pop songs or borrowed music along with some newly written elements. With *2001*, Kubrick pushed those experiments even further, and as he worked, it seemed, at least to Jan Harlan, that there were three important aspects of Kubrick's method for choosing music in the second half of his career:[17]

1. Kubrick had to like [the cue] as a piece of music
2. Kubrick didn't like fading out or cutting
3. If he loved it enough, it didn't have to be that right [it could be historically inaccurate, like some of the music in *Barry Lyndon*, for example]

Directors often put together a rough cut of a film with an ersatz score. This temporary track, or temp track, helps the director and the editor find the rhythm of the film and helps enhance the emotional impact for early viewers of the cut. Because the score for the film is not usually written when the composer is presenting a rough cut, directors sometimes choose classical music or excerpts from the scores of other films as part of the temp track. (A notable exception to this practice was Kubrick's own *Spartacus*, which filmed for such a long time that Alex North was able to record a temp track of his original music. See chapter 2.) As a result, directors sometimes find that upon repeated viewing, the temp track has integrated itself into the narrative, becoming an organic part of the film. If they will not or cannot use the music on the temp track, directors will often ask composers to try to match a preexistent piece in style and mood.[18] Film music critic John Bender calls Kubrick's method of assembling a score "'permanent' temp-tracking."[19]

Kubrick became famous for using classical music albums from his own collection on his temporary tracks. Kubrick used music in the editing room, often editing sequences to specific pieces and even specific recordings: in that way, the piece of music would stay on the finished soundtrack if at all possible. He often edited the music as little as possible, opting to cut or add images rather than compromise the composer's musical idea.[20] Stanley Kubrick's great love of classical music, both canonical and avant garde, encouraged him to experiment with different kinds of music to accompany the images in his films.[21]

Reactions to the use of classical music in Kubrick's films were mixed. Film composers, in particular, dislike the practice of using preexistent music in film, for obvious reasons. Composer Jerry Goldsmith argued against the usefulness of this music because its familiarity and incongruity made it distracting. "It is a mistake to force music into a film, and for me *2001* was ruined by Kubrick's choice of music. His selections had no relationship, and the pieces could not comment on the film because they were not part of it. . . . A score is a fabric which must be tailored to the film."[22] Kubrick did not (or could not) often explain his choices, but about *The Blue Danube*, for example, Kubrick noted: "It's hard to find anything better than 'The Blue Danube' . . . for depicting grace and beauty in turning. It also gets as far away as you can get from the cliché of space music."[23] It may be argued that the source of the music, whether it is the canon of Western art music or the mind of a young film composer, is unimportant. The only thing that should concern any viewer is how well the music serves the film. Some have argued that the scores made of preexistent pieces have served their purposes admirably,[24] a sentiment that rings true especially in the films that use music specifically chosen by the director in prominent structural and narrative functions. Perhaps the best example of this is Kubrick's own *A Clockwork Orange*, which will be discussed in detail in the following chapter.

## ALEX NORTH AND THE LOST SCORE[25]

While shooting *2001*, Kubrick pitched the idea of using all preexistent music on the soundtrack. The idea was flatly rejected by MGM who felt that a project of the magnitude of *2001: A Space Odyssey*—a Cinerama film, an event film—deserved no less than a large orchestral score tailored to it. At the behest of the studio, Kubrick asked Alex North, with whom he had worked on *Spartacus*, to compose the score for the film.[26] North was particularly excited to work on the film because Kubrick described the film as having just twenty-five minutes of dialogue, and North had just finished scoring the dialogue-heavy drama *Who's Afraid of Virginia Woolf?* In December of 1967, North traveled to London to meet with Stanley Kubrick to discuss the project. North's account of this entire process was published in Jerome Agel's *The Making of Kubrick's 2001*. In the meeting they discussed aspects of the score, and North remembers: "[Kubrick] was direct and honest with me concerning his desire to retain some of the 'temporary' music tracks which he had been using for the past years. I realized he liked these tracks, but I couldn't accept the idea of composing part of the score interpolated with other composers."[27] Despite Kubrick's attachment to these pieces, North felt that he would be able to contribute newly written pieces that would match the moods and structures of Kubrick's temporary track, but with updated harmonies and a greater sense of continuity. It has been suggested, however, that Kubrick's "temporary" tracks were never meant to be temporary. Conductor and orchestrator Henry Brant has related an anecdote about the subject in which Kubrick indicated that he commissioned the score as a stopgap measure. Alex North's wife, Anna Höllger-North, remembers the situation similarly.[28]

Regardless of Kubrick's intentions, the director set up North, who had been living in New York's Chelsea Hotel (incidentally also where Clarke was living), in an apartment on the Chelsea Embankment. It was there that he would write the score over a period of weeks. The intensity of the work and the stress of the deadline had a detrimental physical effect on North, who suffered debilitating muscle spasms and consequently was not able to conduct the score. Brant, a composer in his own right, led the very large orchestra. North sat in the control room during these sessions, while Kubrick came by to check on the process now and then. Far from being discouraging, Kubrick made useful suggestions to the composer. North took great pains to match, as closely as possible, Kubrick's choices. One cue in particular, "Bones," which was written to replace Richard Strauss's introduction to the tone poem *Also Sprach Zarathustra*, is quite obviously—even on a first hearing—modeled on the earlier piece. North correctly suspected that even with all the similarities, Kubrick would not part with the Strauss piece.

All told, North composed about forty minutes of music, which was recorded over a period of two weeks. At that point, North was hoping to see the film so that he could spot the music and get an overall sense of what still needed to be done. Kubrick did not send him the film and essentially left him in a holding pattern for eleven days. (Although North mentions that Kubrick was still making suggestions for possible changes during this time.) These days were incredibly stressful for North, who was both frustrated at the lack of communication and anxious to finish the score. In his private notes, he kept track of his correspondence, or lack thereof, with Kubrick. One note says: "explained to his asst. my momentary duress. Willing to go ahead and still working *under Doctor's care*" (emphasis original). Finally, Kubrick responded with a written note, dated 26 January 1968. It reads:

> I tried to phone you several times last night but your phone was busy over a period of several hours. As I've told you several times during the past week, I'm still editing and I won't be able to determine what, if any, further music requirements exist until then. I hope to be able to do that in a few days. Regards, Stanley.[29]

With the release of the film still a couple of months away, North still had no idea which portions of his music would be kept and which would be left unused. In early February, North finally heard from Kubrick about the score, and the message left him more puzzled than ever; Kubrick stated that no more music was necessary and that he was going to use "breathing effects for the remainder of the film."[30] When *2001* was previewed in New York on 1 April 1968, it was the first time Alex North saw the film, and he was very disappointed to find that Kubrick had not used one measure of his music on the film.

For more than two decades, North's score remained largely unheard, except for a few themes that bear a resemblance to parts of later scores like that of the 1981 fantasy film *Dragonslayer* (for which North was nominated for an Original Score Oscar) and 1968's *The Shoes of the Fisherman*. In the latter film, the heroic theme for Kiril, the man who unexpectedly becomes pope, features a particular rhythmic and harmonic gesture that very closely resembles a gesture heard in the cue that was meant to replace Richard Strauss's music in *2001*. Two bright sonorous chords appear, the first both shorter in length and higher than the second. This short-long gesture, played by trumpets and horns in particular, has a sense of majesty about it. It fits equally well in the context of humankind's evolution and in the elevation of a simple, humble man to the highest office of the Roman Catholic Church. This motif becomes one of the most important themes in *Shoes of the Fisherman*. Other cues resemble simple folk music or chorale-like hymns. The main title bears resemblance to a Ukrainian folk song, "Oy ne khody Hrytsyu," which became a popular tune in the U.S. with the title, "Yes My Darling Daughter." Versions exist by Dinah Shore, the Andrews Sisters, and Eydie Gormé.

North mentioned once or twice expanding the raw material from the score into a symphony, his third. Incidentally, North thought that he might dedicate such a piece to the Apollo 13 astronauts, who survived a lunar mission riddled with life-threatening challenges. That project never materialized. One of the cues from North's score, called "Fanfare from *2001*"—the cue meant to replace Strauss—was included on *Hollywood's Greatest Hits, Vol. 2*, a compilation of film music performed by Erich Kunzel and the Cincinnati Pops Orchestra (1993).

In the early 1990s, film music legend Jerry Goldsmith set about recording the score from the manuscript copies.[31] The resulting score differs a bit from North's actual recordings (which were published in 2007 and are discussed below). There is also the erroneous inclusion of a cue that North wrote for a 1967 television series called *Africa* (called "Main Theme" on the track listing). The manuscript for that cue was mixed in with the music for *2001* and was thought to be part of the original score.

Even with its inaccuracies, the release of the score on the Varése-Sarabande label featuring the National Philharmonic Orchestra must have felt like a great vindication for North's estate. Unfortunately, North died in 1991 and did not live to see the completed recording, which could not have been made without the efforts of Jerry Goldsmith, who felt that Kubrick had made the wrong decision in discarding North's score. Reviews of the score were mixed. Some could not get Kubrick's iconic musical choices out of their consciousness, while others addressed how well North had captured the moods in Kubrick's film.

In 2007, Intrada Records, an American label specializing in soundtracks, released a recording of North's personal copies of the recording sessions he did for the film. This is considered to be the definitive version of the score and differs from the Goldsmith version in a few important respects. First, the cue called "Main Title" on the Goldsmith recording is called "Bones" on the Intrada recording, the name given by North and Brant. "Bones" (with the additional title of "and M.T." ostensibly for Main Title) is an important cue because it is the one meant to replace Strauss's *Zarathustra* excerpt. The Intrada release also includes additional takes for three cues in which one can hear slightly different emphases in Brant's interpretation. There is an alternate version of the cue called "Foraging" on the disc, which, because the manuscript for it was not included with the rest of the score, is missing from the Goldsmith recording. Also, the cue from the *Africa* series is gone ("Main Theme" on the Goldsmith recording). One of the most useful aspects of the Intrada recording is the detailed commentary in the CD booklet by film music scholar Jon Burlingame. In addition to historical information about the recording, Burlingame and producer Nick Redman devised timings that allow one to sync up the recording to scenes in the film. Previous to this, a synching guide appeared in the *New York Review of Science Fiction* in 2000, but North's tapes hadn't yet been released.[32] The Intrada recording is also unique because it has the blessing of both Kubrick's estate and North's.

The first cue on the Intrada recording, "The Foraging," was composed for the Dawn of Man sequence. North paints the desolate landscape with a low melody in the cellos, basses, and low woodwinds, which alternate with high pings in the harp. There is a meandering line in the low strings that seems to suggest the disorder of the natural world. Layers of melody eventually work their way up to the higher range and then fade back down again. When the australopithecines arrive on scene, North adds some percussion, a gong, and the texture seems to become a bit more complex. Otherwise, the apes do not have their own music, suggesting that they are just part of this tableau, just another animal in nature, with no special spark. This is made explicit in scenes where the tapirs and australopithecines occupy the same space, show no fear toward each other, and share the same resources. The leopard attack is not dramatized in the music, and this is where the cue would fade out. The alternative cue for "The Foraging" is more heavily orchestrated, more structured, and, one might argue, more dramatic. There are more of the tense, clichéd film music conventions here. Fraught with tension, these musical gestures dramatize the actions on-screen, making it seem like something huge is afoot. There are also echoes of the "Bones" cue.

The next cue, "The Bluff," is meant to accompany the confrontation between two tribes. The "protagonist," Moon-Watcher, leads one of the tribes. North characterized the cue as "barbaric" to emulate the fierce competition between the tribes for a rapidly shrinking watering hole. Although "competition" might be too strong a word here, as the australopithecines just shout at each other. Staccato notes of the low woodwinds and strings begin the cue. The use of percussion, primarily gestures of varying length in the timpani, mirrors the aggression of the apes as they beat the ground and flail their arms to scare off the rival tribe. There are also flourishes in the woodwinds that seem to echo the chatter of the apes. The ending of the cue, which features an almost noble-sounding fragment in the horns, Burlingame says, "suggests the fanfare of [the cue] 'Bones' yet to come." "The Bluff" cue is a bit too long for the scene, as this is one of the scenes Kubrick pared down after initial screenings of the film. The horn fanfare occurs after the scene has faded to black.

The next cue, "Night Terrors," accompanies scenes of the tribe, quiet and frightened, as they try to survive another night. Once again, the low woodwinds create an ominous mood, but instead of the high harp notes of sunrise, the accents are lower. Bass clarinets echo the "Bones" cue. Brass instruments join in—tubas, euphoniums, and flugelhorns—providing warmth with longer-held chords. The music is here is layered, almost as if fear is laid on fear. There are none of the percussive hits of the earlier aggression, although there are two short figures played on timpani, the first for muted timpani marked "near the rim." The second is simply marked *pianissimo*. The meter remains indiscernible, another way North shows the uncertainty of these animals' lives. Emotionally, the high strings, played with harmonics, seem to wail in dissonant anguish, although the apes themselves manage to stay quiet. The addition of prickly gestures on the harp (to be played "near the soundboard") and the low strings add to the tension. These three cues, "The Foraging," "The Bluff," and "Night Terrors," were not replaced in the film with preexistent music. Kubrick in fact used no music at all, which must have been an additional shock to North. It's one thing to be replaced by Richard Strauss, but quite another to be replaced by silence.

In the film, the appearance of the first monolith is accompanied by the music of György Ligeti. The intensity of the cue grows as the australopithecines fearfully approach the mysterious object. Finally, after approaching and retreating, Moon-Watcher reaches out and touches the monolith. This is the object that, as Burlingame observes, "will change the destiny of mankind," and Kubrick's musical choice here infuses the scene with tremendous dramatic importance. North apparently did not compose a cue for this scene. The previous cue, "Night Terrors," ends just as the first ape creature wakes up to see the monolith.

"Bones" accompanies the newly enlightened Moon-Watcher as he plays around with some bones. In doing so, he makes the connection that such an implement can be used as a weapon. This scene, so perfectly captured by the introduction to Strauss's tone poem, is here accompanied by North's similar fanfare. It shares many musical and structural details with the earlier piece. In both, there is a rising arpeggio figure and the use of insistent brass, and in both the organ gets the final word, hanging on after all the other instruments have ceased. In an interview, North described his take on the *Zarathustra* music, "I wrote a piece of equivalent length, only more contemporary, dissonant, harsh, and brassy."[33] North and especially orchestrator Brant show a great sensitivity to the brass section here, using the slightly different timbres of French horn, trombone, and euphonium (and others) to create a full, rich sound that complements the open intervals of the composition. The cue, like the excerpt from Strauss, seems to play on the relationship between the darkness of the minor and diminished chords against the brightness of major triads. There are hits on the cymbals and the timpani that also echo the Strauss.

In the scene following the discovery of the monolith, Moon-Watcher and the tribe eat the raw flesh of a tapir that Moon-Watcher has felled with his bone weapon. The following morning, they return to the watering hole. This scene has no score in the film, but North's cue for the sequence is appropriately harsh to the ears, with strident brass and heavy percussion. Particularly prominent are the timpani. The percussion from "The Bluffs" is here again, even before the confrontation takes place. It foreshadows the upcoming attack and makes the eating of meat seem fraught with portent, as if the meat is responsible for the violence. They eat for a long time, as the sun goes down. The young apes even play with the bones too, the younger generation learning from the older generation. At the watering hole, the two tribes face off. Moon-Watcher steps forward, and a single line in the brass is like his voice, which is then joined by counterpoint. When Moon-Watcher makes the first strike, the music changes. Accents in the piano and percussion alternate with a fast moving line in the strings (doubled by English horns and clarinets). The effect is one of aggression and forward motion, as if the apes will begin to march. North used piano, Hammond organ, chimes, xylophone, and celesta to add color to the scene. As the sense of forward motion picks up, at one point North marks that the piano should play the "five lowest chromatic tones" on the keyboard and that a measure later he or she should play both the five highest chromatic tones and the five lowest. The organ player is told to hit a "palmful" of high and low notes for the same accented cluster. More percussion instruments play, snare drum, cymbal, and bass drum adding to the fracas. Again, Kubrick trimmed this scene, and consequently North's music is too long for the film version. On the original sketch, North wrote "Ess Fleisch und Morder," which became the cue's name after Brant translated it, "Eat Meat and Kill." In his book *The Films of Stanley Kubrick*, Daniel DeVries puts it a different way, "I kill, therefore I am."[34]

Kubrick's first choice for the first scene in the space age was the scherzo from Mendelssohn's *Midsummer Night's Dream*. Many people, including North, have made the point that Kubrick had gotten so attached to the temp track that it was impossible for him to change his mind, but even though he had been using this tune for a while, Kubrick replaced Mendelssohn with Johann Strauss late in the game. Jan Harlan mentioned a similar circumstance that occurred during the production of *Eyes Wide Shut*. Kubrick, who had chosen a particular song for use in the film, kept it for a year but then suddenly changed his mind near the end of production. He found something that served the scenes better. To Kubrick, perhaps the Mendelssohn began to seem too contrived for the scene, although he did not remedy the situation by choosing a more obscure piece of music. Instead, he chose *The Blue Danube* waltz, which is just as recognizable, perhaps even more so.

North's alternative, a cue called "Space Station Docking," begins with a charming and very lively conversation between the strings and woodwinds (strings are both plucked and played with the bow). There are accents on organ, harpsichord, and harp. When the camera gets close to the space station, the music changes a bit, slowing down perhaps to mimic the turning of the station. The harmony becomes more chromatic, and from this point on, dissonant elements never fully leave the harmony. The fluttery lines of the woodwinds are juxtaposed by slower-moving lines in other instruments. Like the waltz, North's cue is dance-like and mimics the effulgent mood of the Strauss except in harmonic language, which is more defiantly dissonant. North's cue also foreshadows the uncertainty ahead; it is more suggestive of what is to come and reflects some of the secrecy and uncertainty of the as yet-unrevealed mystery on the moon. The fluttery conversation keeps grinding to a halt for dissonant chords played by the glockenspiel, celesta, harpsichord, vibraphone, chimes, xylophone, two harps, and a marimba. But instead of having a charming, shimmering quality as one might expect from this collection of instruments, the effect is more unsettling, as the innocence of the journey masks the seriousness under the surface.

North's cue "Space Talk" accompanies the conversation Dr. Heywood Floyd has with his daughter back on Earth. The music of the cue is soft and intimate, meant to underscore dialogue, and features a warm quality with strings, harp, and woodwinds. Trills in the strings seem to add to the magical nature of the cue. There is an underlying sweetness here, with an undercurrent of an emotion Burlingame characterizes as "awe," which is slightly at odds with Floyd's businesslike sense of the ordinary. Floyd doesn't once look out the window to his left to see the Earth passing by. Perhaps North was reflecting his own awe at this future vision. Once again, Kubrick replaced North's music with silence. As in a work like *Paths of Glory*, the absence of music sometimes feels like the absence of humanity. By not using North's sweet music, Kubrick takes some of the humanity out of the scene, and once again Floyd's businesslike demeanor dominates, even as he talks to his own daughter (Kubrick's daughter Vivian played the part).

As Floyd continues on to the moon, the cue "Trip to the Moon" (echoing the title of the classic Méliès brothers' 1902 film), features unique instrumentation, including a harpsichord, two harps, a celesta, glockenspiel, flutes (alto and bass flute included), and strings (without cellos or basses). The delicate orchestration is charming and effervescent. As a companion to the "Space Station Docking" cue, it shares a general overall mood rather than similar musical ideas. Kubrick used *The Blue Danube* again here, giving Floyd's trip continuity, even though it was interrupted by his brief "layover" at the space station. The grace of this cue—the harpsichord making it sound particularly stately—does not mirror the motion on the spacecraft (the Aries 1B). Even though the flight attendant is weightless, the gravity shoes she wears causes her to walk somewhat unsteadily as she attempts to keep her feet on the ground or ceiling as she moves through the craft. Although the cue is given a meter of 3/4 (like Strauss's waltz) it does not share the dance-like quality of Kubrick's ultimate choice. In fact, North seems unconcerned about the meter being discernible, as the musical colors seem to be the most important aspect of the music. The dissonant interludes of the previous cue are absent here for some reason. There is no music for the next fifteen minutes of film, although it appears that North planned to write a second part for the remainder of the voyage to the moon and the landing of the Aries.

Once on the moon, Floyd travels with others to the site of the newly uncovered monolith. The conveyance, called in the script "Moon Rocket Bus," lends its name to North's cue. There is a foreboding mood in this cue, clueing the viewer in to the idea that something important is about to happen. Perhaps the eeriest thing about the cue is North's use of a wordless line for a solo soprano. The voice sounds far off, as insistent strings play in the foreground. Again, the orchestration is inventive and evocative, here featuring an organ and harpsichord. North's mixing of timbres in this case results in an otherworldly sound. The woodwind section, featuring English horns, adds warmth to the timbre. The opening theme of the cue returns, with its agitated strings and single voice. The voice, still echoey and somewhat distant, seems to be getting more insistent as well, until it disappears, leaving a dissonant sound mass as the moonbus lands. Once again, North signals us that something is afoot.

The remainder of the Intrada recording includes the other Dawn of Man cue. In this version, the reference to "Bones" that North merely hinted at in "The Foraging" is made more explicit. The final three tracks are additional takes for "Eat Meat and Kill," "Space Station Docking" (middle section), and "Docking" (coda). The Intrada disc was given a small pressing of three thousand copies and has been out of print since. It is therefore a somewhat rare, but very important, artifact in this story.

One must make note of how often North attempted to capture the mood of Kubrick's chosen pieces. There isn't a one-to-one correlation for all pieces because some of the cues, especially in the Dawn of Man sequence, were replaced by no music at all in the final cut. But there are sufficient similarities in, say, "Bones" (*Zarathustra*) and "Space Station Docking" (*Blue Danube* waltz) to show that North was trying to make good on his promise to provide cues equivalent to those on Kubrick's temp track. In an interview with Michel Ciment, Kubrick, however, claimed that North just didn't get it. Kubrick explained that although he had gone over his selections with North and that the composer agreed to use them as a guide, "he nevertheless, wrote and recorded a score which could not have been more alien to the music we had listened to." Furthermore, Kubrick dubbed the score "inadequate." None of this came up during the recording sessions, when Kubrick was in and out, making suggestions to North and Brant. Perhaps he felt it was too late to make changes, or perhaps he knew the music would not ultimately be used. It's hard to figure out what Kubrick was doing here. He can certainly be forgiven for making choices that ultimately served the film, but it seemed that his reticence lead North on, to a certain extent. Also, he explains to Ciment that North's inadequate score left him in an uncomfortable position. "With the premiere looming up," he said, "I had no time left even to think about another score being written."[35] With this statement, he makes it sound as though using the preexistent music score was a measure he was required to take, out of practical need. Although I don't think anyone at MGM would argue that if Kubrick had wanted to commission another score, the date of release might have been pushed back yet again.

Even though Kubrick was not the first director to discard a newly written score for a film, and he was certainly not the last (other famous examples include the scores for Hitchcock's *Torn Curtain* and William Freidkin's *The Exorcist*), after *2001* he was more cautious in his collaborations with composers. The three composers who contributed to his last four films—Wendy Carlos for *A Clockwork Orange* and *The Shining*, his daughter Vivian for *Full Metal Jacket*, and Jocelyn Pook for *Eyes Wide Shut*—all had a better understanding of how to collaborate with Kubrick.

## *2001: A Space Odyssey*: The Soundtrack

The initial soundtrack release from MGM was far more successful than anyone at MGM could have hoped. It was so profitable that MGM released a second album, this one featuring "Music Inspired by MGM's Presentation of the Stanley Kubrick Production." As its first track, this album included the introduction to Strauss's *Also Sprach Zarathustra*, but no other cut on the album appears in the film. The rationale for this—besides the obvious profit-making opportunity—is that the original soundtrack had inspired in the public a new interest in art music. What better way to serve the public than to put out an album of selections that the public might like as much? MGM included an alternate piece by Ligeti, *Lontano* (which Kubrick would use in *The Shining*), his organ piece *Volumina*, and another excerpt from *Requiem*. There is also another part of Strauss's *Zarathustra* and waltzes from his opera *Der Rosenkavalier*. The liner notes explain that these waltzes are "spacious music for outer space." Also included is the "Berceuse" section of Khachaturian's *Gayane Ballet Suite*. In addition, there is a piece by Leo Delibes, "Coppelia," "Entflieht auf Leichten Kähnen" by Anton Webern, and "Margarethe" by Charles Gounod. In addition, Columbia Masterworks (CBS) released an album called *Selections from 2001* featuring recordings by the Philadelphia Orchestra (under Eugene Ormandy) and the New York Philharmonic (under Leonard Bernstein) of most of the music from the film, including the introduction to *Also Sprach Zarathustra*, Ligeti's *Atmospheres* and *Lux Aeterna*, and Strauss's *Blue Danube* waltz.

### Richard Strauss: *Also Sprach Zarathustra*[36]

Appearances:

0:00:00–0:01:22 Credit sequence
0:11:40–0:13:10 Discovery of bone as weapon/tool by Moon-Watcher
2:07:35–2:09:03 Dave Bowman becomes the Starchild

Richard Strauss wrote *Also Sprach Zarathustra* in 1896. It falls into the genre of the tone poem, a single-movement work with multiple sections and an extra-musical program. Strauss composed a number of these tone poems early in his career, beginning a few years after Strauss left the University of Munich. His first effort in the genre was *Aus Italien* from 1886, followed a few years later by tone poems about Don Juan and Macbeth. This particular type of piece had been pioneered by Franz Liszt in the mid-nineteenth century. The symphony itself had declined in popularity after the deaths of the great symphonists Mozart, Haydn, and Beethoven, and composers began to experiment with new ideas, including writing purely instrumental music meant to function in a narrative sense. Liszt attempted to expand the concert overture, a one-movement musical piece with a dramatic or evocative program, to a piece with as much motivic complexity as a symphony. He was therefore inspired by Beethoven's Sixth Symphony (the *Pastoral*), and Mendelssohn's *Hebrides* Overture. Liszt completed more than a dozen of these pieces, with subjects such as Orpheus, Hamlet, and Prometheus. Although Liszt's symphonic poems have not becoming overwhelmingly popular nor are they often performed, they inspired similar works by subsequent composers, Richard Strauss among them, that have entered the standard repertoire.

Strauss's tone poem *Also Sprach Zarathustra* is loosely based on the eponymous literary work by Friedrich Nietzsche, which the author had completed in 1885. The novel follows the fictional prophet Zarathustra (who shares only his name with the Persian Zoroaster), who travels and teaches his ideas about morality. In the prologue, Nietzsche explains that humans are the link between apes and a new type of being, what Nietzsche calls the Übermensch, or superman. This concept of the development of the human into a being that has achieved its full potential is particularly resonant in the narrative of *2001*, since the monoliths are an external stimulus that helps apes and later humans (as represented by Dave Bowman) achieve such a self-actualization. Again, it is worth noting that Kubrick was not much concerned with the story, but one must admit that, in this case, it fit rather well.

It was the concept of evolution that inspired Strauss's tone poem. The composer explained:

> I did not intend to write philosophical music or portray Nietzsche's great work musically. I meant rather to convey in music an idea of the evolution of the human race from its origin, through the various phases of development, religious as well as scientific, up to Nietzsche's idea of the *Übermensch*.[37]

The section of the tone poem that appears in the film is just the introduction to a work that lasts about thirty minutes. There are nine sections in all, which Strauss named after chapters in Nietzsche's book. The piece begins with the famous introduction, which has the alternate title of *Sonnenaufgang*, or Sunrise. The fanfare in the trumpets begins with three notes, C-G-C. These elemental pitches that form a fifth and an octave represent the beginning of the overtone series, an acoustical phenomenon in music. Strauss has directed the first entrance of this theme to be played "feierlich" or solemnly. These three notes have been called both the dawn motif and the nature motif. All of the instruments in the very large orchestra play the final fortissimo chord at the end of the introduction, although the organ's sonority, because of its long decay, is heard last. One measure of rest separates the introduction from the second section, "Of those at the back of the world." Seven sections follow including *Das Grablied* (the Grave Song, or Dirge) and *Von der Wissenschaft* (Of Science). The latter of these features a fugue with a theme comprised of all twelve notes of the chromatic scale (with the repetition of only two notes), something that would be developed decades later in the twelve-tone music of Arnold Schoenberg.

What must have intrigued Stanley Kubrick in the Sunrise section was its elemental nature. Its builds up from single notes into a bright sonority, like the first hints of sunlight over the horizon into a brilliant blaze of sun. An added bonus of using this section is its brevity. It also comes to a resolution at its end. Kubrick did not have to cut it because it is already self-contained. Furthermore, it is not necessary for the audience of *2001* to know the program of the tone poem because the essence of its meaning is conveyed so well in the music and so appropriately through the visual images.

The use of Richard Strauss's *Also Sprach Zarathustra* has garnered a lot of attention and has become closely associated with the film; once one has seen the movie, it is difficult to hear this work without thinking of the Dawn of Man sequence or the striking visual tableau—moon, earth, and sun—of the opening. Kubrick biographer Vincent LoBrutto argues that the piece adds depth to the philosophical attitude of the narrative.[38] Kubrick had originally planned to have narration over the opening sequence, but it's hard to imagine that now. It's also hard to believe that any words could be more eloquent than the music and the images alone.

The power of the film as a pop culture artifact is clear when one realizes that the opening to *Also Sprach Zarathustra* (and not the rest of the tone poem) has become a well-known piece of music largely because of its inclusion in this film. It has been repeated and parodied and used in animation and advertisement. The film and Strauss's opening gambit for this tone poem have become intertwined, for good or for ill. In Jan Harlan's documentary, *Stanley Kubrick: A Life in Pictures*, Tony Palmer says of this film: "I never knew if the images arose out of the music or the music arose out of the images, but perhaps the true thing to say is that they became, in his imagination, clearly, and so have become in ours, totally inseparable."[39]

### Johann Strauss: *Blue Danube* waltz

Appearances:

0:16:02–0:21:21 Shuttle docking with the Orion space station
0:29:20–0:36:18 Trip to the moon
2:20:26–2:28:37 End credits

Kubrick chose for the scenes of spacecraft flying and docking perhaps the most famous waltz by Johann Strauss, the so-called Waltz King.

Kubrick had previously used a waltz by Strauss in *Paths of Glory*. For the scene in which Kirk Douglas's Colonel Dax goes to the house of Major General Broulard to plead for the lives of his men, we hear Strauss's *Künsterleben*, or "Artist's Life." Here the waltz provides a contrast with the stark percussion of the battlefield. In *2001*, *The Blue Danube* waltz, or *An der schönen blauen Donau*, provides accompaniment to movement.

Johann Strauss composed the work in 1866, and although it is best known as an instrumental work, *The Blue Danube* had words written by the poet of the Vienna Men's Choral Association, Joseph Weyl. There was also another set of words written by Franz von Gerneth, which speak of the beauty of Vienna. The instrumental version, which premiered at the Paris World's Fair of 1867, became extremely popular, becoming something of a nationalistic anthem for Austria. It remains popular today, not just in Vienna but all over the world. In the film score guide to *2001*, Carolyn Geduld mentions that this waltz had been used in the film *A Night to Remember*, which takes place on another ship, the *Titanic*. The regularity of a waltz, in this case a specifically well-known one, offers the viewer something of a comfort. Space travel is no longer a white-knuckled adventure for the highly trained. Now it's like flying to an international location. Geduld calls this travel "measured, polished, choreographed, routine." The music reflects these qualities.[40]

*The Blue Danube* is comprised of short sections with different waltz melodies, and Kubrick uses every one of them over the two space travel sequences. Immediately after the Dawn of Man section, Kubrick starts the cue with the introduction to the waltz. It is not strictly in time yet and it outlines the opening theme, while the strings glisten with tremolos and the woodwinds provide accents. This opening passage is in the key of A major, which is the dominant tonality for D major, the key of the waltz. This key area sets up the feeling of expectation, a sense of anticipation that Kubrick could not have explained theoretically but that works perfectly to transition from the silence of space to the movement of the craft. Each waltz has its own character, and many of the sections have repeats. Kubrick omitted a couple of these repeats in order to make the length of the music fit the length of the visual sequence. The cutting of repetitions, which is sometimes done even in formal performances, is a very unobtrusive way to shorten a piece, and as we understand, Kubrick was loath to make cuts in the middle of melodies, or at any point that was not an organic resting place.

The first space sequence uses all of the waltzes in order from the introduction through the fourth waltz. The sequence covers the docking of the spacecraft and stops just as Floyd arrives at the immigration area at the space station. Kubrick then allows dialogue and the ambient noise of the space station becomes the only sound. The keen ear will hear announcements over the public address system like the finding of a lost cashmere sweater. The human interaction on the space station is as stark and colorless as the decor. It could have been Kubrick's intention to avoid the emotional baggage that music might have brought to these scenes on the station. In the second space sequence—Floyd traveling from the station to the moon—Kubrick returns to the second waltz and continues through to the end of the piece. The moment of the ship's landing is timed perfectly to coincide with the grand pause in the waltz that signals the ending section of the piece. While the craft is lowered slowly into the hold on a pedestal, the final section of the waltz plays, a slower, almost melancholy end to the dance, and then a vigorous few measures conclude the piece. There is no feeling of foreboding or even portent in *The Blue Danube*. The feeling is light, joyful perhaps. There is no indication that there might be anything dangerous or questionable about what will happen on the moon.

Kubrick chose the waltz for the end credits as well. Once again, the piece plays in its entirety. Long after the credit sequence is finished and words "The End" have flashed, Kubrick allows a black screen to remain for minutes as the waltz continues all the way to its end.

## The Music of Gyorgy Ligeti

Appearances of *Atmosphères*

0:00:00–0:2:19 Overture (this is the timing on the DVD; a longer excerpt was played in theaters)
1:52:16–2:00:12 Intermission
2:02:52–2:11:10 Stargate sequence

Appearances of *Requiem* (*Kyrie*)

0:08:20–0:10:54 The monolith appears to the ape creatures
0:50:54–0:54:35 Floyd (and other astronauts) explore the monolith in the Tycho crater
1:56:58–2:02:52 Monolith appears floating in the space around Jupiter, journey through the Stargate

Appearance of *Aventures*

2:11:11–2:14:20 Bowman leaves the pod, entering into the Louis XVI
bedroom

Appearances of *Lux Aeterna*

0:45:33–0:46:51 Floyd and colleagues travel to the Tycho crater on the
Moon Rocket Bus
0:49:06–0:50:51 Moon Rocket Bus continues its journey to Tycho and
then lands

György Ligeti was born in 1923 into a Hungarian Jewish family in the
Transylvanian region of Romania. As a young man, he studied music at
the conservatory in Kolosvár. The Second World War interrupted his studies, and Ligeti was forced to work in a labor camp while other members
of his family were sent to concentration camps. Ligeti lost both his father
and brother in the camps. After the war, Ligeti taught in Budapest, but
communism left him isolated from the musical community outside of the
Soviet Union and other Eastern Bloc countries. In the mid-1950s, Ligeti
moved to Vienna, leaving his early compositions behind, many of which
were never recovered.

Ligeti moved to Cologne and worked with pioneers of electronic
music like Karlheinz Stockhausen, although Ligeti produced only two
electronic pieces. Instead, the work of those at the West German Radio
studio in Cologne inspired him to write instrumental and vocal music
that mimicked textures of electronic music. It was the idea of texture that
became the central focus of Ligeti's creativity. Ligeti's music would create
what he called "sound masses" that he would then shift and manipulate. A
sound mass might consist of many notes, five, ten, twenty, or even more,
played by instruments or sung by voices or both. The notes are often
close together forming a cluster of sound, something Ligeti called "micropolyphony." Some of the vocal pieces use traditional texts, like the *Lux
Aeterna* and the *Requiem*; however, the nature of sound masses renders
these words mostly unintelligible.

Although Ligeti was enjoying some notoriety in the 1960s, it was
Kubrick's use of his pieces in *2001* that introduced the composer to a
massive audience. Brother-in-law Jan Harlan notes that Kubrick's choice
of Ligeti's *Lux Aeterna* was precipitated by a suggestion made by Kubrick's
wife (Harlan's sister) who happened to hear it while painting or sculpting

and listening to Radio 3.[41] According to Harlan, the director found the sound of Ligeti's music "very sophisticated and new."[42] Kubrick would use Ligeti's music in both *The Shining* and *Eyes Wide Shut* as well.

Kubrick's use of Ligeti's music was not without controversy, however. First of all, there have been conflicting reports about whether (and how much) Ligeti knew about Kubrick's desire to use his music.[43] According to some reports, Ligeti's experience of the music in *2001* was the opposite of North's experience. North watched and was disappointed that his music wasn't in the film; Ligeti watched and was surprised by how much of his music was used in the film. Ligeti's publishers were not legally obligated to tell the composer of negotiations with Kubrick's Hawk Films, although it is not unreasonable to imagine that someone should have communicated the details as a courtesy to him.[44] In September of 1968, Ligeti apparently saw the film and was upset with what he saw as the betrayal of C.F. Peters, his publishers. In a letter he wrote to a friend right after he viewed the film, Ligeti claims that "Peters betrayed me" and that the film "is a piece of Hollywood shit."[45] There followed a lawsuit in which Ligeti and his representation complained that his music was not "background music," as the contract suggested, and that the manipulation of *Aventures* (discussed below) violated the contract, which made no provision for tampering.[46]

Furthermore, it has been suggested that on a philosophical level, Ligeti was uncomfortable sharing the score with people like Richard Strauss, whose ambiguous position during the Second World War would be offensive to Ligeti, whose Jewish family was torn apart by the Nazi regime. Later, Ligeti spoke about how well he felt the music fit with the images. In Jan Harlan's documentary about Kubrick, Ligeti, late in his life, seems to have gained some perspective, perhaps understanding how useful Kubrick's films were in popularizing his music. Of the appropriateness of his music in *2001*, he says that the music and the images suggest great speed, perhaps even beyond the speed of light. "And then we enter in another world."[47]

Ligeti's music is so unique and so unlike anything else on the soundtrack that it begs interpretation. The music of the Strausses and Khachaturian seems to represent our known world, perhaps even our humanity. But when the characters on-screen are confronted with the monoliths, something alien, we hear this very different kind of music, representing another world, an "other."[48] In an essay on *2001*, Barry Keith Grant has raised the question of whether or not Ligeti's music can be heard when the monoliths are present. If we are not sure this music can be heard by those on-screen, we cannot be sure of its meaning. Evidence in the film seems to suggest that the voices that accompany the appearances of the monoliths are not heard by the apes, nor are they heard by the astronauts in the Tycho crater. (From a purely scientific standpoint, the moon has no air or atmosphere and no sound can travel.) Perhaps, as Grant suggests, the sound is the fabled "music of the spheres," a sound that modern man has lost the ability to hear.[49]

Kubrick begins the film with *Atmosphères*, a work that begins with a large cluster of sound played by an orchestra. There is no overwhelming feeling of regular meter or rhythm, nor is there functional harmony that creates a sense of expectation. We simply hear the shift of texture over time, as instruments enter and leave the sound mass. The same piece accompanies the intermission. The lack of regular rhythm, meter, melody, and harmony is perhaps a signal from Kubrick, telling the audience to rid itself of the traditional expectations of narrative film. The piece appears again in the Stargate sequence.

A section of Ligeti's *Requiem*, the *Kyrie*, accompanies sequences that feature the monoliths. In this piece, the sound masses are created by a soprano soloist, mezzo soprano soloist, and two choruses. The choruses consist of twenty people, essentially four on a part for soprano, mezzo, alto, tenor, and bass. The orchestra for this piece includes full complements of strings, woodwinds, brass, and percussion and also harpsichord, harp, and an optional celesta. In the section Kubrick used, we hear the voices primarily, with some instrumental accent notes, although the instruments often double the voices. The shifting texture helps build tension, as the voices grow in intensity and dynamics, gradually becoming higher, shriller, louder. In the first appearance of the *Kyrie*, Kubrick times it so that the music reaches a biting climax just as we see the image of the monolith lined up perfectly with the sun and moon. Kubrick then cuts to the silent landscape, an abrupt stop that jolts the viewer and alerts us that the mysterious episode is over, and life continues as usual. Things, however, are about to change. Kubrick must have been unconcerned with cutting this piece in the middle of a phrase because the abruptness of the silence is powerful and because there isn't a discernible regular phrase structure to interrupt.

In the second appearance of the piece, in the Tycho crater, Kubrick allows the voices and instruments to grow in intensity, but instead of letting the voices reach a climax of shrillness, the voices remain in the lower range when the monolith emits its high-pitched signal. This harsh sound continues for an uncomfortably long time while the voices of Ligeti's *Kyrie* fade gently away. When the signal finally ceases, we get a short pause of silence before the beginning of the Adagio from Khachaturian's *Gayane*.

During the Stargate sequence, Kubrick uses two Ligeti pieces in something of a suite. We begin with the *Kyrie* section from the *Requiem* and seamlessly segue from vocal music into the instrumental *Atmosphères*. In the thick texture of many instruments playing at once, time seems to stand still, although with the special effects on-screen, Kubrick achieves a feeling of motion and speed. Just as his vocal music seems to take the individual humanity out of the voice, Ligeti's instrumental *Atmosphères* seems to decrease the identification of individual instruments in the sound complex. The result is a sound that seems simultaneously familiar and otherworldly.

When Bowman "lands" in the Louis XVI bedroom, we hear the eerie sounds of Ligeti's *Aventures*, a work that requires its soloists to chatter, laugh, and sing, say, or yell nonsensical vocables (syllables). (The film's credits, even on the DVD release, do not mention this piece.) The piece also begins with the soloists breathing heavily in rhythm, which fits in quite well with Bowman's breathing noises. In the version in the film, the voices appear to be slowed down at first, making them sound less human, almost as if we are hearing the sounds of the aliens themselves as they observe Dave Bowman making his transition. (The "deformation" of the piece was a central element in the legal troubles between Ligeti and MGM.) Then there is no music for a while, as Dave sees himself older, eating at a table across the room. The only sounds are his younger self breathing and the clink of utensils on plates. The older Bowman gets up, his footsteps echoing against the floor. Sitting back down, he starts to eat again only to knock over a glass. The shattering seems to trigger the breathing sound again as Bowman notices an even older version of himself in bed. This Bowman, possibly dying, reaches out to the monolith at the foot of his bed, but this time Ligeti's *Kyrie* is absent. There is no music at all for a moment. Then, as Bowman becomes the Starchild, Strauss's introduction from *Also Sprach Zarathustra* begins again.

### Khachaturian: Adagio from *Gayane*

Appearance:

0:54:38–0:58:02 Exteriors and interiors from Jupiter Mission
1:03:26–1:07:16 Exterior of the ship, Poole's birthday message, Bowman sleeps, Poole plays chess with HAL, Bowman draws his hibernating colleagues

The history of Aram Khachaturian's ballet, *Gayane*, is quite complicated. Khachaturian composed music for the ballet in 1942, but it contained elements of an earlier ballet that he composed in the late 1930s called *Happiness*, with scenario by Gevork Ovanesyan. The main character is Karine, a simple patriotic woman who works on a collective farm and whose love interest is a border guard named Armen. The music for *Happiness* contained what Khachaturian identified as seven Armenian melodies and many more musical characteristics that were folklike.[50] In 1942, he began revising *Happiness*, with Konstantin Derzhavin reworking the libretto. Derzhavin retained some characters and settings of *Happiness* but changed the plot. He also changed the name of the ballet to that of the story's heroine, Gayane. Khachaturian said that about 60 to 70 percent of the music was new.[51] In this ballet, Khachaturian's music uses Armenian, Caucasian, and Russian folk materials. The melodies, although written in a regular time signature, have unexpected accents to mimic the uneven meters of the indigenous folk music. In the 1950s, a completely new version of the libretto was penned by Boris Pletnyov and Khachaturian revised his music for the work's Bolshoi premiere (although such changes could hardly be defined as a simple revision of the material). This version made the work more of a psychological drama, and it was this latter version that Khachaturian seemed to feel was the best iteration of his ideas. It is the version he chose to record in 1978, and it is the version that appears in the set of his complete works published by Musikverlag Hans Sikorski, Hamburg.

From the 1942 version of the ballet, the composer created three suites that could be played in the concert setting. These helped popularize this music, especially the Sabre Dance from act 4, which is part of the second suite. The Adagio heard in *2001* is from the third of the three suites, but does not appear at all in the 1957 version of the ballet. Although *Gayane* remains one of Khachaturian's most popular works, the many versions of the story and music culminated in what the composer called "the tragic history of my ballet."[52] In 2005, RCA released a recording of its LP of the complete ballet—the 1942 version—on CD. Loris Tjeknavorian conducted the National Philharmonic Orchestra in this performance.

The scenario of *Gayane* involves the title character and her family, who work on a kolkhoz, which is a collective farm. Gayane's husband Giko also works on the farm, but he is an alcoholic who does not pull his weight in the collective. In the story, Gayane and Giko argue, and after a series of events Gayane is imprisoned by her husband. She escapes, and Giko threatens their child, Hripsime, but Gayane will not be moved, so Giko stabs her. Kazhakov, the commander of the Soviet guard, arrests Giko. While Gayane heals, the two fall in love. The ballet ends a year later with the wedding of Gayane and Kazhakov (and others) on the thriving kolkhoz.

The name Gayane has great significance in Armenian culture. In the ethnic area of Armenia, an abbess named Gayane was martyred by Tiridates III. The Roman emperor Diocletian took a nun named Hripsime (the name of Gayane's daughter in the ballet) as his wife. Hripsime and Gayane and thirty-eight other nuns fled to Armenia, but they were found and killed. Gayane was later canonized by the Armenian Apostolic Church, and a church was built in her honor on the spot of her martyrdom.

The Adagio is one of the more somber portions of the 1942 version of the ballet, and it accompanies the first images of the *Discovery* spacecraft as it makes its long silent journey toward Jupiter. As we see *Discovery* from the outside, there is a stunning sense of isolation, as these astronauts are farther away from Earth than humans have yet been. The beginning of the excerpt is a meandering unison line in the strings, and this singular melody does seem to suggest loneliness. The unison line breaks up into harmony, but even then the mood remains subdued.

As Poole jogs around the centrifuge, punching the air, passing by the hibernating bodies of his colleagues, the music continues. Neither Poole nor Bowman seems to hear it, as they very quietly go about their duties on the ship. They are not as inhuman as some have suggested (with the implication that HAL possesses more human qualities than these men). Bowman spends some free time drawing, and of course later we see him show anger and terror. These men certainly have emotions, but they were chosen for this mission in part because they were able to keep them suppressed, under control. Theirs is a measured maintenance of feelings, carefully monitored. *Gayane* helps suggest this façade, this mask. It reflects the astronauts' isolation but also the emotion that they can not or do not show. Of course there are many interpretations of this piece and why Kubrick included it. In the film score guide, Geduld exposits, "This slow and lonely sounding piece underscores the extreme boredom of deep space travel."[53] According to Jan Harlan, Kubrick chose the piece because, to him, it signified "total loneliness."[54]

## Other Music

There are a few additional cues in the film, the Pooles singing "Happy Birthday" to their son, and the opening theme music for a television program in which Bowman and Poole are interviewed. The name of the program is called *The World Tonight*, and it appears on BBC 12. The cue, a jazzy fugue by Sidney Torch, appears for about fifteen seconds. Finally, a few lines of "Daisy Bell," which was composed in 1892 by English composer Harry Dacre, is performed by Douglas Rain, the voice of HAL. Almost seven decades after its composition, the song was sung by a real computer, the IBM 704, in a demonstration of speech synthesis. The discipline of speech synthesis had made great strides in the 1930s with the vocoder (a shortened version of "voice encoder" developed by Bell Labs) and improved upon in the 1940s and 1950s. John Larry Kelly Jr. continued the work with Bell Labs in the 1960s programming the IBM 704 to sing "Daisy Bell" to accompaniment programmed by Max Matthews. Arthur C. Clarke witnessed a demonstration of this feat and adapted it for the *2001* novel. In the film (as in the novel), as Dave Bowman disconnects HAL's memory circuits, HAL appears to suffer a crisis, first claiming that he is afraid and then saying that he can feel his mind going. His voice begins to falter and then slow down. He reverts back to a presentation he might have given right after his activation: "Good afternoon, gentlemen. I am a HAL 9000 computer. I became operational at the HAL Plant in Urbana, Illinois, on the twelfth of January, 1992. My instructor was Mr. Langley and he taught me to sing a song. If you'd like to hear it, I can sing it for you." Dave asks to hear it, and HAL sings it, in his eerily slowing voice. When he is done with the line "a bicycle built for two," which is hardly intelligible, Dave gets the pre-recorded briefing from Floyd about the monolith.

The success of *2001* and particularly of the soundtrack helped to solidify even further Kubrick's reputation as an auteur. Not only did he seem to have authority over every aspect of production—special effects, editing, even the release date—but he began to exert complete creative control over the soundtrack by using preexistent music rather than a traditional score. Far from being a lone wolf, however, Kubrick would still rely on his collaborations with musicians, arrangers, editors, and composers for musical options in his late films.

Music was part of *2001: A Space Odyssey* from the very beginning. Not only did it inspire some storytelling and help in production but Kubrick foresaw in this project a new way to reach his audience. In the 1968 interview in *Playboy* magazine, Kubrick said:

> I tried to create a visual experience, one that bypasses verbalized pigeon-holing and directly penetrates the subconscious with an emotional and philosophical content. . . . I intended the film to be an intensely subjective experience that reaches the viewer at an inner level of consciousness, just as music does.[55]

Kubrick was also very clever to realize that silence could be a powerful part of his story as well. The use of silence helps to let audience members make up their own minds about the emotional content—if there is any— of certain scenes. The astronauts keep their own emotions under a veneer of neutrality, and we, as the audience, don't have music to help us decide how to feel. There is no sinister sting when HAL terminates the life functions of the three hibernating astronauts. There is no music when Poole and his pod go tumbling through space.

The music Kubrick used in the film seems to have had a great influence not only on Kubrick's next project, A Clockwork Orange, but on subsequent works, such as Barry Lyndon and The Shining. Kubrick imbued both 2001 and A Clockwork Orange with a sense of choreography: critics, and even the director himself, have used words like "dance" and "ballet" to discuss the marriage of music and image in these films. In the three years between 2001: A Space Odyssey and A Clockwork Orange, perhaps Kubrick continued his ruminations on the interconnectedness of music and emotion and the choreographic interplay of music and movement.[56] In all of his films, Kubrick proved that these issues were always foremost in his mind.

## NOTES

1. Pauline Kael, Going Steady (Boston: Little, Brown, 1968), 122–123.

2. Vincent LoBrutto, Stanley Kubrick: A Biography (New York: Da Capo Press, 1997), 352.

3. Arthur C. Clarke, 2001: A Space Odyssey (New York: Penguin, 1993), 182.

4. Michel Chion, Kubrick's Cinema Odyssey, trans. Claudia Gorbman (London: BFI Publishing, 2001), 12.

5. Royal S. Brown, Overtones and Undertones: Reading Film Music (Berkeley: University of California Press, 1994), 291.

6. John Baxter, Stanley Kubrick: A Biography (New York: Carroll and Graf, 1997), 225.

7. Arthur C. Clarke, The Lost Worlds of 2001 (New York: Signet Classics, 1972), 146.

8. Clarke, The Lost Worlds of 2001, 29.

9. Clarke, The Lost Worlds of 2001, 18.

10. Clarke, The Lost Worlds of 2001, 31.

11. Clarke, The Lost Worlds of 2001, 45.

12. LoBrutto, Stanley Kubrick, 304.

13. Erno Rapée, Motion Picture Moods for Pianists and Organists (New York, 1924; reprint, New York: Arno, 1974), x.

14. Rapée, *Motion Picture Moods*, v–xii.

15. Interview with the author, April 20, 2011.

16. Michel Ciment, *Kubrick: The Definitive Edition*, trans. Gilbert Adair (New York: Faber and Faber, 1999), 153.

17. Interview with the author, April 20, 2011.

18. Michel Chion, *Kubrick's Cinema Odyssey*, trans. Claudia Gorbman (London: BFI Publishing, 2001), 24.

19. John Bender, "Farewell to the Master," *Film Score Monthly* 4, no. 8 (September/October 1999): 25.

20. Interview with Jan Harlan, *Silverscreen Beats*, 7:30 and 29:30.

21. John Baxter, *Stanley Kubrick*, 225–226.

22. Jerry Goldsmith, interview with Tony Thomas, in *Film Score: The View from the Podium* (South Brunswick: A.S. Barnes, 1979), 228.

23. Stanley Kubrick, quoted in Gene D. Phillips, *Stanley Kubrick: A Film Odyssey* (New York: Popular Library, 1975), 136.

24. Bender, "Farewell to the Master," 25.

25. In 2007, Paul A. Merkley wrote a very thorough article on the musical aspects of *2001: A Space Odyssey*, assembling information, both anecdotal and archival, in order to establish a timeline of Kubrick's musical decisions. "'Stanley Hates This But I Like It!': North vs. Kubrick on the Music for *2001: A Space Odyssey*," *The Journal of Film Music* 2, no. 1 (Fall 2007): 1–34. In 2010, Kate McQuiston and Julia Heimerdinger followed up with even more information on the subject including information specifically about the legal case involving Ligeti in the *Journal of Film Music* 3, no. 2 (2011), McQuiston's "'An Effort to Decide': More Research into Kubrick's Music Choices for *2001: A Space Odyssey*," 145–154 and "'I Have Been Compromised. I Am Now Fighting against It.': Ligeti vs. Kubrick and the Music for *2001: A Space Odyssey*," 127–143. The troubles between North and Kubrick were well documented in LoBrutto's biography, 306–309, and in John Baxter, *Stanley Kubrick*, 226–227.

26. Paul Merkley explains that Kubrick had discussed the score with other composers as well, keeping them "on tap" until final decisions about the score were made. Merkley, "Stanley Hates This," 10–11.

27. Jerome Agel, ed. *The Making of Kubrick's 2001* (New York: Signet, 1970), 198.

28. Both anecdotes are recounted in Merkley, "Stanley Hates This," 21.

29. Alex North's papers at the Academy of Motion Picture Arts and Sciences Archive at the Margaret Herrick Library.

30. Agel, *The Making of Kubrick's 2001*, 199.

31. LoBrutto, *Stanley Kubrick*, 305–309.

32. Richard Cohen, "A Practical Guide to Re-Hearing 2001," *The New York Review of Science Fiction* 12, no. 7 (2000): 10–14.

33. David Cloud and Leslie Zador, "Alex North Interview: The Missing Score for '2001,'" *Los Angeles Free Press*, November 12, 1970, 42.

34. Daniel DeVries, *The Films of Stanley Kubrick* (Grand Rapids, MI: William B. Eerdmans, 1973), 47.

35. Ciment, *Kubrick: The Definitive Edition*, 177.

36. For a complete synopsis of the film, see appendix B.

37. Richard Strauss quoted in Norman Del Mar, *Richard Strauss: A Critical Commentary of His Life and Work, Vol. 1* (Ithaca, NY: Cornell University Press, 1986), 134.

38. Lobrutto, *Stanley Kubrick*, 308.

39. *Stanley Kubrick: A Life in Pictures* (documentary), directed by Jan Harlan (2007, Warner Home Video), 1:00.

40. Carolyn Geduld, *Filmguide to* 2001: A Space Odyssey (Bloomington: Indiana University Press, 1973), 45.

41. This anecdote has been expanded upon in Merkley, McQuiston, and Heimerdinger in the *Journal of Film Music*.

42. Interview with the author, April 20, 2011.

43. Julia Heimerdinger has done an exhaustive study of the documents surrounding the case of Kubrick's use of Ligeti's music in *2001* in "I Have Been Compromised," *Journal of Film Music*, 127–143.

44. Heimerdinger, "I Have Been Compromised," 133.

45. Quoted in Heimerdinger, "I Have Been Compromised," 134.

46. These legal documents are translated from the German and quoted in Heimerdinger, "I Have Been Compromised," 134, 135–137.

47. *Stanley Kubrick: A Life in Pictures*, :57.

48. Geduld, *Filmguide to 2001*, 40.

49. Barry Keith Grant, "Of Men and Monoliths: Science Fiction, Gender, and *2001: A Space Odyssey*," in *Stanley Kubrick's* 2001: A Space Odyssey: *New Essays*, ed. Robert Kolker (New York: Oxford University Press, 2006), 79–80.

50. Victor Yuzefovich, *Aram Khachaturian*, trans. Nicholas Kournokoff and Valdimir Bobrov (New York: Sphinx Press, 1985), 131.

51. Yuzefovich, *Aram Khachaturian*, 137.

52. Yuzefovich, *Aram Khachaturian*, 160.

53. Geduld, *Filmguide to 2001*, 51.

54. Jan Harlan, interview with the author, April 20, 2011.

55. Stanley Kubrick's 1968 interview in *Playboy* quoted in *The Making of Kubrick's 2001*, ed. Jerome Agel (New York: New American Library, 1970), 145.

56. Walker, *Stanley Kubrick Directs* (New York: Harcourt Brace Jovanovich, 1972), 270.

# Chapter Four

———————————————○———————————————

# "It Was Lovely Music That Came to My Aid"

## A Clockwork Orange

IT IS NO ACCIDENT THAT MANY EARLY OPERAS told the story of Orpheus. What better story for a composer to set than one that relies heavily on the power of music? In operas like Monteverdi's *L'Orfeo,* Peri's *Euridice,* and Gluck's *Orfeo and Euridice,* the main character's music is part of the narrative; Orpheus needs it to charm his way into the underworld to his beloved Eurydice. Any work of literature—opera libretto, play, or novel— that deals with music or that features a character who is a composer or musician may only achieve its full realization in a performance medium. In today's culture, the dominant medium for such realizations or adaptations is film.

Much as opera provided the perfect medium for the telling of the Orpheus myth, likewise, the film form, from its invention, has offered a unique opportunity for directors who want to tell stories that rely on music as part of the narrative or stories that have music as an essential part of the setting. Stanley Kubrick saw that potential in Anthony Burgess's novel *A Clockwork Orange,* and he understood, better than many other directors, that *A Clockwork Orange*'s musical aspects were ripe for adaptation into a form that had both visual and aural components. *A Clockwork Orange* stands alone as the most musical of all the raw sources from which Kubrick adapted his films, and it is therefore necessary to discuss the music in the novel in order to understand Kubrick's choices in translating the material to the screen.

Anthony Burgess undertook the writing of *A Clockwork Orange* in 1961 after reportedly receiving a diagnosis of a fatal brain tumor. Burgess wrote three novels in that same year, hoping to leave his widow an income after his death. When it was clear Burgess was going to live, he went on to write many more novels, and some of these also feature musical themes or characters. Music is a recurrent theme in his work, and there is an important reason for this: Burgess was an amateur, self-taught musician and composer. His mother sang and danced professionally (as Beautiful Belle Burgess) and his father was a pianist who occasionally subbed for the cinema pianist in town. Burgess, who was born and grew up in Manchester, England, attended symphonic concerts and even tried his hand at violin lessons as a child. Although the lessons did not last long, his affinity for music would continue until his death.

After working in Malaysia in the 1950s, Burgess considered music as a career, and was as prolific at composition as he was at writing books. It was his wife, however, who urged him to choose one discipline and focus on it. She gave him an ultimatum: write one more piece and send it to the BBC Orchestra. If the BBC accepted the work, he should follow composition. If not, he should focus on writing. Although the BBC rejected Burgess's effort and he became a full-time writer, he continued composing for the rest of his life. He even published a memoir about his musical experiences called *This Man and Music* (1983).

## THE ADAPTATION OF THE NOVEL

Burgess's *A Clockwork Orange* was not even a decade old when Kubrick adapted it for the screen. The main character of the story is Alex, a teenage thug who, with his three friends, perpetrates on innocent citizens what he calls "ultra-violence." Alex has a great love of classical music, which he uses much like a drug, either stimulating him into action or providing a way to come down after causing mayhem. The novel mentions many composers (some of them fictional), while the film boils down Alex's love of music into love of one particular composer: Beethoven. The effects of this choice will be discussed below.

Burgess sold the film rights to *A Clockwork Orange* long before Stanley Kubrick's film version was released. At one point in the 1960s, lawyer Si Litvinoff commissioned a screenplay adaptation of *A Clockwork Orange* from the author himself. Litvinoff was anxious to produce the film. It would have been his first, and he had envisioned Mick Jagger—a fan of the novel—playing Alex. (Although the Rolling Stones were too busy to allow Jagger to star in the film, their album *The Rolling Stones, Now!* (1965) has liner notes written in a style similar to the "Nadsat" language Burgess

developed for the book.)¹ Like Nabokov before him, Burgess's adaptation
was far too long and complicated to be filmed. Litvinoff lost the rights and
the discarded script was thought lost. The rights to *A Clockwork Orange*
were subsequently acquired by Kubrick in 1969.

We know a bit more about Burgess's script now, since it was rediscov-
ered in the author's house in Bracciano, Italy (near Rome), eleven years
after the author's death. Burgess biographer Andrew Biswell describes it:

> [The script] is an elaborate reworking and reimagining of *A Clockwork
> Orange* rather than a straightforward adaptation. It introduces a number
> of Nadsat words not present in the original, as well as a series of ex-
> travagantly bloodthirsty dream-visions . . . [in which Alex is] urged on to
> further atrocities by the classical soundtrack which plays constantly in his
> head. . . . Burgess's stage-directions make it clear that this cinematic Alex
> is intended to represent the suppressed violent desires of the audience.²

Although Burgess would be called to answer for the violence allegedly
inspired by Kubrick's film version, and he took pains to distance himself
from the project at times, Biswell points out that Burgess's script "has an
intensity of violence which is largely missing from Stanley Kubrick's more
euphemistic interpretation."³

Stanley Kubrick turned to *A Clockwork Orange* after the success of
*2001: A Space Odyssey*. Warner Bros. had limited its financial contribution to this new project because of the expected X rating, and Kubrick, in
response, attempted the adaptation himself. The scope of *A Clockwork
Orange* was small enough to make the transition to the big screen without
being oversimplified. This is not to say that Kubrick arrived on set with a
completed screenplay on the first day of filming. His adaptation of the novel
took place during filming. Kubrick would choose scenes from the novel, encourage the actors to improvise, and often film a single take after rehearsals.
This was not Kubrick's usual modus operandi, but it seemed to work for the
actors and the film. The script was typed up after the day was done.

When Burgess first heard of Kubrick's efforts to make a film based on
his novel, in 1970, he recalls that he was a bit skeptical that it would happen. He also felt, rightly, that the matter was very much out of his hands.
He did suspect, however, that if the film was made, Kubrick would show
rape, violence, and frontal nudity, believing that the zeitgeist in American
cinema favored explicit depictions of such acts over suggestive and vague
images.⁴ The film's notoriety lent Burgess a modicum of fame, but he remained ambivalent about the finished project. In 1975, Anthony Burgess
wrote an article for the *New York Times* called "On the Hopelessness of

Turning Good Books into Films." In this article Burgess stated, "Film, seeming to have all the resources, and more, of literature, still cannot produce anything as great as a work of literature."[5] Furthermore, in the mid-1980s, Burgess completed an adaptation of the original text: a stage version, complete with original music that Burgess composed. The "play with music," as he called it, could be accurately termed a singspiel or musical and seems to be—among other things—an attempt to reclaim the story from Kubrick and to reimagine the narrative in a musical perspective. Many other adaptations have followed, including Burgess's own *A Clockwork Orange: 2004* (from 1990), a production mounted by the Royal Shakespeare Company featuring music by Bono and The Edge of U2.

Kubrick's film was financially successful, earning $15.4 million worldwide, a $13.2 million profit over the $2 million in production costs. Burgess sued for his share in 1973 and was conceded (out of court) a "percentage of the film's net income."[6] It is important to note that the book became a best seller only after Kubrick's film; *A Clockwork Orange* is by far Burgess's best-known work, and the average American reader would be hard-pressed to name even one of Burgess's many other novels. The film has also entered into pop culture as fodder for parodies, including parodies in *Mad* magazine and on *The Simpsons* animated television show.

## Comparison of Versions[7]

The film *A Clockwork Orange* allows the audience to experience the sights and sounds of Alex's world in a visceral way. Music reinforces and acts as a counterpoint to the exploits of the characters, especially Alex. In the case of the film *A Clockwork Orange*, the main character's passion for the music of many composers—meticulously described in Burgess's novel—encompasses far fewer composers than in the novel, but the music in the film is acoustically present. In the first scene, which takes place in the Korova Milkbar (an establishment that serves milk spiked with drugs), Kubrick begins with a close-up of Alex, who gradually becomes more distant as the camera dollies back. The music in this scene of the film is a synthesized arrangement of Henry Purcell's *Music for the Funeral of Queen Mary*. By contrast, in the novel, a pop song plays in the Milkbar: a fictional tune called "You Blister My Paint" by Berti Laski.

Kubrick chose to omit some of the scenes of violence and to retain others; he also chose to make the main characters and his friends a bit older than they are in the book. The director's choice of Malcolm Mc-

Dowell in the lead role shifted the focus of the novel from the serious crimes of teenagers (Alex is just fifteen in the book) to the serial crimes of youth (McDowell was actually twenty-eight years old when he played Alex). Because of the actors' ages, teenage delinquency does not seem to be society's problem in the film version; rather, it is the willful misbehavior of young adults who, perhaps, should know better. However, Mr. Deltoid, Alex's "Post-Corrective Advisor," fills the combined role of parole officer and school guidance counselor as he investigates "young" Alex's truancy. The victims of crime—at least three ten-year-old girls in the novel are victims of rape or attempted rape—are played by older actresses in the film, making the crimes less egregious and in one case turning statutory rape into a consensual ménage à trois.

Perhaps the most significant difference between the novel and the film version is that Kubrick chose not to film the final chapter of the novel. Kubrick used the American edition, which was published, at the behest of the New York publisher, without the final chapter. The twenty-first chapter finds Alex restored to his original state after being subjected to the Ludovico treatment, a behavioral therapy that effectively removes from Alex his free will. He is sitting with three new friends (he was betrayed by the original three) in the Korova Milkbar, just as he was in chapter 1. But unlike the beginning of the novel, Alex does not feel like participating in the "ultra-violent" activities they have planned. He goes off on his own and thinks about having a family. Alex believes that he is growing up. The European version of the novel ostensibly ends on a note of hope, but upon a closer reading, it is just as unsettling as the truncated ending. Alex, in thinking about his possible family, realizes that the son he may someday have will indulge in the same kinds of crimes that he himself has perpetrated. Alex will not be able to stop him, neither will his fatherly advice nor his own horrible experiences. Alex's son's destiny is to make the mistakes of his father and suffer accordingly. The twenty-first chapter also underlines the inevitability of patriarchal conditioning that is far more subtle than the Ludovico treatment. By turning his back on youthful, violent behavior, Alex finally conforms and, to a certain extent, relinquishes his free will to conventional gender roles and societal urging. Kubrick came across the final chapter after filming had already begun and did not consider adapting it because it struck him as "unconvincing and inconsistent with the style and intent of the book."[8]

From a musical standpoint, the twenty-first chapter also reveals changes in Alex's musical tastes as he matures. In the first twenty chapters of the book, Alex listens mainly to stentorian orchestral music. In the final chapter, the first time Alex admits that he is tired of destruction, he also reveals that his passion for orchestral thunder has given way to a taste for German *lieder*, "just a goloss [voice] and a piano, very quiet and yearny, different from when it had been all bolshy [big] orchestras and me lying on the bed between the violins and trombones and kettledrums."[9] Alex's outward choice of music reflects the inner change of his character.

Music serves the narrative of *A Clockwork Orange* in ways specific to the medium in which the story is told. In the novel, music serves a largely symbolic function. It is arguable that music, in Kubrick's adaptation, is more important than it was in Burgess's novel, for it is in the film that the music is transformed into a structural element, an aesthetic standard, or an emotional hook. It ceases to be simply a symbol. Instead, music is a visceral connection to the actions on-screen, the cuts in the film, and the experiences of the main character. It is effective for many reasons, but especially because the music Kubrick chose is enjoyable and familiar, packed with its own cultural meanings, meanings that will be parsed in this chapter.

## MUSIC IN THE FILM

Film music scholar Claudia Gorbman has described many functions of music in film, and her definition of narrative film music seems particularly apt as it relates to the score of *A Clockwork Orange*. Narrative film music may cue the audience of a film to associate certain themes with a character, and these connections are repeated throughout the film. For example, a musical theme experienced by a character in the diegesis—sung by the character, for example—may emerge orchestrated on the score later in the film.[10]

Advertisements for the film seem to make an ironic connection between Alex's love of music and the other activities he enjoys. The tagline on one movie poster reads: "the adventures of a young man whose principal interests are rape, ultra-violence and Beethoven." Music is tied into Alex's feelings of power, and far from being a passive interest, it is part of his violent rituals. In Burgess's novel, Alex—during a quiet moment alone at home—muses over an article he read: "Modern Youth would be better off if A Lively Appreciation Of The Arts could be like encouraged. Great Music, it said, and Great Poetry would like quieten Modern Youth down and make Modern Youth more civilized. Civilized by syphilised yarbles [testicles]. Music always sort of sharpened me up, O my brothers, and made me feel like old Bog [God] himself."[11]

Because this connection between music and violence is made so explicit, even in the film, the viewer is made to wonder how Alex developed his tastes. They were not instilled in him by his parents, nor were they born of peer pressure; Alex's friends seem ignorant and indifferent to the music Alex loves. When Dim gives a raspberry to a woman singing in the Korova Milkbar—Beethoven's Ninth in the film and an aria from the fictional opera *Das Bettzeug* in the novel—his slight is punished swiftly and violently by Alex. His parents (Alex calls them Pee and Em) are portrayed as weak-willed, sniveling creatures who listen to silly pop music. Alex's teenage rebellion forms him into his parents' opposite: the thundering id to their cautious, timid egos and the cultured prince to their blue-collar, middle-class kitsch. The girls Alex meets in the record shop also seem ignorant about everything but pop music, "Who you getten, bratty? . . . The Heaven Seventeen? Luke Sterne? Goggly Gogol?"[12] Even highly educated people in the novel and film, as represented by Dr. Brodsky, profess ignorance of music. Alex complains about the use of Beethoven as the soundtrack music for the Ludovico films to which Brodsky explains that the only thing he knows about music is that it's good for heightening emotion. Alex, in both film and novel, plays the role of music critic. He is the only one for whom classical music is special, even sacred, but the reader or viewer can only speculate how it came to be so important to Alex and so intertwined with his violent impulses.

Music may read as a symbolic representation of Alex's free will since his ability to listen to music is lost as a side effect of the Ludovico treatment. Or perhaps Alex's love of music is his only redeeming characteristic, the one thing he shares with the rest of humanity. It certainly allows the viewer to forge a connection to Alex, even subconsciously. From Kubrick's point of view, the score allows the audience to enjoy the music, even when we are upset by the scenes accompanied by the music. Furthermore, Kubrick's use of music allows characters to participate in a visual dance. In an interview with Penelope Houston, Kubrick comments on the choreographic connections of image and music:

> In cinematic terms, I should say that movement and music must inevitably be related to dance, just as the rotating space station and the docking Orion space ship in *2001* moved to the "Blue Danube." From the rape on the stage of the derelict casino, to the super-frenzied fight, through the Christ figure's cut, to Beethoven's Ninth, the slow-motion fight on the water's edge and the encounter with the cat lady where the giant white phallus is pitted against the bust of Beethoven, movement, cutting, and music, are the principal considerations—dance?[13]

Like the spaceships in *2001*, Alex dances through *A Clockwork Orange*. Violent fights take place against the backdrop of music and enemies circle each other as if waiting to partner up, but in the latter film, we aren't shown peaceful docking maneuvers set to a famous waltz, we get loosely choreographed crime, sex, and conflict.

### Henry Purcell: *Funeral Music for Queen Mary*

Appearances:

0:00:10–0:00:53 Credit sequence
0:00:54–0:02:24 Opening shot in the Korova Milkbar under Alex's expository voiceover
0:13:23–0:14:38 Alex and his friends return to the Korova Milkbar
0:16:55–0:18:48 Alex walks home (he whistles the main theme and it is picked up by the score)
1:24:04–1:26:16 Testing the Ludovico treatment's effectiveness
1:38:58–1:43:26 Alex is attacked by his old friends
2:02:18–2:04:20 Alex is in the hospital

Wendy Carlos's realization on the Moog synthesizer of the march from Henry Purcell's *Music for the Funeral of Queen Mary* begins the film, and the title cards are cut to structural points in the music. When the last credit card has flashed, the first shot is of Alex, sitting in the Korova Milkbar, looking boldly at the audience. During the long dolly out, the first voiceover begins as Alex explains who and where he is and introduces us to his friends Pete, Georgie, and Dim. In the credit sequence and the opening shot, the march serves structural, aesthetic, and political functions: the visual cuts coincide with the musical cadences; the march introduces the strange and perhaps "futuristic" sound of the Moog synthesizer and seems to evoke a sense of doom; it perhaps suggests a death knell for some kind of governmental authority. The sense of doom is enhanced by the short quote of the *Dies Irae* plainchant in the excerpt.

Example 4.1.   Dies Irae melody.

The *Dies Irae* is a chant and poetic text from the Roman Catholic Requiem mass. Wendy Carlos's inclusion of it is appropriate in the sense that this was intended as a funeral march. The *Dies Irae* will be discussed in detail in chapter 6. Carlos appropriately revisited this chant for the score of *The Shining.*

Purcell's march also adds "Englishness" because it is by British composer Henry Purcell, in a highbrow, early Baroque style that anticipates Alex's anachronistic musical tastes. The music, although distorted, adds to the "courtlike mood."[14] Henry Purcell (1659–1695), arguably the greatest native English composer of the Baroque period, wrote his *Music for the Funeral of Queen Mary* in 1694, when Queen Mary succumbed to an outbreak of smallpox. Kubrick did not acknowledge the possible political meanings of the work, but his use of it in the film suggests some understanding of these ideas.

The Purcell march appears in scenes in which characters demonstrate authority of some kind. At the beginning of the film, Alex is in control of everything. He holds the audience's gaze, speaks to them via voiceover, and holds court in the Korova Milkbar. His droogs are his subjects and the street is his kingdom. When Alex walks home, he whistles the theme to himself as the march continues playing on the soundtrack. The music is not sourced at that point—it doesn't appear to be coming from anywhere on-screen—but the synchronicity of Alex's whistling along with the piece shows that either Kubrick shot the scene to that piece or made sure it fit after the fact. The march reappears as the gang heads back to the Korova Milkbar for a drink after a night of ultra-violence. After the Ludovico treatment, Alex is subjected to a number of tests in front of an audience. When the topless woman sent to entice Alex comes through the curtain, Purcell's music starts again, this time because *she* holds the power in the room. There are various reaction shots of the audience and of Alex, wide eyed and speechless at her approach. When the funeral music reappears much later in the film, it is changed, with percussive hits added to mirror the beating Alex is getting from his former droogs. Alex is no longer in control; the Ludovico treatment has rendered him utterly helpless, unable even to defend himself. Georgie and Dim, now members of the police force, occupy places of authority and the change in the music reflects the violent way they choose to practice this authority. The return of the music also ironically underscores Alex's lost power. Purcell's march also suggests that the government has taken control and autonomy away from everyone. Alex is made helpless, the beautiful woman is the tool of the doctors who are, in turn, tools of the government. In this political system, everyone is turned into a clockwork orange.

### Edward Elgar: *Pomp and Circumstance*

Appearances:

1:01:35–1:03:30 Minister of the Interior visits the prison looking for a subject (March no. 1)
1:07:25–1:09:52 Alex is taken to the Ludovico treatment center (March no. 4)

Kubrick used the music of another great English composer, Edward Elgar, in scenes dealing with the Ludovico treatment. Two of the marches from Elgar's *Pomp and Circumstance* appear in the film. The first march of the set accompanies the scenes of the Minister of the Interior choosing Alex as the first subject for the Ludovico treatment, while the fourth march appears when Alex is transferred to the Ludovico clinic. Of the marches written for *Pomp and Circumstance*, marches 1–4 were written before the First World War and embody an unabashedly patriotic spirit. Elgar, one of the first composers to record his works onto gramophone records, recorded the first and fourth marches of *Pomp and Circumstance* in 1914. The marches were released during World War I with the following liner notes:

> At a time when patriotism is welling up in the breast of every British-born citizen, Elgar's super-patriotic suite is doubly welcome, especially a performance conducted by the great composer himself. In "Pomp and Circumstance" Elgar reaches great heights of national feeling. The patriotism of the artist shows itself as vividly in this work as in his acceptance, despite his age, of an active part in protective work during the war. . . . No one can listen without experiencing feelings of noble patriotism, such is the nature of its immediate appeal. Every Britisher should possess this unique record. [15]

The trio section of the first march has become known in the U.S. chiefly for being the music played at graduations. In hearing this march accompanying the scenes of Alex being chosen for, and entering the Ludovico treatment, the viewing public would see the process as a kind of rite of passage. Alex is leaving the state jail and moving on. His trip to the clinic is an event sanctioned by the government; he is a test case for the minister's solution to crime. The patriotic feeling of the piece would then seem ironic, given that the government is sending Alex off for what amounts to government-approved torture.[16]

There is no doubt that Kubrick was aware of the use of the march in the United States and the United Kingdom. Since the *Pomp and Circumstance* marches are not mentioned by Burgess in the novel, they were probably chosen by Kubrick for their association with graduation, as Alex moves from one phase of his punishment to the next. Even though the country in which *A Clockwork Orange* takes place remains unnamed, certain aspects of the film, including British actors and locations, must lead the audience to assume the action takes place in England.

## Rossini: Overture to *The Thieving Magpie*

Appearances:

0:04:35–0:09:44 Alex's gang happens upon members of a rival gang, led by Billyboy, who are attempting to rape a woman at the derelict casino; there is a fight between the gangs; when the police sirens are heard, Alex's gang escapes in a stolen car
0:33:26–0:43:38 Alex begins a fight with his own gang because they have challenged his authority; the gang betrays Alex

Gioacchino Rossini's Overture to *The Thieving Magpie* (*La gazza ladra*) is not one of the pieces Burgess included in the novel, but it occupies about a minute and a half more screen time than Beethoven's Ninth Symphony. The overture to the opera, which was composed in 1817, accompanies important scenes of conflict in the film and first appears as Alex and his droogs encounter a rival gang led by Billyboy. In the film, the scene begins with the camera lingering on a fresco on the wall of the theater and slowly panning down past the proscenium arch and onto the stage itself. This graceful motion is accompanied by two sounds, the overture to Rossini's opera and the screams of the woman Billyboy's gang is attempting to rape. Here are Billyboy and his droogs, stripping the clothes off a screaming young woman and trying to force her onto a mattress on the stage. The audience for this act of violence is Alex's gang. When Alex interrupts the proceedings by insulting Billyboy's masculinity, "come get one in the yarbles [testicles], if you have any yarbles, you eunuch jelly, thou," the woman is forgotten and the gangs begin to fight in the theater. What follows is a scene of stylized violence that is similar to a clichéd saloon fight of a Hollywood western: bodies fly through the air, and the participants break chairs, bottles, and panes of glass over each other's heads and shoulders.[17]

It is no accident that Kubrick has chosen to set the action in an abandoned theater that Alex calls the "derelict casino." In the novel, the rival gangs meet at the Municipal Power Plant, not exactly a theatrical location. But one may argue that the gang lives in a world that is nothing but theater, with masks and costumes that flaunt their "inauthenticity."[18] The boys wear these masks and special clothes (and makeup in the film) while indulging in ritualized behavior and speaking in their own argot. The combination of the abandoned theater and the opera overture make the scene feel like a play-within-a-play; the actions of the characters are violent, and instead of a beautiful singing voice to go with the music, there is a girl screaming for mercy.[19]

The scenario of the opera should be noted: *La gazza ladra* may be classified as "rescue opera" because the heroine, Ninetta, is saved from a horrible fate—execution—at the very last minute.[20] In Billyboy's scenario there is also a rescue; Alex's arrival saves a woman from a savage gang rape. In Rossini's opera, the cause of all trouble and misunderstandings is a magpie that steals things, hiding them in her nest. In Billyboy's stage drama, Alex is the thief as he steals the starring role away from Billyboy and takes it for himself. The idea of Alex as thieving magpie is evident in his treatment of music; not only does Alex steal Billyboy's thunder, he robs the works of great composers and uses the music to enhance his dastardly thoughts and actions.[21]

The combination of music and motion—a choreographed and stylized fight scene—has caused more than a few people to discuss the scenes accompanied by the Rossini overture in terms of choreography. Kubrick takes this street scrap and turns it into something graceful, perhaps in a way distancing the audience from the violence.[22] On the other hand, the music, because of its familiarity and liveliness, may help the audience feel the excitement Alex feels during the fight. Perhaps it is not meant to distance but rather to bring us closer to the character and the scene. The overture accompanies the entire fight scene and the scene that follows in which Alex and droogs travel through the night in a stolen car, forcing other cars off the road and searching for a little fun. Rossini's music stays with the gang until they reach a place with a sign in front that says HOME. The overture fades away and is replaced by the doorbell that plays the first four notes of Beethoven's Fifth Symphony. The "Fate Knocking at the Door" motif here is quite apt as the doorbell signals the arrival of Alex and his droogs.

Rossini's overture reappears after the gang regroups the following day, and Pete, Georgie, and Dim question Alex's authority. Alex smoothes things over until the group walks down to the waterfront. As the scene unfolds in slow motion—underscoring its importance to Alex—the voiceover explains the main character's thought process. Thinking, he reasons, is actually for stupid people, while the smart ones are inspired. Taking his inspiration from some unnamed music he can hear through an open window, Alex lashes out at his friends. In the novel, Burgess allows Alex to specify that it is Beethoven's Violin Concerto that encouraged him so.[23]

Rossini's overture plays through the slow-motion fight and through the two scenes that follow: one in which the droogs agree to let Alex remain their leader, and the second in which they go to the house of the "cat lady" (so called because there are a number of cats in her residence). When Alex enters the house, he attempts to charm the woman at first, but as she demands he leave, he reacts to what he perceives as her rudeness. Next to the doorway in which he stands is a rather large ceramic phallus on a table. The woman admonishes him not to touch this "very important work of art." In their conflict, she grabs a small metal bust of Beethoven, swinging it wildly, while Alex holds the phallic sculpture in front of him. The music gets louder, and they circle each other, seemingly waltzing to the accompanying music as they taunt each other with their weapons. The woman manages to hit Alex in the head, which allows her a brief advantage. Ultimately, however, the blow to the head just causes Alex to become angry; he seemed to be enjoying the "dance" with the woman. Alex trips the woman and hits her with the sculpture. The climax of the music enhances the fatal blow,[24] as do the still pictures of the paintings (all paintings were done by Kubrick's wife Christiane) Kubrick cut together. Kubrick does not show the sculpture making contact with the woman's face, nor does he show any gore or blood. In this way, we are spared from the view, like Quilty's death behind the painting in Lolita.

In the earlier scene in the derelict casino, Alex heard sirens in the distance and he whistled for his gang's attention. The music quieted down as well, as if obeying his command. In this scene with the cat lady, once again, the sirens wail outside, and Alex backs away from the body of the woman. He stumbles outside to warn his friends and get away. But there is one more obstacle in his path. The droogs, who have decided to relieve Alex of his leadership, contrive a way to keep Alex at the scene just long enough to be nabbed by the police. Dim stands waiting outside of the woman's house brandishing a glass bottle of milk behind his back. Once again, the important moment is rendered in slow motion. As Dim swings his arm around and the bottle makes contact with Alex's face, the splash of white takes place as if in a dream. The music plays on, Alex screaming that he cannot see. The Rossini overture meshes with the sound of sirens until all sound abruptly ends and the following scene begins. In contrast to the darkness of the night and the loudness of the score, the next scene takes place in a brightly lit and very quiet police station.

Perhaps Kubrick chose the overture simply because of its lively rhythms, because it is a playful template against which the movements of the characters can be placed. There is no indication that Kubrick was aware of the story of the opera or even that he was particularly concerned about whether he was using the overture rather than an aria or a chorus (although works with voices must be used carefully in film so as not to clash with dialogue). As in 2001, Kubrick was concerned with finding pieces that had discrete sections, organic resting points, and the energy appropriate for the scene. Rossini's overture provided all three.

The version of the overture that appears in the film is a traditional orchestral performance, although Kubrick and Wendy Carlos had hoped to present a Moog version of the overture. There wasn't time to complete it, however, and the Moog version does not appear in either the film or on the original soundtrack album. However, a second soundtrack offering was released in 1972 called [Wendy][25] Carlos' A Clockwork Orange, which features her Moog version of the piece.

### Rossini: Overture to *Guillaume Tell*

Appearances:

0:28:10–0:29:25 Alex has a consensual ménage à trois with two girls he meets in the record shop. This is a sped-up Moog version of the Allegro Vivace finale of the overture.

0:47:27–0:48:20 A view of Alex's prison is shown from above. Alex's voiceover explains that this is the sad part of the story (traditional version of the Andante section).

1:32:03–1:37:10 Alex has left the Ludovico center, to return home, but finds that his parents don't want him anymore; he walks through the streets (Andante section).

Another overture by Rossini appears in the film, the overture to *Guillaume Tell*, which was composed in the late 1820s. Two parts of the piece appear. The first excerpt that appears in the film is the Allegro Vivace finale. It appears in a version performed by Wendy Carlos on the Moog synthesizer. In her realization, both the timbre of the piece and the tempo are altered. The overture to *Guillaume Tell* accompanies what, in the film, is the only consensual sexual encounter. Alex meets two young women at the record shop and picks them up to the tune of the march of the fourth movement of Beethoven's Ninth Symphony. He lures them to his home with the promise that he will play their records on his high-quality sound system. The ménage à trois, accompanied by a very fast rendering of the overture to *Guillaume Tell*, is meant to be a moment of levity. The music brings to mind references to the Lone Ranger and the feeling that things are comically rushed. The end of the excerpt slows down to normal speed as Alex meets his friends for the evening.

In the novel, Alex meets Marty and Sonietta in the record shop, two young girls Alex describes as being around ten. He takes them out for lunch and then brings them home. He does indeed play their pop records, as promised, and while he does so, gives them alcohol to drink. When their music is finished, he injects some drugs and puts on Beethoven's Ninth. He rapes Marty and Sonietta while the last movement of the symphony plays (he mentions that he plays it twice through), and afterward the girls are upset but leave him to sleep. In the book, this encounter is one that truly distances the reader from Alex. In the film, to show the incident as written (although Alex is fifteen in the book) would have been devastating to any sense of identification the audience has with Alex. Here, Kubrick takes the incident and changes it to something funny, something that makes us think that Alex is simply a rogue, a cad, but not an evil one.

The other part of Rossini's overture to *Guillaume Tell* is the sad, soulful andante opening, and this excerpt accompanies moments of pathos or the times in which Alex despairs. The first moment of despair is an overhead shot of the prison. Alex opines that we have reached the sad and tragic part of the narrative. Kubrick shows three separate shots of the state jail, from different angles while Alex recalls the trial and the harsh words spoken against him. The music begins to fade so that the transition from Alex (the individual) to prisoner 655321 is unaccompanied by any music.

This section of the overture to *Guillaume Tell* returns when Alex, who has been released from the Ludovico center, is told by his parents that they do not want him to come home. Alex tries to punch the lodger Joe, who is now occupying his old room, but is too sickened from the treatment to do anything. The music begins as his father explains that all of his belongings were taken for victim compensation and that his pet snake "met with like an accident." The music gains more prominence in the scene as Alex's father explains that Joe has already paid next month's rent and will not leave. Alex walks along the waterfront, looking at the water and listening to the birds sing. An old man asks for money and recognizes Alex as one of the young men who assaulted him earlier in the narrative. Seeing that Alex is weak and defenseless, the man gets his revenge, and the music stops.

### Rimsky-Korsakov: *Scheherazade*

Appearance:

0:56:00–0:57:30 Accompanies Alex's fantasies while in prison

While Alex is incarcerated, he reads the Bible and fantasizes about the violence he finds there. Alex, sitting in the prison library with a large Bible open in front of him, imagines himself as a Roman soldier savagely whipping Jesus as he wearily carries his cross to Calvary. The music on the score is an excerpt from Rimsky-Korsakov's symphonic suite *Scheherazade*, composed in 1888. The film cuts back to Alex at a desk in the prison as he dreamily closes his eyes. He then imagines slitting the throat of an enemy in battle while he explains his preference for the sex and violence of the Old Testament over the excessive talking of the New Testament. Alex imagines that he is reclining on a bed of cushions surrounded by three topless women, one looking off into the distance, one feeding him large purple grapes, and the other fanning him with a palm frond. The sequence is accompanied by the solo violin of *Scheherazade*, and here the music is ostensibly supplied by Alex's imagination. The exoticism of the music is a fitting accompaniment to the images of Alex lying between two women in exotic costumes while being fanned by a third. All the women are topless and each wears jeweled head decorations and long strings of beads around her neck. Alex and the women lie under a red canopy and on top of many red pillows. The music is unlike anything we have heard up to this point, and its uniqueness speaks to Alex's new exotic and biblical fantasies.

### "Singin' in the Rain"

Appearances:

0:11:15–0:13:16 Alex sings this song as he and his friends attack and sexually assault a woman, forcing her husband to watch

1:47:15–1:49:38 Alex sings it to himself as he sits in the bathtub at F. Alexander's house

2:13:56–2:16:30 Gene Kelly's version over the end credits

In the novel *A Clockwork Orange*, the attack on F. Alexander and his wife takes place without music. Alex does not provide any either by playing a recording or by singing. Instead, the only sounds are the screams of the two victims. Kubrick wanted some musical accompaniment to the attack in the film. He asked Malcolm McDowell if he knew any songs off-hand and "Singin' in the Rain" was the song he mentioned. The song McDowell used could have just as easily been "76 Trombones" from the *Music Man* or "Surrey with the Fringe on Top" from *Oklahoma!* Each one would have brought extra-diegetic meaning to the film as "Singin' in the Rain," does. One cannot help but think of Gene Kelly's dance number in the eponymous Stanley Donnen classic, especially because Alex dances a bit during the attack. Perhaps Kubrick meant to offer the scene as a parody of musical numbers, just as the fights choreographed to music can be read as a parody of dance. The cries of the couple as well as Dim's off-key backup singing are Alex's only accompaniment. The song is incongruent (although Alex does seem "ready for love") and that is the point of it. If Alex were singing a song about raping and beating, his actions would at least match his words, yet the joy of the song is a sharp contrast to the humiliation and horror of the Alexanders. It also underscores how casual violence can be to Alex. In that respect, it is a far more chilling accompaniment than silence.

The song appears two more times in the film. After Alex has been subjected to the Ludovico treatment and ends up back at F. Alexander's house, he sits in a bath and quietly sings the song. F. Alexander, intrigued by the sound, rolls over to the bathroom door in his wheelchair to hear Alex better. The song plunges him back into the horror of the night he and his wife were attacked. Whether this song could actually be sung by Alex after the Ludovico treatment is doubtful. Even if, as he states for the reporter, he is sickened only by the Ninth Symphony, "Singin' in the Rain" would remind him of violence as well, unless he were singing completely mindlessly. If the song did not cause the sickness, surely the associations he had with it would. One might think of Alex's probable response as being an analogue to that of F. Alexander. Alex too would remember the events of that night and, instead of taking pleasure in those memories, he would be sickened by them. As a dramatic device, however, Kubrick's use of the song as F. Alexander's revelation is very effective.

It is also questionable that Alex would know and take pleasure in a song like that. In the novel and the stage version of the story every piece of music experienced with pleasure by Alex is some form of art music, and every person who enjoys pop music is treated with contempt. The inclusion of "Singin' in the Rain" is problematic because the choice of the song came from the actor, Malcolm McDowell, rather than the character, Alex.[26] Alex has, up to this point, shown that music is important to his life and character, but even the tagline of the film underlines his connection to Beethoven, not to musicals. One could argue that "Singin' in the Rain" is itself a classic and therefore suitable for Alex's tastes, but then his love of art music becomes diluted and less effective as a tool for his destruction. The film, in general, provides a looser interpretation of Alex's love of music. The sharp-eyed viewer may even notice that Alex, in an early scene, removes a tape of pop singer Goggly Gogol from his stereo before putting in Beethoven's Ninth Symphony.

For the Alex of the film, "Singin' in the Rain" and Beethoven's Ninth Symphony are both a source of pleasure in the first half of the film. These two anthems form the soundtrack to his joy.[27] In the second half, the use of these pieces either reflects the evil of those trying to take Alex's free will or, in the case of "Singin' in the Rain," causes Alex to fall into the hands of people willing to sacrifice him to make a political point. The two pieces are juxtaposed rather powerfully in the concluding moments of the film. Alex's final line, "I was cured all right," occurs between the end of the fourth movement of Beethoven's Ninth and the beginning of Gene Kelly's recording of the title song from Singin' in the Rain. Leading up to this moment, Alex has been returned to his natural state. Music once again can inspire images of sex and destruction. In this case, Alex imagines cavorting with a nearly naked woman at a high society affair— the clothing of the onlookers seems to suggest Ascot— to the last bars of Beethoven's Ninth Symphony. The placement of "Singin' in the Rain" over the final credits suggests that Alex will continue on his path of violence and destruction. It also leaves the audience with this enduring sonic "image" of the protagonist.

At the end of the twentieth chapter of the novel—the point at which the film ends—Alex hears the Ninth Symphony (the scherzo, not the fourth movement) and he does have a fantasy, but one that does not involve sex. Instead, Alex dreams of running along, carving the screaming face of the world with a razor. In Alex's final fantasy of the film—he is applauded by the Ascot-ian spectators, a naked woman straddles him and playfully bats his hands away—Alex seems more anti-establishment than violent. He is not hurting anyone, not beating or stabbing anyone. Even the woman he dallies with seems to have a smile on her face; he is not holding her down, he is not in the position of attacker. Alex is simply thumbing his nose at tradition and social mores. "Singin' in the Rain" seems to mirror the playfulness of the image. The song undercuts the seriousness of Alex's "cure" and ignores the implications of his willingness to be a pawn of government again. Kubrick might have changed the ending because he wanted Alex's cure to seem less chilling. Once again, Alex is the cad. He's not wicked, just incorrigible.

## "Popular" Music in the Film

There are two popular tunes heard in the film. One is Terry Tucker's "Overture to the Sun," which appears in the post-Ludovico show. The piece accompanies the staged fight between a rude man and Alex. "Overture to the Sun" has a quasi-renaissance sound to it, with tambourines echoing the strong beats and a reed instrument playing the modal melody. The courtly piece is an interesting counterpoint to the behavior of the man who is being deliberately rude to Alex. Erika Eigen's "I Want to Marry a Lighthouse Keeper" plays as Alex returns to his parents' apartment after being released from the Ludovico treatment center. Catchy and cute but lacking the gravitas of Alex's musical choices, this song is meant to show Pee and Em's lack of taste.[28] Kubrick used it as part of the decoration, like the paintings on the wall or the postmodern sofa and chairs. The song is sourced on-screen; it plays on a radio in the middle of the living room, and Alex's father turns it off once Alex announces that he is back.

Both Erika Eigen and Terry Tucker belonged to a psychedelic folk trio called Sunforest (Freya Hogue was the third member of the ensemble). The three of them pursued their dreams of pop stardom in London, where an executive from Decca Records discovered them in 1969 and helped them record their only album, *The Sound of Sunforest*. Both "Overture to the Sun" and "Lighthouse Keeper" appeared on this album, but Kubrick had Tucker and Eigen re-record their songs for the soundtrack. "Overture to the Sun," for example, is in a higher key.

## Music of the Ludovico Treatment

In his seminal work *Theory of Film: The Redemption of Physical Reality*, Siegfried Kracauer remarks on the way that film lowers the consciousness of the spectator. Likening the effect of film to that of a drug, Kracauer states, the audience is "not prompted by a desire to look at a specific film or to be pleasantly entertained; what they really crave is for once to be released from the grip of consciousness, lose their identity in the dark, and let sink in, with their senses ready to absorb them, the images as they happen to follow each other on the screen."[29] Furthermore, Kracauer explains the effectiveness of film propaganda and the use of tools such as camera angles, lighting, and music to cue the viewer to specific reactions. He refers specifically to the use of "musical themes with stereotyped meanings" to evoke a response from the spectator.[30] Although the "stereotyped meanings" of pieces had been in practice since the beginning of film and literally codified as early as the 1920s, Kracauer mentions these practices in the larger context of the role of music in film.

It would seem that the purveyors of the Ludovico treatment believe, like Kracauer, that films with music are the best way to reach their subjects. There are three elements in the Ludovico treatment: the visual images shown to Alex, the serum he is given before the film sessions, and music (although in the novel, the music comes from various composers). The first soundtrack piece used is Wendy Carlos's original composition, *Timesteps*. The music starts with atmospheric sounds that enter the consciousness slowly.[31] As Alex is readied for the films—he is strapped into a chair and his eyes are forced open—the audience begins to become aware of the strange sounds. Gradually, the sounds become more intrusive, with gongs and other computer-generated sounds banging away at seemingly random intervals. When the quick, rhythmic section of the piece begins, the film starts. The frenetic pace of the music and the schizophrenic changes of tempo and rhythm seem to suit the film, which depicts a vicious beating and a gang rape. On the second day of treatment, Carlos's music is gone and in its place is the music of Beethoven.

Kubrick has given Ludwig van Beethoven central importance in *A Clockwork Orange*. Mozart, Handel, Haydn are never mentioned, nor are any other composers. At crucial moments in the film, excerpts of Beethoven's music and even the composer's likeness appear. The very first notes of Beethoven we hear in the film are the first four notes of the Fifth Symphony; the "Fate Knocking at the Door" motif from the symphony is transformed into the doorbell at the home of F. Alexander and his wife. When Alex rings, the fate of his victims hang in the balance, as does his own fate. Kubrick chose to use Beethoven's music throughout the film as a unifying theme, unlike Burgess who varied Alex's listening choices.

Kubrick's small changes to the novel sometimes have large conse-
quences. In the scene in which Alex fights with the cat lady, she grabs a
bust of Beethoven and swings it at Alex. In the novel, it is Alex who tries
to grab it, but falls in the process. In the film, Kubrick makes it explicit
that Beethoven has now become a weapon against Alex. The cat lady uses
it, the Ludovico clinic uses it (or they follow government recommenda-
tions) to combat Alex's violent images, and F. Alexander uses it to drive
Alex to suicide.

The use of Beethoven in the film might bring to mind the Nazi appropriation of the works of Beethoven and Wagner.[32] Certainly, this point
becomes explicit when the Ludovico film of a Nazi rally is accompanied
by the march from the fourth movement of Beethoven's Ninth Symphony.
The use of this music as the soundtrack for the film seems to echo historical events; conductor Wilhelm Furtwängler, vice president of the Nazi's
Reich Music Chamber, conducted the Ninth Symphony for Hitler's
birthday concert in 1942.[33] Second only to Richard Wagner in popularity, Beethoven enjoyed an important place in the political machine of the
National Socialists. But his place in the Reich was cemented only after
*The Journal of the Reich Committee for the Volk's Health and Service and
the German Society for Racial Hygiene* proclaimed in 1934 that his racial
genealogy was free of undesirable elements.[34] Once he was shown as a
pillar of German history, the use of his music—especially the Third and
Fifth Symphonies—at rallies and as the soundtrack to propaganda films
was encouraged. The Ninth Symphony was not popular with the Nazis
at first; the message of universal brotherhood was not congruent with
their policies; yet manipulation of the work's message over time stressed a
united brotherhood of humanity as the Nazis defined it.[35] In an interview
with Michel Ciment, Kubrick comments on the connection between
music and the Nazis as it pertains to *A Clockwork Orange*: "I think this
[Alex' love of rape and Beethoven] suggests the failure of culture to have
any morally refining effect on society. Hitler loved good music and many
top Nazis were cultured and sophisticated men but it didn't do them, or
anyone else, much good."[36]

Apart from its use in the Third Reich, Beethoven's Ninth Symphony
has a complex history in terms of its genesis, composition, performance,
and reception. It has proven to be one of the most enduring works in the
canon and one of the most popular. In his handbook *Beethoven: The Ninth
Symphony*, David Levy argues that the work's almost universal appeal is
due in some measure to the words of Friedrich Schiller's *An die Freude*,
set in the final choral movement. The poem's "non-specific religiosity"

seems to embrace all listeners and unite many disparate factions in the hope and promise of universal brotherhood.[37] The Ninth Symphony has served as the victorious music celebrating the fall of the Berlin Wall, an offering of atonement at the Mauthausen Concentration Camp in Austria, the joyful music to accompany the beginning of construction of Wagner's Festspielhaus in Bayreuth, and the opening theme to the 1998 Winter Olympic Games.[38] As a universally popular work, Beethoven's Ninth has had many interpretations over the years from Richard Wagner's claims of programmatic idealism to theorist Heinrich Schenker's contradictory assessment of the Ninth as absolute music, that is, music with no narrative or extra-musical meaning.[39]

At the end of the twentieth century, the Ninth Symphony became a battleground for issues of gender and sexuality, perhaps most famously in Susan McClary's interpretation of Beethoven's Ninth as a musical expression of "explosive rage." By withholding cadences, she observes, Beethoven causes a build-up of frustration that bursts forth in a manner akin to an ejaculation. In addition, McClary compares her reading of the symphony to Adrienne Rich's poem "The Ninth Symphony of Beethoven Understood at Last as a Sexual Message," which begins with the line "A man in terror of impotence . . . "[40] Neither Rich nor McClary mentions *A Clockwork Orange* in their work, but these ideas of violence and sexuality as portrayed in the music seem to resonate in the novel, film, and play.

The use of Beethoven's Ninth Symphony in the film has garnered particular attention because of its familiarity and its importance to the narrative. It is the soundtrack of Alex's violent fantasies, his theme song, and a tool for his enemies. Beethoven's Ninth is one of the best-known works from the canon of Western art music, a piece categorized as being perhaps Beethoven's most "valuable" work.[41] Of the four movements of the symphony, only two appear in the film, the second and the fourth. The second movement of the symphony, the scherzo, has a quick tempo, a percussive character, and an imitative opening. The first time it appears in the film is after the night of ultra-violence. Alex returns home, wanting to hear a little "Ludwig van" before he goes to sleep. The version we hear is the traditional orchestral version. The music is not only a soundtrack to the film but also the score to the film Alex sees in his head. As the music plays the camera focuses on the objects in Alex's room, one by one. The opening of the scherzo, a series of downward octave leaps, is accompanied by a fast tracking shot up to the stern face of Beethoven on the window shade. This is the "answer" to the slow dolly backward in the opening scene at the Korova Milkbar. The face of Beethoven is the mirror to Alex's face.

The face of Beethoven is then replaced by the face of a woman painted on the wall. The camera slowly pans down to see Alex's snake Basil slithering along his perch toward the vagina of the painted woman (perhaps she is Eve?). The camera continues its motion down and finds four identical statues of Christ bleeding from the wounds in hands, feet, and side and bearing the crown of thorns. The statues are posed so as to bring to mind a chorus line of dancers. As the camera reaches the statues of Christ, the music takes on a structural function. Kubrick uses Beethoven's sudden fortissimo as the place to begin cutting on the strong beats of measures. The first edit coincides with a fortissimo hit on the timpani, and each subsequent cut, featuring details of the Christ statues, happens on the first beat of each measure. The music in this scene acts as an accompaniment to masturbation (made explicit in the novel), which is suggested only by the tight close-up of Alex's face and the slight movement of his shoulders. The scherzo is particularly effective here because of the rapid-fire editing that matches the music. The religious iconography of the Christ statues suggests that this ritual of music, fantasy, and masturbation is Alex's equivalent of a spiritual experience.

As the music moves into a transition, Alex explains that music helps him to envision violent scenes. The first shot is filmed from directly underneath the gallows of an execution scene. A woman (a stuntman in costume)[42] in a white dress falls through the trapdoor, her shoes coming straight at the camera. The next image of Alex baring his bloody fangs is cut in very quickly; the shot occurs twice more. There are two explosions, one sending dirt and earth into the air, the other a fireball. The cavemen clip is footage from *One Million Years B.C.* (1966); Kubrick must have reasoned that Alex would replay in his mind violent images he had seen in films. Finally, there is a plume of fire that is possibly a pictorial representation of Alex's orgasm. The montage suggests amoral power through religious imagery, explosions, vampirism, and capital punishment.[43] The idea of Alex using the music as the soundtrack to an internal film is a popular one among scholars; Thomas Allen Nelson, for example, calls Alex's fantasies "an internal *horrorshow*, Alex's Cinema of the Id."[44]

The scherzo continues as Alex's mother attempts to wake him in the morning. The camera then follows Alex's mother into the kitchen; it is one of the few times in the film that the camera does not follow Alex. As the music continues, no longer sourced (it is heard equally as loud in Alex's room and the kitchen where Pee and Em speculate on where Alex spends his nights), the scherzo takes on a new function: that of a proxy for Alex's presence.[45] He is not physically in the kitchen with his parents but his presence is strongly felt and his domination of their lives is complete; even asleep in his bed, he is still in control of the family. The scherzo continues as Alex leaves his room—via a door with a combination lock—and struts around the apartment he thinks is empty, yawning and scratching. Here, the music appears to be what is buzzing around Alex's head from the night before. The scherzo comes to a stop, however, when Alex notices guidance counselor/parole officer Mr. Deltoid sitting on his parents' bed.

The scherzo appears once more in the film, toward the end. Alex wakes up to the scherzo—this time realized on the Moog synthesizer—blaring through the floor. F. Alexander and his associates have brought Alex to another house (a traditional Tudor house as opposed to F. Alexander's home, which is a more modern structure) and locked him in an upstairs bedroom. F. Alexander sits in the room directly below—a game room—in which the giant speakers of the stereo lie on a pool table. The associates seem bored, unmoved by the music, one leisurely rolls colored balls into the pocket on the opposite side of the table. Only F. Alexander looks pleased as he glances upward, taking on Alex's role as torturer, using music to do harm. Alex decides the only way out is through the window. He jumps, and Kubrick provided a startling point-of-view shot by throwing a camera out of the window. The music is a catalyst, the serpent in the Garden of Eden that perpetrates Alex's literal "fall" from grace. When Alex regains consciousness in the hospital, his free will has been restored to him, as has the ability to listen to music. We can also think of this music as the catalyst that closes the circle; the weapon of music is returned to its original owner.

The main vocal theme of the fourth movement of the Ninth Symphony—what most people would identify as the most recognizable segment of music—occurs twice in the film: when Alex and his droogs return to the Korova Milkbar, a woman sings a capella "Freude schöner Götterfunken, Tochter aus Elysium / wir betreten feuertrunken, Himmlische, dein Heiligtum." After she sings, Dim answers her with a raspberry, which Alex punishes with a rap from his cane. This is the first sign of any dissension in the ranks. Alex's hasty retribution for mocking the singer leads ultimately to his betrayal by the droogs. Placing the protection of music above loyalty to his friends proves detrimental. The theme's second appearance occurs as the accompaniment to one of the Ludovico films.

There are two other sections of the fourth movement that appear in the film, the alla marcia section and the final prestissimo section. The alla marcia first appears as the accompaniment to Alex's trip to the Music Bootick. This version of the march is realized on the Moog. The timbre of the Moog makes the piece sound as if it were played by toys; the cymbal hits sound like a child hitting pots and pans. At the beginning of the scene, the camera focuses on a blond woman licking a phallic lollipop. She's standing next to a board labeled "Top Ten," each slot of which lights up in a different color. Alex enters the Music Bootick and walks a circuit around the store back to his starting place. Alex passes panels of brightly colored plastic, shiny silver walls, and flashing colored lights. The music is ecstatic and the visuals complement the sound. Instead of covering the exposed lights with gels, Kubrick allowed the lights on the ceiling to cause lens flares. The sequence in the Music Bootick is an overload of sights and sounds. Alex's outfit and walking stick could have been modeled on a famous statue of Beethoven in Heiligenstadt.[46]

Alex holds court in the music shop, walking around in his royal purple coat with its ornate cuffs and collar, his walking stick and manner of speech making him seem ever the courtly gentleman. The music in the scene seems to be sourced because Alex speaks loudly over it. The tenor vocal line of the alla marcia section has also been fed through a Vocoder (a synthesizer for the voice) resulting in a strange, otherworldly sound. The tenor voice sings "Froh" (joy) just as Alex turns to notice the two beautiful girls.

The march, realized on the Moog synthesizer, also appears as the score to one of the films Alex is forced to watch in the Ludovico clinic. The scene depicts a Nazi rally (possibly Nuremberg) in which thousands of Nazi soldiers goose-step seemingly to the cadences of Beethoven's march; bombers of the German Luftwaffe in flight; the blitzkrieg across Europe; Nazi paratroopers jumping out of airplanes; a tank moving through a field; members of the military searching houses; and a city burning behind a sculpture of children playing. When the camera focuses on Alex again, strapped to the chair in the Ludovico cinema, his voiceover speaks of his realization that the only sound present is the sound of Beethoven's Ninth Symphony, fourth movement. The practitioners of the Ludovico treatment appropriate the music of Beethoven for their therapy in a manner akin to the way the Nazis appropriated the music of Beethoven and Wagner for political rallies, and indeed the way any group appropriates music for propaganda. The Nazis knew, just as the doctors at Ludovico know, that music is an effective way to get into people's heads. The doctors' choice of Beethoven seems completely coincidental, and consequently music is the unwitting pawn in this chess game. When Alex—during the Ludovico treatment—insists that the use of this music as the soundtrack to the film is "a sin," he claims that the appropriation of Beethoven for their purpose is wrong; but this is hypocritical as his own use of it was no better.

When the main vocal theme begins with the words "Freude schöner Götterfunken, Tochter aus Elysium" ("Joy, beautiful divine spark, daughter of Elysium"), Alex pleads that it isn't fair that he must hear this music while feeling so ill. Dr. Brodsky and colleague seem surprised that Alex knows what the music is, but reason that this unfortunate side effect cannot be helped. Because of the length of the scene, Kubrick omitted some music so that the end of the scene would coincide with the end of the movement. To get the two excerpts to fit together organically, Wendy Carlos changed the end of the earlier section to more closely match the beginning of the later excerpt. As we hear the last twenty measures of the movement, and indeed of the entire symphony, Dr. Brodsky's proclamation, "In less than a fortnight now, you'll be a free man," has a sense of finality.

When Alex wakes in the hospital after attempting suicide, it becomes clear that his free will has been returned. The backlash against the government has been swift and powerful, explained by newspaper headlines painting Alex as a powerless pawn ruthlessly used by this totalitarian regime. The Minister of the Interior asks Alex for his support and in return, the government will make sure he is well treated. As an act of goodwill, the minister gives Alex a stereo with ridiculously large speakers. As these are rolled in, the score is already playing the end of the fourth movement from the symphony (although it's not clear if the music is actually coming from the stereo). Assistants run in with large baskets of flowers, photographers jockey for position to snap pictures of the minister with his arm around Alex. The music continues and Alex's "Cinema of the Id" starts up again. During the four measures marked *Maestoso*, Alex begins fantasizing. As in the fantasy sequence from the first half of the film, edits are done on structural points in the music. Kubrick cuts from the reality of the photo op to the images in Alex's head on the downbeat of a measure. The meter changes and the tempo becomes prestissimo; Alex is seen cavorting in slow motion with a woman, while well-dressed men and women applaud. When the music hits the final cadence, Alex proclaims—as an analogue to Brodsky's comment—"I was cured, all right."

The role music plays in the novel is limited to the imagination of the reader—in terms of the allegorical compositions—and to his or her familiarity with the actual preexistent music Burgess describes. Adaptation to the film medium allowed Kubrick to expand the role and functions of music in the narrative. Music is still an important emotional experience for Alex, fuel for his deviant fantasies and inspiration for violent deeds, but it is also a visceral experience for the audience. The connection between music and violence also hints that if Alex enjoys violence and music as visceral pleasures, he is the most truly alive and fully realized character in the drama. He is the most human, although he is not humane. Alex's love of music also makes him the Other, an anomaly in a society where pop music seems to be the choice of young and old. The Alex of the book describes pop music as a sweet kid's drink served in an expensive goblet. He has no taste for it. To him, Mozart and Beethoven are worth hearing; pop music doesn't make the grade.

In addition to serving the narrative as a comment on the main character or society, the music, to Kubrick, often suggested movement and dance. The rhythms of the music often inspired Kubrick's editing, and Carlos's interpretations allowed alterations in tempo to better match the mood of the scene. The music also allowed Kubrick to stylize sex and violence. The music acts as a buffer to the violent images. In this way, it takes on the same function that the Nadsat language performs in the novel. Burgess, in the introduction to the 1986 American edition of the novel, said, "Nadsat, a Russified version of English, was meant to muffle the raw response we expect from pornography."[47] In other words, because our translation of the words is not instantaneous, we are spared the gut reaction we might otherwise have. Similarly, because the score allows us to see the images on-screen as dance-like, they are easier to accept.

## CLASSICAL MUSIC AND VIOLENCE IN FILM

Most of the music that appears in the novel, film, and stage versions of *A Clockwork Orange* comes from the established canon of Western music. The role of music in the film goes beyond a simple narrative function; it speaks to the role of classical music in modern culture. At the time of the film's release, *Time Magazine* art critic Robert Hughes said this of the film, "No movie in the last decade (perhaps in the history of film) has made such exquisitely chilling predictions about the future role of cultural artifacts—paintings, buildings, sculpture, music—in society, or extrapolated them from so undeceived a view of our present culture."[48]

Music has been thought to have a calming effect, but in film, classical music is often used as an accompaniment to violence or as the music of choice for dastardly villains. Using classical music in this way has cultural resonance both in the filmic tradition and in other aspects of popular culture. The average audience viewer has come to expect the cliché of educated criminals who possess an appreciation of classical music. The portrayals of violence in connection with classical music affect readings

of the music. One may argue that we, as a culture, somehow begin to associate classical music with violence outside of film or perhaps even begin
to see classical music as deviant in and of itself. Film music is extremely
effective at contributing to cultural mythology and encoding it the narrative structure of the medium.[49]

Forty years before *A Clockwork Orange* presented "the adventures
of a young man whose principal interests are rape, ultra-violence and
Beethoven," Fritz Lang's *M* (1930), one of the first masterpieces of sound
film, tells the story of a man whose principal interests are pedophilia, murder, and Grieg. The film was based on true events, a series of child murders
in Dusseldorf. Peter Lorre plays Hans Beckert, a pedophile with a taste
for two things: little girls and Edvard Grieg's *Peer Gynt* Suite, specifically
the theme from "In the Hall of the Mountain King." It is his whistling of
this music—there is no background score—that identifies him as surely as
the white chalk "M" that a pursuer places on the shoulder of his coat. The
blind balloon-seller remembers that he heard a man whistle the music as
he bought a balloon for a young girl, Elsie, who was later found murdered.
Beckert can no more stop his nervous whistling than he can control his
twisted impulses. Later in the film, the balloon-seller hears the music again
and remembers the man who bought Elsie's balloon. The recollection starts
a chain of events that leads to Beckert's capture. Lang must have chosen
Grieg's *Peer Gynt* because it was easily recognizable, but it is unclear why he
chose that rather than a folk or popular tune. Unlike Malcolm McDowell's
choice of "Singing in the Rain," we do know that the whistling (and perhaps
the song) were not Peter Lorre's choice; the actor could not whistle. Fritz
Lang did all of Beckert's whistling in the film. Grieg wrote the incidental
music for Ibsen's play in 1874; he later popularized the music into a suite.

In *M*, the use of a familiar piece is particularly effective because there
is no other music in the entire film; its starkness is ominous and its playfulness is a striking contrast to the character's murderous activities. Incidentally, the film was later used by the Nazis in propaganda dealing with the
evils of deviant sexual behaviors. Fritz Lang was half-Jewish and fled from
the Nazis and his own wife—a devout follower of Hitler—in 1933.[50] The
Nazis' use of music has been discussed above, and their connection to this
repertoire has become something of a film cliché. Even films made when
the Nazis were in power painted them as lovers of great music, and since
then screenwriters and directors have portrayed the ironic combination of
their musical knowledge and their violent actions. In the film *The Life and
Death of Colonel Blimp* (1943), one character says of Germans: "They sink
undefended ships, shoot innocent hostages, and bomb and destroy whole
streets in London, killing little children. And then they sit down in the

same butcher's uniform and listen to Mendelssohn and Schubert. There's something horrid about that."[51] The character is not referring to the Nazis since the comment is made during World War I, but the film itself was made during the Second World War, and the significance of the statement could hardly have been lost on the audience.

Even recently, a filmic depiction of Nazis is incomplete without some act of horror, torture, or violence accompanied by classical music that seems utterly indifferent to the cruelties on-screen. In *Schindler's List* (1995), for example, in a scene with Nazi thugs clearing out a Jewish ghetto, one of them stops for a moment, amid the gunfire and screams, to play Bach's English Suite on a piano.

Bach's music as enjoyed by the well-ordered criminal mind is something of a cliché itself.[52] In Thomas Harris's best-selling book *The Silence of the Lambs*, serial killer Hannibal Lecter is a both a cannibal and classical music aficionado. He, like Alex before him, uses classical music as a backdrop to his violence. When director Jonathan Demme adapted the novel into an Oscar-winning film in 1991, he used the music Harris described in the novel—Bach's Goldberg Variations—as a chilling counterpoint to a series of brutal murders.[53]

Classical music as the accompaniment to torture is an important aspect of Ariel Dorfman's 1992 play *Death and the Maiden*. Both the play and its 1994 film adaptation tell the story of a woman, Paulina, who was tortured and sexually molested by a man who played Schubert's *Death and the Maiden* quartet while he abused her. When Paulina's husband brings a mysterious man home one evening—fifteen years after the torture—Paulina believes that the guest was her tormentor. The *Death and the Maiden* quartet forms part of the film's score.[54]

Whether the connection between classical music and deviant behavior and violent characters is due to the coding of classical music in film from the age of silent films or if it is the influence of famous characters like Hans Beckert in *M* or Alex in *A Clockwork Orange,* the practice lives on in film. It should be noted that, according to filmic depictions, not all criminal minds are amenable to classical music. There are many film characters who commit crimes and listen to popular music or no music at all, but it seems that those criminals who love classical music are those either wholly committed to their life of crime and who do not see the immorality of their actions (through amoral behavior, compulsion, or by indulging in a completely divergent worldview), like Alex and Hans Beckert; or those whose minds are so meticulously well ordered that classical music is the only sufficiently complex diversion for them, like Hannibal Lecter. It is interesting to note that in the real world, classical music is often used as a deterrent for criminal behavior, effectively repelling muggers and drug dealers from public parks, train stations, and parking lots.[55]

## The Struggles of Beethoven

Canonical music accompanies many of the scenes in *A Clockwork Orange*. Competing for the most screen time are Beethoven's Ninth Symphony and Rossini's overture to *La gazza ladra*. Beethoven's music occupies a place of lesser importance in the novel than in the film, although admittedly, the Ninth is the only piece that Burgess mentions more than once. In Burgess's stage version—written twenty-five years after the novel and fifteen years after the film—songs based on Beethoven's work are featured in every part of the play.[56] It seems odd that Burgess should place such great emphasis on Beethoven's music; in the novel, the most significant pieces (i.e., the one that leads to the betrayal of friends or the one that drives him to suicide) are fictional compositions. Perhaps he did not want to assign "responsibility" to pieces that actually existed.

We can analyze the use of Beethoven's music in the play as a reaction to Kubrick's use or misuse of music in the film (in Burgess's estimation). Burgess could also have seen the music of Beethoven, wrought through struggle and difficulty, as an analogy to the struggle of the main character.[57] Beethoven is known for his progressive deafness, his staunch individuality as an artist, his personal problems (familial and romantic trouble), and his aggressive, overbearing nature; he is consistently associated with a narrative of overcoming.[58] Beethoven, like Alex, was uncompromising, and in the music of Beethoven there seem to be more and greater personal struggles than there are in the music of the preceding classical period. Burgess has said this of Beethoven's music:

> The conflict is prolonged, and when resolution comes it is delayed and hard-won. Periods of peace balance phases of struggle, and slow movements are represented as visions of beatitude. The struggle is not physical . . . it can only be moral, an attempt to win through to the light of the good after wrestling with the forces of darkness. Beethoven's private despairs and triumphs confirm this.[59]

### Wendy Carlos, Switched on Beethoven

Wendy Carlos (b. 1939) is similar to Anthony Burgess in that her career has been a combination of two disciplines, in this case music and technology. Carlos composed her first piece at the age of ten and built her first computer at age fourteen. As a child, she won a scholarship at the Westinghouse Science Fair for a project she made involving computers. At sixteen, she was altering the tuning on the family piano.[60] At seventeen, Carlos built a music studio of her own and recorded electronic compositions based on the fundamentals of *musique concrète,* using tape recorders to manipulate found sounds. At Brown University, where Carlos studied both music and physics, she ran small, informal workshops to teach the basics of electronic music to her fellow students and colleagues. As a student at Columbia, specifically the Columbia-Princeton Electronic Music Center, she continued composing and championing the work of other electronic composers. To that end, she helped Leonard Bernstein assemble a program of electronic music for a concert at Philharmonic Hall, Lincoln Center. During this period, Carlos had two of her electronic pieces recorded. In the late 1960s, Carlos began working with engineer Bob Moog and was introduced to, and developed significant modifications for, the Moog synthesizer.

The works of Beethoven, Purcell, and Rossini performed on a Moog synthesizer seemed to Stanley Kubrick to be suitable musical accompaniment to the action in *A Clockwork Orange,* although he hadn't originally planned on using synthesized recordings. Carlos's producer, Rachel Elkind, sent Kubrick a copy of *Switched on Bach* and *The Well-Tempered Synthesizer* after photography on the film had largely been completed. Intrigued by the timbre of the synthesizer, Kubrick immediately sent for Elkind and Carlos. The Moog realizations in *A Clockwork Orange* had unforeseen implications due largely to the popularity of Wendy Carlos's *Switched on Bach* album, which appeared three years before Kubrick's film. *Switched on Bach* was the first classical album to sell more than a million copies. Its appeal was broad; it was a must-have album for fans of both classical and pop music. Its influence was far reaching, inspiring numerous electronic interpretations of preexistent music and worrying musicians who feared that the Moog synthesizer could jeopardize their careers.[61] It drew rave reviews from many, including famed Bach-interpreter Glenn Gould, who called *Switched on Bach* "the record of the decade,"[62] and began what can be termed the age of the synthesizer.

The album introduced many listeners to the sound possibilities of electronic instruments and did so with the lively and tonal music of the Baroque. Up until the late 1960s, the synthesizer was only used at institutions that could afford a studio and the electronic instruments. Those who experimented with synthesizers were considered a fringe group dealing in "weird space sounds."[63] *Switched on Bach* made Wendy Carlos famous and, in a larger sense, brought the synthesizer to the general public and lent it a sense of legitimacy as an instrument for new music.[64]

With the success of *Switched on Bach*, Carlos was approached about possibly scoring science fiction films liked *Marooned* (which ended up with a soundtrack of computer sound effects and little to no ambient music) but had her first collaboration in film with Stanley Kubrick. Carlos has the distinction of being one of the few composers who worked with Kubrick on more than one film; in the 1980s, she and producer Rachel Elkind recorded tracks for Kubrick's *The Shining*. The success of *Switched on Bach* inspired many imitations and created a cottage industry for Carlos and Elkind. To date, Carlos has recorded *Switched on Bach 2*, *Switched on Brandenburgs*, *The Well-Tempered Synthesizer*, *Wendy Carlos by Request*, and *Switched on Bach 2000*.

Like the soundtrack to *2001: A Space Odyssey*, the soundtrack to *A Clockwork Orange* was also quite successful, spending thirty-one weeks on the Billboard Top 100.[65] Three months after the soundtrack to *A Clockwork Orange* debuted, Carlos released *[Wendy] Carlos' Clockwork Orange*, a collection of music that was intended for the film but which was not finished or had not been used by Kubrick (see the track list below). This album spent nine weeks on the Billboard chart.[66] It includes the composition *Timesteps* in its entirety and the Moog version of the overture to *La gazza ladra* "as we would have done it, had there been time," say Chris Nelson and Wendy Carlos in the liner notes. The album also features an original composition called "Country Lane." Carlos meant for this music to accompany the scene in which Alex's former droogs beat and nearly drown him. The music weaves in themes from *La gazza ladra*, the *Dies Irae* plainchant (which Carlos would use again in *The Shining*), the sounds of actual rain, and a synthesized voice performing a distorted version of "Singin' in the Rain."[67]

### Track lists of *Stanley Kubrick's A Clockwork Orange* (1972) and *[Wendy] Carlos' Clockwork Orange* (1972)[68]

*Stanley Kubrick's A Clockwork Orange*: 1972
   Side A

1. Title Music from A Clockwork Orange (from Henry Purcell's Music for the Funeral of Queen Mary)

Composer: [Wendy] Carlos and Rachel Elkind
Tempi Music BMI
Performed by: [Wendy] Carlos 2:21
2. The Thieving Magpie (Abridged)
Composer: Gioacchino Rossini
Performance: A Deutsche Grammophon recording 5:57
3. Theme from A Clockwork Orange (Beethoviana)
Composer: [Wendy] Carlos and Rachel Elkind
Tempi Music BMI
Performed by: [Wendy] Carlos 1:44
4. Ninth Symphony, Second Movement—Abridged
Composer: Ludwig van Beethoven
Performance: A Deutsche Grammophon Recording 3:48
5. March from A Clockwork Orange (Ninth Symphony, Fourth Movement—Abridged)
Composer: Ludwig van Beethoven, Arr. [Wendy] Carlos
Tempi Music BMI
Performed by: [Wendy] Carlos, Articulations by Rachel Elkind 7:00
6. William Tell Overture—Abridged
Composer: Gioacchino Rossini
Performed by [Wendy] Carlos, 1:17

   Side B

1. Pomp and Circumstance March No. I
Composer: Sir Edward Elgar 4:28
2. Pomp and Circumstance March No. IV—Abridged
Composer: Sir Edward Elgar 1:33
3. Timesteps (Excerpt)
Composer: [Wendy] Carlos, Tempi Music BMI
Performed by: [Wendy] Carlos 4:13
4. Overture to the Sun
Composer: Terry Tucker, Mills Music ASCAP 1:40
5. I Want to Marry a Lighthouse Keeper
Composer: Erika Eigen, Mills Music ASCAP
Performed by: Erika Eigen [no timing]
6. William Tell Overture—Abridged
Composer: Gioacchino Rossini
Performance: A Deutsche Grammophon Recording 2:58

7. Suicide Scherzo (Ninth Symphony, Second Movement—Abridged)
   Composer: Ludwig van Beethoven: Arr. [Wendy] Carlos, Tempi Music
   BMI
   Performed by: [Wendy] Carlos 3:07
8. Ninth Symphony, Fourth Movement—Abridged
   Composer: Ludwig van Beethoven Performance: A Deutsche Gram-
   mophon Recording 1:34
9. Singin' in the Rain
   Composed by: Arthur Freed, Nacio Herb Brown, Robbins Music
   ASCAP
   Performed by Gene Kelly, an MGM Recording 2:36

*[Wendy] Carlos' A Clockwork Orange: 1972*
   Side 1

1. Timesteps—[Wendy] Carlos
   (BMI—13:50)
2. March from A Clockwork Orange
   (BMI—7:00) (Beethoven: Ninth Symphony: Fourth Movement,
   Abridged)
   Articulations by Rachel Elkind
   Arr. [Wendy] Carlos

   Side 2

1. Title Music from A Clockwork Orange
   (BMI—2:21)
   (from Purcell's "Music for the Funeral of Queen Mary")
   [Wendy] Carlos and Rachel Elkind
2. La Gazza Ladra
   (P.D. 5:50)
   (The Thieving Magpie, Abridged)
   Gioacchino Rossini
3. Theme from A Clockwork Orange
   (BMI—1:44)
   (Beethoviana)
   [Wendy] Carlos and Rachel Elkind
4. Ninth Symphony: Second Movement
   (P.D.—4:52)
   Ludwig van Beethoven

5. William Tell Overture, Abridged
   (P.D.—1:17)
   Gioacchino Rossini
6. Country Lane
   (BMI—4:43)
   [Wendy] Carlos and Rachel Elkind

In 1998, Carlos and Elkind released *Wendy Carlos's Complete Original Score* of *A Clockwork Orange*. In addition to "Country Lane," this album features two additional tracks that were left unused for the film: "Orange Minuet," which was composed for the stage scene after the Ludovico treatment (Terry Tucker's "Overture to the Sun" was used instead), and "Biblical Daydreams," which was intended to accompany Alex's fantasies while in prison. Carlos describes these pieces in the liner notes to the re-release and she also explains why Kubrick did not end up choosing them:

> A few other cues were left "on the cutting room floor." One was Biblical Daydreams, to underscore the images Alex fantasizes while reading the Bible in the prison library. That scene had an amusing incongruity that we picked up on using subtle musical "wink-nudges" (for the crucifixion procession the music nastily jokes "I love a parade," while in the harem it slyly observes "I want a girl, just like . . . ") Instead Kubrick used Rimsky's *Scheherazade*, the same temp track we'd tried to replace. That often occurs in film making; Stanley Kubrick is hardly alone. One often gets locked into whatever is seen or heard the first several dozen times (while editing), which makes anything else at all, no matter how good, seem not to work as well. Kubrick and his lovely wife, Christiane, had become quite excited by an old fashioned style Orange Minuet cue I'd written for the stage sequence. They definitely wanted it in their film and even suggested a single (!) of it. But by now the scene's Overture to the Sun temp track had begun to sound like the "only possible cue," so our piece was left out, as no other suitable location could be found (they did try, and regretted the loss).[69]

Also in 1998, Carlos recorded *Tales of Heaven and Hell*, which featured "A Clockwork Black" a piece featuring choral samples and references to the borrowed music of the film.

When *A Clockwork Orange* premiered, the sound of the Moog was already familiar to many in the audience, and critics of the time lauded the synthesizer's innovative sound. Although it must have been a "futuristic" sound for audiences in 1971, the Moog now dates the film as a product of late 1960s and early 1970s aesthetic. Carlos's realizations combined an eerie-sounding prescience with a detachment from humanity (the synthesized voice in the Ninth Symphony emphasizes this quality) that proved a good fit for the film. Because of Kubrick's penchant for using preexistent music in his films, Carlos was a good choice for collaborator; she was able to offer, transformed through the synthesizer, some of the preexistent pieces he wanted to use. Carlos explained, "[Kubrick] was getting his cake and eating it too."[70]

Kubrick's choice of the Moog may have served, at least in 1971, Burgess's desire to keep the story free of any reference that would anchor it in the past. When Anthony Burgess wrote *A Clockwork Orange* in 1961, he was inspired by the argot of the "mods" and "teddy boys" as he wrote the story. However, Burgess knew that he could not actually use this slang for the story; to use it would be to freeze the action of the story into a definite time in the past. Instead, Burgess invented the Nadsat slang for Alex and his friends. He also used fictional composers who might—in his imagination—be contemporary to the story, but chose not to name any composers who were alive when he wrote the novel. Burgess achieved a sense of timelessness in the story, one that makes it more able to survive as a relevant cultural artifact. The characters in the novel, especially Alex and his friends, use this timelessness as a way to relieve themselves of responsibility to contemporary society; they transcend it through their mode of dress, speech, or action. The droogs are timeless and therefore not subject to the laws and rules of their time and place.[71]

Alex's quirk, his love of classical music, is also carefully crafted in the novel to keep the reader from associating Alex with a particular time period. This ahistoricism is a key part of fables and parables. Burgess mentions the canonical figures of Mozart, Bach, and Beethoven but he also mentions fictional composers: Otto Skadelig, Geoffrey Plautus, Adrian Schweigselber, and Friedrich Gitterfenster. In addition to allegorical meanings in the names, the author is able to suggest the scope and breadth of Alex's love of music. The character's passion for music is not just limited to canonical composers or the old masters; the composers Burgess mentions might be writing during Alex's time. These fictional composers also offer a wistful window into a world of music that does not exist, and through this window the reader comes to trust Alex as an authority on this music and the only person who can truly speak of its beauty.[72]

There is a further possible meaning to the use of Moog versions of certain pieces. The second movement of the Ninth Symphony appears in both orchestral and synthesized versions. The first time the piece appears is after a typical night of ultra-violence for the main character, Alex. When it appears a second time—this time in the Moog version—Alex can no longer enjoy it. He has undergone the Ludovico treatment and classical music makes him so physically ill that he wishes for death. The scene ends with Alex attempting suicide. The transformation of the work in the second occurrence can be seen as an analogue to the character, Alex. He has been changed, altered, mechanized in some way because the Ludovico treatment has taken away his freedom of choice, and thus—according to Burgess—his humanity. The title *A Clockwork Orange*, described by F. Alexander (the author of the eponymous book-within-a-book), refers to "the attempt to impose upon man, a creature of growth and capable of sweetness, to ooze juicily at the last round the bearded lips of God, to attempt to impose, I say, laws and conditions appropriate to a mechanical creation."[73] Since Alex has been changed and mechanized, the music—also mechanized—reflects this.[74] When Alex chose music for himself, it was the traditional orchestral version; as accompaniment for the Ludovico films or as torture for Alex (its most unpleasant forms) it appears transformed in the Moog version.

If viewed in this respect, the music through the Moog represents an ungodly transformation. Just as Alex has been contaminated by the treatment and removed from his original state, the music has been transformed through mechanical "contamination." Yet this reading is at odds with the positive response to *Switched on Bach* both critically and commercially. The negative implication of the synthesizer sound may also be tempered by some sequences in which the Moog is heard and Alex is happy. Alex seems to enjoy the Moog version of the alla marcia section from the fourth movement of Beethoven's Ninth Symphony the first time it appears in the film. The alla marcia excerpt first appears as the accompaniment to Alex's trip to the Music Bootick. The meaning of the Moog realization as a contaminated version of something organic fits better during the second appearance of the alla marcia. It appears as the score to one of the films Alex is forced to watch in the Ludovico clinic. Once again the music is ecstatic, yet the film depicts images of violence perpetrated by the Nazis.

The familiar music of Beethoven played on a Moog synthesizer, especially in the case of the alla marcia section of the fourth movement and the main theme of the second movement, turns from an enjoyable experience for Alex to one of torture, yet the Moog versions of these excerpts may sound even more ecstatic than their orchestral counterparts. What version of the music does Alex hear? Is he aware of the difference between the second movement of Beethoven's Ninth Symphony that is heard in the first third of the movie and the version used to torture him later in the film? Perhaps the difference in the versions is meant to signify for the audience the way that the music sounds to him at the time of his torture. The music has ceased to be an organic product, hewn through the genius of his beloved "Ludwig van" and played by many talented hands. It becomes the output of a machine, the product of one human hand, playing a note at a time, with voices—disconnected from their humanity—ironically singing about universal brotherhood. However, the argument that the Moog realizations are Alex's perception of music after the Ludovico treatment would be sounder if the alla marcia excerpt did not appear in Moog version while Alex circled the Music Bootick.

In many of the scenes, the music is clearly sourced, as in the Ludovico sequences or those in which Alex makes verbal reference to the music. There are other scenes, however, in which it is unclear whether or not Alex can hear the music. As mentioned earlier, Alex seems to speak louder over the music that may or may not be sourced. In the slow-motion fight sequence at the waterfront, Alex proclaims that he heard music through an open window, but the audience cannot be sure that the music he describes is the piece on the soundtrack. Some scenes, like the fantasies he indulges in while in prison, are accompanied by music, perhaps from Alex's own mind. The music he imagines, an excerpt from Rimsky-Korsakov's *Scheherazade*, for example, is played by a traditional orchestra.

The sound of the Moog opens the film and is present before any significant visual image. Wendy Carlos's realization on the Moog synthesizer of the march from Henry Purcell's *Music for the Funeral of Queen Mary* begins the film. As the accompaniment to the first scene, the synthesizer performs an important function: with one note, the audience is told to be on its guard for strange things. At the time of the film's release, the first few seconds must have seemed to explain that the story to follow is not about the present time, but a time in the future, a time in which the cutting edge of technology is used to play music. The transformation of the music, in this case, is as much a part of setting the scene as costumes and furniture. Purcell's music continues as the scene opens in the Korova Milkbar. Alex and his friends are drinking "milk plus," which Alex describes as milk infused with drugs like "synthmesc" and "drencrom." It is not clear whether the music in the scene is sourced or scored, and one may wonder if the Moog version of Purcell's funeral music is what Alex hears through his "milk plus" high.

*A Clockwork Orange*, which is considered by many to be controversial for its depictions of rape and violence, may act as a kind of Ludovico treatment, causing the audience to associate the sound of the Moog with violence. For today's viewers, the age of the Moog as cutting-edge technology has long passed. Yet the success of the soundtrack and its offspring, the continued success of Wendy Carlos's work, and the use of the Moog by contemporary artists indicate that the age of the synthesizer is still ongoing. Perhaps it is best to say that the timbre of the Moog indicates a concept of the future. To those in the 1960s and 1970s, the Moog hinted at a possible future still to come; to the audience of today, it suggests a quaint retro-future vision that exists only in clothing, design, and music.

## Notes

1. Anthony Burgess devised an argot for the book he called Nadsat. It combines English with some Russian words, Cockney rhyming slang, and neologisms. It is spoken by Alex and his friends. The word "nadsat" is the suffix meaning–teen, as in seventeen.

2. Andrew Biswell, *The Real Life of Anthony Burgess* (London: Picador, 2005), 338.

3. Biswell, *The Real Life of Anthony Burgess*, 338.

4. John Baxter, *Stanley Kubrick: A Biography* (New York: Carroll and Graf, 1997), 247–248.

5. Anthony Burgess, "On the Hopelessness of Turning Good Books into Films," *The New York Times,* April 20, 1975, 2, 15.

6. David Hughes, *The Complete Kubrick* (London: Virgin Publishing, 2000), 172.

7. A complete synopsis of the film can be found in appendix B.

8. Michel Ciment, *Kubrick: The Definitive Edition,* trans. Gilbert Adair (New York: Faber and Faber, 1999), 157.

9. Anthony Burgess, *A Clockwork Orange* (New York: Ballantine Books, 1962; reprint, New York: Norton, 1986), 186. All page citations are to the reprint edition.

10. Claudia Gorbman, *Unheard Melodies: Narrative Film Music* (Bloomington: Indiana University Press, 1987), 83.

11. Burgess, *A Clockwork Orange,* 42.

12. Burgess, *A Clockwork Orange,* 43. There is a similar line in the film. The names refer to fictional singers, but the eighties synthpop band Heaven 17 took their name from the film.

13. Interview between Stanley Kubrick and Penelope Houston quoted in Vincent LoBrutto, *Stanley Kubrick: A Biography* (New York: Donald I. Fine Books, 1997), 339.

14. Alexander Walker, *Stanley Kubrick Directs* (New York: Harcourt Brace Jovanovich, 1972), 270.

15. *His Master's Voice Records* (October 1914), 3, quoted in Lewis Foreman, "The Winnowing-Fan: British Music in Wartime," in *Oh, My Horses! Elgar and the Great War*, ed. Lewis Foreman (Rickmansworth: Elgar Enterprises, 2001), 121.

16. Randy Rasmussen, *Stanley Kubrick: Seven Films Analyzed* (Jefferson, NC: McFarland, 2001), 113.

17. Pauline Kael, *Deeper into Movies* (Boston: Little, Brown, 1973), 376.

18. Sam Johnson, "'What's It Going to Be Then, Eh?' Deciphering Adolescent Violence and Adult Corruption in *A Clockwork Orange*" in *Portraits of the Artist in A Clockwork Orange: Papers and Music from the Anthony Burgess Centre's International Symposium 'The Avatars of* A Clockwork Orange,' December 7–8, 2001, ed. Emmanuel Vernadakis and Graham Woodroffe (Angers, France: Presses de l'Université d'Angers, 2003), 32.

19. Rasmussen, *Stanley Kubrick: Seven Films Analyzed*, 118.

20. Richard Osborne, "La Gazza Ladra," in *New Grove Opera*, ed. Stanley Sadie (New York: Macmillan Press, 1992), 366.

21. Rasmussen, *Stanley Kubrick: Seven Films Analyzed*, 113.

22. Jan Dawson, "A Clockwork Orange," *British Film Institute Monthly Film Bulletin* 39, no. 457 (February 1972): 29. Similar points have been made in both Kenneth von Gunden and Stuart H. Stock, *Twenty All-Time Great Science Fiction Films* (New York: Crown Publishers, 1982), 232, and in David Zinman, *Fifty Grand Films of the Sixties and Seventies* (New York: Crown Publishers, 1986), 215.

23. Thomas Allen Nelson, *Kubrick: Inside a Film Artist's Maze* (Bloomington: Indiana University Press, 1982), 153. The music Alex hears in the novel is "a bar or so of Ludwig van (it was the Violin Concerto, last movement)" (*A Clockwork Orange*, 53).

24. Arthur Gumenik, "*A Clockwork Orange*: Novel into Film," *Film Heritage* 7, no. 4 (Summer 1972): 12.

25. The original vinyl album releases of the soundtrack and its "sequel" list Walter Carlos as the composer. All subsequent rereleases list Wendy Carlos. Where the original credits are listed, Wendy will appear in brackets, as it is the composer's legal name.

26. Peter J. Rabinowitz, "A Bird of Like Rarest Spun Heavenmetal: Music in *A Clockwork Orange*," in *Stanley Kubrick's* A Clockwork Orange, ed. Stuart Y. McDougal (New York: Cambridge University Press, 2003), 124.

27. Rasmussen, *Stanley Kubrick: Seven Films Analyzed*, 113.

28. Nelson, *Kubrick: Inside a Film Artist's Maze*, 160

29. Siegfried Kracauer, *Theory of Film: The Redemption of Physical Reality* (New York: Oxford University Press, 1960), 159–160.

30. Kracauer, *Theory of Film*, 162.

31. Scans of the score of *Timesteps* are available on Wendy Carlos's website, http://www.wendycarlos.com/+wcco.html#t-steps.

32. Rabinowitz, "A Bird of Like Rarest Spun Heavenmetal," 118.

33. Sam H. Shirakawa, *The Devil's Music Master* (Oxford: Oxford University Press, 1992), 271–279. See also Celia Applegate and Pamela Potter, "Germans as the 'People of Music': Genealogy of an Identity," in *Music and German National Identity,* ed. Celia Applegate and Pamela Potter (Chicago: University of Chicago Press, 2002), 1–35.

34. David B. Dennis, *Beethoven in German Politics, 1870–1989* (New Haven, CT: Yale University Press, 1996), 149.

35. Dennis, *Beethoven,* 151–152. See also Dennis, "'Honor Your German Masters': The Use and Abuse of 'Classical' Composers in Nazi Propaganda," *Journal of Political and Military Sociology* 30, no. 2 (Winter 2002): 273–295.

36. Ciment, *Kubrick: The Definitive Edition,* 163.

37. David Levy, *Beethoven: The Ninth Symphony,* revised ed. Yale Music Masterworks Series (New Haven, CT: Yale University Press, 2003), 8.

38. Levy, *Beethoven: The Ninth Symphony,* 5–8.

39. Nicholas Cook, *Beethoven: Symphony No. 9,* Cambridge Music Handbooks (Cambridge: Cambridge University Press, 1993), 81–83.

40. Susan McClary, *Feminine Endings* (Minneapolis: University of Minnesota Press, 1991), 128–129.

41. Bruno Nettl, *Heartland Excursions* (Chicago: University of Chicago Press, 1995), 31. The political use and reception history of this work has been the subject of Esteban Buch's *Beethoven's Ninth: A Political History,* trans. Richard Miller (Chicago: University of Chicago Press, 1999).

42. This clip seems to be an outtake from the 1965 film *Cat Ballou* (1965). A very similar scene occurs at 1:34:07 in which Cat is hanged but is then rescued by a friend hidden underneath the gallows. *Cat Ballou,* prod. by Harold Hecht, dir. by Elliot Silverstein, 97 min, Columbia/Tristar, 1965, DVD version 2003.

43. Rasmussen, *Stanley Kubrick: Seven Films Analyzed,* 127.

44. Nelson, *Kubrick: Inside a Film Artist's Maze,* 153. This point is stressed by Sam Johnson in his article "What's It Going to Be Then, Eh?" 32.

45. Ellen Shamis Roth, "The Rhetoric of First Person Point of View in the Novel and Film Forms: A Study of Anthony Burgess' *A Clockwork Orange* and Henry James' *A Turn of the Screw* and Their Film Adaptations," Ph.D. diss., New York University, 1978, 206.

46. A picture of this statue appears on the website "Meet Beethoven at Heiligenstadt," http://www.lvbeethoven.com/MeetLvB/AustriaHeiligenstadtStatueHanlein.html.

47. Burgess, *A Clockwork Orange,* x.

48. Robert Hughes, "The Décor of Tomorrow's Hell," *Time* magazine, December 27, 1971, reprinted in Mario Falsetto, ed. *Perspectives on Stanley Kubrick* (New York: G.K. Hall, 1996), 185.

49. Royal S. Brown, *Overtones and Undertones: Reading Film Music* (Berkeley: University of California Press, 1994) 30.

50. David A. Cook, *A History of Narrative Film,* 3rd ed. (New York: Norton, 1981), 350.

51. Quoted in Royal S. Brown's "Film and Classical Music," in *Film and the Arts in Symbiosis: A Resource Guide*, ed. Gary R. Edgerton (New York: Greenwood Press, 1988) 206.

52. Scott Timberg, "Is Bach Playing? Look Out!" *Los Angeles Times*, August 24, 2003, sec. E, 34–35.

53. Thomas Harris, *The Silence of the Lambs* (New York: St. Martin's Press, 1988), 234–237.

54. Ariel Dorfman, *Death and the Maiden* (New York: Penguin Books, 1992). The film *Death and the Maiden* (1994) was directed by Roman Polanski and stars Sigourney Weaver and Ben Kingsley.

55. An article in the *Los Angeles Times* states that in London Underground stations where classical music is played, robberies have been reduced by 33 percent, assaults by 25 percent, and vandalism by 37 percent. Scott Timberg, "Halt, or I'll Play Vivaldi!" *Los Angeles Times*, February 13, 2005, sec. E, 35 and 40.

56. See Christine Gengaro, "'It Was Lovely Music That Came to My Aid': Music's Contribution to the Narrative of the Novel, Film and Play A Clockwork Orange," Ph.D. Dissertation, University of Southern California, 2005. See also Jim Clarke, "'Homesick for Sin': Why Burgess Revisited *A Clockwork Orange*," in *Portraits of the Artist in* A Clockwork Orange: *Papers and Music from the Anthony Burgess Centre's International Symposium 'The Avatars of* A Clockwork Orange,' December 7–8, 2001, ed. Emmanuel Vernadakis and Graham Woodroffe (Angers, France: Presses de l'Université d'Angers, 2003), 69–78.

57. In an unpublished prologue to the play found in the Anthony Burgess collection at the Harry Ransom Humanities Research Center at the University of Texas, Austin, Alex is Adam in the Garden of Eden. Eve is Marty, Alex's girlfriend at the end of the play. Beethoven's Ode to Joy appears at the moment at which Marty eats the forbidden fruit, appropriately, a ticking orange. See Paul Phillips, "Alex in Eden: Prologue and Music to Burgess's Dramatization of *A Clockwork Orange*" in *Portraits of the Artist in* A Clockwork Orange: *Papers and Music from the Anthony Burgess Centre's International Symposium 'The Avatars of* A Clockwork Orange,' December 7–8, 2001, ed. Emmanuel Vernadakis and Graham Woodroffe (Angers, France: Presses de l'Université d'Angers, 2003), 113–129.

58. Beethoven's personal struggles with deafness have been noted in, among others, William Kinderman, *Beethoven* (Oxford: Oxford University Press, 1995), 60–64.

59. Anthony Burgess, *This Man and Music* (New York: McGraw-Hill, 1982), 82.

60. Trevor Pinch and Frank Trocco, *Analog Days: The Invention and Impact of the Moog Synthesizer* (Cambridge: Harvard University Press, 2002), 132.

61. Pinch and Trocco, *Analog Days*, 132.

62. Quoted in Mark Prendergast, *The Ambient Century: From Mahler to Trance—The Evolution of Sound in the Electronic Age* (New York: Bloomsbury, 2000), 71.

63. Interview with Jon Weiss in Trevor Pinch and Frank Trocco, "The Social Construction of the Early Electronic Music Synthesizer," in *Music and Technology*

*in the Twentieth Century,* ed. Hans-Joachim Braun, (Baltimore: Johns Hopkins University Press, 2000), 75.

64. Prendergast, *The Ambient Century,* 70.

65. The album peaked at position 34. Joel Whitburn, *Billboard: Top Albums 1955–2001* (Menomonee Falls, WI: Record Research, 2001), 1002.

66. *Walter Carlos's Clockwork Orange* peaked at 146 on the Billboard chart. Joel Whitburn, *Billboard: Top Albums 1955–2001,*134.

67. Chris Nelson, liner notes to *Walter Carlos' Clockwork Orange,* prod. Rachel Elkind, Columbia KC 31480, 1972, record album.

68. These are the track lists exactly as they appear in the liner notes of the original albums. *Stanley Kubrick's A Clockwork Orange,* produced by Rachel Elkind, Warner Brothers 2573, 1972, record album. *Walter Carlos' Clockwork Orange,* produced by Rachel Elkind, Columbia KC 31480, 1972, record album.

69. Wendy Carlos, "Looking Back at *Clockwork,*" from the liner notes to *Wendy Carlos' Complete Score* for *A Clockwork Orange,* prod. Rachel Elkind, 1998, ESD 81362.

70. Jeff Bond, "A Clockwork Composer: Wendy Carlos," *Film Score Monthly* 4, no. 2 (March 1999), 21.

71. Johnson, "'What's It Going to Be Then, Eh?'" 32.

72. Rabinowitz, "A Bird of Rarest Spun Heavenmetal," 110.

73. Burgess, *A Clockwork Orange,* 21–22.

74. Walker, *Stanley Kubrick Directs,* 271.

*Chapter Five*

─────────────────○─────────────────

# "I Was Lucky Enough to Have Superb Material to Work With"

## Barry Lyndon

STANLEY KUBRICK'S WORK ON *A Clockwork Orange* seems to have greatly influenced his next film, *Barry Lyndon*. Although on the surface, the two films might seem very different, there are aspects of the adaptations and the stories themselves that seem to suggest a connection between them. First, they are both period pieces—*Barry Lyndon* takes place in the eighteenth century, while *A Clockwork Orange* occurs in some unspecified future time. Second, they feature protagonists who are callow and selfish young men. And third, in both cases, Kubrick changed or omitted small details from the source material to make the protagonist more sympathetic. The music in *Barry Lyndon* likewise seems to bear the marks of Kubrick's experience with the music in *A Clockwork Orange*. His collaboration with Wendy Carlos must have convinced Kubrick that what he truly needed on *Barry Lyndon* was an arranger—someone to manipulate Kubrick's chosen excerpts in a way that would suit the film without interfering with the music's integrity. By setting out to hire an arranger, Kubrick was fully embracing his method of "scoring" films using preexistent sources while also assuring that he would have the musical expertise of a composer without having to deal with a composer's ego.

Once again, Kubrick drew from a literary source, this time William Makepeace Thackeray's 1844 novel *The Luck of Barry Lyndon*, later published as *The Memoirs of Barry Lyndon, Esq.* In both *A Clockwork Orange* and Thackeray's book, the main characters' points of view are strikingly similar. Both novels are narrated in first person, and both main characters are rogues, who, despite their selfishness and questionable morals, can, at times, be charming. They are unreliable narrators in that they rationalize

147

their behavior, fully believing in the rightness of their actions. In *A Clockwork Orange*, Kubrick achieved a great intimacy between the protagonist and the audience by letting Alex narrate his own story, as he had in the book. Kubrick decided against this in *Barry Lyndon*. Instead, we have three title cards and an unnamed narrator. We lose some of the intimacy with the character, and sometimes Barry's motivations remain obscure, whereas we are hardly ever in the dark about why Alex is doing something. The Redmond Barry of the book is very honest and forthcoming about his motives, and he is usually driven by greed or revenge.

In an interview with Michel Ciment, Kubrick explained his decision to give the voiceover announcements to a neutral narrator. While acknowledging that Thackeray's use of the unreliable narrator made the book "more interesting," he claims that such a device "could not be repeated on the screen. It might have worked as comedy by the juxtaposition of Barry's version of the truth with the reality on the screen, but I don't think that *Barry Lyndon* should have been done as a comedy."[1] Ciment does not ask about the use of the device in *A Clockwork Orange*, which does sometimes add comedic elements, but does not in any significant way turn the film into a comedy. Kubrick retains much of the language of the book in the film's narration, thereby retaining some of Thackeray's tongue-in-cheek descriptions.

In *Barry Lyndon*, Kubrick—as he did in *Clockwork Orange*—changes the intended ending and, in the process, alters Redmond Barry's fate. In Thackeray's book, Redmond narrates his story from prison, where he spends nearly the last two decades of his life. In Kubrick's film, the narrator states that it was rumored that Barry traveled to the Continent, mentioning only that he continued to gamble, unluckily. We are therefore spared specific knowledge of his low demise, and his fate is left to our imaginations. The narrator's final words are, "He never saw Lady Lyndon again," a choice that suggests the real tragedy of Barry's life was his lost love and failed marriage. While Thackeray's novel is a satirical look at an antihero who wants nothing more than to become a gentleman, Kubrick's film ends up being what one writer calls "an elegy for the destruction of the low-born hero by an unyielding class system."[2]

## EARLY IDEAS FOR THE SCORE

The music in *Barry Lyndon* performs a multitude of functions. As in many films, music acts as an element of setting, denoting times and places. In

*Barry Lyndon*, Kubrick also uses music to differentiate motifs and phases in the life of Redmond Barry.[3] As is typical of his style, Kubrick relies on the visuals and music to tell the story, allowing the music to fill in gaps that would normally be filled by dialogue. In the opening scene of the film, for example, Redmond Barry plays cards with his cousin, Nora Brady, a woman for whom Redmond has developed romantic feelings. The two characters speak very little, but there is subtext, and the music does much to complement the work of the actors. Instead of allowing the emotions of the characters to be explicitly stated in heavy-handed dialogue, the quiet, yearning cue conveys what the characters cannot say to one another.[4] The musical cues in *Barry Lyndon* also provide connective tissue that draws together two, three, and even four scenes. Kubrick interviewer Michel Ciment says that this function of the music turns "music into a textual mark of significant fragments, a creator of textual patterns."[5]

To find music for the film, Kubrick cast his net wide, starting with composers contemporary with the story. Kubrick's attention to detail, as always, was astonishing, and his desire for authenticity was of paramount importance, although as we will see, he was willing to make allowances when he felt it served the film. Finding the music for the score for *Barry Lyndon* was a complicated process, as was the search for an appropriate arranger for the music Kubrick would end up choosing. Correspondence saved in the Stanley Kubrick Archive at the University of the Arts in London paints a picture of a production interested in exploring many options. At one point, Kubrick considered hiring André Previn to "conduct and orchestrate the score" for $32,500. About two weeks after Kubrick floated this idea, executive producer Jan Harlan informed him that Previn was too busy to participate on the film.[6] Kubrick's next choice for musical director appears to have been Nino Rota, who is best known for scoring films by Federico Fellini and Luchino Visconti. (Rota went on to win an Academy Award for the score to *The Godfather Part II* in 1974.) An interoffice memo dated 31 July 1975 from Larry Marks to Stanley Belkin at Warner Brothers states that Nino Rota was to be engaged to "write, arrange, orchestrate, adapt and conduct the score for the motion picture for a flat fee of $32,500." From the beginning, Rota was concerned that Kubrick intended to include little to no original music. Riccardo Aragno, the man who translated Kubrick's films into Italian, conveyed Rota's sentiments to Kubrick in a letter from Aragno in August of 1975. (Aragno ostensibly translated Rota's original letter, which must have been in Italian.) Kubrick's camp, while suggesting that there might be an opportunity for some original composition, had clearly stated that Rota's main duty would be to arrange and orchestrate the director's choices. According to Aragno, Rota expressed worry that any music he did write might be thrown out at the last moment (à la Alex North's score for *2001*), and also stated that since Kubrick really wanted an arranger, the job might be better suited to a less well-known composer. Aragno finishes the letter, "So Nino came to the conclusion that—in all friendship, mutual esteem and graceful accord—it would be better for him to bow out at this point." Aragno seemed intent to make it clear that Rota still felt warmly toward Kubrick and in no way had hard feelings about the situation. There isn't a formal response from Kubrick in the archive, but there is a half-typed, half-written letter to Rota. It is not signed and bears no date. The written-in edits are underlined and the crossed out portions appear crossed out in the draft of the letter:

> Although I do understand how you feel, I am nevertheless ~~disappointed and a little~~ sad about the way things have ended. <u>Aside from being one of the nicest people I have ever met</u>, I think you are the best film composer in the world, and if you were prepared to do the film, ~~it~~ I would have been ~~a very good very fortunate thing indeed. I appreciate everything you have done, and how far you tried to bend in order to.~~ I hope that in the future I will do a film where classical themes are not what I want, and that you will still be willing to work with me. <u>Good luck and love from everyone</u>...

Before Kubrick ironed out the details about who would be the musical director of the production, he was busy choosing musical cues for the film. He was aided greatly in this endeavor by executive producer Jan Harlan. In a letter from 29 August 1973, Harlan corresponded with Hans B. Eggers from Deutsche Grammophon:

> As we discussed, we will need a large amount of all types of 18th century and 17th century music—dances, folk songs, minuets, gavottes, etc. I think it would be a marvelous idea if Deutsche Grammophon could provide us with a large choice of what's available along these lines, including all the big master works for orchestra and chamber music of this extremely rich period.

Harlan also asked Polydor Records for a list of early Italian operas, and Hanno Rinke from Polydor A&R wrote back on 21 April 1975 with a list of "Italian Opera Repertoire from Monteverdi Till Early Verdi." Between 1974 and 1975, Harlan also corresponded with Stan Hibbert, the assistant secretary from the Musician's Union about the use of certain recordings for the film. About one piece, dances by Mozart (K. 605), Hibbert stated:

The Union does not, as a matter of course, authorise the use of gramophone records for use in the sound-track of films; we prefer that special
sessions are mounted for the recording of music for specific feature
films. However, we are prepared to accede to your request, subject to a
payment of 18 pounds to each of our members involved in the original
gramophone recording session.

Dominic Frontiere from Leslie Stevens Productions sent a lengthy letter
to the production team of *Barry Lyndon* (2 July 1973) suggesting music
for the film that would be historically accurate and noting that the most
popular composers of the historical time period were Handel, Purcell,
J. C. Bach, and Scarlatti. Frontiere also suggests that Kubrick might find
that the music of composers anachronistic to the story might be equally
as effective as those from the time period, including Frederick Delius
and Hamilton Harty. He adds, "You have many choices in styles of music
to choose from [appropriate for the time period]: harpsichord and organ
music was very popular; religious music abounded; thousands of hymns
were composed." He ends with: "Enclosed are some of the songs that
were popular at the time of the Seven Years' War. If there is any specific
research you would like done, please write." Included with this correspondence is the sheet music for the following pieces: "Johnny Cope," "The
Marquis of Granby," "Why Soldiers Why," "Hot Stuff," "Tenth Regiment,"
"See the Conquering Hero Comes," "The British Grenadiers," "Over the
Hills and Far Away," "Lilliburlero." Of these songs, Kubrick ended up using only "The British Grenadiers" and "Lilliburlero."

The archive also contains lists of records they wanted to obtain, and
one list (undated) includes Haydn, Johann Melchior Molter, Beethoven's
German dances, Mozart's dances, Purcell trumpet tunes, Purcell's *Fairy
Queen*, and Vivaldi's Trumpet Concerto and *The Four Seasons*. Another
list (from 12 June 1975) includes numerous Haydn symphonies, "Nina
Pazza Amore" from Paisiello's *Barber of Seville*, Mozart piano sonatas,
selections from Gluck's opera *Orfeo*, Mahler's *Songs of a Wayfarer*, and
Donizetti's *Elixir of Love*. Because the beginning of the film takes place
in Ireland, Kubrick was interested in having authentic Irish songs on the
soundtrack. The production team was in contact with arrangers familiar
with this repertoire, including Dermot Graham and Patrick J. Power.

As for finding an arranger, Kubrick eventually got in touch with
Leonard Rosenman after the film had been completed. Rosenman (1924–
2008) had majored in music at UC Berkeley, earning a B.A., and he went
on to study composition with twentieth-century masters Arnold Schoenberg and Roger Sessions. Around the time he turned thirty, Rosenman

began to write scores for film and television. One of his first assignments was the Elia Kazan film *East of Eden*. One of his most famous scores was written for another James Dean film, *Rebel without a Cause*. Occasionally still writing for films, Rosenman moved on to television, much like former Kubrick collaborator Gerald Fried.[7] Rosenman composed scores for episodes of *The Twilight Zone*, *The Alfred Hitchcock Hour*, *The Virginian*, and *Marcus Welby, M.D.* He taught and composed into the 1990s when he was diagnosed with degenerative dementia.

Despite his impressive credentials as a composer, Rosenman's skills as an arranger were what Kubrick wanted. Certainly one of the high points of Rosenman's career was working on *Barry Lyndon*, especially because he won an Academy Award for the film, for Best Original Song Score and/or Adaptation. The collaboration with Kubrick was not without difficulty or friction, but in the final tally Rosenman did an admirable job. He, at one point, expressed concern that Kubrick had perhaps overused one of the cues,[8] a sarabande attributed to Handel that Kubrick featured (in slightly different variations) no less than ten times in the course of the film. But when Rosenman was asked if he deserved an Oscar for his efforts, he responded, "I'd have been an idiot to turn it down. . . . My award was for best adaptation, and I was lucky enough to have superb material to work with."[9]

This is a list of the "superb material" Kubrick chose, as it appears on the original soundtrack album (two cues missing from the soundtrack will be discussed at the end of the chapter):

### *Barry Lyndon: Original Soundtrack Album*

Side A

1. Sarabande—Main Title—Handel
   National Philharmonic Orchestra; Leonard Rosenman, arr. and cond.
2. Women of Ireland—Sean Ó Riada
   Chieftans
3. Piper's Maggot Jig—Traditional
   Waterford Glass Band
4. The Sea-Maiden—Traditional
   Chieftans
5. Tin Whistles—Sean Ó Riada
   Paddy Moloney and Sean Potts
6. British Grenadiers—Traditional
   Fifes and Drums, Rosenman, arr. and cond.

7. Hohenfriedberger March—Frederick the Great [attrib.]
   Leonard Rosenman, cond.
8. Lilliburlero—Traditional
   Fifes and Drums, Rosenman, arr. and cond.
9. Women of Ireland—Sean Ó Riada
   Derek Bell, harp
10. March from *Idomeneo*—Mozart
    EMI Records
11. Sarabande—Duel—Handel
    National Philharmonic Orchestra, Rosenman, arr. and cond.

   Side B

1. Lilliburlero—Traditional
   Leslie Pearson, arr. and cond.
2. German Dance No. 1 in C Major—Schubert
   National Philharmonic Orchestra, Rosenman, arr. and cond
3. Sarabande—Duel—Handel
   National Philharmonic Orchestra, Rosenman, arr. and cond
4. Film Adaptation of the Cavatina from *Il Barbiere di Siviglia,* Paisiello
   National Philharmonic Orchestra, Rosenman, arr. and cond
5. Cello concerto in E-minor (third movement), Vivaldi
   Pierre Fournier, Cello, Festival Strings, Lucerne, Ralph Baumgartner,
   cond. Deutsche Grammophon
6. Adagio from Concerto for 2 Harpsichords and Orchestra in C minor,
   J. S. Bach
   Karl Richter and Hedwig Bilgram, harpsichords, and the
   Munich Bach-Orchestra, Deutsche Grammophon
7. Film adaptation of Piano Trio in E-flat op. 100 (second movement),
   Schubert
   Ralph Holmes, Violin; Moray Welsh, Cello; Anthony Goldstone,
   Piano; Rosenman, arr.
8. Sarabande—End-Title, Handel
   National Philharmonic Orchestra, Rosenman, arr. and cond.

## Making the Chosen Music Fit

Once Kubrick had a rough idea of the music he wanted for the film, the challenge was fitting the cues into the shots without compromising the

integrity of each cue. As Jan Harlan explained, Kubrick did not want a
cue that had to be awkwardly cut or faded.[10] For those works that were
arranged, Kubrick had more control over the length of each cue; however,
in some cases, Kubrick used the cue in more than one place in the film,
each place requiring different timings. Many of the papers in the *Barry
Lyndon* files of the Kubrick archive in London deal with the challenge of
making the music fit. There are packets of papers discussing the cues,
where they will start and end in the film, where the arrangements should
be recorded, and other considerations. The following are some excerpts
from these notes.

After the duel between Redmond and Quin, notes read, "After Quinn
[sic] is Dead 1 min 4 2/3 second; This would be a bigger version of the
Sarabande, starting after 'Is he dead?' and ending on the long shot kissing
Mother." For the appearance of "Lilliburlero" the note reads:

> Tony [film editor Tony Lawson] has to work the length back to the front
> of the ship shot, to make sure the beat falls correctly on the first shot of
> the marching. There should be a ruffle of drums on the first cut of the
> prow of this ship. SK [Stanley Kubrick] to discuss with Leonard. The
> music should last 20 secs. longer than the scene requirements.

One note refers to a "Love Theme—Violin Version." Although it is not
clear what this "Love Theme" is, the note explains that "The Sea-Maiden"
could be used instead:

> Version of March 10, 1975 has, for 8 M 4 [reel]—Love Theme—Violin
> Version
>
> 1. Starts while Chevalier is reading the letter, and ends at the end
>    of the scene.
> 2. Tony and SK to select exact place and check it against the music.
>    We are well covered with the music
> 3. An alternative piece of music would be to use the "Sea-maiden" if
>    the Love Theme sounds corny.

For the appearance of *Idomeneo* that accompanies Redmond's escape from
Prussia, the notes explain how precisely the cue must be timed:

> 1. To be backed in from the coach drive-away, and to start as Ryan gets in.
> 2. This is a dubious music cue, and will have to be heard to be believed.
> 3. If we use it, we will use the EMI recording.

## G. F. Handel: *Sarabande*[11]

Appearances:

0:00:04–0:00:55 Opening credits (strings and continuo version)
0:21:09–0:25:06 Duel variation—for the Duel with John Quin
0:25:07–0:25:55 Harpsichord variation—Barry rides away from his home
after duel
2:20:27–2:25:03 Barry teaches Bryan fencing; Barry buys Bryan a horse
2:26:55–2:30:29 Low strings variation—Bryan dying after the accident
2:30:29–2:31:41 Variation with drums—Bryan's funeral (slight alteration
at the end)
2:31:41–2:33:26 Quieter variation—Barry's drinking problem and Lady
Lyndon's devotion
2:39:40–2:50:44 Duel variation—Lord Bullingdon demands a duel with
Barry
2:53:32–2:54:25 Injured Barry plays cards with his mother
3:01:15–3:04:36 Big version, solo string version, full orchestra and
drums—continues over credits

Handel composed numerous suites for keyboard. A suite is simply a
collection of stylized dances, and the sarabande is a dance in a triple meter. The particular sarabande in *Barry Lyndon* is part of Handel's Keyboard
Suite in D Minor, which was published in the 1730s, though, as is common of many of Handel's keyboard works, it is difficult to determine an
exact date of composition. Most of his keyboard works were written before
1720, likely meant for teaching and intended for private use. The Suite in
D Minor has five parts: Prelude, Allemande (a duple meter dance supposedly from the German tradition, hence the name), Courante (a slow, triple
meter dance), Sarabande, and Gigue (a lively triple or compound meter
dance). Handel composed the theme of this sarabande with two variations,
using the so-called folia chord progression as a basis. This succession of
chords is often attributed to French Baroque composer Jean Baptiste Lully
(although of Italian descent, he reached his greatest fame as the court composer for King Louis XIV). The folia structure certainly predates Lully, but
his version in 1672 is one of the most famous. An earlier folia exists, but it
was the later version that was used by many of the best-known composers
of the Baroque period: Corelli, Scarlatti, Geminiani, Vivaldi, and, of course,
Bach. Later composers who revisited the folia are Liszt in the nineteenth
century and Rachmaninoff in the twentieth century.

Handel's sarabande is a simple tune, just sixteen measures long, but through Rosenman's different arrangements achieves a number of different emotional states. Variations of the piece occupy more than thirty minutes in the film. One single cue lasts eleven minutes. The opening credits and closing credits are accompanied by the sarabande, providing a dramatic opening and close to the film. In the first half of the film, we hear the sarabande three times: the opening credits, the duel with Captain Quin, and Redmond's departure from home. It does not appear again until almost two hours later, as Redmond teaches his son to fence. It draws the beginning section of the film to the end section of the film, bookending them. This bookending feature is something Kubrick exploited with Schubert's Piano Trio as well.

One version, featuring low strings (playing pizzicato) and tremolo accents, is used twice in the film, in both cases to accompany the scenes of duels. In a way, the scenes are mirror images of each other, and the music draws them together. In the first, at the beginning of the film, Redmond Barry demands satisfaction from the Englishman Captain John Quin. The issue at hand is Quin's proposal to Redmond's cousin, Nora, with whom Redmond is in love. The tremolo accents seem to underline the nervousness of the participants, especially Quin, who is visibly shaken and does not seem to want to go through with the duel. Redmond seems braver and in fact successfully shoots his opponent. What Redmond does not know is that Nora's family rigged the duel in order to ensure the financial support of Captain Quin. Redmond hits him not with a musket ball but with a plug of tow—flax or hemp fibers. Convinced by Nora's brothers that he has killed Quin (who faints upon being "shot"), the sarabande plays through one more cycle, although in the harpsichord version.

In the mirror duel scene at the end of the film, Barry Lyndon (as he is now known) is the one challenged, this time by his stepson, Lord Bullingdon (an event that does not occur in the original source material). Again, Barry seems less shaky than his opponent, who is not only visibly nervous but vomits when it is time for him to stand his ground. Again, the tremolo accents in the sarabande cue provide a musical analogue to Bullingdon's nerves. Bullingdon's first shot misfires, but Barry does not shoot him, instead firing into the ground. Rather than allowing that act to settle the matter, Bullingdon takes a second shot, this time hitting Barry in the leg, which must be amputated below the knee.

The sarabande is heard in a scene in which Barry is teaching his beloved son, Bryan, how to fight with a sword. The appearance of the cue in this context may perhaps be a reference to Redmond's duel with Quin as a young man. This version of the sarabande, with the cello as soloist, lends a sense of foreboding to the otherwise lighthearted scenes of Barry doting on his son. The narrator confirms this feeling of foreboding by saying, "Fate had determined that [Barry] should leave none of his race behind him. And that he should finish his life poor, lonely, and childless." The music continues as Bryan asks his father for a horse. A violin solo takes up the tune and the cello returns as Lady Lyndon tells Bryan not to ride unless he is with his father. Barry further warns him that he will be flogged if he goes to see the horse before his birthday. The cue ends as Mr. Runt enters Barry's room presumably the next day to tell him that Bryan was not in his bed in the morning. The music begins again, violin and low strings together as Bryan lies injured, paralyzed except in his hands. Barry assures him that he will recover from the accident, but the child seems to know that he is dying. He asks his parents not to quarrel so that they can all be reunited in heaven.

A passionate version of the sarabande, with full orchestra and timpani, accompanies the scene of young Bryan's funeral procession. His white coffin rides in the same golden carriage that carried him at his birthday party. A quieter version accompanies the aftermath of the tragedy: Barry's drinking problem and Lady Lyndon's fervent religious devotion. The use of the sarabande over the end credits ties the film together, and we understand that the elements of this story have formed a dramatic, tragic tale.

### Sean Ó Riada: "Women of Ireland"

Appearances:

0:02:08–0:06:16 Nora hides a ribbon on her person for Barry to find
0:09:35–0:13:16 Barry and Nora talk the woods; Barry makes trouble for Nora with Quin
0:15:30–0:17:03 (Harp version) Dinner in which Quin and Nora announce their engagement
0:55:47–0:58:01 (Harp version) Barry meets a woman on his way to Holland

This particular cue seems to represent Redmond Barry's youth in Ireland and his early romances. It accompanies the very first scene of the film, in which Redmond and cousin Nora are playing a game of cards. She hides some ribbon in her cleavage and bids Redmond to find it. He is too shy to look for it, but she gives him a hint and guides his hand to it.

They share a kiss afterward. Later, Redmond and Nora walk in the woods and talk while a lonely fiddle plays the tune in the background. Redmond is upset that Nora has given her attentions to Captain Quin, and Nora's explanation—that Quin is a man while Redmond is only a boy—further agitates the young man. The music continues with the addition of tin whistle and other fiddles, while the captain courts Nora in a field. Redmond marches up to them, giving Nora back her ribbon. The image here, of Redmond and Nora against a backdrop of rolling green hills, is visually stunning, and the play of light and shadows in the scenery behind them suggests a landscape painting. Quin, suspicious of their relationship, attempts to leave, and it is on his angry reaction that the song stops. Nora's brothers patch up the situation offscreen, and in the next scene, the harp version of "Women of Ireland"—featuring harpist Derek Bell—plays as Redmond joins the family for dinner. The cue plays on, with other instruments added, as Nora and Redmond exchange glances over the table. The music ends just as Redmond's uncle stands to announce Nora and Quin's engagement. Redmond, who is unwilling to allow this to stand, challenges Quin to a duel.

The harp version of "Women of Ireland" is heard once more in the film, when Redmond—after having escaped from the British service—meets up with a woman on his way to Holland, a neutral place during the Seven Years' War. The harp version of the song plays as they join hands, and she asks him to stay with her for a few days. They share a tearful goodbye some unspecified time later. There is a melancholy air about the music, and it perfectly complements the sadness of Redmond and the woman parting ways. The yearning quality of the music evokes in one instance the frustrations of young love and Redmond's desire for Nora and, in the other instance, Redmond's sadness upon leaving the young woman.

Although the song sounds—to the ears of those unfamiliar with Irish music—as though it could be a traditional folk song from the eighteenth century, it has been attributed to Seán Ó Riada, an Irish composer and musician, who likely penned the song in the 1960s. Although the cues in the film are instrumental, Ó Riada set an eighteenth-century poem by Peader Ó Dornín to the tune. Ó Riada, whose early career was centered upon composition using modes and twelve-tone techniques, became heavily involved in Irish folk music around 1960. He arranged, orchestrated, and performed many folk songs with a band he formed called Ceoltóirí Cualann. The ensemble consisted of piano and harpsichord (to mimic the traditional Irish harp, the clarsach), flute, pipes, tin whistles, accordion, fiddle, and bodhrán, a shallow frame drum. In addition to the arrangement, performance, and recording of preexistent Irish songs, Ó Riada composed new songs in a traditional style.

An original member of Ceoltóirí Cualann, Paddy Moloney, eventually founded the Chieftans and plays tin whistle, Uilleann pipes, button accordion, and bodhrán in the band. He also arranges much of their music and, in addition to performing on their recordings, produces them as well. It was the Chieftans who performed the Irish music for the soundtrack to *Barry Lyndon*. The Chieftans' appearance on the *Barry Lyndon* soundtrack was a great opportunity for the group, which is still active today. This opportunity formed some of the publicity pieces for the film. In a newspaper piece from 1973, the Chieftans explain that Kubrick personally wrote them a letter praising their music and telling them he wanted to discuss using some of their music in *Barry Lyndon*.[12] Another piece, in London's newspaper *Daily Express*, reports that Paddy Moloney visited Kubrick's home to watch sequences from the film. Author Victor Davis stated that their appearance on the soundtrack would give the Chieftans a boost: "Look what Kubrick did for those old squares, the Strausses, in *2001: A Space Odyssey*."[13]

### Traditional: "Piper's Maggot Jig"

Appearance:

0:08:19–0:09:32 Nora dances with John Quin

The Waterford Glass Band recorded this traditional jig for *Barry Lyndon*. It plays as Nora dances with John Quin at the celebration that takes place ostensibly after the British regiment (including men who have joined up from this Irish town) makes its grand display. Kubrick, again wanting authenticity, sent the actors, Gay Hamilton and Leonard Rossiter, to London to learn the proper steps of the jig. Not only did the two learn it perfectly, but they also performed it flawlessly on the first take. Kubrick, however, asked for numerous takes, perhaps, as Gay Hamilton surmises, to make it seem almost careless, "like we'd been doing that dance all of our lives."[14] The piece is lively and rhythmic, and the joy of the jig and the participants' enjoyment of the dance are contrasted against Redmond's dismay at seeing Nora and Captain Quin together.

**Traditional: "The Sea-Maiden"**

Appearances:

0:27:19–0:29:33 Barry says goodbye to his mother and goes to Dublin
0:47:38–0:49:39 After Captain Grogan's death, Barry wants to get out of
the service

    Another Irish air, "The Sea-Maiden," accompanies two scenes. In the first, Redmond bids farewell to his mother and flees to Dublin. Although the tune seems to suggest a sense of melancholy for the boy who has just left his home and mother for the first time, the narrator explains that Redmond must, as any young man in the same situation, be excited about the possibilities of independence.
    In the second appearance of this tune, Barry has just seen his friend, Captain Grogan, die in battle. As he reflects on the event, he realizes that he wants to escape the service. The tune accompanies a scene of the regiment burning a farm and leaving with the animals, and one of Redmond carrying buckets of water. It is on this errand that Redmond sees a chance of escape, and he takes the opportunity, stealing the horse and uniform of an officer.

**Sean Ó Riada: "Tin Whistles"**

Appearance:

0:29:45–0:33:34 Barry meets Captain Feeny

    As Redmond travels to Dublin, he stops briefly at an inn to get a drink of water. A man sitting at a table outside bids Redmond hello and asks him to stay and join him for a meal. Redmond refuses, saying he must be on his way. A little while later, Redmond rides down the road to the strains of "Tin Whistles," and he meets the same man on the road, who identifies himself as Captain Feeny—a name seemingly recognized by Redmond. Feeny and his son are thieves and they rob Redmond of everything but the clothes on his back. With no money and no other choice, Redmond joins the British Service.
    The cue begins with a ruffle on the bodhrán, and a lone tin whistle plays a meandering melody. The second time through the melody, a second tin whistle joins the first in harmony. The two musical lines, played

by the Chieftans' Paddy Moloney and Sean Potts, meet and diverge as they weave two melodies together. The two tin whistles end on a haunting unison note as Redmond walks away from Feeny and all of his worldly possessions.

## Traditional: "British Grenadiers"

Appearances:

0:06:22–0:08:02 Scene of British regiment marching in Ireland
0:43:41–0:45:24 Ship traveling; battle (drums alone continue until
    0:47:37)
1:47:33–1:47:58 Barry in a brothel, soldiers singing the song

Early in the film, the narrator states, "The whole country was alive with war's alarms. Three kingdoms ringing with military music." One of the military tunes that was undoubtedly heard was "The British Grenadiers," a march used by British armies. As the name implies, it is a song about a regiment whose members dropped grenades, an especially dangerous endeavor. It is currently the official march of a number of groups including the Royal Regiment of Canadian Artillery and the Corps of Royal Engineers. The provenance of the tune is not entirely clear, having possible British or Dutch origins. The best-known text for the tune comes from the War of Spanish Succession, which lasted from 1702 to 1713. Parts of the text refer to the specific clothing and equipment of the grenadiers and speak of the bravery and persistence of the group.[15] The refrain, "Sing tow, row, row, row, row, row, the British Grenadiers" is paired with lines like, "But our brave boys do know it [the force of gunpowder], and banish all their fears," or "Here come the Grenadiers, my boys, who know no doubts or fears!"[16]

Redmond Barry's time in the British service is symbolized by this traditional military tune. As one might expect, the drum cadence is suitable for marching, and the fife and drums arrangement is entirely appropriate for battlefield performance. We hear the music for the first time when the British soldiers led by Captain John Quin march through Redmond's town. Redmond looks upon the display of the regiment, which, according to the narrator "filled Barry with envy." Soon enough, because of the robbery at the hands of Captain Feeny, Redmond is wearing the same red uniform and marching in formation. The music accompanies film of a ship at sea, presumably carrying Redmond's regiment to a battle against a small

French rear guard, and the cue continues into the battle itself, with the drum cadence lasting almost two minutes after the melody has finished.

It is in the battle that Redmond loses his friend and protector Captain Grogan. Grogan, who was Redmond's second in the duel with Quin, previously informed Redmond that Nora's family rigged the duel and that Quin and Nora have indeed gotten married. When Redmond sees him shot in battle, he carries the man into the woods and they share some words before Grogan dies of his wound. The experience sours Redmond on the service, and soon his thoughts turn to escape. The first two cues featuring "The British Grenadiers" are both instrumental, but the final time we hear the song, a group of men (two of them in British uniform) sings drunkenly in what might be a bar or a brothel. Redmond, who at this point is married to Lady Lyndon, is enjoying the attentions of two topless young ladies, while the men sing a verse of "The British Grenadiers" in the background.

## Traditional: "Lilliburlero"

Appearance:

0:39:54—0:41:05 Barry sees Captain Grogan again

"Lilliburlero" appears in a scene in which Redmond's regiment is being joined by another group of soldiers, including his old friend Captain Grogan. As Grogan's men parade by Redmond and the others, Redmond and Grogan share a look of recognition. The music for the march "Lilliburlero" has a murky history. The tune is often attributed to British composer Henry Purcell, because it appears in his 1689 collection *Music's Handmaid* under the name "A New Irish Tune." It is highly doubtful, however, that Purcell was the creator of the tune, and it is much more likely that he adapted some preexistent folk tune for his collection. The BBC World Service has used the "Lilliburlero" tune as the signature tune for their news since 1955, and on their website they claim that the first appearance of the tune with the words "There Was an Old Man of Waltham Cross" is in a 1661 collection called *An Antidote against Melancholy*.[17] This volume is described on the title page as being "Compounded of Choice Poems, Jovial Songs, Merry Ballads, and Witty Parodies" and contains no actual music notation, just the poems. Under the heading "A Catch," these words appear:

> There was an old man at Walton Cross, [Waltham]
> Who merrily sung when he liv'd by the loss;
> *Hey tro-ly loly lo.*

He never was heard to sigh a hey ho
But he sent it out with *Hey troly loly lo.*
He chear'd up his heart,
When his goods when to wrack[,]
With a hem, boy, Hem!
And a cup of Old Sack;
Sing, *hey troly loly lo.*[18]

To further confuse the history of this tune, there is also a French version called "Marche du Prince d'Orange," which is attributed to Lully and another composer who worked for King Louis XIV. In subsequent years, the tune has also served as a drinking song, a song about the Protestant army in Northern Ireland, and a satirical song about the Confederacy in the American Civil War.

"Lilliburlero," in the time of *Barry Lyndon*, was known as a political protest song against King James II, last of the Catholic monarchs, who fled England when the Dutch invaded England under the command of his Protestant nephew (who was also his son-in-law), William III of Orange. James attempted to regain the throne in 1689 with the help of Irish Catholic supporters, but his effort was thwarted at the Battle of Boyne in 1690. James spent the last decade of his life at a French court that was under the aegis of his friend and relative King Louis XIV.

Heading the opposition against James II was Thomas Wharton, first Marquess of Wharton. Wharton was a member of Parliament and later served England as the lord lieutenant of Ireland early in the eighteenth century. Wharton penned lyrics to the Lilliburlero tune to give voice to the British opposition to Catholics.[19] The refrain of "Lilliburlero"—"Lero Lero Lilliburlero / Lilliburlero bullen a la"—has a number of possible sources, like the mispronunciation of Irish words, which could refer to lilies, the flowers, or to William Lilly, who predicted there would be a Catholic King of England, to the use of "Lilli" as a nickname for William.

## Frederick the Great (attrib.): Hohenfriedberger March

Appearances:

0:51:14–0:52:25 Redmond escapes British service in the guise of Lieutenant Fakenham

0:58:05–0:59:16 Redmond rides through the countryside

1:01:15–1:01:53 Rides with Potzdorf, song is taken up by the men singing in the pub; fades out at 1:03:49 as Potzdorf calls for Barry's arrest

1:04:32–1:08:37 Fife and drum version; Barry's fellow Prussian soldier gets beaten; Barry saves Potzdorf

The Hohenfriedberger March represents the period after Redmond's escape from the British service. Sick of the difficulties of life in the regiment and disheartened after the death of Captain Grogan, Redmond is unwilling to finish out the years left in his commission. The march begins, in grand fashion, as Redmond rides through land occupied by the Prussian army (allied with Britain in the war). In his disguise as British officer Lieutenant Fakenham, Redmond hopes to reach Holland. Before he can get there, however, Redmond meets up with Captain Potzdorf, an officer in the Prussian army. As they ride off together, the march begins anew. Potzdorf suspects that Fakenham is not who he says he is and, through a series of questions and some flattery, lures Redmond into lies to discover his deception.

Potzdorf takes Redmond to the mess hall where the march (to this point played by an orchestra) is taken up by soldiers who sing the song. The music goes from being part of the score to being part of the action, "sourced" on-screen.[20] This was a particular challenge because Kubrick wanted the instrumental version and the sung version to be in the same key, nearly seamless to the ear. In the notes about the musical cues, it says:

1. [The cue] starts from Hardy [the actor portraying Potzdorf] riding away, and ends just before the singing in the Prussian Mess.
2. Check if we can make a reasonable transition from the end of the melody, which does end properly, to the Prussians singing, to see whether they are close to being in the same key.
3. If they're not in the same key, the tempophon[21] could probably change the key, or we might consider doing it again.

Potzdorf, who interrupts the singing to call for the arrest of "Fakenham," gives Redmond a choice: go to prison (or be executed by the British army for desertion) or volunteer for the Prussian army. Redmond chooses the latter. At first, life in the Prussian army seems worse than life in the British service. A fife and drums version of the march accompanies a Prussian soldier running the gauntlet for some unknown minor offense.

Redmond, however, proves his mettle and earns himself a reward when he saves Potzdorf in battle. Redmond frees the captain from a support beam that has fallen on him and, as he had for Captain Grogan, carries the injured man to safety. In this case, Potzdorf survives and Redmond is rewarded. When the war is over, Redmond continues in the Prussian service as a spy. It is this assignment that helps Redmond transition to the next phase in his life.

The Hohenfriedberger March is attributed to Frederick the Great, who was the king of Prussia from 1740 to 1786. Frederick studied music in his youth and had no designs on his father's crown, attempting to run away from his responsibilities as heir to the throne. He eventually ascended to the throne and ruled Prussia during the Silesian Wars, the second of which featured the Battle of Hohenfriedberg. It was supposedly Frederick's victory in this battle that inspired him to the write the Hohenfriedberger March.[22] Frederick, an accomplished composer and flautist, surrounded himself with some of the most talented musicians of the day, including C. P. E. Bach (son of J. S. Bach) and noted flautist, composer, and treatise-writer Johann Joachim Quantz.

## Mozart: March from *Idomeneo*

Appearances:

1:10:27–1:11:11 Voiceover explaining the end of the war
1:13:23–1:14:50 Barry begins his new assignment
1:26:57–1:27:32 Barry leaves country disguised as the Chevalier

When one of the marches from Mozart's opera *Idomeneo* first appears, the Seven Years' War is over and the narrator explains that Redmond's regiment was garrisoned in the capital of Prussia, Königsberg. The cue plays over footage of carriages riding up and down a grand avenue, either side of which are lush palaces. The cue ends as Redmond enters the office of the minister of police, Potzdorf's uncle. The final two chords nearly match up with Redmond's military two-step arrival at Herr von Potzdorf's desk. Redmond's new assignment will be as part of the police bureau, and he must spy on the Chevalier de Balibari, a libertine. As Redmond is about to accept the assignment, the excerpt from *Idomeneo* begins again and plays as Redmond and Captain Potzdorf discuss the details of Redmond's made-up backstory. The march ends as Redmond presents himself to the Chevalier. In the novel, the Chevalier turns out to be Redmond's uncle (his father's brother), but here he is simply something of a father figure (and a fellow Irishman). Redmond reveals his true identity to the Chevalier, and together they work to conceal information from the Prussian police.

The final appearance of the march signals the end of Redmond's time in Prussia. The Prussian police plan to send the Chevalier out of the country, but instead the Chevalier and Redmond hatch a plan. The Chevalier crosses the border in secret in the night, and the next day, Redmond, disguised as the Chevalier, is escorted to the front by two Prussian officers. The last eight measures of the march play as the carriage begins its journey. As the march reaches its conclusion, the end of this phase of Barry's life is given a sense of finality.

Mozart's opera *Idomeneo* was composed in 1780 to be premiered in Munich and employs innovative orchestration and dramatic singing especially sensitive to the emotions in the text.[23] Its story line, made into a libretto by Giambattista Varesco (after a French libretto by Antoine Danchet), is a love story of Ilia, daughter of King Priam of Troy, and Idamante, son of Idomeneo, King of Crete. This love story is complicated by a promise made by Idomeneo–thought to be lost at sea—to Neptune, namely that he will sacrifice the first person he sees if only he be allowed to survive a shipwreck. The first person to greet Idomeneo is his own son, Idamante. In the end, Idamante, who is willing to sacrifice himself to fulfill his father's promise, is spared, and Neptune commands that Idomeneo yield the throne to the young lovers, who become the new rulers of Crete. Perhaps because of Mozart's trip to Paris two years previous to the composition of *Idomeneo*, the opera retains certain aspects of French style, including choruses, ballets, and marches (one of which is the excerpt used in *Barry Lyndon*).[24] This particular march is one of three in the opera and occurs in the middle of act 2.

### Schubert: German Dance No. 1 in C Major

Appearances:

1:56:24–2:00:06 Bryan's birthday party
2:03:40–2:05:52 Barry tries to get a title

This playful piece is heard twice in the film. In the first instance, it accompanies the festivities for Bryan's eighth birthday party. A magician does tricks for Bryan, while an audience of family and local nobility watch. Although the scene is ostensibly about Bryan, it begins with a shot of Lord Bullingdon, and the narrator explains the growing tension between Bullingdon and Barry: "his hatred for Barry assumed an intensity equaled only by his increased devotion to his mother." The music continues as Barry and his mother put Bryan to bed.

Schubert's German Dance is also the theme music for Barry's attempts to get a title of his own. Barry's mother, always looking out for her
son's advantage, warns him that if anything happened to Lady Lyndon, all
of her fortune would go to Lord Bullingdon, who would not provide for
Barry. So Barry, using a combination of charm, gifts, and possibly outright
bribery, attempts to get a title. Schubert's dance serves to underscore the
game Barry is playing, spending money quickly and foolishly, throwing lavish events to impress important people, and outfitting a company of troops
to fight in the American Revolution. The cue ends as Barry is presented
to King George III. Barry's hopes for a title are dashed, however, when he
and Lord Bullingdon engage in a very public brawl. Schubert composed
this piece early in his career, when he was about sixteen years old. It is
scored for string quartet (two violins, viola, and cello) and shows the influence of the classical style of Mozart and Haydn.

**Giovanni Paisiello: "Saper bramate" from *Il Barbiere di Siviglia***

Appearances:

1:18:36–1:22:28 (instrumental) Barry serves the Chevalier when he plays
    cards
1:27:16–1:30:26 (with voice) The Chevalier and Barry run a gaming table

Paisiello's cavatina from act 1, sc. 6 of *Il Barbiere di Siviglia* or *The
Barber of Seville* is the music that accompanies the Chevalier's card game.
In this version, the vocal line is played by a cello, perhaps to keep it from
interfering with the narrator's explanation of how Redmond helps the
Chevalier cheat. The cue continues as the prince of Tübingen accuses
the Chevalier of cheating. The aria appears again, as the Chevalier and
Redmond—now a free man—run a gaming table (again with dishonest
methods). The narrator explains that Redmond Barry is beginning his
"professional work as a gamester." In this version of the aria, the vocal
line is indeed sung. It is hard to figure out why Kubrick used the different
versions of the aria, since in both instances there is narration and quiet
conversation over the music. The aria comes to an end as Redmond has a
swordfight with a man who owes him a gambling debt.
    Paisiello's opera *Il Barbiere di Siviglia* was composed in 1782 and
proved to be the composer's greatest success. The librettist Giuseppe
Petrosellini adapted the story from a French play by Pierre Beaumarchais.

The story line involves a count who falls in love with a woman named Rosine. To ensure that she will fall in love with the man and not his fortune, he dresses up as a poor student named Lindor. The titular barber, Figaro, helps the count meet up with Rosine, who is trapped in the home of her guardian, Doctor Bartholo. The opera ends with the marriage of the count and Rosine. The excerpt from the opera that is used in the film, "Saper bramate," is a cavatina sung by the count, in the guise of Lindor, the poor student. Unable to offer her any material treasures, he can only offer loyalty, constancy, and adoration. Gioachino Rossini composed an opera called *Il Barbiere di Siviglia* in 1816 with a libretto by Cesare Sterbini and achieved great success as well, actually eclipsing the success of Paisiello's opera.[25]

## Vivaldi: Cello Concerto in E Minor, Third Movement

Appearances:

1:44:30–1:47:33 Redmond Barry is now married to Lady Lyndon; young Lord Bullingdon complains about Barry to his tutor; Bryan is born
1:49:33–1:53:16 Lady Lyndon sees Barry cheating; Barry apologizes
2:16:08–2:23:49 Barry contemplates Bullingdon's departure; Lady Lyndon signs for Barry's debts

The third movement of Vivaldi's Cello Concerto in E Minor is a melancholy theme that seems to represent the uneasy and sometimes unhappy union between Redmond—now known as Barry Lyndon—and Lady Lyndon. It is first heard in the scene immediately following the wedding (which took place a year after Lady Lyndon became a widow). Barry sits in their carriage smoking a pipe. Lady Lyndon asks him to refrain from smoking for a while, and, tellingly, he does not stop but instead blows smoke in her face. The narrator explains that Lady Lyndon would come to "occupy a place in Barry's life not very much more important than the elegant carpets and pictures" in his home. The music continues as Lord Bullingdon in the other carriage tells his tutor, Mr. Runt, that he is upset his mother has quickly and foolishly married an opportunistic man. The music connects these scenes in the carriages with the birth, a year later, of Bryan Patrick Lyndon, the beloved son of Barry and Lady Lyndon. It is notable that, in this instance, Kubrick does not allow the musical cue to come to a satisfying resting place, instead interrupting the peaceful tableau of mother, father, and child with a cut to a scene in which Barry kisses two topless women at a brothel, while men sing drunkenly in the background. Kubrick would never have allowed such a jarring interruption of the music unless it served the film, and here the cut suggests the discord Barry's behavior will cause in his marriage.

Three scenes later, Lady Lyndon, Lord Bullingdon, and Mr. Runt take a walk outside. The only sounds are the wind, the rushing water of a brook, and the birds singing. The three see Barry across the brook, kissing the maid who is tending to Bryan. Without a word, Lord Bullingdon takes his mother's hand as the Vivaldi cue begins again. Barry looks up and knows he is caught. The narrator says, "Lady Lyndon tended to a melancholy and maudlin temper, and left alone by her husband, rarely happy or in good humor. Now she must add jealousy to her other complaints, and find rivals even among her maids." The cue continues into the next scene as Lady Lyndon plays cards with her friends, seeming distracted and sad. In the next scene, Lady Lyndon sits motionless in the bath, staring into the distance, while two maids attend to her. Barry enters the room and asks to be left alone with his wife. He apologizes, and the two reconcile. This time, the movement is allowed to come to its proper cadence at the end.

The third and final appearance of this excerpt from Vivaldi comes in the aftermath of Lord Bullingdon and Barry's very nasty public argument. Because of the nature of the argument, which devolved into fisticuffs, Barry's bid for a title is dashed and most of his friends leave him. Because of this, Barry's creditors descend upon him at once to get their money, and Lady Lyndon nearly signs away her fortune as Barry sits motionless. The final cadence of the movement arrives as Barry and Bryan sit in a boat in the stream and fish. Vivaldi, a notable composer from the High Baroque period, is best known for his set of concertos *The Four Seasons*. Vivaldi was incredibly prolific, writing more than five hundred other concertos, many for violin, but some for other instruments like the flute and cello. The fast movements of Vivaldi's concertos are often characterized by lively, virtuosic passages, but his slow movements, as evidenced by this piece, can suggest pensiveness and perhaps even unrest.

### J. S. Bach: Adagio from Concerto for Two Harpsichords and Orchestra in C Minor

Appearance:

2:11:21–2:13:12 Concert at which Bullingdon publicly humiliates Barry

Lady Lyndon and Mr. Runt, on harpsichord and flute, respectively, play a concert for a group of guests. It is a delicate tune, with pizzicato accompaniment from the string orchestra. Lady Lyndon and Mr. Runt each play lines that wind around each other in imitation. The sound of footsteps interrupts the peacefulness of the performance, but Lady Lyndon and the orchestra do not stop playing until Bryan and Lord Bullingdon reach the harpsichord. Bullingdon is in his stocking feet, while Bryan wears his half brother's shoes. In the silence after the interruption, Lord Bullingdon expresses to his mother his disgust at the "shameful nature of [Barry's] conduct towards your ladyship, his brutal and ungentlemanlike behavior, his open infidelity, his shameless robbery and swindling of my property and yours." Bullingdon explains to her and to all present that he is going to leave home. Lady Lyndon leaves in tears, and Barry reacts by punching Bullingdon in the back, starting a brawl that horrifies all present. It is only through the intervention of the guests that Barry does not kill Lord Bullingdon.

As he did with the Vivaldi piece, Kubrick chose the slow movement of Bach's concerto, in this case to convey a sense of delicacy. J. S. Bach is one of the best-known composers from the Baroque period, and it was in the time period in which *Barry Lyndon* takes place that his music was beginning to fall out of favor. Bach's complex counterpoint was being replaced by a emotional and less complex simple style exemplified by the music of C. P. E. Bach, Mozart, and Haydn. Court and private performances continued, of course, but elements of the Baroque style faded gradually from new music.

### Schubert: Piano Trio in E-flat, Op. 100, Second Movement

Appearances:

1:32:00–1:39:06 Barry sees Lady Lyndon; they play cards; Barry kisses her (measures 1–66,1–20, 1–56, 1–34)
2:57:11–3:01:13 Barry, now with one leg, leaves the inn to return to Ireland (measures 1–40 altered, 187–end)

The second movement to Schubert's Piano Trio bookends the relationship between Redmond and Lady Lyndon. It is the cue that is playing when he sees her for the first time at the spa, walking with her husband, Sir Charles Reginald Lyndon, her son Viscount Bullingdon, and Lady Lyndon's chaplain, Mr. Samuel Runt. As Kubrick sweeps with great care across a garden full of people in exquisite costume walking amidst the beautiful scenery, the narrator explains that Redmond's experiences had rid him of romantic notions, instead instilling in him the desire to "marry a woman of fortune and condition." It just so happens that Lady Lyndon, whom Redmond closely watches, is, as the narrator describes her, "a woman of vast wealth and great beauty."

Some time later, at the gaming table, Redmond and Lady Lyndon gaze at each other, their faces lit by candlelight. She steps outside and does not seem at all surprised when Redmond follows her a few minutes later, nor does she protest when Redmond wordlessly takes her hands and kisses her. The narrator explains that "six hours after they met, her Ladyship was in love." The cue, which connects the scenes of Redmond's courtship, ends as Redmond addresses Sir Charles while he plays cards with some friends. He expresses to Redmond that he knows what's going on between Redmond and Lady Lyndon, but Redmond denies any impropriety. Sir Charles works himself into such a lather over their conversation it appears that he suffers a heart attack. The voice of the narrator reads his obituary as the scene and the voice fade out, replaced by a black screen and then the intermission card.

The second and last time we hear the cue, Barry Lyndon, "utterly baffled and beaten," returns to Ireland so that he won't be arrested. He leaves the inn where he convalesced after the duel with Lord Bullingdon and the amputation of his lower leg. With crutches he makes his way to the carriage, his mother by his side, and the narrator explains, as the frame freezes, that "he never saw Lady Lyndon again." We cut then to the Lyndon estate where Lady Lyndon and Lord Bullingdon sit with Mr. Runt and Graham while she signs notes for payment. The note that she must sign to pay Barry Lyndon's annuity does not pass her unnoticed, and even Bullingdon waits to see what she will do. This cue features the ending of this movement of the trio, a section of the music we have not yet heard before. There is modal mixture here, both minor and major harmonies, complementing what might be described as Lady Lyndon's mixed feelings. She pauses briefly at seeing the name "Redmond Barry," but finally signs. When it is done, she stares straight ahead, perhaps remembering her love for Redmond Barry, Bullingdon watching her closely. The moment passes and she returns to the present, while the trio begins its final cadences. The last chords are heard just as the epilogue title card appears: "It was in the reign of George III that the aforesaid personages lived and quarreled; good or bad, handsome or ugly, rich or poor they are all equal now." Schubert began composing the piano trio in November of 1827 and it was likely heard in public in March of 1828, the year he died.[26] The slow movement of the trio conveys Schubert's mastery of the melancholic. Like many of his songs, it mixes major and minor modes and exemplifies the term "bittersweet."

There are two additional cues that appear in the film, but are not on the recorded soundtrack. Jean-Marie LeClair's sonata a trois "Le Rondeau de Paris" plays while Kubrick shows what could be a family portrait of Lady Lyndon with young Bullingdon and the infant Bryan. Visually, there is very little movement in this tableau except for Bryan in his bassinet. The narrator explains that Barry and Lady Lyndon are leading separate lives; Barry goes out and enjoys himself while Lady Lyndon stays at home with her two sons. The narrator says, "She preferred quiet, or to say the truth, [Barry] preferred it for her." As a mother, Lady Lyndon should lavish attention on her children and "should give up the pleasures and frivolities of the world, leaving that part of the duty of every family of distinction, to be performed by him." The music that is playing under this scene becomes the focal point of the next scene as it is revealed that Lady Lyndon, Mr. Runt, and Lord Bullingdon are performing the music. Bullingdon plays a cello, Lady Lyndon plays harpsichord, and Mr. Runt plays the flute. They would be the picture of a perfect family, but, of course, Mr. Runt is not Lady Lyndon's husband. Jean-Marie LeClair's claim to fame is as one of the founders of the French violin school. Although the sonata in the film features the flute as a solo instrument, LeClair was known for writing violin sonatas.[27]

The other musical cue that does not appear on the soundtrack is a brief excerpt of a Schubert piano piece. It is the first five measures of the first impromptu of the four collected in Schubert's op. 90. The first chord of this twenty-second clip first appears at the end of part 1, as Sir Charles Lyndon suffers his heart attack (1:42:00–1:42:20). The screen fades to black and the intermission title card appears. The same excerpt is played over the title card for part 2, which reads, "Containing an account of the misfortunes and disasters which befell Barry Lyndon." Melancholy in character, the Schubert excerpt matches well with the ominous title card. Everything about these five measures conveys a feeling of uncertainty, from the open octaves of the opening chord, which deny a feeling of major or minor, to the presence of a fermata on this chord that thwarts any sense of rhythm we might have. The key signature suggests that we might be in E-flat major or C minor, but the open Gs point to C minor. The phrase that follows this chord, however, meanders from B natural (not in the key signature), up to E-flat, down to A natural (not in the key signature), and back up to D, leaving the listeners with a sense that we still don't know quite what key we are in. Kubrick was almost certainly unaware of the theoretical reasons that make this excerpt so fitting for the intermission, a point in the story where many things are very much "up in the air," but it is undeniably an excellent choice.

## Differences between Novel and Film

There are two notable differences between Thackeray's novel and Kubrick's *Barry Lyndon*, the first of which involves the nature of marriage between Barry and Lady Lyndon. In the film, at least, Kubrick suggests that Barry at some point is inspired to apologize to Lady Lyndon for his indiscretions, and there is no subsequent indication that Barry is unfaithful to her. Only Bullingdon's speech about Barry's behavior suggests otherwise. In fact, in the scenes before Bryan's accident, the family—with the exception of Lord Bullingdon—seems content. Despite their troubles, Barry and Lady Lyndon appear to have genuine feelings for each other. When Lady Lyndon signs for Barry's annuity, it is an emotional moment; the final sad words about Barry are: "He never saw Lady Lyndon again." The Barry of the film doesn't seem as bad compared to the Barry of the book, who comes off as shallow, conniving, and sometimes cruel.

In Thackeray's book, there is no indication that Barry loves or even likes Lady Lyndon. He says: "Few men are so honest as I am; for few will own to their real motives, and I don't care a button about confessing mine. . . . I made the acquaintance of Lady Lyndon with ulterior views."[28] After the death of Sir Charles, the Lady Lyndon of the book is being actively courted by Lord George Poynings, a man to whom she eventually turns to help her escape her marriage, which has become unbearable. Barry admits to using her, ignoring her, mistreating her, and not allowing her to see her own son if she is disagreeable. Furthermore, he knows that if he shows her the slightest affection, she will do what he asks. The only reason he is ever kind to her is to gain some sort of advantage.

Although she is described in the film as a woman of great wealth and great beauty, and she is played by actress and model Marisa Berensen, the Barry of the book does not find Lady Lyndon attractive at all. In describing her, and the staff that traveled with her, the Redmond of the book says, "In another [carriage] would be her female secretary and her waiting-women;

who, in spite of their care, never could make their mistress look much better than a slattern."[29] After a year a marriage he says of her:

> She had grown very fat, was short-sighted, pale in comparison, careless about her dress, dull in demeanour; her conversations with me characterized by a stupid despair, or a silly blundering attempt at forced cheerfulness still more disagreeable: hence our intercourse was but trifling, and my temptations to carry her into the world, or to remain in her society of necessity exceedingly small. She would try my temper at home, too, in a thousand ways.[30]

The second important difference between the novel and the film is Kubrick's addition of the duel between Barry Lyndon and Lord Bullingdon. The event does not happen in the book, but its presence in the film provides a single point of conflict that effectively separates Barry and his mother from the Lyndon family. It puts the dissolution of the marriage in the hands of Lord Bullingdon, rather than Lady Lyndon. The duel also allows Kubrick to show Barry's basic decency—he refuses to shoot Bullingdon, even when given a clear shot. The reward for his decency is a bullet in the leg. Bullingdon comes off worse here, especially because we haven't seen more evidence of Barry's indiscretions. In fact, Barry looks less like an evil conniver and more like a careless spendthrift with ambitions, however foolish, of moving up in class.

## CONCLUSION

The music in *Barry Lyndon* is an extremely important part of the film, but it is Kubrick's visual achievements that have garnered the most discussion. In addition to Leonard Rosenman's Oscar for Best Score/Adaptation, the film received three additional Academy Awards. John Alcott won for Best Cinematography; Ken Adam, Roy Walker, and Vernon Dixon won for Best Art/Set Direction; and Ulla-Britt Sölerlund and Milena Canonero won for Best Costume Design. In total, *Barry Lyndon* received seven nominations, including three for Kubrick, for Best Adapted Screenplay, Best Picture, and Best Director.[31]

Kubrick had beautiful scenery and sets to film, and he took great pains to show the lush rolling green hills and modest homes of Redmond's native Ireland and the extravagance of the palaces of Europe. Kubrick's art directors transformed various castles, palaces, and estate houses in

Ireland, England, and Scotland (with some exteriors done in Germany) for nearly all of the locations. In filming in these castles, Kubrick was inspired to shoot scenes with natural light whenever possible, and in some cases, to shoot by candlelight. Such a feat would not have been possible were it not for the Zeiss camera lenses Kubrick used on the film. Developed for the Apollo moon landings, the Zeiss lens featured a wide aperture and fixed focal length that allowed Neil Armstrong and Buzz Aldrin (among others), to take pictures in the low light on the moon's surface. With the Zeiss lenses, and the modifications made by a few technical innovators, Kubrick was able to capture the candle-illuminated faces in *Barry Lyndon*.[32]

In such scenes, and in many other conventionally lit scenes, Kubrick opted for a fixed camera and very little movement from the actors. The result in some cases are tableaux—living paintings. This is not surprising as the production lavished the same amount of research on the visual art of the eighteenth century as they did on the music of the time. Among those works they studied were the landscapes and portraits of Thomas Gainsborough, Jean-Antoine Watteau, and William Hogarth. Their influence on the look of the film is clear.

The importance of the music cannot, however, be discounted. Every single cue for the film was preexistent, and Leonard Rosenman did a brilliant job of arranging Kubrick's choices into viable music cues. Kubrick once again showed that his instincts were dead on, especially considering the amount of musical excerpts that he must have heard in the course of production. The musical choices convey everything from yearning to delicacy to grief to playfulness to melancholy. The use of a single cue for more than one scene draws those scenes together thematically or recalls earlier references. Kubrick develops a musical language within this score and effectively expresses the hope and then tragic downfall of Redmond Barry.

Final note: The sharp-eyed viewer of *Barry Lyndon* will notice that Kubrick used three actors who appeared in his previous film, *A Clockwork Orange*: the minister from *A Clockwork Orange*, Anthony Sharp, plays Lord Hallom in *Barry Lyndon*, the man with whom Barry discusses getting a title; Patrick Magee, who played the victim and later torturer F. Alexander in *A Clockwork Orange,* plays the Chevalier de Balibari; and Alex's father in *A Clockwork Orange*, Philip Stone, plays Graham, one of Lady Lyndon's advisors. Stone also appears in Kubrick's next film *The Shining*, as the previous caretaker of the Overlook Hotel before Jack Torrance, Delbert Grady, making him the only actor to appear in three consecutive Kubrick films.

## NOTES

1. Michel Ciment, *Kubrick: The Definitive Edition,* trans. Gilbert Adair (New York: Faber and Faber, 1999), 170.
2. Peter Cosgrove, "The Cinema of Attractions and the Novel in *Barry Lyndon* and *Tom Jones,*" in *Eighteenth-Century Fiction on Screen,* ed. Robert Mayer (Cambridge: Cambridge University Press, 2002), 21–22.
3. Kubrick did this to great effect in *2001,* where the music of Ligeti represented encounters with alien intelligence.
4. Gene D. Phillips and Rodney Hill, "Leonard Rosenman," in *Encyclopedia of Stanley Kubrick* (New York: Checkmark Books, 2002), 300.
5. Luis M. Garcia Mainar, *Narrative and Stylistic Patterns in the Films of Stanley Kubrick* (Rochester, NY: Camden House, 1999), 57.
6. All letters discussed in this section were found in the Stanley Kubrick Archive, University of the Arts London, *Barry Lyndon* files.
7. Another thing Rosenman had in common with Gerald Fried was writing for *Star Trek.* Rosenman provided the score for 1986's *Star Trek IV: The Voyage Home.*
8. Phillips and Hill, "Leonard Rosenman," 301.
9. Marshal Berges, interview with Leonard Rosenman, "Home Q&A with Marshal Berges," *Los Angeles Times Home Magazine,* 40.
10. Interview with the author, April 20, 2011.
11. For a complete synopsis of the film, see appendix B.
12. "Chieftans' Big Chance," *Evening Herald,* October 24, 1973.
13. Victor Davis, "Film Boost for Chieftans," *Daily Express London,* September 30, 1975.
14. Vincent LoBrutto, *Stanley Kubrick: A Biography* (New York: Da Capo Press, 1997), 398.
15. http://footguards.tripod.com/06ARTICLES/ART27_BritGren.htm.
16. William E. Studwell, *The National and Religious Song Reader: Patriotic, Traditional, and Sacred Songs from around the World* (Philadelphia: Haworth Press, 1996), 55.
17. http://www.bbc.co.uk/worldservice/institutional/2009/03/000000_ws_sig_tune.shtml.
18. Reprinted in *Choyce Drollery: Songs and Sonnets*: To which are added the extra songs of *Merry Drollery,* 1661, and *An Antidote against Melancholy,* 1661. Edited, with Special Introductions, and Appendices of Notes, Illustrations, Emendations of Text, &c., by J[oseph] Woodfall Ebsworth, M.A., Cantab. Boston, Lincolnshire: Printed by Robert Roberts, Strait Bar-Gate. 1886, p. 151. From the Ebook and Texts Archive from the University of Toronto Robarts Library http://www.archive.org/details/choycedrolleryso00ebswuoft.
19. http://the-american-catholic.com/2011/04/09/lilliburlero/.
20. This distinction is sometimes referred to as diegetic music and non-diegetic or extra-diegetic music. The former is music that is part of the diegesis, the milieu on-screen, and the latter refers to the score.

21. A tempophon is a device that allows one to modify the pitch or speed of something recorded on magnetic tape. In Germany, where the device was pioneered, it is called *zeitdehner*, or time-stretcher, and in English, it is also known as a rate-changer. http://www.granularsynthesis.com/hthesis/gabor2.html.

22. Frederick's authorship of this piece is doubtful. Eugene Helm and Derek McCullough, "Frederick II," in *The New Grove Dictionary of Music and Musicians*, ed. Stanley Sadie (London: Macmillan, 2001), 219.

23. Charles Osbourne, *The Complete Operas of Mozart* (New York: Da Capo Press, 1978), 143.

24. Osbourne, *Complete Operas of Mozart*, 156.

25. Michael F. Robinson, "Giovanni Paisiello," in *The New Grove Dictionary of Music and Musicians*, ed. Stanley Sadie (London: Macmillan, 2001), 911.

26. John Reed, *Schubert: The Final Years* (New York: St. Martin's Press, 1972), 173.

27. Neal Zaslaw, "Leclair," in *The New Grove Dictionary of Music and Musicians*, ed. Stanley Sadie (London: Macmillan, 2001), 446.

28. William Makepeace Thackeray, *The Memoirs of Barry Lyndon, Esq.*, ed. Andrew Sanders (Oxford: Oxford University Press, 2008), 188.

29. Thackeray, *Barry Lyndon*, 184.

30. Thackeray, *Barry Lyndon*, 244.

31. AMC Filmsite, http://www.filmsite.org/aa75.html.

32. Tim Robey, "Kubrick's Neglected Masterpiece," *The Telegraph*, February 5, 2009, http://www.telegraph.co.uk/culture/4524037/Barry-Lyndon-Kubricks-neglected-masterpiece.html.

# Chapter Six

─────────────────○─────────────────

# Midnight, the Stars, and You
## The Shining

With *Barry Lyndon*, Kubrick came close to perfecting the use of music as an element of time and place. The music, carefully chosen and expertly arranged, became an element of setting that suffused the beautiful images and static scenes with additional significance. From *2001* through *A Clockwork Orange* and *Barry Lyndon*, Kubrick's musical choices were becoming ever more precise and effective. His next film, 1980's *The Shining*, continued this process, achieving what some consider the pinnacle of his success in marrying music to film: "*The Shining* (1980) exemplifies a level of both sophisticated interaction of music and moving image, and general reliance on music for contextual, characterization and narrative purposes, rarely equaled in his output."[1] As Kubrick had put his stamp on black comedy, science fiction, and the period drama, *The Shining* allowed the director to bring his unique vision to the genre of horror. Those who appreciate this vision have discussed the film as a high artistic watermark for the genre.[2]

Kubrick's adaptation of Stephen King's *The Shining* would not be as eerily effective without his musical choices. The aural landscape of *The Shining* features *Lontano* by György Ligeti, whose music Kubrick had already used to great effect in *2001*; Bela Bartók's *Music for Strings, Percussion, and Celesta*, which lends an eerie, lonely sound that seems to mirror the isolation of the Overlook Hotel; the *Dies Irae* plainchant realized on the synthesizer by Wendy Carlos, suggesting the specter of death at the Overlook Hotel; and the music of Krzysztof Penderecki, which accompanies some of the most terrifying moments of the film. These musical choices effectively evoke both desolation and Jack's descent into madness, but *The*

*Shining* also features the 1930s-era tunes Jack hears in the Gold Room. Far from being a comforting respite from the atonal music of the hotel, this music appears in the context of Jack's visions, as the hotel gradually causes Jack to slip away from sanity.

## TECHNOLOGICAL INNOVATION

Kubrick did the unthinkable in *Barry Lyndon*, lighting scenes with only candles, pushing the envelope of technological innovation to its limit. Kubrick continued to make films on the cutting edge of technology by using a fairly new invention in *The Shining*, a camera stabilization system invented by Garrett Brown in the early seventies and eventually sold by the Tiffen Company. Called the Steadicam, the system allows a camera to be mounted on an armature that absorbs any unsteady movement made by the camera operator, resulting in fluid movement without the limitations of a dolly track. In her book about the Steadicam system, Serena Ferrara describes how the device works:

> The Steadicam isolates the camera from all but the largest movements of the operator by means of the stabilizer arm and gimbal. The gimbal prevents unwanted effects from the angular movements of the operator (and allows the camera to be aimed with the lightest possible touch), and the arm's two-spring system absorbs the up-and-down jerks caused by the operator's movements through exploiting the high inertia of the rig (camera and electronics) and the flexibility of its support (the arm).[3]

In the context of *The Shining*, the fluidity of the movement contributes to a sense of large space, as the camera travels through the hallways and rooms of the hotel—and later through the hedge maze—with a startling level of freedom. Kubrick likened it to a magic carpet, and it allowed the camera an even more intimate way of inhabiting the scenes, especially as it follows young Danny on his explorations of the hotel.[4] When Kubrick first wrote to Ed Di Giulio of Cinema Products Corporation, after seeing a demo reel, he was already thinking about filming from a low angle. The last thing he said in his communication to Di Giulio was, "Is there a minimum height at which [the Steadicam] can be used?"[5] He might have been thinking about shooting from Danny's point of view, or perhaps he was thinking of the sequence in which Wendy drags the unconscious Jack into the pantry. The use of the Steadicam on a low mode rig—essentially with the rig turned upside down to allow the camera to move across the floor—

was one of two unique innovations that were developed on the set of *The Shining*.[6] The other innovation was Garrett Brown's use of the so-called two-hand technique, in which one hand controls the arm of the Steadicam to control position and height, while the other hand pans and tilts.[7]

*American Cinematographer* made *The Shining* its cover story in August of 1980. One of the articles dedicated to the film explored the challenges of using the Steadicam system, including how to design lighting that was actually part of the set (and looked like it was part of the hotel), so the camera could move and turn freely without running into or revealing the theatrical lighting.[8] The Steadicam also contributed to the narrative, as the freedom of movement suggests a presence that is not bound in regular "earthly" ways. Serena Ferrara believes that Jack's descent into madness "makes itself felt almost in a material dimension, through which the Steadicam moves."[9] After seeing the film, Di Giulio wrote to Kubrick and said of the Steadicam, "It was like a malevolent POV. Evil was following the kid."[10]

## THE SHINING IN POPULAR CULTURE

Although *The Shining* was the first Stanley Kubrick film since *Paths of Glory* not to receive an Academy Award nomination, it was among the top ten highest grossing movies in the year of its release and among the top fifty moneymakers of the decade. It has become a pop culture touchstone, parodied on the mainstream animated television shows *The Simpsons* ("Treehouse of Horror V," segment titled "The Shinning"), *Family Guy* (episode "Peter, Peter, Caviar Eater," in which Stewie encounters twin girls who ask him to come play), and Cartoon Network's *Venture Brothers* (in which father Rusty Venture advises his son Hank that "not all black men have 'the Shining'"). Excerpts of *The Shining* are seen at a drive-in during the film *Twister*. As a tornado destroys the drive-in screen, a famous scene from the film—the "Here's Johnny" scene—can still be recognized as it is projected on a wall of rubble as it travels through the air. *The Shining* has also been mentioned on numerous other television shows, even recently; a 2012 episode of USA Network's comedy *Psych* featured a *Shining*-themed episode called "Heeeeeere's Lassie."

In addition to its presence in popular culture, there is perhaps no other Kubrick film that has inspired so much speculation as to hidden meanings. It is full of symbols and symbolism, and it lends itself to multiple readings. In 2011, Rodney Asher created a full-length documentary,

*Room* 237, which outlines some of the most prominent theories that have been shared in various media since the release of the film in 1980. In many of these readings of *The Shining*, the Overlook Hotel is often interpreted as a stand-in for America, an America that is powerful, secretive, or corrupt. And many of these theories originate in one particular deviation from Stephen King's source material. While taking the Torrances through the Overlook Hotel in the film, Wendy asks, "Are all these Indian designs authentic?" to which the manager Ullman replies, "Yeah, I believe [they're] based on Navajo and Apache motifs." He goes on to explain that, "The site [of the hotel] is supposed to be located on an Indian burial ground, and I believe they actually had to repel a few Indian attacks as they were building it." The inclusion of news like that—in light of Kubrick's rigorous attention to detail—suggests that it is not a casual piece of information. Perhaps Kubrick simply wanted to convey that the site of the Overlook was a contested piece of land, the final resting place of spirits who have never been able to find peace. (A similar idea was used in the 1982 film, *Poltergeist*, in which a family whose house is built over a supposedly relocated cemetery is terrorized by hostile ghosts.) The production design's choice of Native American decorative motifs throughout the hotel is another aspect of the film that has no antecedent in King's novel.

One of the first interpretations of *The Shining* was presented by David A. Cook in 1984, who viewed the film as a metaphor for "the murderous system of economic exploitation which has sustained the country" since our ancestors came here and made an Indian burial ground of the entire country.[11] Another prominent theory also draws upon the Indian burial ground theme. In 1987, journalist Bill Blakemore suggested that the film refers to the genocide of Native Americans.[12] Blakemore sees meaning in the presence of cans of Calumet baking powder in the pantry, a brand named after a Native American peace pipe and featuring in the logo a stylized Native American in a headdress. Blakemore argues that the cans represent treaties, some honest, but most broken, dishonest, and false. The presence of former caretaker Grady's twin daughters (not described as twins in the book) represents the duplicity of the white man.[13] In 2012, Blakemore published additional commentary on his original 1987 article online.

Like Blakemore, Geoffrey Cocks has seen a hidden agenda about genocide in *The Shining*, but in this case Cocks sees a connection to the Holocaust. We know that Kubrick showed an interest in making a film about the Holocaust for part of his career and that a few years after completing *Full Metal Jacket*, he collected voluminous materials for a film on the subject called *Aryan Papers*, which he planned to film in the 1990s. *Aryan Papers* was based on the 1991 novel *Wartime Lies* by Louis Begley. Although he never made this film, Kubrick's interest in a project on the Holocaust never seemed to wane. We do not know, however, if the subtle references to the Holocaust, as outlined by Cocks, were indeed Kubrick's filmic exploration of the phenomenon, but Cocks dedicated an entire book to patterns in Kubrick's career as a filmmaker that seem to refer in ways both subtle and overt to the Holocaust. In *The Wolf at the Door: Stanley Kubrick, History, and the Holocaust*, Cocks suggests that *The Shining* is Kubrick's meditation on the Holocaust. If this is true, Kubrick's interest in making *Aryan Papers* is puzzling, but perhaps he wanted to approach the subject in a less covert manner and perhaps he was inspired by *Wartime Lies*.

In the very first chapter of *The Wolf at the Door*, Cocks refers to the scene in *The Shining* in which a torrent of blood pours out of an elevator covering a hallway (and eventually the camera) with blood. He says of this scene, which has no analogue in Stephen King's novel, "The ocean of blood flowing from the elevator in *The Shining* is the blood of centuries, the blood of millions, and, in particular, the blood of war and genocide in Kubrick's own century."[14] Music is a significant part of Cocks's argument for *The Shining* as a Holocaust film since Kubrick's choices bear "the heavy historical weight of the Holocaust"[15] because they represent the work of Central and Eastern European composers, something we will discuss later in this chapter.

The idea that the Apollo 11 moon landing was a hoax rather than a real historical event has occupied conspiracy theorists for decades. It has been suggested that Kubrick might have been the filmmaker responsible for the footage of the allegedly faked moon landing, a possibility explored in French filmmaker William Karel's 2002 "mockumentary" *Dark Side of the Moon*. Rather than stating Kubrick's involvement as fact, it provokes the viewer to understand that footage and interviews taken out of context can, in fact, be used to support an unsubstantiated claim and provides an example of "hyperreality," the theory that media can change or color our understanding of events. The film had the blessing of people like Kubrick's wife and representatives from NASA, who agreed to read scripted lines for the camera.

The idea of Kubrick as filmmaker of an Apollo hoax was taken up in earnest by occultist and filmmaker Jay Weidner. In his 2011 film *Kubrick's Odyssey: Secrets Hidden in the Films of Stanley Kubrick; Part One: Kubrick and Apollo*, Weidner explains that *2001* was Kubrick's practice for filming

the moon landing and that *The Shining* is Kubrick's admission of his involvement in the hoax. As Weidner states in the narration, *The Shining* is a film
that "described the ordeal of faking the Apollo Moon landing." But why
would Kubrick need to make such a film? Weidner argues that Kubrick was
weighed down by guilt and could not have confessed to the filming of the
moon landing outright because he might have been killed by the powers that
be. *The Shining*, Weidner suggests, is Kubrick's covert confession.

Weidner explains the addition of information about the Indian burial
ground is a way to make the hotel a stand-in for America (just as Cook
argued). The character of Jack Torrance, who represents Kubrick, is
charged with maintaining the hotel or, in this case, maintaining the U.S.
An early snowstorm represents the Cold War, while the bears and eagles
found around the hotel are the Russians and the Americans, respectively.
In the film's "most crucial scene" Danny plays with trucks on the rug,
and the rug's hexagonal design seems to echo the shape of launch pad
39a, where Apollo 11 blasted off; in this scene, Danny's sweater also has
a rocket labeled "Apollo 11" knitted into it. He stands up—literally lifting
off from the rug launch pad—and goes to room 237, which was changed
from 217 in the book—according to Weidner to represent the 237,000-
mile distance between the earth and the moon.[16] To Weidner, room 237
is the fake moon set. Kubrick's replacement of Grady's daughters with
twins is another signal, as the NASA program previous to Apollo was the
Gemini program, and the astrological sign Gemini is represented by twins.
Finally, Weidner suggests that Jack's repeatedly typed phrase, "All work
and no play makes Jack a dull boy"—invented for the film—is yet another
attempt to describe Kubrick's ordeal. Weidner interprets the "All" of the
beginning of the phrase as "A-11," a code word for Apollo 11.

Although Kubrick was known as something of a recluse, he did grant
quite a few interviews over the course of his career, and in none of those
did he confirm any of these theories. In an interview with Michel Ciment
about *The Shining*, Kubrick did say this: "People can misinterpret almost
anything so that it coincides with views they already hold. They take from
art what they already believe."[17]

## PRE-PRODUCTION FOR THE FILM

Kubrick spent some time after completing *Barry Lyndon* looking for a new
project. He was briefly considered to direct Paddy Chayefsky's film *Network*, but Chayefsky—interested in being an auteur like Kubrick—ended

up directing the film himself. Kubrick searched novels for ideas, and an executive at Warner Bros. sent a copy of Stephen King's novel to Kubrick. Unlike the vast majority of things sent to the director, *The Shining* caught his attention right away. It had elements of the supernatural and psychological, and the filming of it would put forth cinematic challenges that must have intrigued Kubrick.[18]

On any Kubrick film, factual details about settings are very important, and *The Shining* is no exception. In the archives at University of the Arts London, there are a dozen or so letters written to hotels that could possibly stand in for the Overlook Hotel. In addition, there are letters about locations, props, information on the snowfall in Colorado, requests for pictures of Sno-Cats, and correspondence with the Denver airport (for the brief scene that takes place there). The decoration of the Overlook Hotel, an establishment that has hosted "all the best people," in the words of the manager, Mr. Ullman,[19] required the use of many photographs. Instead of providing new staged photographs, Kubrick borrowed prints from Warner Bros.'s considerable photograph archive to hang on the walls of the Overlook Hotel. Every possible detail of pre-production was scrutinized, and every effort was made to prepare a physical set that would serve the narrative and accommodate the use of the Steadicam. The lighting design, for example—wiring the set of the hotel with all of the necessary lights including lights to simulate natural light—took four months.[20]

Once again, the choice of appropriate music occupied the production team, and once again, there was correspondence with various entities suggesting possible tunes for the film. Jan Harlan wrote to Rudi Fehr, an executive at Warner Bros., to ask for a list of popular songs from 1920 to 1935. In response, Fehr provided a comprehensive list of more than 150 songs. In his letter of 23 December 1977, he offers to make tapes of songs for Harlan, but explains that time is a factor as he is about to start work supervising the dubbing of *Close Encounters of the Third Kind*.[21] For the years 1930 and 1931, for example, Fehr provided the following titles:

> 1930—"Beyond the Blue Horizon," "Bidin' My Time," "Body and Soul," "But Not for Me," "Bye Bye Blues," "A Cottage for Sale," "Cryin' for the Carolinas," "Dancing with Tears in My Eyes," "Embraceable You," "Exactly Like You," "Fine and Dandy," "I Got Rhythm," "I'm Confessin' That I Love You," "It Happened in Monterey," "Just a Gigolo," "Little White Lies," "Love for Sale," "On the Sunny Side of the Street," "Rockin' Chair," "Ten Cents a Dance," "Three Little Words," "Time on My Hands," "You Brought a New Kind of Love to Me," "You're Driving Me Crazy."

1931—"All of Me," "As Time Goes By," "Between the Devil and the Deep Blue Sea," "Cuban Love Song," "Dancing in the Dark," "Good Night, Sweetheart," "Got a Date with an Angel," "Heartaches," "I Found a Million Dollar Baby," "I Surrender, Dear," "I've Got Five Dollars," "Just One More Chance," "Lazy River," "Life Is Just a Bowl of Cherries," "Minnie the Moocher," "Mood Indigo," "Nevertheless," "Out of Nowhere," "Paradise," "Peanut Vendor," "Soft Lights and Sweet Music," "Sweet and Lovely," "When I Take My Sugar to Tea," "When It's Sleepy Time Down South," "Where the Clue of the Night Meets the Gold of the Day," "Yours Is My Heart Alone," "You're My Everything."

The archive also contains a handwritten list of popular songs from the late 1920s and early 1930s. In the list, the unknown author states that the criteria for popularity was sheet music sales, gramophone record sales, or "consistent performances of stage and radio." A memo from Jan Harlan to Kubrick, Douglas Twiddy, and Brian Cook dated 12 April 1978, suggests "The Strolling Vagabond" for the film, while another letter provides a list of Scott Joplin records, as recorded by pianist Joshua Rifkin. There are documents listing albums ordered by Harlan from the record store Imhofs, for review by Kubrick. One from 26 January 1978 lists the following recordings of opera and their price: *Gianni Schicchi* no. 76563 £3.79; *Faniculla del West* SLS.5079 £8.95; *Tosca* 5BB123-4 £6.95. He also ordered the following from Imhofs: *Madam Butterfly* SET584-6; *Manon Lescaut* SLS962; *Rondine* DPS 2055; *Turandot* GOS 622-4. Kubrick ended up including no music from opera in *The Shining*, none of Joplin's works, and just four popular songs from the 1930s.

## THE WORK OF WENDY CARLOS

Despite all of the research into preexistent music, Kubrick was still willing to entertain the possibility of working with Wendy Carlos on the score to *The Shining*. Kubrick and Carlos had, of course, shared a very successful and fruitful collaboration on *A Clockwork Orange*. In fact, Kubrick began working with Carlos and producer Rachel Elkind before any footage was shot, asking them to read the novel and come up with musical ideas. To help get into Kubrick's mind-set, they asked if Kubrick was listening to anything specific, and Kubrick mentioned a Sibelius piece, *Valse Triste*.[22] They recorded many cues before the film was shot, and once they saw footage, they scored scenes that would never make it into the final cut of the film. In addition, they made multiple albums of sound effects, some of which ended up being used in conjunction with Kubrick's final musical choices. In discussing the unused sounds and music, Carlos stated the following in Jan Harlan's documentary, *Stanley Kubrick: A Life in Pictures*:

> We were working with the material that was in the book, and trying to make music that fit the mood of a sort of updated gothic horror story, which is what *The Shining* is, really, I mean, as a novel, in any case. And of course the stylization that came out from the filming was not present in the book. And so we failed in our attempt. Which is why there is a great deal of other music put into the movie.[23]

Copies of the albums produced by Carlos and Elkind can be found at the Stanley Kubrick Archive at the University of the Arts London. The following are track lists as they appear on the album covers that Carlos and Elkind sent to Kubrick for review.

### *THE SHINING*—ALBUM—MUSIC BY W. CARLOS AND R. ELKIND

Side A

1. Title Music
2. High-Low
3. Danny Bells
4. Heartbeat Passage #1
5. Heartbeat Passage #2
6. Danny

Side B

1. Thought Clusters, Danny's 1st Esp (VerA)
2. Thought Clusters, Danny's 1st Esp (VerB)
3. Food Larder ESP
4. Psychic Shout Up Into Room 237 & Out
5. Psychic Shout & Room 237-While Seq.
6. Danny At Dart Board
7. Danny & Grady Twins
8. Single Loud Scream-Efx

Although there are many tracks on this album, the one that intrigued Kubrick the most was the opening track "Title Music." The cue incorporated the *Dies Irae* chant, and in further explorations it would continue to return, eventually ending up as the opening cue for the film. Carlos and Elkind continued offering Kubrick choices for the film, and producing other albums, the next one with an emphasis on vocal effects provided by Elkind.

### DISC 2, *THE SHINING*: MUSIC BY WENDY CARLOS AND RACHEL ELKIND

Side A

1. Thought Transfers
2. Low And High
3. Low And High-Rich
4. Rich & High ESP
5. DC-10 @ 8 AM

Side B

1. The Shining—Title Music (New Mix)
2. The Shining—Title Music (Version of 7)
3. Winter Maze
4. Dream Man
5. Keepin' Out of Mischief Now

The first three tracks on this disc feature a buzzing sound that suggests insects. Perhaps Carlos and Elkind were inspired by Stephen King's scene (unused in the film) about a wasp nest. Jack removes a wasp nest from the roof of the Overlook and gives the empty nest to Danny. In the middle of the night, however, the nest is somehow once again infested with the stinging insects. The buzz of "Low and High" seems to approach the unpleasant buzzing of a dentist's drill. The track "DC-10 @ 8AM" has a low sustained dissonant chord that sounds like it's played low on an organ. Carlos and Elkind revisited the *Dies Irae* of "Title Music," adding twangs and buzzes and lip trills. "Winter Maze" suggests iciness and cold with the addition of heartbeat and percussion effects. This long cue features vocal sounds both high and low, and moans and wails that sound almost inhuman. There is a bell sound now and then throughout the track, with more buzzing appearing. Some of the sounds of these tracks hearken back to a seminal piece of electronic music called *Poème Electronique* by Edgard Varèse. The last two tracks are tunes that Carlos and Elkind might have recorded for the 1920s party scene. "Dream Man" is a piano tune with male vocals, almost bluesy in character. The piano is out of tune, giving it an eerie sound. The final song is a version of the Thomas "Fats" Waller song, "Keepin' Out of Mischief Now."

The next disc continues with the vocal experiments of Elkind and dispensed with clever titles, describing each track with phrases like "Low groaning moans" and "Small high shrieks."[24] Once again, the album begins with a version of the *Dies Irae*. In this case it's a wordless vocalization, very free in performance. There is a note on the album indicating that the track "Vocal Glissandi" was intended for Jack's entrance into room 237. The same scene would also use the track "Whisperings," which features unintelligible voices that suggest auditory hallucinations. The low groaning moans are mixed so that they are heard out of phase from both the left and right speakers. On this album, there are some sound experiments with traditional instruments such as a cue of piano strings being rubbed by soft mallets, recalling composer Henry Cowell's innovative pieces *Aeolian Harp* (1923) and *The Banshee* (1925), in which the piano strings are swept or plucked from inside the piano. On side B of this disc, Carlos and Elkind recorded another sound experiment with the autoharp, this time adding a boinging sound to the *Dies Irae* chant. This combination of elements was well on its way to becoming what would be the opening track of the film.

What followed were more recordings with even more descriptive titles. The album Carlos and Elkind called *Two Track #2 "Loops"* had ten tracks, many of which featured an eerie sound element they called "Ghosties." For one of the tracks, a handwritten note describes the cue as "Ligeti like." The tracks also feature moans, sighs, and screams. Someone has noted on the album that the first three cues—including one called "Rocky Mountains"—resemble "Apocalypse Now helicopters" (which suggests that someone was still listening to these cues and making notes after *Apocalypse Now* premiered in August of 1979). Carlos and Elkind's album *Two Track #5 Wind and Textures* had mostly atmospheric cues with wind and other effects. The *Dies Irae* appears here as well, in a cue they called "The Snow." Their recording *Two Track #6 Piano and Autoharp Efx and Synth* has just seven tracks, mostly sound effects. The first side ends with a cue played on the Polymoog[25] called "Blood Bath." This track was ostensibly conceived as the accompaniment to the elevator bloodbath Kubrick invented for the film. On side B of the album, there are both Polymoog and piano versions of the *Dies Irae* chant. Next to the listing of the tracks on the B side, someone has written in marker: "Shrieks and hums v. sustained suspense redrum pre-walking around the room."

In the end, Kubrick chose just a few of the cues and effects Carlos and Rachel Elkind produced for *The Shining*. The opening of the film is their version of the *Dies Irae*, complete with vocal effects and the autoharp boinging sounds heard on the third album Carlos and Elkind presented to Kubrick. The only other cues of theirs that appear in the film are "Rocky Mountains," an atmospheric piece that accompanies the Torrances' drive to the Overlook Hotel on closing day, and a cue I call "Shining/Heartbeat," which accompanies the scene where Hallorann receives a "shine," alerting him to problems at the Overlook, and the scene in which Jack sees the woman in room 237. Two of these cues, the final version of the *Dies Irae* (just called "The Shining" on the soundtrack) and "Rocky Mountains," appeared on the original soundtrack album for *The Shining*, an album that was pulled because of problems with the licensing of the music. It has never been re-released, and original vinyl copies of the soundtrack are rare and expensive. One scholar who has written about the film, K. J. Donnelly, referred to the "the unheard, imagined missing score" of Wendy Carlos and Rachel Elkind as another "ghostly aspect" of the film.[26] A few years ago Carlos mentioned that she and Elkind recorded what she described as "a ton of electronic and orchestral music . . . that has never seen the light of day."[27] That music, however, eventually came to light. Carlos released many of the cues on two albums she recorded in 2005 called *Rediscovering Lost Scores, Volumes I and II*.[28] In total, Carlos included thirty-one previously unheard tracks from *The Shining* (see appendix C for a complete listing of the tracks of these recordings). *Rediscovering Lost Scores, Volumes I and II* include the lion's share of the work Carlos and Elkind did for the film, although copies of these two albums are also quite rare.

## THE TWO SOUND WORLDS OF *THE SHINING*

Although there are many musical cues in *The Shining*, they seem to fit into one of two categories. On one hand there are the avant garde, possibly atonal, amelodic cues that are extra-diegetic, that is, accompanying the narrative but assumed not to be heard by the characters within the narrative. On the other hand, the other music is diegetic—heard by the characters within the film's world—and tonal, tuneful, and pleasant. As Mainar explains:

In *The Shining* extradiegetic music is ominous and lacks melody, matching the horror story, whereas the diegetic music heard at the ball is
melodic, soft, and friendly. Music helps to contrast the two worlds, to
indicate the passage from one to the other, and to suggest the ambiguous
attraction of the world of the past (of mental disturbance) has not only
for Jack but also for the audience.[29]

One moment in the film that is devoid of any music, and in the hands of
another director might have called for a dissonant sting, is Ullman's admission that the hotel is built on an Indian burial ground. Ironically, though,
the ghosts in the hotel are not Native Americans. Instead, as James
Naremore points out, they are "descendents of the white barbarians who
destroyed the Indian culture—in particular by jazz-age sophisticates."[30]
Donnelly echoes this, explaining that the atonal, amelodic music of
Bartók, Penderecki, and Ligeti is not part of the music of the haunting, but
is simply music to accompany the sublime elements,[31] which happen to be
horrific. The big band music is part of the nostalgic lure that pulls in Jack,
perhaps attempting to absorb his soul. The music represents a time and
place that Jack seems to become somewhat nostalgic about, yet it is not
his own past he is nostalgic for, but an idealized past where everything is
genteel and beautiful. The past has an ugly underside, not available at first
glance. The songs aren't exactly correct for the time period represented by
the activities in the Gold Room. The songs are from the 1930s, about a
decade off. Kubrick—a stickler for detail—made allowances for musical
choices if they were particularly effective for the film. We saw a similar
thing in *Barry Lyndon*, in Kubrick's choice of Schubert, an anachronistic
composer for the eighteenth century. Donnelly explains such fuzzy time-
lines as part of Jack's false nostalgia:

> The songs appear as an embodiment of memory—not necessarily our
> personal memory but more a collective memory of some sort. Indeed,
> pop songs often serve this function. . . . It may be that when music or
> song articulates memory, particularly a collective memory as an aesthetic
> repository, it might possess the power to unearth bad things from the
> past that we would rather forget, like slavery, starvation or mass murder,
> more than some individual sexual repression or personal neurosis.[32]

Since the release of the film, the two sound worlds of the film have occupied scholars, especially since Kubrick chose not to name all of the
specific pieces in the credits of the film. There is a card that says "Music
By," followed by a credit for Bartók's *Music for Strings, Percussion, and*

*Celesta*. After that, there is a card that says Krzysztof Penderecki, followed by one that says "György Ligeti." This seems like an odd choice, especially from a legal standpoint, but the need for it might have been very practical. Gordon Stainforth, whose contribution to *The Shining* will be described in the next section, explained that it was very difficult to keep track of all of the clips he had used, since there were multiple versions of scenes and the different clips were sometimes layered together. Add to that the naturally hectic atmosphere of film completion and Kubrick's penchant to change things until the very last second, and it is easy to see how these details slipped through the cracks.[33] Donnelly argues that the choice was intentional by Kubrick to convey the sense that these works formed "an indistinct sonic backdrop."[34]

## The Contribution of Gordon Stainforth

Instead of using the services of an arranger, as he had on *Barry Lyndon*, or one composer as he had done on *A Clockwork Orange*, Kubrick's main musical collaboration would be with music editor, Gordon Stainforth.[35] Stainforth's work on the music of *The Shining*, which has been detailed by Jeremy Barham in an article from 2009, shows that what Kubrick wanted were options. Early in the scoring process, Kubrick was already showing a preference for the music of Penderecki and Bartók, and he "gave Stainforth large amounts of recorded examples to sift through."[36] As he had done with Alex North on *Spartacus*, Kubrick gave Stainforth a list of places where he wanted music, and like the list he had given to North for the earlier film, he made brief descriptions of what he wanted. Stainforth then went ahead and cut music to scenes, often giving Kubrick a few musical options for each scene. Barham is careful to point out that Kubrick didn't give much thought to the history of the repertoire under consideration, nor did he particularly worry about a critical analysis of the pieces. Instead, he told Stainforth what he wanted of the music in a practical, functional sense. And unlike many of the other aspects of filmmaking, Kubrick allowed Stainforth to "score" different versions of the scenes without his immediate supervision. When it came time to choose the appropriate version to cut into the film, however, the decision lay entirely with Kubrick.[37]

In his work creating options for Kubrick, Stainforth was sometimes aided by film editor Ray Lovejoy, who could shave off extraneous frames or perhaps add some to scenes if the musical cue called for such alterations. This technique was particularly useful when Stainforth wanted to cut to structural points in the music—as Kubrick preferred. Of this process Stainforth says there was a lot of "trial and error on my part."[38] The collaboration went smoothly, without prolonged discussions, and Stainforth believes that he and Kubrick shared a fundamental understanding of how best to use the chosen music in the film. Of the process of cutting the chosen music to the scenes, Stainforth has said: "[Kubrick] quite definitely entrusted it to me."[39]

### Wendy Carlos: "The Shining (featuring the *Dies Irae* melody)"[40]

Appearance:

0:00:00–0:03:03 Jack drives to the Overlook Hotel for his interview

At one point in pre-production, Kubrick asked Wendy Carlos about appropriate music for graves and death, and she suggested the chant commonly known from the Roman Catholic Requiem mass, the *Dies Irae*. One of the chant's most famous appearances is in the final movement of Berlioz's *Symphonie Fantastique* from 1830, a piece that Carlos recommended to Kubrick. In typical Kubrick fashion, it had a strong effect on him, and like Prokofiev's score to *Alexander Nevsky* that he owned as a child, he played it, Carlos estimates, more than a hundred times. In that time, he forged a deep connection to the music.[41]

The *Dies Irae* is arguably the most famous excerpt from the canon of chant for the Roman Catholic Church, and it is one with a very interesting history. The text is ascribed to Thomas of Celano, a Franciscan monk, and dates from the mid-thirteenth century. (An earlier version of the poem exists from the previous century, and Thomas's status as possible originator of the poem has been called into question.)[42] The poem was set to a chant and became an addition to the liturgy called a Sequence. The Sequence began as a prose form before 1000, but in later years began to take on the qualities of poetry.[43] Although there was no one set form for the Sequence, many were constructed with rhyming couplets. The text and music of the Sequence changed from day to day, hence part of the "Proper" of the mass—as opposed to the "Ordinary" chant texts that remained unchanged through the year—and was usually placed after the Alleluia. It became part of the Requiem mass, the mass for the dead, sometime during the fourteenth century in Italy.[44] When the Catholic Church reflected on its practices in the mid-sixteenth century at the Council of Trent (1543–1563), one of the many aspects under discussion was the proliferation of nonliturgical additions to the mass. The Council decided to excise the vast repertoire of more than four thousand Sequences with the exception of just four, one of which was the *Dies Irae* (a fifth was reintroduced in the eighteenth century).

The *Dies Irae* poem has eighteen stanzas (and a nineteenth added by an anonymous author) with the lines of text written in trochaic meter (each foot is made of one stressed syllable and one unstressed syllable), and there are four trochees per line. The melody for each of the four opening stanzas repeats twice more in the course of the chant, and the repetition, unusual in Sequences, gives the music an overall sense of unity. (See the musical excerpt of the *Dies Irae* in chapter 4.)

Since the Middle Ages, the *Dies Irae* text has appeared in many settings of the Requiem mass, from Mozart, Verdi, Britten, and others. Some composers have set the text as a stand-alone piece.[45] The *Dies Irae* melody has made appearances in compositions from the nineteenth and twentieth centuries. It is so well known that even the inclusion of a few notes of the opening melody suggests the symbolism of the Day of Wrath (a literal translation of "Dies Irae"), the final judgment, and of course death in general. Franz Liszt explored the melody in variations in his *Totentanz* of 1848. Sergei Rachmaninoff, who seemed particularly fond of the theme, used fragments of the melody in pieces like his *Rhapsody on a Theme of Paganini* (1934) and his *Symphonic Dances for Orchestra* (1940). Ildebrando Pizzetti, who used the melody in his own a cappella Requiem setting of 1922, revisited the chant tune in his 1958 opera *Assassini Nella Catedrale* (Murder in the Cathedral). In the 1970s George Crumb quoted the melody in his work for electric string quartet, *Black Angels: Thirteen Images from the Dark Land*, a meditation on the Vietnam War.[46] French composer Camille Saint-Saëns used a pleasant, major-key, waltz-like version of the chant in his charming *Danse Macabre* (1874), a joyous, playful dance of the dead. The *Dies Irae* has also been quoted in film scores. Film music scholar William Rosar has discussed the *Dies Irae* in *Citizen Kane*, as a melodic quote of the chant by film composer Bernard Herrmann via Rachmaninoff's symphonic poem *Isle of the Dead* (1945).[47] And of course, Wendy Carlos quoted the *Dies Irae* in her setting of Henry Purcell's *Music for the Funeral of Queen Mary* in *A Clockwork Orange*, a direct musical connection between the two films that Donnelly refers to as a "worm-hole."[48]

Carlos's cue "The Shining" plays as the film begins. A helicopter is moving along the water in a valley between two mountains. The seemingly effortless gliding of the helicopter prefigures the swift, smooth movement of the Steadicam in the hotel. The image of the valley dissolves to a shot over land (with some water still visible on the left side of the screen) as a small yellow car is driving up a winding road. The camera approaches the car, as if chasing it, but finally passes it and heads out over the water again. The camera cuts to the car again—which we momentarily lose in a tunnel, but find again on the other side of it. The camera continues to follow the car at a distance until the camera focuses on the Overlook Hotel itself.

Carlos begins the cue with the first two phrases of the *Dies Irae* chant, holding the last note of the second phrase for a moment before moving on. This music would coincide with the text that can be translated, "Day of wrath, day that will dissolve the world into ashes." Skipping the music for third phrase of the stanza—"as David testifies with Sybill," Carlos sets the opening phrase of the music that would accompany the third stanza (the first two stanzas share the same music). The text set to this music would be "Tuba mirum, spargens sonum," or "The trumpet sounding a wondrous sound."[49] At the end of this phrase, the vocal embellishments of Rachel Elkind begin, and other sounds, like those of the autoharp strings, begin to dominate. Carlos returns in a moment to the opening phrase of the chant, this time accompanied by Elkind's vocals, and the cue ends with a repeat of "Tuba mirum" phrase. The vocal flourish at the end, somewhere between a cry and a moan, echoes just for a moment after the synthesizer line ends, providing an eerie effect that is undercut by the lack of music and the "normal" atmosphere of the scene Kubrick titles "The Interview."

## Wendy Carlos: "Rocky Mountains"

Appearance:

0:17:41–0:19:48 The Torrances drive the mountain road to the Overlook Hotel

This atmospheric cue plays as the Torrance family drives the road up to the Overlook Hotel, echoing the drive Jack took at the beginning of the film. The mood in the car is subdued, but grows a bit tenser as the family shares some small talk about the Donner Party and cannibalism. The cue begins with a low note that moves down by fifths as the shot from the helicopter comes over the woods and finds the small yellow Volkswagon on the road. The cue becomes quieter as Kubrick cuts to the interior of the car, and the conversation becomes the focal point of the scene. When the conversation ends, and the helicopter shot continues through the mist, the music becomes prominent again, with Carlos adding voices to the mix, forming a dissonant cluster of sound. The pitches rise up briefly, glissing from note to note, until the music takes a downturn, and the notes slide further and further down as the Overlook comes into view. The sinking chords at the beginning of the cue infuse the scene with a sense of foreboding.

### Wendy Carlos: "Shining/Heartbeat"

Appearances:

1:10:53–1:12:05 Danny "shines" to Hallorann that there is trouble at the Overlook (layered, near the end of the cue, with Penderecki's *The Awakening of Jacob*)
1:19:05–1:20:30 Wendy and Jack talk while Danny has visions
1:31:39–1:36:28 Wendy devises a plan for escape; Danny screams "Redrum"; Jack disables the radio; Hallorann flies to Colorado

This cue features a high-pitched sound, almost like the high buzzing of a dentist's drill. The sound is meant to be jarring, even unpleasant, like the "Thought Transfer" cues from the albums. It is accompanied by a heartbeat sound and intermittent vocal effects that are similar to those heard in the *Dies Irae* cue. The high-pitched sound seems to be what "shining" sounds like. All three appearances of the cue occur within about twenty minutes of the film in which things start to go downhill very quickly, as Danny's visions send him into a trance, Jack becomes agitated, and Wendy is beginning to grasp the family's isolation.

### György Ligeti: *Lontano*

Appearances:

0:21:21–0:22:17 Danny turns to see the twins in the game room; they smile and walk away
0:27:19–0:28:01 Danny hears Dick ask him if he wants ice cream
0:46:10–0:47:57 Danny and Wendy play in the snow; Jack writes; Wendy discovers the phones are dead

The music of György Ligeti provides a connection among *2001*, *The Shining*, and *Eyes Wide Shut*—not bad for a composer who began his "collaboration" with Kubrick against his will and without proper notification or compensation. In addition to the music that appeared in *2001*, Ligeti's *Lontano* appeared on MGM's album of music *Inspired by 2001*. Ligeti composed *Lontano* in 1967, a year after his a cappella *Lux Aeterna*, which appeared in *2001*. In contrast to that piece, *Lontano* (the Italian word meaning "far") is entirely instrumental, scored in fact for "large orchestra," but the use of "micropolyphony" and tone-clusters suggests a very strong connection between them, and in fact, Ligeti scholar Michael D. Searby calls them "sister works."[50] *Lontano* is also a departure from the works immediately previous to it because it has a semblance of a tonal center, although it is not by any means a tonal piece in the traditional sense. The pitch center lends a structural element and allows the micropolyphony to have a feeling of focus and drive.[51] Because of the focus given to texture and timbre, the presence of melodies or individual lines within the texture escapes many listeners; but in *Lontano*, the construction of texture out of melodic elaboration seems to be Ligeti's intent. Nevertheless, it is the overall effect of the sound that is most compelling about *Lontano*, and it has been described thus:

> *Lontano* is a study in opalescence, in slowly evolving timbral and harmonic transformation heard through polychromatic mists of sound. Within these vaporous textures, timbres and harmonies ebb and flow. Sometimes the sonic mists almost clear, to reveal for a moment tangible chordal shapes, before slowly enveloping them again as other shapes coalesce in sharper focus, before they too recede.[52]

The excerpt from *Lontano* is taken from the middle of a movement, something unusual for Kubrick, although this is a single-movement work with continuous sound. The piece is written in traditional notation, with a meter and bar lines, although as the notes in the score explain, "The bar lines serve only as a means of synchronization; bar lines and beats never mean an accentuation; the music must flow smoothly, and accents (with a very few, precisely indicated exceptions) are foreign to the piece." The notes go on to explain that all instruments should enter with as quiet and unnoticeable attacks as possible and that changes in bow direction for the strings should be staggered among the players so they are not noticeable.[53] Kubrick and Gordon Stainforth simply needed to find the timbre they wanted to use and then fade into a particular measure and fade out when the scene ended. The nature of the piece makes such excerpting easy and unobtrusive. The style of writing also unintentionally mimics typical suspense music from film scores, in which the strings hang on a single pitch to create tension. Ligeti's choice to construct *Lontano* in a single movement proved to be something of a challenge in this style. It is difficult to sustain sound masses over time, especially in large-scale pieces. He got around this in *Lux Aeterna* by having smaller movements and different syllables for the singers. Ligeti worked through the challenge with *Lontano*, attempting to use pitch references as a way to articulate a musical structure.[54]

The excerpt from Ligeti's *Lontano* seems to be another sonic signal for "shining," as it appears first when Danny sees the twins in the game room. He is playing darts alone, but suddenly turns around to see the twins in their blue dresses, holding hands and staring at him. Danny and the twins stare at each other for a moment, before the twins look at each other and walk out. The sounds in this section of *Lontano*, from around measure fifty, feature a sustained high harmonic in the strings and low notes in the contrabass clarinet (a rare instrument for orchestras, sometimes used in bands) and the contrabassoon. The brass instruments enter as well, until finally the string harmonic sound gives way to a more traditional string sound, and the brass drop out. The music fades out at the beginning of the next scene, as Ullman shows Wendy and Jack their apartment for the winter.

In the next appearance, Dick Hallorann is giving Wendy and Danny a tour of the kitchen. As the three of them step into the walk-in pantry, the high whistle sound of the string harmonic is clearly heard, and the low woodwind sound emerges underneath. What Hallorann is saying to Wendy fades into a distant echo, and Hallorann "shines" to Danny, "How'd you like some ice cream, Doc?" This time the cue fades out while the strings are still sustaining the harmonic.

The third time the cue appears, winter has definitely arrived. Wendy and Danny play in the snow while Jack appears to watch them with an odd look on his face. The music continues through the next title card, "Saturday," as Jack types in the lounge and Wendy discovers the phones are dead. This excerpt in the music is longer and continues into a section with a thicker texture. Oddly, this appearance of the cue does not accompany "shining" per se, but it does seem to suggest that there is something encroaching into the lives of the Torrances, like the snow covering the grounds. After this point, music for "shining" seems to be accompanied by Wendy Carlos's "Shining/ Heartbeat cue," which did not appear on the soundtrack album.

### Bartók: Music for Strings Percussion and Celesta

Appearances:

0:38:09–0:40:26 Danny and Wendy enter the hedge maze; Jack bounces a ball in his writing room

0:41:18–0:43:48 Danny rides around on his tricycle and ends up in front of room 237; Jack writes at the typewriter; cue stops when Jack pulls out paper

0:52:36–0:56:59 Danny asks Jack if he likes the hotel and if he would ever hurt him or Wendy

Béla Bartók was a Hungarian composer who, in addition to writing and teaching music, also collected folk music from Eastern Europe. His studies of the peasant music of Slovakia, Hungary, Bulgaria, and Romania made him one of the first important ethnomusicologists, a group that included fellow composer and pedagogue Zoltán Kodály. Bartók drew upon many influences in his writing, including the art music of the late nineteenth and early twentieth centuries—the music of Debussy and Richard Strauss was particularly important—and his own encounters with folk music from various peasant cultures. Antifascist in his beliefs, Bartók emigrated to the U.S. after the Nazi Party came to power and Hungary came under its influence.

Bartók composed *Music for Strings, Percussion and Celesta* in 1936 for the tenth anniversary of the Basel Chamber Orchestra, and the piece was premiered by that group in January of 1937. There are four movements, but Kubrick used music only from the Adagio third movement. This movement is an illustration of a type of music Bartók referred to as "Night Music." In his mature style, it was common for Bartók to write slow movements in this idiom, and there are, perhaps, more than a dozen pieces with movements in the "Night Music" style. Bartók used the term without defining it specifically, but it is generally seen as an evocation of the sounds of nature at night in the same vague way that Chopin's piano nocturnes painted pictures of the night. One of the most explicit evocations of "Night Music" happens in the fourth movement of Bartók's *Out of Doors* suite, which he dedicated to his second wife, Ditta.[55]

In *The Shining*, the first appearance of the piece occurs as Wendy and Danny enter the hedge maze. At this point, the weather is still mild, and there is no snow on the ground. As they reach the mouth of the maze, the cue begins at m. 20 in the score. A dissonant chord in the muted strings—held with tremolos—adds to a feeling of suspense. Ascending and descending glissandi in the second violins and the meandering line in the solo violin and the celesta add to the eerie feeling. The chromatic line that seems to wander, echoes the movements of Wendy and Danny in the maze who wander through, making wrong turns, and eventually finding the center. Jack, who is inside the hotel, has been throwing a ball against a wall instead of writing, and when the scene cuts to him, the ball hits the wall right at m. 31 in the score, just when the piano, celesta, and solo violin reach a chord together. The xylophone enters, as does the timpani, which plays ascending and descending glissandi. Jack walks over to a model of the hedge maze, and music suddenly changes character just as the camera angle changes. We appear to be seeing the maze model from Jack's point of view, but a closer look (and a closer listen, as we can hear them talking) shows that Wendy and Danny are in the center of the maze. The part of Bartók's piece that accompanies this camera trick features flowing arpeggios in the piano, harp, and celesta, with an underpinning of tremolos in the strings. Kubrick cuts back to Wendy and Danny, and the music seems to grow in intensity (Bartók has marked a crescendo in the strings, and the arpeggios drop out for the last two measures) as Wendy asks Danny, "You didn't think it was gonna be this big, did you?" To which he replies, "Nope." The tremolos in the strings continue to grow louder until the scene ends abruptly with a fortissimo strike on a cymbal. The strike matches perfectly with the next title card, which reads "Tuesday." The movement goes on after this, but Gordon Stainforth made a cut right after the cymbal hit, quickly fading out the chords that would have continued.

In the second appearance, just a minute or so later, the music begins a few measures earlier than it did in the previous cue. We hear a couple of hits of the xylophone, a short, five-note phrase in the cellos, and then the same dissonant chord we heard at the hedge maze. The glissandi in the second violins begin just as Danny rides his tricycle past room 237, finally realizing where he is. He gets up and tries the knob of the door—just as the string glissandi stop and the xylophone enters—but finds it locked. He sees a vision of the twins as the timpani glissandi start, and he looks up at the door as he gets back on the tricycle to ride away. The arpeggios begin as we see Jack from the back. He is sitting in the lounge, typing, and the camera gradually moves toward him. Kubrick reverses the angle, and we see Jack's face, intently look at the page in his typewriter. As we switch again to the angle looking at Jack from behind, Wendy enters the lounge where her husband writes, and when she reaches him and asks him how it's going, he pulls the paper out of the typewriter just as the cymbal crashes again. The music stops as Jack and Wendy have a conversation that ends with Jack angrily telling her she is not to disturb him when he is writing.

The last time it appears, Danny goes to his room to get a fire engine toy and is instructed by Wendy not to wake Jack. Jack, however, is awake, sitting up on his bed. This time the cue begins at the start of the third

movement, with the xylophone plinking with increasing intensity. The timpani adds accents and then the violas enter with a mournful line. Danny
asks permission to get his fire engine, but Jack wants to talk to him first.
As Danny goes to Jack, the second violins begin a line of their own, the
two lines—violin and viola—winding around each other. Soon chromatic
gestures are heard here and there in many of the string parts, staggered,
as if they are passing the gestures around. As the music moves toward the
section with the string glissandi, Danny asks Jack if he likes the hotel. The
music continues, and as the timpani glissandi enter, Danny asks Jack if he
would ever hurt him or Wendy. Jack assures him that he would not, and
the arpeggios begin, although there is a slight alteration to make the cue
fit. Stainforth cut a few measures of the arpeggios so that the scene could
end with the cymbal hit and a title card that says "Wednesday."

## THE MUSIC OF KRZYSZTOF PENDERECKI

Born in 1933 in Debica, Poland, Penderecki experienced the Second
World War as a child. Although little is written about his early life, there is
no doubt that the cataclysm of the war had a great impact on Penderecki,
both as an artist and as a person. In the 1950s and 1960s his reputation
as an innovator grew; he experimented with extended techniques for instruments and graphic notation (to better convey his musical ideas).[56] He
gained popularity with his St. Luke's Passion, a retelling of Christ's crucifixion that is grand in scale and very dramatic. Despite living in postwar com-
munist Poland under Stalinist policies, Penderecki continued to produce
many forward-looking pieces. He was helped in great measure by the death
of Stalin and the subsequent abandonment of Stalinism after Khrushchev
came to power. One of Penderecki's most famous works is one associated
with the end of World War II. Originally called 8' 37", the later renamed
Threnody to the Victims of Hiroshima (1960) reflected the composer's
thoughts about history and about human suffering.[57] Like the music of
Ligeti, Threnody—which predates Ligeti's Lux Aeterna and Requiem—also
deals with texture and sound masses as a unifying paradigm. Penderecki's
pieces in The Shining date from 1961 to 1974, and the later pieces seem
to focus more on melodic elements and lyricism, although they are still
unmistakably driven by sound rather than tonal or melodic organization.[58]
        Penderecki's status as a witness to the Second World War, and com-
mentator on its human toll, is a central issue of Geoffrey Cocks's assessment of hidden themes in The Shining. In an article from 2006, Cocks

makes explicit the connection between Penderecki's music as a reaction to the war and Kubrick's placement of the music in the film:

> Penderecki's music accompanies the actual horrors of the Overlook Hotel past and present. This is significant, for Penderecki's own father was a lawyer during World War II when the Nazis killed 70 percent of the lawyers in Poland. Born in 1933, Penderecki watched Jews being taken away by the Germans and devoted his musical career to the exploration of tolerance and intolerance. . . . As Danny envisions the elevator gushing blood and Jack dreams of murder, on the soundtrack is Penderecki's *The Awakening of Jacob* (1974). Jacob, aside from being the name of Kubrick's father, is he in the Bible who is renamed Israel and whose sons are the ancestors of the twelve tribes. The text is Genesis 28:16. . . . Kubrick similarly utilizes Penderecki's *Utrenja* ("Morning Prayer," 1969–70) from the Eastern Orthodox liturgy for Christ's entombment and resurrection to underscore savagely the hotel's final manifestations of its accumulated horrors. [59]

There is no arguing that Penderecki's discovery of new sounds through the use of extended techniques helped to convey the sublime at the Overlook Hotel, but it is unclear whether Kubrick had any idea—or even wanted to know—of Penderecki's proximity to the war. What concerned him, of course, were specific qualities of the pieces and how well they served the narrative. We may assume then that Penderecki's sound resources must have been intriguing to Kubrick, since so many of his pieces form part of the score. It contributes to the viewer's sense of unease, as the sounds are sometimes unfamiliar and form a middle ground between music and sound effect.

One of the most challenging things about analyzing the soundtrack to *The Shining* is one of the very things that makes the soundtrack particularly effective: the freedom and flexibility with which Kubrick and Gordon Stainforth used the music of Penderecki. From about an hour and forty minutes into the film until the end of the film, many of the musical cues are layered one on top of another. It is exceedingly difficult to parse out the different cues in some instances, but where it is possible, I have made a note of the places where there is layering. Because Stainforth often offered many choices to Kubrick, the labeling of these multiple cues was not always meticulously done.[60]

In table 6.1, I have attempted to account for all the cues used from 1:41:15 to 2:19:26. Where the layering made identification of a work uncertain, I marked the most likely piece with an asterisk (*). There are three places (about a minute and a half in total) of unidentified music, labeled

**Table 6.1.  Soundtrack of *The Shining***

| Begin Cue | End Cue | Piece(s) | Actions |
|---|---|---|---|
| 1:41:15 | | *Polymorphia* | Argument between Wendy and Jack |
| 1:49:10 | | Add layer—*Kanon Paschy* | Wendy hits Jack with the bat |
| 1:49:25 | | *Polymorphia* becomes prominent again (beginning to m. 38) | Wendy drags Jack to the pantry |
| | 1:53:20 | *Polymorphia* fades out | |
| 1:53:20 | | *De Natura Sonoris #1* | Wendy runs out to check Sno-cat |
| 1:53:48 | | Add layer—*Polymorphia** | Wendy sees Sno-cat has been sabotaged |
| | 1:54:20 | *Polymorphia** ends | |
| | 1:54:26 | *De Natura Sonoris #1* ends | |
| 1:54:26 | 1:57:40 | No music | Grady and Jack talk; wind SFX |
| 1:57:41 | | *De Natura Sonoris #2* (beginning to about m. 14) | Halloran drives through the snow / redrum |
| | 2:00:54 | *De Natura Sonoris #2* ends abruptly | |
| 2:00:55 | | *Ewangelica*—opening "Rattle" only | Jack puts an ax through the door |
| | 2:01:03 | "Rattle" ends | |
| 2:01:04 | | *Kanon for Orchestra and Tape* | Wendy and Danny try to escape through the window |
| 2:04:12 | | Add layer—*Kanon Paschy* | Jack axes through the bathroom door and says, "Here's Johnny!" |
| | 2:04:32 | *Kanon* and *Kanon Paschy* fade out | |
| 2:04:32 | 2:08:30 | No music | Sno-cat sound / wind SFX |
| 2:08:30 | | *Ewangelica* (from the beginning of the movement) | Jack axes Halloran; Danny runs away |

(*continued*)

**Table 6.1.** (*continued*)

| Begin Cue | End Cue | Piece(s) | Actions |
|---|---|---|---|
| 2:09:49 | 2:10:12 | Add layer—*Polymorphia**<br>*Polymorphia** ends | Wendy sees man in bear suit |
| 2:10:12 | 2:10:22 | *Ewangelica* continues<br>*Ewangelica* ends | |
| 2:10:22 | 2:10:46 | Unknown | Jack turns on lights outside in the maze |
| 2:10:52 | 2:12:02 | *Kanon for Orchestra and Tape*<br>*Kanon* ends | Jack chases Danny into the maze |
| 2:12:02 | 2:12:24 | No music | Wind and SFX |
| 2:12:24 | | *Ewangelica* (from beginning)<br>Add layer—*Kanon for Orchestra and Tape* | Wendy finds Hallorann and the injured guest |
| 2:12:54 | 2:13:24 | *Ewangelica* ends; *Kanon for Orchestra and Tape* continues | Jack and Danny run through the maze<br>Wendy sees skeletons in the hotel lobby;<br>Danny retraces his steps |
| 2:14:36 | | Add layer—*Kanon Paschy* | Wendy sees blood from the elevator |
| | 2:14:43 | *Kanon for Orchestra and tape ends; Kanon Paschy* continues | Jack loses Danny in the maze |
| | 2:15:44 | *Kanon Paschy* ends | |
| 2:15:44 | 2:16:11 | Unknown | |
| 2:16:11 | | *Kanon for Orchestra and Tape*<br>Add layer—*De Natura Sonoris #2* | Jack looks for Danny; Danny escapes the maze |
| 2:17:30 | 2:18:00 | *Kanon for Orchestra and Tape and De Natura Sonoris #2* fade out | Wendy and Danny get in the Sno-cat |
| 2:18:00 | 2:18:42 | No music | Jack's incoherent yelling |
| 2:18:42 | 2:19:26 | Unknown | Jack wanders around the maze |
| 2:19:30 | End | "Midnight, the Stars, and You" | Picture of the July 4 party |

"unknown." For the places where Kubrick and Stainforth used excerpts from *Utrenja II*, I simply used the name of the movement in question, either *Kanon Paschy* or *Ewangelica*.

### Appearances of *De Natura Sonoris No. 1*

0:49:13–0:51:11 Danny rides through the hotel and sees the twins in the hallway
1:53:20–1:54:26 Wendy realizes that Jack has sabotaged the Sno-cat (layered with *Polymorphia*)

### Appearances of *De Natura Sonoris No. 2*

1:01:09–1:04:06 Danny walks in, injured; Wendy blames Jack; Jack walks to the Gold Room
2:17:30–2:18:00 Wendy runs out of the hotel and finds Danny coming out of the maze; they get into the Sno-cat; Jack calls out for them (layered with *Kanon for Orchestra and Tape*)

### Appearances of *The Awakening of Jacob*

0:10:32–0:12:09 Danny talks to Tony while brushing his teeth; he blacks out
0:57:05–1:01:05 Jack has a nightmare; he tells Wendy about it
1:11:46–1:16:07 Jack goes to room 237 and sees the woman in the bathtub (layered with "Shining/Heartbeat" cue)

### Appearances of *Polymorphia*

1:41:20–1:53:21 Wendy finds Jack's writing; they argue (layered with *Utrenja II—Kanon Paschy*); Wendy drags Jack into the pantry
1:53:46–1:54:20 Wendy realizes that Jack has sabotaged the Sno-cat (layered with *De Natura Sonoris No. 1*)

### Appearances of *Kanon for Orchestra and Tape*

2:01:04–2:04:32 Jack is using the axe to break down the door to the apartment and the bathroom (layered with *Utrenja II—Kanon Paschy*)
2:10:52–2:12:02 Jack chases Danny into the maze
2:12:54–2:14:43 Jack and Danny in the maze (layered with *Utrenja II—Ewangelica* and *Utrenja II—Kanon Paschy*)

## Appearances of *Utrenja II: Ewangelica*

2:00:55–2:01:03 Jack puts an ax through the apartment door
2:08:30–2:10:22 Jack kills Hallorann; Danny runs from Jack; Wendy sees
   a man in a bear suit
2:12:24–2:13:24 Wendy finds Hallorann's dead body; she runs into the
   injured guest

## Appearances of *Utrenja II: Kanon Paschy*

1:49:10–1:49:25 Wendy hits Jack with the bat; Jack falls down the stairs
2:04:12–2:04:32 Jack breaks through the bathroom door with an axe
2:14:36–2:15:44 Wendy sees blood coming from the elevator; Jack loses
   Danny in the maze

*The Awakening of Jacob* appears early in the film, as Danny converses with "imaginary friend" Tony and while Jack talks to Wendy on the phone. Tony at first refuses to tell Danny why he doesn't want to go to the Overlook, but then Danny has a vision. Blood spills out of the elevator at the hotel, rushing up to the camera and moving the furniture in the flow. Danny also sees the twins, and the camera briefly shows Danny's horrified face. The blood covers the camera and fades the scene to black. The sounds are low, intermittent chords in the orchestra, each one getting louder and more dissonant. The cue fades out as the doctor checks on Danny. It's ironic that this piece accompanies Danny's loss of consciousness and his vision of something horrible, as the biblical text that inspired the piece is about Jacob waking up and being assured of God's presence. ("When Jacob awoke from his sleep, he thought, 'Surely the Lord is in this place, and I was not aware of it'" Genesis 28:16.)

The second appearance of the piece occurs when Danny is playing in the hallway by room 237. Again, we hear the intermittent chords. Danny finds the room open, but we don't see him enter as the scene fades to Wendy checking on the boiler. She hears Jack yelling and runs upstairs to find him having a nightmare. As he screams, the high notes in the strings sound, but then the low dissonant chords return. As he explains that he dreamed he killed Wendy and Danny, the lines in the strings glissando upward, and tone clusters cover a large range. Danny walks in to the lounge and there's a percussive sound followed by sustained notes played on the musical saw and slide whistle. Those sustained notes are the beginning of *De Natura Sonoris No. 2*, which continues as Jack heads for the ballroom.

*The Awakening of Jacob* returns as Jack goes to check on room 237. As he walks there, Wendy Carlos's "Shining/Heartbeat" cue plays, mirroring perhaps Jack's nervously beating heart. The high-pitched sound fades into the low intermittent chords as Jack finally sees what's in the room: a beautiful naked woman, who wordlessly kisses Jack. This is the same music that accompanied his nightmare a few scenes ago, and indeed this fantasy turns into a nightmare, as the beautiful woman transforms into a decomposing crone who laughs at Jack as he backs away from her in terror. The music ends as Jack leaves room 237 and locks the door behind him.

As their titles suggest, *De Natura Sonoris Nos. 1* and 2 explore the nature of sounds, something of a preoccupation for Penderecki. On his profile page for the Schott Publishing Company, he is quoted as saying, "I have spent decades searching for and discovering new sounds."[61] Composed in 1966 and 1971, respectively, *De Natura Sonoris Nos. 1* and 2 use unusual sound resources including rare instruments and extended techniques. Penderecki's *De Natura Sonoris No. 1* accompanies Danny's surprise encounter with the twins in the hallway. He is riding his tricycle and turns a corner to find the twins standing there, hand in hand. They ask him to come and play, but he sees visions of them dead, covered in blood. He tells Tony he is scared, and Tony reminds him that Hallorann said the visions were like "pictures in a book." The cue is tense, almost from the beginning, which fades in a few measures into the piece as the woodwinds and strings are sustaining very high notes. The horns and trumpets provide accents in their high registers. A percussive crash coincides with Danny seeing the twins. Low woodwinds accompany the twins' request for Danny to come play. Clatters in the gong, tam-tam, and bells follow. Then there are instrumental surges upward, first in the woodwinds, then in the brass, and finally in both groups. Danny claps his hands over his eyes just at the end of the second one, and after the third one he looks again, and the twins are gone. The music becomes quieter once more, as Danny talks to Tony, fading out for the next title card, "Monday."

*De Natura Sonoris No. 1* reappears as Wendy, who intends to escape with Danny on the Sno-cat, runs out to check on the machine. To her horror, she finds that the Sno-cat has been disabled. Here, Kubrick and Stainforth layered the excerpt from *De Natura Sonoris No. 1*—much of the cue used for Danny's encounter with the twins in the hallway—with part of the prickly section of *Polymorphia*. The accents from *Sonoris* provide unexpected jolts (including percussive hits on timpani, drums, gong, and piano) while the pizzicato and discomfort of the high strings in *Polymorphia* perfectly mirror Wendy's rising panic. The gong crash brings us to Jack who is sleeping in the walk-in pantry. The music fades away, and there is a knock at the door.

Penderecki's *De Natura Sonoris No. 2* appears a few times in the film. The first time it fades in just as *The Awakening of Jacob* is fading out. Jack has just had a terrible nightmare at his desk, and Danny walks in, sucking his thumb. Wendy, seeing that the boy is injured, blames Jack, and the music grows more dissonant as she screams at him. Jack, who believes he is innocent, stalks to the Gold Room, muttering angrily to himself, his physical lashing out coinciding with one of the entrances in the piece. He looks for alcohol in the bar and when he realizes there is none he intones, "I'd give my goddamned soul for just a glass of beer." High notes in the slide whistle (*Flauto a coulisse*) and musical saw (*Sega*), slide downward as they die away, and the cue ends.

In the second instance, the cue begins as Hallorann drives the Sno-cat to the Overlook. It begins with a percussive sting on the cymbals, followed by the high notes in the slide whistle and saw. The notes glissando downward and die away, as the violas enter with a long-held note. The string instruments enter and in some cases, the notes stay sustained, while in others the instruments split into tone clusters. The extended techniques on the instruments are unsettling to the ear, even startling, and add tension to the scene. The cue ends as we return to Hallorann in the Sno-cat.

The first time Penderecki's *Polymorphia* is heard it plays once through entirely, then begins again immediately and fades into *De Natura Sonoris No. 1*. It is a very long cue and, like the two *De Natura Sonoris* pieces, experiments with sounds and extended techniques. *Polymorphia* was composed in 1961. Written for forty-eight string instruments, it is a continuation of the sound experiments with strings Penderecki had begun with *Threnody to the Victims of Hiroshima*. Like the earlier piece, Penderecki used a system of graphic notation he devised to convey the extended techniques he desired. At one point in the middle of the piece, half of the violins and all of the violas are playing from wavy-line notation that could be an EKG or an EEG. In addition to glissandi, the sound landscape of the piece also includes tone clusters—often eight different notes played simultaneously—and percussive plucking or tapping of the strings. This particular piece has a section of prickly pizzicato sounds and sections played *legno battuto* (striking the string with the wood part of the bow) that are especially uncanny.

Wendy locks Danny in the apartment so she can go talk to Jack. When she tells Danny to stay put, Tony answers her. Walking down to the lounge where he has been writing, Wendy's movements are accompanied by low, unrelenting notes in the strings. Going to his desk, she finds that Jack has typed "All work and no play makes Jack a dull boy" over and over again on what looks like hundreds of pieces of paper. This discovery is accompanied by a long-held high note in a dozen violins. The violas begin frantic glissandi, completely uncoordinated, and are soon joined by some of the violins. The glissandi grow in volume and intensity, until Jack shows up. Some of the players then use their fingertips to tap the strings behind the bridge, and some hit the strings with the wood of the bow rather than the hair. Kubrick cuts to Danny, who seems to be hearing what Jack is saying and who is experiencing the vision of the blood coming from the elevator. The prickly section ends, and the long-held clusters return, expanding and contracting as Jack backs Wendy up the stairs. He begins threatening her, and she swings a bat at him to keep him away. Long, wide tremolos are heard with accents as Jack reaches for her and she hits him in the hand and then in the head. *Polymorphia* begins again as she drags his semi-conscious body to the pantry, locking him in. It continues to play as they speak through the door to each other. He tries to bargain with her and play on her sympathies as the glissandi begin. She tells him she's going to take Danny to Sidewinder (a nearby town) in the Sno-cat, but he informs her—as the prickly section begins again—that she's "not going anywhere." The piece fades into *De Natura Sonoris No. 1* as she runs out into the snow to check on the Sno-cat, which Jack has sabotaged. Part of the prickly section of this piece is layered with *De Natura Sonoris No. 1* as Wendy discovers the sabotage.

*Utrenja* (1970–1971) is a religious choral piece that marks a follow-up to Penderecki's famous *St. Luke's Passion*, which was composed in 1963–1965.[62] The first part of *Utrenja* deals with the entombment of Christ, after his crucifixion, while the second part—from which Kubrick took two excerpts—deals with Christ's resurrection. The first movement of the second part, *Ewangelica*, or *Gospel*, is not sung in a traditional way, but chanted like rhythmic spoken words. One particular musical feature of the movement, a "sting" of sorts on percussion, that begins the movement is used numerous times in this final section of the film to punctuate particularly horrifying events. It first appears just after Danny writes "Redrum" on the door in lipstick. He screams, "Redrum," and Wendy wakes up and holds him, only to see "Murder" in the mirror. Just as this happens, Jack uses an ax to break through the door of the apartment. Stainforth doesn't allow the cue to continue, but instead cuts quickly to *Kanon for Orchestra and Tape*. The sting appears again as Jack surprises Hallorann with an ax to the chest. Here the cue is allowed to continue and we hear the rhythmic chanting of the choir, which is very sibilant. Another rattle occurs about half a minute into the movement, and this one accompanies Danny running from the cupboard in the kitchen and Jack limping after him. The movement continues with more chanting as Wendy looks for Danny. Again we hear the sting when Wendy happens upon a man in a bear suit leaning over into the lap of a man in a tuxedo; when they look up at Wendy, there is another sting. The sibilant chanting continues for another thirty seconds. When Wendy comes upon Hallorann's corpse, we hear the sting again, followed by the rhythmic chanting. Another sting enters when Wendy sees a party guest who appears to have a head injury. The chanting continues as we cut to the hedge maze. Jack is chasing Danny, and the chanting is layered with *Kanon for Orchestra and Tape*. Jack, slow because of his limp, warns Danny, "I'm right behind you," as the next sting occurs. The music becomes more frantic, mirroring both Jack's insanity and Wendy's panic.[63]

The other excerpt from *Utrenja II, Kanon Paschy* or *Easter Canon*, starts at the beginning of the movement, with three heavy, low chords in the brass followed by two flourishes upward in the strings and woodwinds. This cue is first used as Wendy hits Jack with the baseball bat. The cue begins when she hits his hand; when the bat makes contact with Jack's head, it matches perfectly with the first flourish. Stainforth used this part of the cue twice in quick succession. Jack falls down the stairs, and as Wendy drags him to the walk-in pantry, *Polymorphia* begins again. Later, when Jack is using the ax to break through the bathroom door, we hear the beginning of *Kanon Paschy*. Jack says, "Here's Johnny" between the two flourishes in the strings. As before, Stainforth repeats the opening gesture—three low brass chords followed by two upward strings flourishes—and then allows the movement to continue with more brass chords and a dissonant vocal entrance of the choir. It continues over into Hallorann's POV as he's driving up to the Overlook. After that, it's just the sound of the Sno-cat followed by the howling wind. As Wendy runs through the hotel, she sees the wave of blood coming from the elevator to the low brass chords and flourishes. It continues as Jack loses Danny's trail in the maze.

### Jack Hylton and His Orchestra: "Masquerade"

Appearance:

1:20:49–1:21:20 Jack, upset at Wendy, hears this tune from the hallway

Jack Hylton was a British bandleader after the First World War. Born in 1892 as John Greenhalgh Hilton, Hylton achieved success as a bandleader and arranger in the 1920s and recorded numerous albums for both the HMV and the Decca labels. In the 1940s, he became a theatrical producer, and in the 1950s he worked in television. "Masquerade," a waltz, was recorded in 1932 on the Decca label.[64]

Wendy suggests that Danny needs medical help, and Jack is angry that she would have him leave his responsibilities at the Overlook. But he must succeed . . . As he storms out of their room, he hears muffled music in the hallway by the kitchen. He turns a corner to find balloons and streamers in the hallway, almost as if a party has just taken place.

### Ray Noble and His Orchestra: "Midnight, the Stars, and You"

Appearances:

1:22:13–1:25:26 Jack enters the Gold Room to find a party in full swing; he orders a drink from Lloyd and then bumps into Grady who takes him to the men's room to help him clean up
2:19:34–2:22:51 The camera closes in on a picture of the 4 July 1921 party at the Overlook Hotel; as the camera gets closer and closer, we realize Jack is in the picture; closing credits

Written in 1932, this tune accompanies Jack's entry into the party in the Gold Room. It has one other appearance, and that is just before (and over) the closing credits. Al Bowlly is the singer on this recording. Born in 1899 in Mozambique, Al Bowlly grew up in Johannesburg, South Africa. He played with bands around Africa and Southeast Asia until gaining some fame with a recording of Irving Berlin's song "Blue Skies." In 1930, he signed a recording contract with Ray Noble and His Orchestra, and over the next few years he put more than five hundred songs on wax. Bowlly is thought of as one of the originators of "crooning," a style of singing that can be described as intimate, gentle, and often romantic. It was made possible by the development of microphones, which allowed even quiet singing to be heard live. Bowlly is credited with a book about the technique of crooning called *The Modern Singing Style*. Bowlly was also one of the very first singers of the era to achieve as much name recognition as a bandleader—something quite unusual at the time. He was popular among the ladies too, who clamored for his autograph after shows. Bowlly's nickname was "The Big Swoon." He died in London in the Blitz in 1941. Ray Noble eventually moved to California where he worked in film and radio. Crooning would continue to be popular until the early 1950s. One of his most famous songs was "Midnight, the Stars, and You," written by Harry Woods, Jimmy Campbell, and Reg Connelly. It speaks of a magical night of dancing under the stars that the singer promises to remember for the rest of his (or her) life. This song perfectly captures the ending of the film, which is quite different from the ending of the novel.

In Stephen King's novel, one of Jack's most important duties as caretaker is "dumping" the boiler. Because the Overlook is a very old hotel, Watson, the maintenance man, warns him that Jack must keep an eye on the boiler's pressure: "Now you got to remember to come down here twice a day and once at night before you rack in. You got to check the press. If you forget, it'll just creep and creep and like as not you an your fambly'll wake up on the fuckin moon. You just dump her off a little and you'll have no trouble."[65] As Jack becomes more and more preoccupied with the hotel's past, he starts neglecting his duties. And as Jack—possessed by the hotel—attempts to "correct" Wendy and Danny, he forgets the dump the boiler. In the end, the boiler explodes, and the hotel is destroyed. Jack is killed in the cataclysm, and the hotel is gone for good, a somewhat satisfying end. King treats us to an epilogue in which Danny, Wendy, and Halloran are spending the summer at the Red Arrow Lodge in Maine. Wendy is still recovering from her physical wounds, and Danny's nightmares are getting less frequent.

In the film, however, the hotel remains unchanged. It will continue to have guests and presumably to haunt caretakers. It also appears to have absorbed Jack into itself. In an epilogue in the film that Kubrick cut, Ullman visits Wendy in the hospital where he tells her that Jack's body has not been found. In the version of the film without an epilogue, we are shown that Jack's body froze to death in the hedge maze, but then we see him again, in a photograph from the July Fourth party at the hotel. Jack has now become part of its grand history, although some imagine that Jack was always in that picture and that his return to the hotel was something of a trick of reincarnation. Or perhaps the photo is his reincarnation.[66] The haunting melody of "Midnight, the Stars and You" captures this chilling ending, history repeating itself, as Kubrick slowly moves closer and closer to this picture, aiding our gradual recognition of the protagonist, spiffily dressed in a tuxedo, with his arms outstretched.

### Ray Noble and His Orchestra: "It's All Forgotten Now"

Appearance:

1:25:47–1:29:01 Jack and Delbert talk in the red bathroom

The recording of this song is somewhat muffled because the song is ostensibly coming from the Gold Room, although the scene takes place in the men's room. Delbert Grady has spilled some drinks on Jack and takes him into the men's room to clean him up. It's interesting that this song plays as Jack and Delbert discuss the things they do not remember. When Jack learns Delbert Grady's name, he tells him that Grady killed his family and committed suicide. Grady claims not to remember this happening. According to Grady, Jack is—and always has been—the caretaker at the Overlook. Like "Midnight, the Stars and You," "It's All Forgotten Now" was published in 1934, which of course makes it anachronistic to the 1920s party that is going on. The flapper fashion and accessories suggests a 1920s soiree.

### Henry Hall and the Gleneagles Hotel Band: "Home"

Appearance:

1:29:10–1:31:34 Continues after "It's All Forgotten Now," while Delbert and Jack are still in the red bathroom

Henry Hall was an English bandleader who worked for the London Midland and Scottish Railway chain of hotels, which included the five-star hotel the Gleneagles. Hall helped promote the Gleneagles by doing radio broadcasts with the band. He played with groups all around England, even leading a band on the *Queen Mary*'s maiden voyage in 1936. He signed a recording contract with Columbia, with whom he put out a few records; then he recorded on Decca. "Home" was recorded in the 1930s for Decca, with vocals by Maurice Elwin.

The muffled tunes of the band continue with "Home" as Grady warns Jack that Danny is calling for help from Hallorann. Grady also explains that he had trouble with his family, but he "corrected" them, and he suggests that Jack do the same with Wendy and Danny. This is the only one of the band tunes that appeared on the original soundtrack album, perhaps because of timing issues.

## OTHER MUSICAL CUES

There are a few other musical cues, but most of them are sourced from televisions or the radio. At the beginning of the film, as Jack is having his interview at the Overlook, Danny eats a sandwich and watches cartoons; the sound effects and music from a Warner Bros. cartoon are very distinctive (0:04:17–0:05:08). Later in the film, when Danny is in a trance—only Tony will communicate with Wendy—Danny sits again watching cartoons. This time it's the theme song to *The Road Runner Show*, followed by the music and sound effects of a Road Runner cartoon (1:39:25–1:41:08). Even this cue was carefully chosen and placed in the scene. The cartoon plays as Wendy leaves the apartment, taking a baseball bat with her for protection. Gordon Stainforth has said of the cue in this scene: "I was particularly proud of the way I 'choreographed' the cartoon music on the TV with Wendy's movements. There was then a long dissolve, as the cartoon music faded, to Wendy entering the Colorado lounge. After a pause I then gently faded in the start of the Penderecki music as Wendy walks towards Jack's desk."[67]

A short theme song to Miami News, Channel 10 is heard just before Hallorann receives a "message" from the Overlook that all is not well (1:09:46–1:10:10). The news reports that Miami is experiencing a record heat wave, while in Colorado there is record snowfall. As Hallorann is driving from the Denver airport to Durkin's to rent a Sno-cat, we hear a brief jingle from the radio station KHOW, Radio 63 (1:38:37–1:38:43).

## CONCLUSION

The soundtrack to *The Shining* is a tour de force of the use of preexistent music. Kubrick and music editor Gordon Stainforth took the lessons learned in *2001*, *A Clockwork Orange*, and *Barry Lyndon* to create a unique soundscape. They were aided in this by the musical choices, which, because of their structures, atonal language, or focus on sound over melody, made extreme flexibility possible. The sounds dip in and out of consciousness. The band tunes alert the Torrances that they are not alone in the hotel. Dramatic flourishes in the art music punctuate the uncanny events. *The Shining* influenced filmmakers in the horror genre, introduced Penderecki and Bartók to a mass audience, and spawned countless theories as to its true meaning. Perhaps its most chilling message is that we are vulnerable not just to the dangers of the outside world but to the evil that lies dormant in the people we love—and in ourselves. In the film, the Overlook still exists, the July Fourth party continues eternally, and Jack has sacrificed his family and himself to be part of it forever.

## NOTES

1. Jeremy Barham, "Incorporating Monsters: Music as Context, Character and Construction in Kubrick's *The Shining*" in *Terror Tracks: Music, Sound and Horror Cinema*, ed. Philip Hayard (London: Oakville, 2009), 137.

2. David Code, "Rehearing *The Shining*: Musical Undercurrents in the Overlook Hotel," in *Music in the Horror Film: Listening to Fear*, ed. Neil William Lerner (New York: Routledge, 2010), 133.

3. Serena Ferrara, *Steadicam: Techniques and Aesthetics* (Oxford: Focal Press, 2000), 19.

4. Michel Ciment, *Kubrick: The Definitive Edition*, trans. Gilbert Adair (New York: Faber and Faber, 1999), 189.

5. Telex reprinted in Garrett Brown, "The Steadicam and *The Shining*," *American Cinematographer* 61, no. 8 (August 1980): 786.

6. Ferrara, *Steadicam*, 31.

7. Brown, "The Steadicam and *The Shining*," 826.

8. Interview with Herb Lightman with director of photography of *The Shining* John Alcott, "Photographing Stanley Kubrick's *The Shining*," *American Cinematographer* 61, no. 8 (August 1980): 781.

9. Ferrara, *Steadicam*, 80.

10. Quoted in Vincent LoBrutto, *Stanley Kubrick: A Biography* (New York: Da Capo Press, 1997), 453.

11. David A. Cook, "American Horror: *The Shining*," *Film Literature Quarterly* 12, no.1 (1984): 2.

12. Blakemore gave these details about his article: "My 1987 article on Kubrick's *The Shining* was written for, and edited by, *The Washington Post*. It was published on the front page of the *Post*'s Sunday entertainment section on July 12, 1987, under the headline, 'Kubrick's *Shining* Secret: Film's Hidden Horror Is the Murder of the Indian.'" http://williamblakemore.com/Blakemore-%20Kubrick%20 Shining.pdf.

13. Kubrick biographer Vincent LoBrutto suspects that Kubrick may have been inspired to use twins instead of just sisters because of two images: photographer Diane Arbus's iconic image of twins from 1967—an idea put forth by Arbus' biographer Patricia Bosworth—and another image that Kubrick himself took when he worked for *Look* magazine in which two sisters stand side by side in front of the men who saved them from carbon monoxide poisoning. LoBrutto, *Stanley Kubrick*, 444–445.

14. Geoffrey Cocks, *The Wolf at the Door: Stanley Kubrick, History, and the Holocaust* (New York: Peter Lang, 2004), 2.

15. Cocks, *The Wolf at the Door*, 246.

16. In James Howard's *Stanley Kubrick Companion*, Howard claims that Kubrick changed the number of the room "as a favour" to the Timberline Lodge in Oregon, on which the Overlook Hotel is based. The Timberline had a room 217, but its association with the disturbing events in *The Shining* might have caused some problems. The Timberline did not have a room 237, so there was no problem there. James Howard, *Stanley Kubrick Companion* (London: B.T. Batsford, 1999), 151.

17. Ciment, *Kubrick: The Definitive Edition*, 196. He went on to say, "I wonder how many people have ever had their views changed by a work of art?"

18. LoBrutto, *Stanley Kubrick*, 411.

19. LoBrutto, *Stanley Kubrick*, 417.

20. LoBrutto, *Stanley Kubrick*, 418.

21. Letter, "From the office of Rudi Fehr 12/23/77," in the Stanley Kubrick Archive, University of the Arts London.

22. Although this cue was not used in the film, it did appear at the end of Vivian Kubrick's documentary *The Making of The Shining*, which is included on the DVD release of the film.

23. *Stanley Kubrick: A Life in Pictures*, directed by Jan Harlan (2007, Warner Home Video), 1:41.

24. See full track listings of these albums in appendix C.

25. The Polymoog was probably best known as the synthesizer used in Gary Numan's song "Cars." The instrument was manufactured from 1975 to 1980 by the Moog Music company.

26. K. J. Donnelly, *The Spectre of Sound: Music in Film and Television* (London: BFI Publishing, 2005), 53, note 15.

27. LoBrutto, *Stanley Kubrick*, 448–449.

28. wendycarlos.com/discs.html#BR.

29. Luis M. Garcia Mainar, *Narrative and Stylistic Patterns in the Films of Stanley Kubrick* (Rochester, NY: Camden House, 1999), 56.

30. James Naremore, *On Kubrick* (London: BFI, 2007), 193.

31. Donnelly mentions Christopher Hoile's 1984 article "The Uncanny and the Fairy Tale in Kubrick's *The Shining*," in *Literature Film Quarterly* 12, no. 1 (1984): 5–12. In it, Hoile discusses the influence on *The Shining* of Freud's essay "The Uncanny" and Bruno Bettelheim's *The Uses of Enchantment* from 1976. Donnelly, *The Spectre of Sound*, 52.

32. Donnelly, *The Spectre of Sound*, 50.

33. Leonard Lionnet, "Mysteries of the Overlook," *Film Score Monthly* 9, no.1 (January 2004): 46–47.

34. Donnelly, *The Spectre of Sound*, 46.

35. A reprint of Stainforth's summary music chart for *The Shining* can be found in Barham, "Incorporating Monsters," 62–64.

36. Barham, "Incorporating Monsters," 145.

37. Barham, "Incorporating Monsters," 145.

38. Howard, *Stanley Kubrick Companion*, 153.

39. Howard, *Stanley Kubrick Companion*, 153. http://www.gordonstainforth.co.uk/.

40. Please see the plot synopsis of *The Shining* in appendix B.

41. LoBrutto, *Stanley Kubrick*, 448–449.

42. The poem also shares similarities with texts from other traditions like *Une thae tokef*, a Hebrew chant for Yom Kippur, and a seventh-century Advent hymn. From Robert Chase, *Dies Irae: A Guide to Requiem Music* (Lanham, MD: Scarecrow Press, 2003), 509.

43. Richard L. Crocker, John Caldwell, and Alejandro E. Planchart, "Sequence," in *The New Grove Dictionary of Music and Musicians*, ed. Stanley Sadie (London: Macmillan, 2001), 91.

MIDNIGHT, THE STARS, AND YOU          217

44. John Caldwell and Malcolm Boyd, "Dies Irae," in *The New Grove Dictionary of Music and Musicians*, ed. Stanley Sadie (London: Macmillan, 2001), 332.

45. Caldwell and Boyd, "Dies Irae," 332.

46. Incidentally, Penderecki wrote a *Dies Irae* in 1967 to commemorate the men and women who lost their lives in Auschwitz, but it features neither the text nor the chant; it instead mixes textual source material from various sources. Caldwell and Boyd, "Dies Irae," 333.

47. William Rosar, "The *Dies Irae* in *Citizen Kane*: Musical Hermeneutics Applied to Film Music," in *Film Music: Critical Approaches*, ed. K. J. Donnelly (New York: Continuum, 2001), 103–116.

48. Donnelly, *The Spectre of Sound*, 42.

49. A full rendering of the text in both Latin and English can be found at http://www.franciscan-archive.org/de_celano/opera/diesirae.html.

50. Michael D. Searby, *Ligeti's Stylistic Crisis: Transformation in His Musical Style 1974–1985* (Lanham, MD: Scarecrow Press, 2010), 8.

51. Searby, *Ligeti's Stylistic Crisis*, 37.

52. Richard Steinitz, *György Ligeti: Music of the Imagination* (Boston: Northeastern University Press, 2003), 153.

53. Ligeti, *Lontano* (Mainz: B. Schott's Söhne, 1967).

54. Searby, *Ligeti's Stylistic Crisis*, 145.

55. Nicky Losseff, "The Piano Concerto and Sonata for Two Pianos and Percussion," in *The Cambridge Companion to Bartók*, ed. Amanda Bayley (Cambridge: Cambridge University Press, 2001), 125.

56. Adrian Thomas, "Penderecki," in *The New Grove Dictionary of Music and Musicians*, ed. Stanley Sadie (London: Macmillan, 2001), 305.

57. Thomas, "Penderecki," 306.

58. Thomas, "Penderecki," 307.

59. Geoffrey Cocks, "Death by Typewriter: Stanley Kubrick, the Holocaust, and *The Shining*," in *Depth of Field: Stanley Kubrick, Film, and the Uses of History*, ed. Geoffrey Cocks, James Diedrick, and Glenn Perusek (Madison: University of Wisconsin Press, 2006), 211.

60. Leonard Lionnet attempted to make a similar chart in the article "Mysteries of the Overlook: Unraveling Stanley Kubrick's Soundtrack to *The Shining*," *Film Score Monthly* 9, no.1 (January 2004): 44–47, although he does not make note of the overlapping cues, and in the hedge maze sequence he leaves the credits as simply "Various."

61. http://www.schott-music.com/shop/persons/featured/krzysztof-penderecki/index.html.

62. Thomas, "Penderecki," 307.

63. As an interesting side note, it is worth mentioning that Kubrick again used music on set to create mood. In a documentary on *The Shining* filmed by Kubrick's daughter Vivian (included on the DVD release), she captures the filming of the hedge maze chase, and in the excerpt Kubrick is playing a tape of Igor Stravinsky's ballet *The Rite of Spring* and directing Danny in his escape. There is no evidence to

suggest he ever considered using the music for Stravinsky's ballet for the film, and there is no footage of him using Penderecki's musical selections to create mood, although they can be quite unnerving in the right context.

64. http://www.jackhylton.com/.

65. Stephen King, *The Shining* (New York: Pocket Books, 1977), 28.

66. Ciment, *Kubrick: The Definitive Edition*, 194.

67. http://www.visual-memory.co.uk/faq/html/shining/shining.html.

# Chapter Seven

———————⊙———————

# Kubrick's Final Word

## Eyes Wide Shut

Two years after the release of *Full Metal Jacket*, Kubrick had once again returned to the idea of telling the story of Napoleon Bonaparte, even thinking he might adapt the story for a multiepisode television series. But the notion didn't last long. Kubrick switched to another idea, the adaptation of Louis Begley's *Wartime Lies*, which was to become the film *Aryan Papers*. This project never made it past pre-production because it would have come out after Steven Spielberg's *Schindler's List*. The decision to postpone the project was made by Kubrick and then CEO of Warner Bros., Terry Semel. Kubrick moved on instead to a possible adaptation of Brian Aldiss's short story *Super-Toys Last All Summer Long*, even collaborating with Aldiss to create a working screenplay. When their efforts yielded nothing to Kubrick's satisfaction, the director worked with other writers, including Arthur C. Clarke, to hash out a scenario. In the end, Kubrick put aside the project ostensibly for a very practical reason; the state of special effects in the late 1980s could not possibly have accommodated what Kubrick envisioned for the film.[1] It was Steven Spielberg's *Jurassic Park* in 1993 that inspired Kubrick to return to the *Super-Toys* adaptation. Kubrick met with special effects gurus Dennis Muren and Ned Gorman from Industrial Light and Magic to discuss possible effects for the film (the two men had done visual effects for *Jurassic Park* and many other films).[2] When production of *Eyes Wide Shut* was finally announced by official Warner Bros. press release in 1995, the statement also confirmed that Kubrick was still planning to make the *Super-Toys* film—now called *A.I.*—after he completed *Eyes Wide Shut*.[3]

219

Kubrick eventually offered *A.I.* to Steven Spielberg after a year of pre-production, believing Spielberg to be better suited to make the film. Spielberg worked on other projects in the late 1990s, but after Kubrick's death, Christiane Kubrick encouraged Spielberg to revisit *A.I.* He agreed, fast-tracking the film into production and releasing *A.I. Artificial Intelligence* in 2001. *Eyes Wide Shut* would be Kubrick's last film. He died three months before the film was released in theaters, and although we hear that Kubrick had, in fact, completed editing, we can imagine that he might have continued to fiddle with the final product up until the release date. He was known to do such a thing, even working on edits *after* the release date in the cases of *2001* and *The Shining*.

Kubrick's interest in adapting Arthur Schnitzler's 1926 novella *Traumnovelle* (sometimes translated as *Dream Story* or *Rhapsody*) seems to go all the way back to the late 1960s, when Kubrick read a translation of the story around the release date of *2001*.[4] In an essay about *Eyes Wide Shut* by Hans-Thies Lehmann, there is a photograph of a note made by Kubrick about the acquisition of the rights to *Rhapsody* on 22 May 1968. It says, "Rhapsody . . . agent says $40,000 but obviously high."[5] Kubrick bought the rights to the property in 1970, but the idea of making it into a film remained on the back burner for quite some time.[6] Interestingly, Schnitzler wrote *Traumnovelle* in his early sixties, about the same age Kubrick was when he finally got around to beginning production on *Eyes Wide Shut*.[7]

When he finally decided to make the film, Kubrick engaged the services of screenwriter Frederic Raphael to help adapt Schnitzler's story to a filmable form. Raphael wrote about their collaboration in his book *Eyes Wide Open: A Memoir of Stanley Kubrick*. Most scholars agree that it "is a source to be used with caution."[8] At issue, among other things, are the lengthy conversations Raphael somehow quotes verbatim. In an interview a few months after Kubrick's death, Christiane Kubrick stated that Raphael's memoir was one of the two most unreliable sources of information about her husband.[9] Nevertheless, Raphael makes some interesting comments, even if they must be taken with a grain of salt.

Arthur Schnitzler began writing *Traumnovelle* in 1925, and installments of the story appeared in *Die Dame* magazine. The book was published as a whole in 1926 and takes place in 1920s Vienna. Schnitzler's use of dreams in his aptly named *Dream Story* brings to mind Sigmund Freud, a contemporary of the author and also a resident of Vienna. When Schnitzler turned sixty, he received a letter from Freud, who explained why the two had never met: Freud said that he had not reached out to

him for fear of seeing his own "doppelganger." Schnitzler, like the character Nachtigall in *Traumnovelle* (Dream Story), had studied medicine but
instead ended up pursuing the arts. Schnitzler's medical background was
something he had in common with Freud, and the author read Freud's
work with interest. The degree to which Schnitzler's work was influenced
by Freud's work has been the topic of some speculation,[10] and one can
imagine the two would have a lot to discuss regarding their common interests: hypnosis, dreams, hysteria, and human sexuality.

There are connections between Schnitzler and Kubrick as well. In
this case, the two men lived at different times and in different cities, but
their work is linked by more than just literary interest on Kubrick's part.
Schnitzler provides a direct connection between Kubrick and legendary
film director and auteur Max Ophüls.[11] Ophüls is recognized as a great
influence on Kubrick, and in 1950 Ophüls produced a film adaptation
of one of Schnitzler's most controversial plays, *Reigen* (often translated
*Round Dance*). Schnitzler's original was intended only for the eyes of his
friends but was performed in public in 1920 and 1921, drawing a strong
negative response, including many anti-Semitic comments. The film version of *Reigen,* called *La Ronde*, features conversations between sexual
partners. Ophüls cast actors who were some of the best and most respected of the time period.[12] In Ophüls's *La Ronde*, the director adds two
things: a master of ceremonies and a carousel. The added character comments on the interactions of the couples, maintains the carousel (which at
one point breaks down), and acts as an omniscient presence. The character even contrasts his all-seeing eye with the limited view that men share:
"Men never know but one part of reality. And why? . . . Because they only
see one aspect of things."[13] A similar sentiment is echoed in a line spoken
by the main female character, Alice, in *Eyes Wide Shut*. In response to the
notion that what women really want is security and commitment, Alice
says: "If you men only knew."

In the late 1990s, playwright David Hare adapted *Reigen* once again,
this time into an English version called *Blue Room*, which premiered in
London and was directed by Sam Mendes. It went on to open on Broad-
way in December 1998. The star of this play when it premiered—the actor
who played all five of the female parts in the show—was Nicole Kidman.[14]
(Her male costar, Iain Glen, played all the male roles.) In Ben Brantley's
review of *Blue Room* in the *New York Times*, he praises Kidman but opines
of the production, "There is none of the visual sumptuousness, set off by
swirling waltzes and equally swirling camera movement, of the famous
French film version."[15]

The main character of *Traumnovelle*, Fridolin, is a doctor, and he is married to Albertine.[16] At the beginning of the book, Fridolin and Albertine, who are saying good night to their young daughter, are anxious to continue a conversation they were having about the masquerade ball for Carnival they attended the previous day. The film, in contrast, begins with the couple—now Bill and Alice, who live in late-twentieth-century New York City—getting ready to leave for a Christmas party. Bill and Alice are played by Tom Cruise and Nicole Kidman, who were married when the film was made. The party is thrown by a wealthy friend and patient of Bill, Victor Ziegler, and the event allows the audience to assess the marriage of Bill and Alice before any crisis in the narrative. It also introduces the character of Ziegler, an invention of Kubrick and Raphael. Ziegler has been called the only "unambiguously evil" character in the film, because he is involved in a mysterious secret society that must protect at all costs the identities of its members ("If I told you their names—I'm not gonna tell you their names—but if I did, I don't think you'd sleep so well") and because he treats women as objects (he refers to a deceased young woman as "the one with the great tits who OD'd in my bathroom"). This supposedly evil nature is hidden beneath a layer of geniality and a seemingly genuine concern for Bill's safety.[17] James Naremore describes the way Sydney Pollack played the character: "[Pollack] gives the impression of an intelligent, kindly and rather earthy father-figure, and his performance creates a disjunction between the character's outward charm and actual corruption."[18] Michel Chion adds Ziegler to Kubrick's collection of flawed father figures alongside the drill sergeant in *Full Metal Jacket*, Humbert Humbert in *Lolita*, Jack Torrance in *The Shining*, and General Broulard in *Paths of Glory*.[19] Sydney Pollack was not the first choice for the role; Kubrick had originally envisioned Harvey Keitel for Ziegler, a choice that might have made Ziegler's questionable nature a bit more readable. Harvey Keitel has often played criminals or corrupt men (Mr. White in *Reservoir Dogs* and the title role *Bad Lieutenant*—both from the 1990s—leap to mind) in his film career, while Sydney Pollack is best known as a director. In fact, Pollack directed one of Tom Cruise's biggest successes from the 1990s, *The Firm*.

The film takes place at Christmastime, and Kubrick makes the most of Christmas lights for the lighting design. The effect is similar to the one in *Barry Lyndon*, in which faces are often illuminated by candles, a source of light that creates a soft glow. There is no definite motive for this change, although Raphael mentions writing parts of his first draft during the Christmas season. The Christmas lighting did have a great technical advantage in that the ubiquity of the light source in certain scenes allowed the camera operator free range of movement. The curtains of gold lights at Ziegler's party and Millich's shop might also be a reference to the sometimes-erotic artwork of Gustav Klimt. who had a "Golden Phase" in his artwork and who lived in Vienna at the same time as Schnitzler and Freud.[20]

The addition of Christmas to the film narrative, and the deletion of any reference to Judaism, is another thing that makes the film a bit different from the source material. There are a few places where Schnitzler made reference to Jews or Judaism in *Traumnovelle*. At one point in the story, Fridolin is menaced by a group of anti-Semitic fraternity boys, and Nachtigall (Nightingale in translation, Nick Nightingale in the movie), the piano player, is identified as Jewish. When Fridolin first runs into him by chance, Nightingale talks to him in what Schnitzler describes as "a soft Polish accent that had a moderate Jewish twang."[21] And as Fridolin remembers details about his friend, Schnitzler goes on to describe a man who was "the son of a Jewish tavern owner in a small Polish town," who had "left home early and had come to Vienna in order to study medicine." While still a student he played music in some fashionable homes, but this ended when he had an altercation with one of his hosts. After an affront, the host, "outraged, though himself a Jew, hurled a common insult at [Nightingale]." Nightingale responded with a slap to the host's face, effectively ending his career playing in fashionable homes.[22]

Because he was to update the story to modern-day New York, screenwriter Raphael believed he could preserve these Jewish references but, according to him, Kubrick did not agree. "He wanted Fridolin to be a Harrison Fordish goy and forbade any reference to Jews." In fact, Raphael explains that Bill and Alice's last name, Harford, could be a shortened version of "Harrison Ford."[23] Part of Kubrick's desire to make the characters non-Jews might have come simply from his desire to cast specifically Cruise and Kidman in the roles of Bill and Alice.[24] It is interesting that the only character "coded as Jewish" is Victor Ziegler,[25] the morally ambiguous character who is the flawed father figure, or perhaps even Bill's shadowy doppelganger. Regardless of these readings, Ziegler is most certainly the character who "represents the economic and political power elite."[26]

Despite its lack of reference to Kubrick's familial heritage, *Eyes Wide Shut* can be read as an intensely personal story for Kubrick. James Naremore outlines some of the connections between the film and the life of the director: the Harfords' apartment resembles the New York apartment where the Kubricks lived in the 1960s; Christiane's paintings decorate the walls of the Harford home (as do works by daughter Katharina Kubrick Hobbs); and Nicole Kidman's glasses and hairstyle seem to resemble those of Christiane. There are also numerous in-jokes in the film. At one point, Alice watches a film on television that was directed by Paul Mazursky, who played Sidney in Kubrick's very first feature, *Fear and Desire*. Bill buys a newspaper from an uncredited Emilio D'Alessandro, Kubrick's chauffeur and assistant. The name Leon Vitali shows up in the newspaper article Bill reads in Sharky's café; Vitali, after playing the adult Lord Bullingdon in *Barry Lyndon*, became one of Kubrick's trusted assistants.[27] The story in the paper covers the death of ex–beauty queen Amanda Curran, whom Bill believes to be the mysterious woman who "redeems" him at the masked ball. In the article, it says:

> After being hired for a series of magazine ads for London fashion de-
> signer Leon Vitali, rumors began circulating of an affair between the
> two. Soon after her hiring, Vitali empire insiders were reporting that
> their boss adored Curran—not for how she wore his stunning clothes in
> public, but for how she wowed him by taking them off in private, seduc-
> tive, performances.

Leon Vitali also acts in the film; he plays the authoritative masked man in the red cloak at the masked ball.

*Eyes Wide Shut* also recalls *Killer's Kiss*, the only other Kubrick film that takes place in New York City, Kubrick's hometown. Both take place over three days, and both films are love stories of a sort featuring couples whose destiny hangs in the balance until the very last moment. There are other little details as well. At the beginning, people in an apartment are getting dressed to go out. Also, Nick Nightingale supposedly goes back to his family in Seattle, just as Davey was preparing to do in *Killer's Kiss*.[28] Ciment interprets the relationship between the two films a little differently, calling *Eyes Wide Shut* a "pentimento" for *Killer's Kiss*. A pentimento, from the Italian word for "repent," is a change in a painting that shows the artist has re-thought a particular part of the image. We know a change has been made because there is evidence of the original, like a sketch underneath the paint or something that has been painted over. In 1953, just after finishing *Fear and Desire*, Kubrick spoke about shooting "A 'Love Story of New York'" that would use locations from all over the city. Whether that idea turned into *Killer's Kiss*, we cannot be sure, nor can we know if Kubrick felt like *Eyes Wide Shut* was a "do-over" for the earlier film, but it is an interesting theory.

Production on *Eyes Wide Shut* took an unusually long time, even for Kubrick. Some reports say that the film was in production for four hundred days—a record for a live-action film.[29] Although because Kubrick preferred—as Harlan explains—"to put his money into time, having as few people as possible on set," Kubrick often worked with a skeleton crew, which greatly lowered production costs on a day-to-day basis.

An interesting side note: in searching Kubrick's motives for making a story with such an important focus on sex, Raphael recalls Kubrick telling him about a conversation the director had with Terry Southern (screenwriter for *Dr. Strangelove*) about making a "blue movie with name actors and great photography." In 1970, Terry Southern penned a novel called *Blue Movie*, in which a famous genius auteur, Boris Adrian (who goes by "B"), directs an expensive pornographic film with established movie stars. Many have assumed that the character of "B" is based on Kubrick, and indeed Southern describes "B" thusly: "Although he was thought of as a 'director' he was really a *film-maker*—in the tradition of Chaplin, Bergman, Fellini—an artist whose responsibility for his work was total, and his control of it complete."[30] The book's dedication reads: "To the great Stanley K."

## CENSORSHIP

Kubrick was no stranger to controversy during his career. Kubrick was the first major filmmaker to attempt an adaptation of *Lolita*; he pulled *A Clockwork Orange* from theaters in England after reports of copycat crimes; he subjected global politics to brutal satire in *Dr. Strangelove*. *Eyes Wide Shut*, likewise, was not without controversy. In the original U.S. version, in order to garner an R rating from the Motion Picture Association of America, Warner Bros. had to digitally add figures into the masked ball sequence to obscure some sexual acts. Jan Harlan explains that Kubrick would likely have changed the scenes himself rather than having Warner Bros. do it for him. Had he lived, Kubrick would have likely shifted the focus from the participants to Bill and the other voyeurs.

If the alterations had not been made, the film would probably have gotten an NC-17 rating, which would have limited possibilities for distribution. The version available on DVD in the United States does not have the digital figures, and no such alterations were needed in international theatrical versions. There was also a complaint from the American Hindus Against Defamation citing the use of a sacred chant in the masked ball scene (see below). When the film was released on DVD, there were a few other minor alterations, including Nicole Kidman's redubbing of a line from "we made love," to "you and I made love," to make it clear she was talking about her husband and not someone else.

## CHOOSING MUSIC

Music, as one might expect, is a very important part of the film. In *Eyes Wide Shut*, Kubrick, as he had in earlier films like *2001*, gave music the important job of conveying information, making it as important as dialogue or the voice in carrying the story.[31] The dialogue is, at times, banal, perhaps purposefully so. And the parroting of lines slows down the rhythm of the words said by the characters. Bill in particular repeats the things that people say to him, as when Ziegler says, "I had you followed," and Bill replies, "You had me followed?" Music also signifies Kubrick's presence in a way because the audience has come to expect more from his musical choices than those of other directors.[32] In *Eyes Wide Shut*, music shows us Bill and Alice's idealized marriage, rather than one that has trouble brewing under the surface; music points to those times when Bill is feeling fearful; and music underpins Alice's dreams and fantasies. Kubrick again chose a piece by Ligeti for the score, the second movement of *Musica Ricercata*, marking the composer's third appearance in a Kubrick film. There is also a brief excerpt from the "Rex tremendae" from Mozart's Requiem, *Nuages gris*, a piano piece by Liszt, and a waltz by Russian composer Dmitri Shostakovich. There are also jazz standards and Chris Isaak's bluesy "Baby Did a Bad, Bad Thing." Kubrick also worked with contemporary composer and violist Jocelyn Pook.

### SOUNDTRACK

The commercially available soundtrack to *Eyes Wide Shut* featured many of the pieces used in the film. The first music heard in the film, Shostakovich's Waltz for Variety Orchestra, is actually the second track on the CD. The first track on the CD is a piece that has come to be very closely associated with the film: the second movement from Ligeti's *Musica Ricercata*. This stark piano piece caught viewers' attention and is, in some ways, the anthem of the film. The version of Jocelyn Pook's "Naval Officer" on the soundtrack features a solo cello that Pook did not use in the film version, because it would have been too distracting. Track 9, "Migrations," has been the source of some controversy because it appears at the masked ball—as Bill roams from room to room watching various couples and threesomes engage in sex acts—and it features the recitation of a verse from the sacred Hindu text, the Bhagavad Gita (part of the Mahabharata). In a letter to Warner Bros. in August of 1999, the American Hindus Against Defamation protested the use of the *shloka* (recitation) in the film saying, "there appears to be no connection, or apparent justification for the use of this *shloka*." The letter also translates the verse "paritranaya sadhunam, vinasaya ca duskritam, dharma-samstapanarthaya, sambhavami yuge yuge," as "For the protection of the virtuous, for the destruction of the evil and for the firm establishment of Dharma [righteousness], I take birth and am incarnated on Earth, from age to age."[33] Although Warner Bros. did not make any changes in the U.S. theatrical version (they cut the chanting from the UK version, which was released after the U.S. version), they removed the chanting from all DVD releases. All recordings of the soundtrack, however, seem to have the chanted excerpt. A complete listing of the cues on the soundtrack are as follows:

1. Musica Ricercata, II (Mesto, rigido e cerimoniale)—György Ligeti (performed by Dominic Harlan)
2. Waltz 2 From Jazz Suite [sic]—Dmitri Shostakovich (Riccardo Chailly and the Royal Concertgebouw Orchestra)
3. Baby Did a Bad, Bad Thing—Chris Isaak
4. When I Fall in Love—The Victor Silvester Orchestra (Victor Young and Edward Heyman)
5. I Got it Bad (and That Ain't Good)—Oscar Peterson Trio (Duke Ellington and Paul Francis Webster)
6. Naval Officer—Jocelyn Pook
7. The Dream—Jocelyn Pook
8. Masked Ball—Jocelyn Pook
9. Migrations—Jocelyn Pook
10. If I Had You—Roy Gerson (Shapiro, Campbell, and Connelly)
11. Strangers in the Night—the Peter Hughes Orchestra (Snyder, Singleton, and Kaempfert)
12. Blame It on My Youth—Brad Mehldau (Oscar Levant and Edward Heyman)
13. Grey Clouds [Nuages Gris]—Franz Liszt (performed by Dominic Harlan)
14. Musica Ricercata, II (Mesto, rigido e cerimoniale) [Reprise]

Even late in his career, Kubrick's musical collaborations retained some of the expected interactions between director and composer: Kubrick asked for a cue; the composer brought him some music; Kubrick made suggestions to help the cue fit the scene better. What sets Kubrick apart, of course, are two things: first one may assume, based on the sheer number of cues composed for *The Shining*, that Kubrick required a rather large number of musical options from which to choose, more perhaps than a composer would be expected to produce on another director's film; second, and most important, Kubrick might ask for cues without showing the composer any film. Kubrick asked Carlos (on *The Shining*) and Pook to write music without showing them footage. Without the opportunity to "spot" the film for the music, Carlos and Pook essentially scored their cues "blind," and once Kubrick heard something he liked, he worked with the cues the same way he worked with the music of Beethoven or Mozart.[34] The composers were of course free to do whatever they wished with the unused cues.

The pieces Kubrick chose are only part of the story; Kubrick's unused choices are interesting as well. Kubrick, at one point, thought he might use a song from Richard Wagner's set of songs, the Wesendonck Lieder. Wagner, of course, is best known as an opera composer, and almost none of his non-operatic works are still performed today with the exceptions of the instrumental piece *Siegfried's Idyll* and the Wesendonck Lieder. The set was published in the late 1850s under the title *Fünf Gedichte von Mathilde Wesendonck für eine Frauenstimmen und Klavier* (*Five Songs by Mathilde Wesendonck for Female Singer and Piano*). The five songs are (in English translation) "The Angel," "Stand Still!," "In the Greenhouse," "Sorrows," and "Dreams." Both "In the Greenhouse" and "Dreams" were what Wagner called "Studies" on musical themes he would use in his opera *Tristan und Isolde*. "In the Greenhouse," Kubrick's choice for *Eyes Wide Shut*, was the last of the songs to be written. Jan Harlan describes Kubrick's choice:

> Something that might interest you, because really nobody knows, we had a variation of the piano accompaniment of "In the Greenhouse" (for soprano), and he loved it. Forget the singer. We had the piano accompaniment. It was transparent and we tried different variations. So for a year, he had this piece of music again and again through the film.

The choice of the Wesendonck Lieder would have been perfect for the film in terms of the music's historical context. Although Kubrick was unaware of the history behind the song cycle—he didn't really care to know, and besides, he didn't think that highly of Wagner as a person[35]—he intended to use it for about a year before tossing it out.

At the time Wagner composed the cycle, he was living on a small house on the property of the Wesendoncks, a wealthy husband and wife who supported Wagner's work. Wagner, who had been living in Dresden with his wife Minna, had become part of a revolutionary group who staged an uprising in 1849. The May Uprising was quashed, and Wagner fled. He settled eventually in Zurich, but endured difficulties both health related and financial. He continued to write operas and essays, and in 1852 met Otto Wesendonck and his wife Mathilde. Wagner appears to have been enchanted both by Mathilde's personality and her poetry. He stopped working on the Ring Cycle (his massive, four-opera epic) in order to focus on a story of forbidden love, *Tristan und Isolde*, and a set of songs using Mathilde's poetry. (*Die Walküre*, one of the Ring Cycle operas, does owe some inspiration to Mathilde, as Wagner made notes in his manuscript to her, especially in scenes between the destined lovers, Sigmund and Sieglinde.)[36] Details about an affair between Wagner and Wesendonck are scant, although whatever did transpire between them happened under the noses of both Wagner's wife and Mathilde's husband. To whatever extent the two were involved, the "affair" ended after Minna intercepted a package meant for Mathilde and read the eight-page letter Wagner had attached. Although the letter says nothing specifically incriminating, Minna's interpretation of the letter was damning enough.[37] Wagner's professional relationship with both Wesendoncks continued, however, and both parties appear to have been influenced favorably in their art by the experience. Jan Harlan describes that Kubrick ultimately decided not to use it: "Maybe six weeks before he died, he tossed it out, because he thought it was too beautiful, so he used the biting Ligeti piece. Dominic [Harlan] recorded it because Stanley wanted the hammering."

Once again, Kubrick demonstrated that his highest priority was finding music that worked for the film. Its historical context didn't matter, and even if something pushed the boundaries of being chronologically acceptable—like the 1930s tunes at the 1920s party in *The Shining* or the Romantic Schubert piece in the Classical time period of *Barry Lyndon*—he was willing to make those concessions if the music fit the scene best. And in the case of the Wagner piece, Kubrick put aside his own feelings for the work, and Harlan seemed to admire Kubrick's uncompromising way of doing what was best for the narrative:

> This is someone who lives in the cutting room for a year with the Wesendonck lieder, and then kicks it out although he loves it. He didn't

love the Ligeti in the same way, but he loved it for the narrative. The
Ligeti had the biting element of jealousy and sexual fantasy, which is the
poison in almost all relationships. It ruins you.[38]

From Harlan's comments, we might assume that "In the Greenhouse" was
going to be used instead of Ligeti's *Musica Ricercata*, perhaps all five times
that it was used, but we cannot be certain of that. In the end, Kubrick's
choice was the right choice, as the Ligeti piece made a huge impression
on filmgoers, appearing in a trailer and TV spots advertising the film and
becoming indelibly intertwined with *Eyes Wide Shut*.


## ECHOES OF BEETHOVEN

The music of Beethoven does not appear in the film, but the composer
does make an important cameo appearance in *Eyes Wide Shut*. In Schnitzler's book, the password to the party is "Denmark," which is incidentally
where Albertine had seen the man with whom she was willing to be
unfaithful (as she describes to Fridolin). In the film, instead of making
the password Cape Cod, which is where Alice is tempted by the naval
officer, Kubrick (and Raphael, perhaps) chose the name of Beethoven's
only opera, *Fidelio*. The opera is a rescue story in which a wife, Leonore,
saves her husband from certain death because of her loyalty both to him
and to his political beliefs. To this end, Leonore dresses up as a boy
named Fidelio so that she can work at the prison where her husband is
being held. The opera idealizes marriage and the conjugal bond, something Beethoven hoped desperately for but never experienced. The name
"Fidelio" has symbolic meaning as well because it is derived from the
word "fedele," or "faithful."


### Minor/Major Seconds

There is a musical gesture that seems to link together some of Kubrick's
musical choices, and that is the interval of the second. A second is simply an interval that goes from a pitch to its neighbor. A minor second is
a half step, the smallest distance one can travel on a piano and still go
somewhere. The Ligeti piece *Musica Ricercata* (second movement) is
based on the minor second between E-sharp and F-sharp. Jocelyn Pook's
"Migrations" likewise begins with a minor second, this time between D
and E-flat. Pook says the use of the particular interval at the beginning of

the piece is a "complete coincidence," but the coincidence, unintentional though it may have been, links the music together in an almost subliminal way. The major second covers the distance of a whole step, and it is an interval we can hear at the beginning of "Strangers in the Night" and in the backward voice of "Masked Ball."[39]

## Shostakovich: Waltz 2 from Suite for Variety Orchestra

Appearances:

0:00:00–0:01:45 Opening credits; Bill and Alice get ready for Ziegler's party
0:20:43–0:22:19 Bill and Alice's daily activities
2:33:27–2:38:46 (End) Closing credits

The first music heard in the film is a waltz arranged by Russian composer Dmitri Shostakovich. It is part of an eight-movement work that has been collected from some of his works including the film scores. Shostakovich wrote many film scores, beginning with music intended for live performance with the silent film *New Babylon* in 1929. From then on, he wrote perhaps one or two scores a year until 1941. When the Nazis invaded Russia in 1941, Shostakovich's duties as a composer for the state took up most of his time, and he composed patriotic music—including his Seventh Symphony—for the cause. He started writing film music again in 1944 and continued writing scores until 1970. The eight-movement Suite for Variety Orchestra appears to use music from films from the 1940s and 1950s, like 1940's *The Adventures of Korzinkina* (from which the first and last movements from the suite are drawn), *The Gadfly* (1955), and *The First Echelon* (1956), which is the source of the waltz in *Eyes Wide Shut*. The suite was performed publicly for the first time outside of Russia in London in 1988.[40]

On Riccardo Chailly and the Royal Concertgebouw Orchestra's recording *Shostakovich: The Jazz Album*, the Suite for Variety Orchestra is misnamed Jazz Suite No. 2, but in fact the actual Jazz Suite No. 2—a three-movement work written in the late 1930s—was lost.[41] However, in 1999, piano sketches for Jazz Suite No. 2 were discovered, and in 2000 British composer Gerard McBurney used the sketches to produce a fully orchestrated version of the piece.

Kubrick had chosen the Waltz 2 from Suite for Variety Orchestra for *Eyes Wide Shut* long before the first frame was shot, and it appears three times in the film. It accompanies the opening credits and bookends the film by appearing over the closing credits as well. In its first appearance, Bill and Alice get ready for Ziegler's party. In between credit cards, Alice appears naked as she tries on and rejects a dress. The waltz plays under the couple's conversation, and although it seems like it's part of the score, it turns out to be sourced from a stereo on-screen when Bill turns it off as they leave for the party. This is a narrative sleight of hand that shows how permeable the boundary is between the Harfords' reality and the reality of the film experience wherein a scene is scored with music.[42] Bill will switch off music again, later, in a scene with a prostitute.

The choice to call the film *Eyes Wide Shut* might seem puzzling, but there is a clue to its meaning as it pertains to the narrative at hand. In this opening scene, Alice asks Bill, "Is my hair okay?" to which he answers, "It's great." But Alice correctly notes that he's "not even looking at it." In marriage, familiarity—as evidenced by Bill's presence in the bathroom while Alice uses the toilet—can lead to a couple becoming blind to each other. Michel Chion also suggests that the title is a reference to dreaming as "a dreamer's eyes are at once both open and shut."[43]

Its second appearance accompanies a montage of Bill and Alice's daily activities. Bill works in his office, seeing patients. He seems to be a general practitioner because he sees patients of different ages and seems to be treating a wide variety of ailments. Again there is nudity: one of the patients—a beautiful young woman—appears topless during an exam, and Alice again appears naked as she gets dressed. Alice eats breakfast with Helena, the Harfords' daughter, who is watching a Warner Bros. cartoon. (The scene calls to mind Wendy and Danny at the beginning of *The Shining*.) Alice also helps Helena get ready, wraps Christmas presents, and sits down with Bill in the evening as he watches a football game. This is the Bill and Alice the world sees: he's a successful doctor and she's the perfect wife and mother. The music represents the image Bill and Alice "like to have of themselves, that they would like us to have of them."[44] The waltz fades out—replaced by the sounds of the football game on the television—after Helena goes to bed. Their perfect image takes a hit when Alice rolls a joint from some marijuana she has hidden in a Band-Aid container in the medicine cabinet, and it is further damaged—perhaps irreparably?—when Alice confesses that she was tempted by a man on their vacation.

The waltz finally reappears over the final credits, suggesting that Bill and Alice have reached a détente, in which they are willing to put indiscretions behind them and move forward together. Alice says, "The important thing is we're awake now, and hopefully for a long time to come." In their final exchange, Alice says, "And you know, there is something very important that we need to do as soon as possible." Bill asks what that is, and Alice answers simply, with one word: "Fuck." Kubrick leaves a few seconds of silence before bringing the waltz back and starting the credit sequence.

### Chris Isaak: "Baby Did a Bad, Bad Thing"

Appearance:

0:19:49–0:20:42 After Ziegler's party, the Harfords begin to kiss in front of their bedroom mirror

Chris Isaak released the song "Baby Did a Bad, Bad Thing" on the 1995 album *Forever Blue*. The song gained notoriety because of its risqué video featuring model Laetitia Casta and Chris Isaak. Kubrick chose the song early on, and it appeared in advertisements for the film. Isaak's lyrics are written from the point of view of someone whose lover appears not to care about hurting him.

After Ziegler's party, Alice is standing naked in front of a mirror in the bedroom, taking off her earrings. The song appears to be sourced onscreen because Alice seems to move to the beat. Bill comes up to her and begins kissing her neck. Alice removes her glasses, but still watches herself in the mirror as Bill kisses her. At the beginning of the scene, we see Alice's bottom from behind and her breasts in the mirror, but by the time Bill enters the frame, the camera has tightened in on the scene, and we do not see Bill's bottom. The gaze seems to be aimed at Alice here—even her own gaze, as Bill ends up half-hidden by his wife.

### The Music of Jocelyn Pook

Jocelyn Pook's musical background includes classical training, but she has also collaborated with pop artists, choral artists, and dance companies. It was the choreographer for the masked ball sequence in *Eyes Wide Shut*, Yolande Snaith, who brought Jocelyn Pook's music to a rehearsal, specifically her "Backwards Priests."[45] Once Kubrick heard the piece—music critic Mike Zwerin characterized it as sounding like "medieval punk"—a track from Pook's album *Deluge*, he knew that the composer would be right for the film. According to Pook, Kubrick got in touch with her the very day he first heard her music. They spoke on the phone, he asked her for samples of her work, and just a couple of hours later, a car came to pick up the cassette she had compiled. The next day, the car returned to pick her up. At their meeting, Kubrick played some of the music that he had chosen for the film, including Liszt's piano piece *Nuages Gris*. Once Kubrick had decided to hire Pook for the film, "we got to work immediately," she says. "I was writing music well before a single frame of film was shot. He would describe the atmosphere of the scene to me, filling in some specific details, and then I would go away and write. When I had a completed demo, I'd come back and we'd discuss it."[46] Kubrick ended up with four pieces by Pook: "Masked Ball" (a reworking of "Backwards Priests"), "Migrations," "Naval Officer," and "The Dream."

"He delighted in music, and had so much respect for musicians," Pook says, noting one of her first impressions of the director. Aware of Kubrick's unique use of music in his films—especially *2001*—Pook was at first intimidated; but in the end she found Kubrick extremely personable, "even fatherly." Since Kubrick stayed close to home, Pook recalls that he would invite musicians to perform concerts, like small salons, in his home. In that way, music came to him. In the years since *Eyes Wide Shut*, Pook has been involved in many film projects, still performs with various groups, and still writes music for the concert hall, even composing a commission for Queen Elizabeth II's Diamond Jubilee festivities in 2012.

## Pook: "Naval Officer"

Appearances:

0:31:44–0:36:20 Alice tells Bill about the naval officer
0:37:22–0:37:49 While in a taxi to the judge's house, Bill imagines Alice with the naval officer
0:45:37–0:45:59 Bill walks through the city and thinks about Alice and the naval officer
1:08:51–1:09:14 In a taxi to Somerton, Bill imagines Alice with the naval officer

When Alice tells Bill about the first time she saw the naval officer in Cape Cod, her description is accompanied by this cue. The harmonies move slowly at first, and Kubrick allows Alice's voice to be the most important sound. Bill listens, the illusion of his secure world shattering around him in his silence. The layers that the instruments create move in and out of dissonance. Pook's cue works under the surface, the rich sounds of the string instruments underpinning the monologue. The conversation is interrupted by a phone call, and Bill is called away to visit the family of a patient who has just died. When he leaves Alice, his own sexual adventure is beginning, and he is urged on by the jealous feelings he has about Alice's story. In a taxi on the way to his patient's house, he imagines what it might have been like if Alice had actually slept with the naval officer. It's his fantasy of her fantasy because Bill isn't imagining something that actually happened; he's imagining what Alice thought, or perhaps what might have happened. The music accompanies Bill's fantasy. After leaving the judge's house (and Marion, who just professed for love for Bill and kissed him), he walks through the streets, obviously still troubled by his wife's story. After seeing a couple on the street kissing, Bill imagines Alice and the officer together, kissing, his hand wandering down between her bare legs. Bill claps his hands in anger, as if willing the mental movie to stop, and the music stops at his command.

Pook is a violist by training, and for this work she chose strings for the instrumentation. Part of this ostensibly came from her level of comfort with these instruments, but she has also said that although she wanted to use an oboe or a horn, the texture didn't seem to work best for the scenes.[47] Chion called the work "beautiful, mysterious."[48] In an interview, Pook explained that the strings allowed the music to be more unobtrusive: "[The cue] had to be quite subliminal, quite low in the mix in the end with these sections. I actually added the solo cello for the CD version of 'Naval Officer,' which I couldn't use in the film version because it was too intrusive."[49] In the film, certain voices rise out of the texture, like that of a single violin or viola, or a pair of instruments playing a melodic line, while the other strings undulate a throbbing accompaniment.

## Pook: "The Dream"

Appearances:

1:33:42–1:38:25 Alice tells Bill of the dream she was having when he woke her up

1:47:34–1:47:53 Bill sits in his office during the day and imagines Alice with the naval officer

1:54:01–1:54:47 Bill sits in his office at night and thinks about Alice with the naval officer

Musically speaking, Pook's cue "The Dream" has a lot in common with "Naval Officer." This similarity was by design as the two fantasies are both written for Alice. They connect to each other and to the life of her imagination. This cue is somewhat more troubled and tense than the music of "Naval Officer." There are still undulating lines, seemingly echoing the earlier cue, but there are more pronounced dissonances and downward glissandos in the strings that seem to add to a sense of foreboding. As Alice says, "I was fucking other men," the music swells in the higher strings, and a sinuous melody emerges in the solo cello before the cue fades down into underscore again. The music is replaced by the sound of street noise in the next scene.

A brief excerpt of the piece appears as Bill sits in his office thinking about Alice and the naval officer. Again, his jealous feelings spur him on to action. He has not yet consummated any kind of affair yet, but he is also concerned about the woman in the headdress from the previous night's masked ball. At Bill's mock trial, she offered herself in Bill's place, and he is concerned that something has happened to her. He cancels his afternoon appointments and drives his own car back to Somerton. Later that day, Bill returns to the office, and he again sees the image of Alice having sex with the naval officer. A short excerpt of music, about forty seconds, accompanies this image of Alice and the officer having sex with the officer on top, and Alice underneath, seemingly crying out in ecstasy. The fantasy inspires Bill to call Marion, the judge's daughter. We do not know what he was planning because Marion's fiancé answers and Bill hangs up the phone.

### Pook: "Masked Ball"

Appearance:

1:11:54–1:18:22 Nick Nightingale is seen and heard playing this at the beginning of the masked ball

This piece features chords in the strings combined with a recording of a Romanian priest reciting a part of a liturgy. The priest's recitation is played backward. There is also an insistent driving rhythm low in the mix early in the cue. This is, in fact, Pook's "Backwards Priests," the piece that Kubrick heard Yolande Snaith play at the rehearsal. The exoticism of both this work and "Migrations," which follows right afterward, adds to the feeling that Bill is somewhere decidedly new and different. There is also something dreamlike about the music and Bill's observation of this ritual.[50] Pook had offered Kubrick a number of additional options instead of this piece, but in the end, nothing fit better than what he first heard.

Nick Nightingale appears to be playing this piece on a synthesizer, although it was performed with actual strings. The backward voice is "activated" by a sampler that Nick can reach to his left. In order to make sure

Nick's movements matched the music, Kubrick shot and edited the scene to the cue. During the ritual that Bill observes, women wearing cloaks and masks kneel in a circle. A red-clad figure in the center of the circle, who holds an incense censer, taps his staff on the floor, signaling the women to bow and then return to a kneeling position. Standing and shedding their robes simultaneously, they reveal that they each wear only a mask, a thong, and high-heeled shoes. They again kneel, and each masked woman "kisses" the woman to her right in the circle. At this moment, Pook's music becomes more dramatic. A new, higher voice recites faster in a more singing manner, and the pitches of the sustained chords become higher as well. A masked man watching the proceedings from a level above nods at Bill, who nods back. The red figure, called Red Cloak in the credits, then signals individual women to leave the circle. A woman in a large feathered headdress leaves the circle and goes to Bill. As they walk away from the ritual, new music begins. There is little eroticism to this scene, as the nude women are almost like statues rather than real women; the masks further distance them from the audience. In this scene and the scenes that follow, Kubrick achieves tableaux that bring to mind Hieronymous Bosch's triptych *The Garden of Earthly Delights*.

The presence of synthesizer and sampler might seem at odds with the ritualistic manner of the masked ball. Why not an organ or a grand piano? Why modern, electronic instruments? Obviously, Kubrick had to figure out how to show a source for his chosen piece and had to give Nick something to do, especially because the only reason that Bill is there is because Nick "just plays the piano" at these events. Perhaps, the party-goers care only that the music works for the situation, not necessarily that it is "authentic" in any way. One analysis put it this way: "The emphasis on modernity lends credence to the idea that this is really just a bunch of super rich white men getting their ya yas on with little interest in historical context or implications of their actions."[51]

## Pook: "Migrations"

Appearance:

1:18:23–1:22:45 Bill wanders around the party, watching people engaging in sexual activity

The work, newly composed for the film, begins in the film with the vocalization of a female singer. The opening of the cue features a minor second that seems to prefigure Ligeti's *Music Ricercata, II*, which will soon

be heard. The mysterious woman in the large feathered headdress urges
Bill to leave the party. After she goes away with another person, drums enter the cue, giving it a rhythmic drive, and Manickam Yogeswaran's vocals
enter. Yogeswaran's vocals had actually been recorded for a different piece,
but Pook appropriated them for the "Migrations" cue and found that they
fit rather well.[52] Bill walks through various rooms in the mansion, watching
couples and threesomes engaging in various sexual activities. The figures
watching the couples and threesomes are quite still, almost as if they are
mannequins, or figures in a painting. Unlike music that cues the audience
emotionally, this piece is more part of the setting. The use of the Indian
singing—which includes the *shloka* from the Bhagavad Gita (present only
on the soundtrack)—lends a feeling of exoticism that seems to refer to the
newness of the experience for Bill. Pook called it a "counter layer" to the actions on-screen.[53] The woman in the headdress reappears, leading Bill away
into a different room, where the music changes to "Strangers in the Night."

### Peter Hughes Orchestra: "Strangers in the Night"

Appearance:

1:22:39–1:24:11 A masked woman urges Bill to leave the masked ball;
    Nick is led away

The woman in the headdress again urges Bill to leave because he
is in danger, but he asks her to come with him. "That's impossible," she
says. He wants to see her face, but she refuses to show him and warns
him one more time to leave before she walks away. A man in a gold mask
tells Bill that his taxi driver is waiting for him and leads him away. At the
same time, Nick is being led—blindfolded—through a dance floor, where
couples, some of them same-sex, are dancing to the song. The song is
heard the loudest where the dance floor is, but there is no visible source
for the music. The song is heard as if from a distance, as Bill walks down
a hallway. At the end of the hallway, the music stops, as Bill sees some
sort of tribunal set up for him.

### The Delvets: "I Want a Boy for Christmas"

Appearance:

1:39:18–1:41:08 Bill searches for Nick

The obscure all-girl doo-wop group the Delvets (also spelled Delvetts) recorded "I Want a Boy for Christmas" in 1961 for George Goldner's label End Records. They issued two 45s both featuring the same A side, "Repeat after Me." One of the B sides was "Will You Still Love Me in Heaven," an answer to the Shirelles' much bigger hit "Will You Still Love Me Tomorrow." On the other 45 release, the B side was "I Want a Boy for Christmas."

The morning after the masked ball, as Bill searches for Nick, he returns to the Sonata Café, only to find it closed. He goes to the diner next door and orders a coffee. He asks the waitress if she knows Nick, adding, "It's very important that I get in touch with him this morning." She knows where he's staying, but tells Bill only after he confides that he's looking for Nick because of a "medical matter." Here is a song that comments on the narrative. Bill is looking for Nick, and the music says, "I Want a Boy for Christmas."

Some have also read into this song a veiled reference to homosexuality or gay subtext in the narrative.[54] Earlier in the film, Bill is accused by a group of frat boys of playing for the "pink team," and in the scene immediately following the scene in Gillespie's, Bill goes to the hotel and asks the man at the hotel to ring for Nick. The desk clerk, played by Alan Cumming, appears to be flirting with Bill, peppering his conversation with innuendo. When he describes the two men who came in with Nick at 4:30 in the morning, he says they were "big guys" and holds his hands out, palms facing inward, in a gesture that is often used to illustrate the length of something.

## Ziegler's Party Music

There are two "parties" in *Eyes Wide Shut*. There is Ziegler's fancy Christmas party, and there is the masked ball that Bill infiltrates. There is something parallel to these two parties. The first is polite, full of upper-class people who exchange niceties, but lust and dishonesty seethe under the surface. Ziegler—whose wife we see at the beginning of the party—appears with an unconscious naked young woman whose name he can barely remember. An older man propositions Alice, and two young women flirt with Bill, attempting to take him somewhere, but we never find out where (one of Ziegler's assistants asks Bill to help with the unconscious woman). At the second party, lust is now overt, a central theme of this ritualistic "celebration." So, although everyone is in masks at the second party, the partygoers' true intention is unmasked.[55]

At Ziegler's party, the music consists of instrumental versions of standards. For the film viewer who is familiar with this genre of songs, the game becomes hearing the tune well enough to identify the title and then noticing how appropriate the title is for the situation. In all of his films, Kubrick tended not to play these kinds of games, but sometimes the choice of song is so perfect, one can't help but think Kubrick was having a laugh. As Alice and Bill dance at the party, their amorous mood is commented on by "I'm in the Mood for Love." (Alice and Bill are not, perhaps, amorous for each other as evidenced by their flirting with other parties in subsequent scenes.) When Alice dances with distinguished older man Sander Szavost, we hear "I Only Have Eyes for You," and "When I Fall in Love." Later, at the second party, the masked ball, everyone wears a mask, and "Strangers in the Night" plays in the background. Ciment calls the placement of these songs "maliciously ironic."[56]

The live band at the party is represented on the soundtrack by the Victor Silvester Orchestra. They play five standards over the entire seventeen-minute party scene. Their first song is "I'm in the Mood for Love" (2:45–4:29). It plays as Alice and Bill arrive at the party and are greeted by Ziegler and his wife, Ilona. Bill and Alice then dance and exchange small talk until Bill recognizes Nick Nightingale playing piano. In between their first and second songs, the band takes a break and what we must imagine is a recording of "It Had to Be You" (played by Tommy Sanderson and the Sandmen) fills in the silence of their break time. In this span—from 4:50 to 7:11—Bill says hello to Nick, and Alice meets Sandor Szavost and the two begin to flirt. A new song begins, ostensibly played by the band (a prominent solo violin is heard, and the bandleader is seen holding a violin when he announces the break). The new song is "Chanson d'Amour" (7:15–10:13). Alice and Sandor continue to flirt while Bill talks to two younger women. As the scene switches to Bill's conversation with Gayle and Nuala, the tune becomes "Old Fashioned Way." During the same song, we return to Alice and Sandor, who is explaining why women get married. A man interrupts Bill's conversation with Gayle and Nuala and leads Bill up to Zieger's bathroom (10:16–13:21).

Shortly after Bill arrives in Ziegler's well-appointed bathroom, "When I Fall in Love" begins to play (13:24–18:35) followed by "I Only Have Eyes for You" (18:38–19:49). During the course of these two songs, we switch back and forth between Alice and Sandor, whose flirting is becoming less hypothetical, and Bill, Ziegler, and Mandy in the bathroom. Bill has been able to wake Mandy, who was unconscious from an overdose.

Ziegler is hoping to get her away from the party as soon as possible, but Bill suggests she stay a little while to recuperate. He also counsels Mandy that she should go to rehab. Before Bill leaves, Ziegler asks him to keep what's happened "just between us," to which Bill answers, "of course." As Alice tries to leave Sandor, he says that he must see her again, but she says, "That's impossible," the same phrase Bill will hear from a mysterious woman at the masked ball. The music of the party cuts suddenly to Chris Isaak's "Baby Did a Bad, Bad Thing."

### Oscar Peterson Trio: "I Got It Bad (and That Ain't Good)"

Appearance:

0:51:12–0:52:22 Domino kisses Bill

This music provides a sourced sonic backdrop for Bill's encounter with the prostitute Domino. Bill has been walking and thinking about his wife's imagined affair with the naval officer. He feels emasculated by her confession, and to add to his humiliation, he is menaced on the street by a group of frat boys who call Bill a "faggot," and a "mary." They knock him down and intimidate him, pretending to be disgusted by him. One of them claims that he is an "exit only" so that Bill will not be attracted to him (assuming of course that the man is talking about his anus). Later when Bill enters the Sonata Café, a large sign reads "All Exits are Final."

It is in this mood that Bill meets Domino, who invites him to her apartment. She is very sweet, and her gentleness disarms him. Once inside her apartment, she asks him "What do you want to do?" and he responds with the question, "What do you recommend?" Domino would "rather not put it into words." They discuss a price, and the scene cuts to Alice at home, eating cookies and milk and watching television. When we return to the scene, Domino kisses Bill, while "I Got It Bad (and That Ain't Good)" plays. Considering that we later find out that Domino is HIV positive, this is rather an appropriate song choice. They don't get any further than one kiss because Alice calls Bill's cell phone and he turns off the music, ostensibly to hide his whereabouts. Bill seems startled by Alice's call, and he tells Domino that he thinks he has to go, although he has made it clear to Alice that he might not be home for a while. He could of course stay, but the moment has passed, and Bill continues on his journey. His next stop is the Sonata Café.

**"If I Had You"**

Appearance:

0:54:59–0:56:17 We hear just the end of this song as Bill enters the So-
    nata Café at the end of Nick's set.

**"Blame It on My Youth"**

Appearance:

0:56:57–1:01:22 Nick and Bill talk in the Sonata Café

This slow instrumental accompanies a conversation between Nick
and Bill. They catch up on their marriages and family, and Nick confesses
that he has another gig that same evening, vaguely explaining that he plays
these kinds of gigs blindfolded. Bill is intrigued. While they are talking,
Nick gets a phone call telling him the password for the party. Nick writes
it on a napkin, aided by Bill, who reads the name, Fidelio, that Nick has
written. "What is this?" Bill asks. "It's the name of a Beethoven opera, isn't
it?" Nick says, finally admitting it's the password. Bill insists that Nick
take him to the party, but Nick is hesitant. He explains that first of all Bill
would need a costume and a mask. The scene then cuts to a taxi pulling
up in front of Rainbow Fashions, Millich's shop.

**Music Ricercata: Ligeti**

1:24:18–1:27:33 Bill is discovered at the masked ball and Red Cloak asks
    for the house password
1:29:07–1:29:34 The woman in the headdress is led away, and Bill asks
    what will happen to her
1:48:59–1:51:56 Bill returns to the mansion the next day only to receive
    a typed letter
2:01:23–2:04:38 Bill notices someone following him
2:05:42–2:06:37 Bill reads about the girl who had the overdose
2:24:04–2:27:35 Bill returns home and finds the mask from the masked
    ball on his pillow next to Alice

*Musica Ricercata* was composed by Ligeti in the early 1950s. At that
time, Ligeti was a professor at the Budapest Academy, where he taught

harmony and analysis. Hungary was one of the Eastern Bloc countries, and as a composer, Ligeti's developing style was at odds with the political climate of Stalinism. In order to maintain his reputation, Ligeti was compelled to create choral arrangements of folk songs.

The ricercar, from which Ligeti named the *Ricercata*, is a type of instrumental work dating from the sixteenth century. In the late Renaissance, the term "ricercar" was used almost interchangeably with other types of improvisatory instrumental pieces like the toccata or the prelude, but later ricercars had one trait that would become the defining characteristic of the form: imitative counterpoint. In the Baroque period, the ricercar would eventually become the fugue, a piece with strict imitative counterpoint based on a musical theme called a subject. In fact, the last movement of Ligeti's *Musica Ricercata* features fugal treatment of the twelve-tone row. Ligeti called this movement "(Omaggio a Girolamo Frescobaldi) Andante misurato e tranquillo." Here Ligeti makes reference to Frescobaldi, an important and influential keyboard composer who died in 1643. The movement is not a strict fugue because it doesn't follow all the conventions of voice leading, but there is plenty of imitative counterpoint. The term "ricercar" also refers to a seeking out, as some ricercars explored key areas or motifs.

*Musica Ricercata* was born into a climate of oppression and fear. Because of the despotism of Hungary at the time, *Musica Ricercata* was an example of "the unexpected, unwanted music that mostly went into [Ligeti's] desk drawer."[57] The work is made up of eleven pieces for solo piano (although versions of this piece have been arranged for wind quintet and for a Russian accordion called a *bayan*). For each of the pieces, Ligeti limits the number of pitches that he can use, and as the set goes on, each new piece has one more possible pitch. The very first piece in the set uses just two tones (and their octave transpositions). The second piece—the only one heard in *Eyes Wide Shut*—has three pitches. The third has four, the fourth has five pitches, and so on. At the end, the eleventh piece in the set, Ligeti uses all twelve tones of the chromatic scale. In the first piece of the set, "Sostenuto—Misurato—Prestissimo," the pitch A is used almost exclusively for the entire piece. Ligeti creates interest by concentrating on rhythmic aspects and by building a large dynamic crescendo. At the end, we finally hear the other note, D. In the second piece, the one heard in the film, the main musical gesture is just a half step from E-sharp to F-sharp. While the first piece in the set seemed almost playful in its rhythmic interest (polyrhythms, gradual acceleration of tempo), the second piece seems more serious and grave. It is marked "Mesto, rigido e

ceremoniale," emphasizing both the rigidity of the music and the ceremo-
nial mood. There are shifting meters and a concentration on using the different ranges of the piano. The first half of the piece consists of the pianist
rocking between the E-sharp and the F-sharp. About halfway through the
movement, after a pause, Ligeti introduces the third pitch, G. These three
pitches may represent Bill's three problems: "temptation, sin, and retribution."[58] Once the G appears, the pianist is directed to accent the new pitch
and repeat it faster and faster until the pianist repeats the pitch as quickly
as he or she can ("Tone repetition as dense as possible"). The E-sharp and
F-sharp return, faster, louder, in the low register. Ligeti marks this section
"Intenso, agitato." The repeated Gs eventually die away and the movement
is over. In *Stanley Kubrick: A Life in Pictures*, Ligeti himself comments on
the piece and its personal meaning: "I was in Stalinist terroristic Hungary
where this kind of music was not allowed, and I just wrote it for myself.
. . . For me, when I composed it, in the year [19]50 . . . it was a knife in
Stalin's heart." The repeated G—the knife in Stalin's heart—often appears
at the point of highest tension. Perhaps it is the hammering of Bill's heart,
or perhaps it arrives when Bill is at his most vulnerable.[59]

   In the first appearance of this movement, Bill is led to the main room
of the mansion where the masked ball takes place under the pretense that
his taxi driver has asked for him. Arriving there, he sees the red-clad figure
sitting in a throne-like chair, flanked by two figures in dark purple robes.
The man in the middle asks Bill to come forward, and as he does the surrounding crowd fills in behind him, trapping him. The man in red asks for
the password, to which Bill replies, "Fidelio." But when the man asks for
the house password, Bill says that he's forgotten it. The murmuring crowd
immediately signals that he has made a mistake, and Bill is asked to take
off his mask and then his clothes. Up to this point, we have heard only
E-sharp and F-sharp, but the entrance of the pitch G begins hammering,
as if it's the panicking heart of Bill. The music continues as Bill attempts
to talk his way out of this. The mysterious woman appears alone on the
second level, and she shouts, "Stop!" The music obeys. She offers herself
in Bill's place, and he is allowed to leave unharmed, so long as he promises
to keep the evening's events silent. An excerpt of the piece is heard again
as the mysterious woman is taken away.

   The second time, it is the next day and Bill returns to the mansion to
find out what happened to the woman. He carefully approaches the locked
gate and sees that a camera is watching him. A car drives down from the
house, and a man gets out. He gives Bill an envelope, and when Bill takes
it, the pitch G emerges and hammers away, as Bill sees that it is his name

typed on the outside of the envelope. The letter tells him to "give up your inquiries" and "consider these words a second warning." The music is replaced by street noise and ostensibly an exterior shot of the Harford home.

After Bill is inspired to meet up with Domino again, only to find out that she's HIV positive, he walks through the streets of Greenwich Village alone. Bill looks back to see a man on the otherwise deserted street. The Ligeti cue begins as he walks, even before he realizes the other man is there. He attempts to hail a cab to escape, but cannot find one. In front of a newsstand, he turns to look at the man following him. It is at this stalemate that the G hammers away. Bill buys a *New York Post* that has the headline "Lucky to Be Alive." Eventually, the man walks away, and Bill takes refuge in a café called Sharky's. Only a minute or so later, the piece returns as Bill opens the paper to read a story called "Ex–beauty queen in hotel drug overdose." The story, easily read in freeze-frame, concerns former Miss New York Amanda Curran (possibly the Mandy from Ziegler's party). There are some glitches in the text, like repeated lines, but it's a fully written story. Amanda's sister Jane is quoted as saying, "The overdose must have been an accident. Mandy and I were as close as sisters can get. If there had been anything wrong, she would have told me." The piece continues as Bill goes to New York Hospital to see her, where she is reportedly in critical condition. In this instance, the piece never gets to the hammering G. Bill feels in control. The music stops when he talks to the receptionist. He finds out that Amanda Curran died at 3:45 that afternoon. Bill is led down to the morgue to see the body.

Finally, the Ligeti cue plays as Bill arrives home, at the end of his odyssey. Alice has placed Bill's mask on the pillow next to her, but when he gets home he doesn't go to bed right away. He turns off the lights on the Christmas tree in the living room, getting himself a beer from the refrigerator. When he enters the bedroom, he sees the mask, and the pounding G begins, his hand is over his heart. He sits down on the bed and begins crying, and when Alice wakes up, he says, "I'll tell you everything." The music is replaced once again by street sounds.

For Jan Harlan and perhaps Stanley Kubrick, the piece represented jealousy, "the poison in almost all relationships." For Michel Chion, the Ligeti piece represents "the Law."[60] For Ligeti, it was, "a knife in Stalin's heart." It is also the kind of piece that Kubrick seemed particularly fond of, a work that could possibly be film music, but that over time reveals itself to be something else. [61] Ligeti's work fulfilled this criterion in both *2001* and *The Shining*. Penderecki's music in *The Shining* could easily fit this category as well.

## Mozart: "Rex Tremendae" from the Requiem

Appearance:

2:04:38–2:05:42

The presence of Mozart's Requiem on the score, even for a minute, is to make manifest the presence of death in music (see chapter 6). Historically, the Requiem Mass is the Roman Catholic liturgy that is performed upon someone's death. There are Gregorian chants that make up the liturgy, the most famous being the *Dies Irae* (heard famously in *The Shining*), but in Mozart's time, it was customary to set the texts of the mass to new music. In 1791, Mozart received a mysterious commission for a Requiem Mass. The man who was paying for the commission preferred to remain anonymous, sending an emissary to Mozart in his place.[62] They negotiated a price and the mysterious man paid half up front, intending to pay the other half upon the Requiem's completion. Unfortunately, Mozart died before finishing the piece, and in order to collect the rest of the money, Mozart's widow—who had been left in a difficult financial situation—employed the help of her husband's assistant, Franz Xaver Süssmayer, to complete the work.

The part of the Requiem that appears in *Eyes Wide Shut* is the opening of the choral movement called "Rex tremendae." The text of this movement is actually a part of the Sequence of the mass, the text that begins "Dies Irae, dies illa." Mozart broke down the very long *Dies Irae* text into different movements including the "Tuba mirum," which precedes the "Rex tremendae," and the "Recordare" and "Confutatis," which follow. The text of the "Rex tremendae" is short, just one stanza of the Sequence. It can be translated as:

> King of tremendous majesty,
> Who freely saves the worthy,
> Save me, source of mercy

There is no specific justification for Kubrick's use of this particular segment of the Requiem, as many others would have fit well enough in the scene.

The piece is heard—ostensibly sourced on-screen—at Sharky's café. Bill opens up the *New York Post* and reads the article about Amanda Curran. The excerpt from the Requiem likely continues in Sharky's but it is replaced, in Bill's mind and heart at least, by the Ligeti piece. It has been suggested that the placement of this piece is another one of Kubrick's commentaries: Bill reads about a dead girl and we hear the Requiem, but it should be noted that Bill is reading about a girl who is still alive, as far as he knows. If this is Kubrick's commentary, the soundtrack is omniscient, knowing of her death before Bill finds out.

The Requiem's explicit reference to death brings up one of the most important tropes of the film, and that is the relationship between sex and death, eros and thanatos. At the beginning of the film, Marion, the judge's daughter, professes her love for Bill while the two are in the room with her father's corpse. Domino, the prostitute with whom Bill would have had sex—were it not for the interrupting phone call of his wife—finds out she has an incurable sexually transmitted disease. Bill asks to see the body of Amanda Curran and is led down to the morgue after learning of her death. He leans over her, possibly compelled to touch her, but he does not. He wants to know if this is the same woman who "saved" him, but ultimately he can't tell.

## Liszt: *Nuages Gris*

Appearance:

2:08:22–2:09:59 Bill sees the body of Amanda Curran in the morgue

When Franz Liszt composed *Nuages Gris* (Gray Clouds), the nearly seventy-year-old composer had been well known for writing extremely virtuosic piano works. *Nuages Gris*, however, represented a departure from this aspect of Liszt's style. It is a short piece, exceedingly simple, but it is infused with interesting and haunting harmonies. It prefigures the work of impressionists like Debussy,[63] and it was composed at a difficult time in Liszt's life. At the beginning of July 1881, Liszt fell down a flight of stairs and ended up in bed for two months. The fall started the seventy-year-old composer on a path of ill health that included a cataract in one of his eyes, insomnia, and edema (known then as dropsy).[64] *Nuages Gris* was composed on 24 August 1881, near the end of Liszt's convalescence. The words "restless" and "unresolved" have been used to describe the harmonies and mood of the piece.[65] Tremolos in the left hand add to a feeling of uneasiness; the dynamic level stays quiet. There is repetition and regular phrase structure, but the harmony is approaching a level of nonfunctionality, meaning that the internal harmonic logic of much Western music—in which one chord logically leads to another—is disappearing. This would happen more and more in music at the turn of the century, leading eventually to atonality and different modes of structuring musical pieces.

As Bill looks at the corpse of the woman, he hears the mysterious woman's voice from the party. She warns him that she cannot show her face to him "because it could cost me my life, and possibly yours." After hearing this in his head, Liszt's music begins. Leaning down, it looks as if Bill might kiss her on the forehead, but he stops a few inches away. The orderly stays turned away from this intimate moment, as the tremolos in the pianist's left hand build tension that instantly dies away as Bill pulls back. In Schnitzler's original text, Fridolin does touch the body:

> Instinctively, as though compelled by and directed by an invisible power, Fridolin touched the forehead, the cheeks, the shoulders, and the arms of the dead woman with both hands, and then entwined his fingers with those of the corpse as though in love play. Rigid as they were, it seemed to him that the fingers tried to move, to seize his; yes, it seemed to him as though from underneath the half-closed eyelids a vague and distant look was searching for his eyes, and as though pulled by a magic force, he bent over her.[66]

He is interrupted by his colleague, and Fridolin places her arms at her sides again at once. In the film, Bill walks down the hallway of the hospital, obviously still troubled, but his thoughts are interrupted by his ringing cell phone. The music stops at the interruption.


## OTHER MUSIC/SOUNDS

The sound design of the film captures New York more authentically than even the elaborate set. Sirens, car horns, and construction sounds linger around the quiet conversations. When Bill and Alice are having their serious conversation at the beginning of the film, a loud siren goes by, perhaps warning them of this dangerous territory. Notably, after Bill confesses "everything" to Alice, and we see her with red-rimmed eyes the next morning, you can hear the sounds of a jackhammer outside. It is the sound of morning in the city, the sounds of construction, rebuilding, which are wholly appropriate after the destruction brought about by Alice and Bill's actions and confessions. The sounds of the city also provide a great sense of space and give the feeling that, despite all of the troubles of these characters, life goes on as usual outside. Worlds collapse and are rebuilt, and all the while time marches on.

When Bill leaves the apartment after Alice tells him about her temptation, she calls him to find out when he'll be home. She is watching a movie on television, and we hear the music and dialogue of that film twice, at 50:57–51:11 and 52:28–53:08.

The Christmas carol "Jingle Bells" appears while the Harfords are shopping at F.A.O. Schwarz (2:28:53–2:30:50). The happiness of the song and the liveliness of the surroundings appear in stark contrast to Bill and Alice, who seem to be cautiously and vaguely discussing what they should do about their current situation. It fades out during their final conversation, allowing their conclusions to be the central focus of the scene.

## MUSIC INTERRUPTUS

So many times in the film Bill is a passive character. His reaction to Alice's initial confession is silence, yet in Schnitzler's original novel, Fridolin at least responds with a confession of his own. The Bill of the film is often led around by other people. He believes he is in control of his life, but allows himself to be moved all the time. At Ziegler's party, he is led away from Gayle and Nuala by one of Ziegler's associates. At the masked ball, Bill is led around by the woman in the headdress and then led out by the man in the gold mask. At Domino's apartment, he allows her to take the lead, unsure how to proceed.

Bill is also at the mercy of interruptions, as is the music of the film. The weight of Alice's story about the naval officer is hanging heavily in the air when a phone call interrupts not just his thoughts, but Jocelyn Pook's music as well. Alice's phone call to Bill later that evening stops Bill from sleeping with Domino (and in response to the call, Bill turns off the music) and urges him on to the next part of his odyssey. In the judge's house, Marion's confession is interrupted by the arrival of her fiancé. As Bill is walking away from the morgue, his thoughts are interrupted again by a ringing cell phone, this time asking him to come to Ziegler's place. And in one final blow to Bill's sense of self-empowerment, Ziegler suggests that the tribunal that singled out Bill from the other partygoers was a charade put on for his benefit. It could also be that Ziegler is just trying to protect Bill from the harsh truth. Since Ziegler is an unreliable character at best, it's difficult to know where his motivations lie, and Bill seems utterly at the mercy of the whims of others.

The reaction to *Eyes Wide Shut* was mixed. Some complained that it wasn't sexy enough, while others said that they just didn't get it. Nicole Kidman's performance was widely praised, while Tom Cruise's performance—of an admittedly more thankless part—paled in comparison in some estimations. One of the problems, if we can call it that, of interpretation of the film is that the film itself does not "impose on us a hierarchy of what is important and what is not."[67] We are left to make our own decisions about the lesson of the story and perhaps what really happened. Was the whole mock trial at Somerton real or staged for Bill? Was the Mandy from Ziegler's bathroom the same woman from the masked ball and the dead girl at the morgue? Can we believe Ziegler? Were parts of Bill's odyssey a dream? Some of his experiences certainly seem dreamlike. What about Alice's final word? If she and Bill "fuck," will it solidify their new commitment to each other? Will this act conceive a child? Michel Chion interprets the film as a story told from the point of view of this possible child—this starchild, if you will—who comes into being only because of his parents' mistakes, indiscretions, and confessions.[68] The best indication of Kubrick's success on *Eyes Wide Shut* is the simple fact that every time the film is brought up in a group of intelligent adults, it begins a conversation.[69] It stirs up strong feelings, differing opinions, and interesting theories. The passionate discourse it inspires seems to indicate that Kubrick, as always, was onto something.

Kubrick considered *Eyes Wide Shut* to be, in the words of Jan Harlan, "his greatest contribution to the art of filmmaking." One wonders then what he might have done after it, had he lived. Perhaps he would have returned to *Aryan Papers* or started developing something entirely new. Since the death of Stanley Kubrick, which occurred a week after he showed the completed version of *Eyes Wide Shut* to Cruise, Kidman, and Warner Bros. executives, Kubrick has not really left the movies. *Eyes Wide Shut* premiered in the U.S. on 16 June 1999. Since then, Kubrick's name appears in film credits of more than a dozen films to date, receiving dedications (the end credits of *A.I. Artificial Intelligence* say "For Stanley Kubrick"), special thanks, grateful acknowledgment, and inspirational thanks. Film directors who never met him, but still consider him a mentor, will continue to honor Kubrick with praise and gratitude for generations.

## CONCLUSION

Over the course of his career, Kubrick worked with hundreds of people on his films. It is certain that he found the work of these individuals indispensable and important. He undoubtedly learned from these colleagues and worked with some again and again. Music was an aspect of filmmaking that Kubrick absorbed so much information about in his formative years, and it was something that he made unique decisions about as he developed his style. From his earliest films, in which he collaborated with Gerald Fried, to the later films, which prominently featured preexistent tunes, it seems that the music in every project had something to teach Kubrick, and Kubrick was always willing to learn.

The aim of this book has been to illuminate the intricacies of Kubrick's relationship with music, to put to rest notions of Kubrick's "rejection" of traditional scoring techniques, and to show that he was not the proverbial lone wolf. It has also offered an opportunity to delve deeper into the meanings of the preexistent musical pieces themselves, perhaps not known by Kubrick but still there, influencing our readings of the films, our interpretations of the stories. Kubrick's musical choices were often made with the gut or the heart, and that is where they hit us. All of us—fans and scholars alike—may want to understand why something has touched us so, and that is why we research and write and attempt to explain an emotional or visceral response to a work of art. It is a testament to Kubrick's art that we continue to do this, with no signs of stopping.

In 1972, Kubrick said, "The thing a film does best is to use pictures with music, and I think these are the moments you remember."[70] It was an idea he lived by, making musical choices a priority in his films long before he loaded film into a camera. His films have a distinct sound to them, a sophistication for the ear that is often overlooked in favor of Kubrick's incredible eye. He did not make explicit the reasons for his musical choices, did not seek out pieces based on historical background or extra-musical meaning, but what he did create is a sound world of film that was unlike anything that had come before. Every filmmaker who uses music in such a creative way stands on Stanley Kubrick's shoulders and builds on the work of the master.

Kubrick's last whisper about music came in *A.I. Artificial Intelligence*, and it is a personal stamp that is undeniably his. In addition to having thousands of drawings made for the film, and working with numerous people on a screenplay, Kubrick had chosen a piece of music that he wanted to appear in the film, a waltz from Richard Strauss's opera *Der Rosenkavalier*. In an interview on one of the DVD extras for *A.I. Artificial Intelligence*, composer John Williams mentions honoring Kubrick's request:

> Incidentally, this quotation of Richard Strauss was the one piece of music that Stanley Kubrick requested that Steven leave in the film. We don't know why. The waltz . . . was the one thing he stipulated. It should be that melody from Richard Strauss in some area. Very difficult for me

to find a place where it fit, but there's a section for about thirty seconds where they drive through those great faces, you know, across the bridge into Rouge City, where on top of my own music, I threaded the waltz theme from *Rosenkavalier* as an homage to Kubrick completely without fully realizing what the connection in his mind was.

There is a sense of majesty, of grandness to the waltz. There is also a sense of movement, because it is a waltz, a dance. Kubrick was fond of waltzes, using them in *Paths of Glory*, *2001: A Space Odyssey*, and *Eyes Wide Shut*.

The thirty seconds of Strauss's majestic waltz was Kubrick's last chosen piece, but the musical influence he had on filmmakers in general, even those too young to have seen one of Kubrick's films first-run in a theater, is strong. Filmmakers and musicologists will continue to look to his films for inspiration, and we will continue to talk about what we see and hear for decades to come. In speaking about the waltz in *A.I.*, Jan Harlan could have been talking about Kubrick's musical sensibility in films as it continues to live on in new filmmakers: "Listen very carefully," he says. "It's there."

## NOTES

1. James Howard, *Stanley Kubrick Companion* (London: B.T. Batsford, 1999), 176.

2. Michel Ciment, *Kubrick: The Definitive Edition,* trans. Gilbert Adair (New York: Faber and Faber, 1999), 258.

3. Howard, *Stanley Kubrick Companion*, 177.

4. Michel Chion, *Eyes Wide Shut*, trans. Trista Selous (London: British Film Institute, 2002), 16.

5. Hans-Thies Lehmann, "Film/Theatre: Masks/Identities in *Eyes Wide Shut*," in *Stanley Kubrick Guide* (Frankfurt am Main: Deutsches Filmmuseum), 235.

6. According to executive producer and brother-in-law Jan Harlan, Kubrick purchased the rights to *Traumnovelle* in 1970 (interview with author).

7. Chion, *Eyes Wide Shut*, 13.

8. Chion, *Eyes Wide Shut*, 17.

9. Baxter was the other one. Nick James, "At Home with the Kubricks," *Sight and Sound* 9, no. 9 (September 1999): 12–18.

10. See Lorenzo Bellettini, "Freud's Contribution to Arthur Schnitzler's Prose Style," *Rocky Mountain E-Review of Language and Literature* 61, no. 2., http://rmmla.wsu.edu/ereview/61.2/articles/bellettini.asp.

11. For a detailed account of Ophüls and Kubrick see Katherine McQuiston's forthcoming title with Oxford University Press.

12. Susan B. White, *The Cinema of Max Ophuls: Magisterial Vision and the Figure of Woman* (New York: Columbia University Press, 1995), 239.

13. White, *The Cinema of Max Ophuls*, 240. This is White's translation from the script of the film.

14. David Thomson suggested that Kubrick should have had Kidman portray every female role in *Eyes Wide Shut*, "so that Tom Cruise can't help seeing her everywhere." Quoted in Patrick Webster, *Love and Death in Kubrick: A Critical Study of the Films from* Lolita *through* Eyes Wide Shut (Jefferson, NC: McFarland, Inc. 2011), 150.

15. Ben Brantley, review of *Blue Room, New York Times,* December 14, 1998, http://theater.nytimes.com/mem/theater/treview.html?html_title=&tols_title= BLUE+ROOM,+THE+(PLAY)&pdate=19981214&byline=By+BEN+BRANTLEY &id=1077011432284.

16. There are some variations in the spelling of these names in different translations.

17. Jonathan Rosenbaum, "In Dream Begin Responsibilities," in *Depth of Field: Stanley Kubrick, Film and the Uses of History*, ed. Geoffrey Cocks, James Diedrick, and Glenn Perusek (Madison: University of Wisconsin Press, 2006), 249.

18. James Naremore, *On Kubrick* (London: British Film Institute, 2007), 240.

19. Chion, *Eyes Wide Shut*, 21.

20. Naremore, *On Kubrick*, 228.

21. Arthur Schnitzler, *Night Games and Other Stories and Novellas*, trans. Margaret Schaefer (Chicago: Ivan R. Dee, 2002), 220.

22. Schnitzler, *Night Games*, 221–222.

23. Frederic Raphael, *Eyes Wide Open: A Memoir of Stanley Kubrick* (New York: Ballantine Books, 1999), 59.

24. Naremore, *On Kubrick*, 227.

25. Naremore, *On Kubrick*, 227.

26. Cocks, *Wolf at the Door,* 146.

27. Naremore, *On Kubrick*, 276.

28. Webster, *Love and Death in Kubrick*, 161–162.

29. Howard, *Stanley Kubrick Companion*, 179.

30. Terry Southern, *Blue Movie* (New York: Grove Press, 1970), 15. Emphasis original.

31. Ciarán Crilly, "The Bigger Picture: Ligeti's Music and the Films of Stanley Kubrick," in *György Ligeti: Of Foreign Lands and Strange Sounds,* ed. Louise Duschesneau and Wolfgang Marx, 245–254 (Woodbridge: Bydell Press, 2011), 250.

32. Claudia Gorbman, "Ears Wide Open: Kubrick's Music," in *Changing Tunes: The Use of Pre-Existing Music in Film*, ed. Phil Powrie and Robynn Stilwell, 3–18. Nurlington, VT: Ashgate, 2006.

33. Letter from Ajay Shah Convenor to Warner Bros, August 3, 1999, http://www.hindunet.org/anti_defamation/eyes/newpage1.htm.

34. Gorbman, "Ears Wide Open," 14.

35. Wagner, in addition to being a composer of epic operas, was also an unapologetic anti-Semite. Although Wagner died in 1883, his music of course lived on and became a favorite of Hitler and the Third Reich. Wagner's importance as a composer is sometimes obscured by these historical facts.

36. Ernest Newman, *The Life of Richard Wagner: Volume II, 1848–1860* (Cambridge: Cambridge University Press, 1933), 526.

37. Newman, *The Life of Richard Wagner*, 541.

38. Interview with Harlan, April 20, 2011.

39. Chion, *Eyes Wide Shut*, 33–34. Also pointed out in Gorbman, "Ears Wide Open," 15.

40. Note 6, chapter 5 of Ian MacDonald, *The New Shostakovich*, new edition updated by Raymond Clarke (London: Pimlico, 2006), 401.

41. Laurel E. Fay, *Shostakovich: A Life* (New York: Oxford University Press, 2000), 113.

42. See Randolph Jordan, "The Mask That Conceals Nothing: On the Concepts of Marital Fidelity and the Lo-Fi Soundscape in *Eyes Wide Shut*," in *Stanley Kubrick: Essays on His Films and Legacy*, ed. Gary D. Rhodes (Jefferson, NC: McFarland, 2008), 157–169.

43. Chion, *Eyes Wide Shut*, 21.

44. Gorbman, "Ears Wide Open," 8.

45. Mike Zwerin, "Kubrick's Approval Sets Seal on Classical Crossover Success: Pooks Unique Musical Mix," *New York Times*, 27 October 1999, http://www.nytimes.com/1999/10/27/style/27iht-pook.t.html.

46. Jeff Bond, "Once in a Lifetime," *Film Score Monthly* 4, no. 8 (September/October 1999): 25.

47. "Jocelyn Pook on *Eyes Wide Shut*," interview with Rudy Koppl, *Soundtrack: Cinemascore and Soundtrack Archives*, http://www.runmovies.eu/index.php?option=com_content&task=view&id=311&Itemid=57.

48. Chion, *Eyes Wide Shut*, 33.

49. "Jocelyn Pook on *Eyes Wide Shut*."

50. Gorbman, "Ears Wide Open," 14.

51. Jordan, "The Mask That Conceals Nothing," 166.

52. "Jocelyn Pook on *Eyes Wide Shut*."

53. "Jocelyn Pook on *Eyes Wide Shut*."

54. Gorbman, "Ears Wide Open," 16.

55. Norman Kagan, *The Cinema of Stanley Kubrick*, 3rd ed. (New York: Continuum, 2000), 243.

56. Ciment, *Kubrick: The Definitive Edition*, 261.

57. Paul Griffiths, "György Ligeti," in *The New Grove Dictionary of Music and Musicians*, ed. Stanley Sadie (London: Macmillan, 2001), 690.

58. Crilly, "The Bigger Picture," 251.

59. Gorbman, "Ears Wide Open," 12.

60. Chion, *Eyes Wide Shut*, 33.

61. Gorbman, "Ears Wide Open," 11.

62. Count Franz Walsegg was the mysterious man in question. He kept his identity a secret because he likely wanted to pass the completed Requiem off as his own composition.

63. Ben Arnold, "Piano Music: 1861–1886," in *The Liszt Companion*, ed. Ben Arnold (Westport, CT: Greenwood Press, 2002), 140.

64. Alan Walker, *Franz Liszt: Volume Three, The Final Years 1861–1886* (New York: Alfred A. Knopf, 1996), 403.

65. Leonard Ratner, *Romantic Music: Sound and Syntax* (New York: Schirmer, 1992), 267.

66. Schnitzler, *Night Games*, 269.

67. Chion, *Eyes Wide Shut*, 25.

68. Chion, *Eyes Wide Shut*, 17.

69. Ciment, *Kubrick: The Definitive Edition*, 258. "At a time when many contemporary artists are regularly praised in the media for repeating themselves, even Kubrick's final work failed to generate anything like critical agreement. It is the surest sign that Stanley Kubrick is more *alive* than ever." Emphasis original.

70. Interview with Philip Strick and Penelope Houston, 1972, in *Stanley Kubrick Interviews*, ed. Gene D. Phillips, 126–139 (Jackson: University Press of Mississippi, 2001).

# Appendix A

───────○───────

# Films and Their Source Material

*The Killing: Clean Break* by Lionel White
*Paths of Glory: Paths of Glory* by Humphrey Cobb
*Lolita: Lolita* by Vladimir Nabokov
*Dr. Strangelove: Red Alert* by Peter George
*A Clockwork Orange: A Clockwork Orange* by Anthony Burgess
*Barry Lyndon: The Luck of Barry Lyndon* by William Makepeace Thackeray
*The Shining: The Shining* by Stephen King
*Full Metal Jacket: The Short-Timers* by Gus Hasford
*Eyes Wide Shut: Traumnovelle* by Arthur Schnitzler

## Unmade Projects

*Napoleon* project: *Napoleon* by Felix Markham
*Aryan Papers: Wartime Lies* by Louis Begley
*A.I.: Super-Toys Last All Summer Long* by Brian Aldiss

For a full rendering of all Kubrick's unmade projects see appendix 12 in Patrick Webster's *Love and Death in Kubrick: A Critical Study of the Films from Lolita through Eyes Wide Shut* (Jefferson, NC: McFarland, 2011), 243–246.

# Appendix B

─────────○─────────

# Film Synopses

## 2001: A SPACE ODYSSEY

AT THE DAWN OF HUMANKIND, a group of apelike creatures try to survive in the harsh African desert. Fearful of wild animals, they also compete with another group of hominids for control of a small watering hole. Driven away from the watering hole, one group spends the night among some rocks. When they wake up, they see a large black rectangular stone. They cautiously venture out and touch it. Soon after, one of these apelike creatures discovers that a bone can be used as a weapon. Killing a tapir and eating its flesh, the group grows strong. Back at the watering hole, one of the apelike creatures bludgeons a member of the other group with the bone weapon. As he throws the bone up in the air in triumph, we cut to an orbiting satellite, far in the future.

Dr. Heywood Floyd is traveling to the Clavius moon base, but first he has a brief layover on an orbiting space station. There, he makes a video phone call to his daughter and runs into some Russian scientists on their way back to Earth. When the scientists ask Dr. Floyd about rumors of an epidemic at the moon base, Dr. Floyd does not share any information. Once at Clavius, Floyd tells base personnel that he is there to investigate an artifact that appears to have been buried on the moon millions of years ago. Floyd takes a team down to the object, called Tycho Magnetic Anomaly One (TMA-1), and when there, a very loud radio signal is emitted from the object.

Eighteen months later, the spaceship *Discovery* is on its way to Jupiter. There are two astronauts awake on board, Dr. David Bowman and Dr.

259

Frank Poole (three other astronauts are in hibernation). They are aided in their daily duties by HAL, a computer that speaks to them in a human voice. HAL predicts the malfunction of *Discovery*'s main antenna, but the astronauts examine the antenna and find no problem with it. Bowman and Poole ask mission control what to do, since HAL is supposed to be "incapable of error." The astronauts on board discuss possibly deactivating HAL if he proves to be wrong. They hold their discussion in an EVA pod to keep HAL from hearing them, but he reads their lips.

While Poole is out of the ship to reattach the antenna, HAL disconnects Poole's oxygen hose, killing him. Dave, unaware that HAL is responsible, uses one of the pods to attempt a rescue. While Dave is outside of *Discovery*, HAL terminates the life functions of the hibernating astronauts. Upon his return to the ship, Dave is refused entry by HAL. Although he has no helmet, Dave uses manual controls to get himself back onto the ship. He begins to disconnect HAL. The computer seems to experience something like fear as Dave disconnects his memory circuits. HAL's disconnection triggers a pre-recorded message from Dr. Floyd. Floyd explains the discovery of the monolith on the moon and that its only communication was sending a radio signal to Jupiter. It is still unknown why.

Dave leaves *Discovery* in a pod, encountering a monolith in orbit around Jupiter. He enters into some kind of space tunnel, traveling at an impossibly fast speed, ending up in a Louis XVI–style bedroom where he watches himself age until he is reborn—a Starchild—watching over the Earth.

## A CLOCKWORK ORANGE

Alex, a teenager, and his three friends drink drugged milk at the Korova Milkbar while they decide what to do with the evening. Their activities will consist of what Alex likes to call "ultra-violence." They attack an old homeless man, have a fight with a rival gang, steal a car, and arrive at a place called HOME. At HOME, the group vandalizes the property, destroying the writings of the man who lives there. Alex performs a rendition of "Singing in the Rain" while cutting off the clothes of the man's wife before forcing the man to watch as they sexually assault her.

Returning to the milk bar where they began the evening, the group hears a woman singing the main theme from Beethoven's Ninth Symphony. When one friend ridicules the woman, Alex punishes him for being uncivilized. The episode seems to cause some tension within the group, but nothing comes of it, and they all return to their homes. Alex ends his night by listening to classical music and imagining violent acts.

The next morning, Alex—who has stayed home from school—receives a visit from the truancy officer who cautions Alex to change his ways. Alex then goes to the record shop to pick up an album that he has ordered. While there, he meets two young women whom he takes home and seduces. As evening falls, Alex meets up with his friends, and one of them questions Alex's authority. To reassert his place as the alpha male, Alex starts a physical fight with his friends. Afterward, Alex and his injured friends have a drink at a bar where Georgie suggests they rob the house of an old woman. Thinking he is a magnanimous leader, Alex agrees with the plan.

The robbery is merely a setup so Alex will be caught by police. Before the police arrive, however, Alex attacks the woman of the house with a sculpture; she dies from her injuries. Deserted by his friends and arrested, Alex arrives at the state jail. Working in the prison chapel, Alex indulges in violent fantasies based on biblical stories. He asks the prison chaplain about a rumored experimental treatment that would commute his sentence. The chaplain expresses dismay that the treatment takes away one's free will.

The Minister of the Interior visits the prison, choosing Alex for the experimental treatment. At the Ludovico center, Alex is given injections and forced to watch violent films. The films begin to make him feel sick. In the next session, Alex notices the soundtrack for the films is Beethoven's Ninth Symphony; he protests the use of music in this way. Alex completes the treatment.

Alex is subjected to humiliation to prove his docility. Satisfied, the minister releases him. He returns home to find his parents have taken in a boarder. With nowhere to go, Alex walks the streets. He runs into the homeless man his gang attacked earlier in the film, and the man attacks Alex and soon others join in. The thought of violence makes Alex sick, so he is unable to defend himself. When the police arrive, Alex believes he has been saved, only to find that the police officers are two of his former friends. They take him into the countryside, beat him, and leave him for dead.

Alex wanders to the closest house, which is HOME. Because Alex wore a mask during the earlier attack, his former victim doesn't recognize him right away, but Alex unintentionally gives himself away. The man, F. Alexander—an outspoken critic of the government—decides to use Alex to further his cause. A woman comes to interview Alex, and he reveals that the Ninth Symphony has become unbearable to him. F. Alexander drugs

Alex, waking him up to the sound of Beethoven. Sickened by the sound and unable to stop it, Alex attempts suicide.

While unconscious, Alex is de-conditioned. He has no memory of this except for vague dreams. A doctor tests his de-conditioning, finding that it has been successful. The Minister of the Interior visits Alex for a photo-op, presenting him with a stereo as a gesture of goodwill. When he hears it the Ninth Symphony, he lapses into fantasies, proclaiming himself cured.

### BARRY LYNDON

Young Irishman Redmond Barry is in love with his cousin, Nora. She plans to marry Captain John Quin, an English soldier. Challenging Quin to a duel, Redmond shoots his rival and is forced to go to Dublin. Given some money from his widowed mother, Redmond is robbed by highwayman Captain Feeney. He joins the English army, running into old friend Captain Grogan, who informs Redmond that he didn't actually kill John Quin. Redmond's pistol was filled with tow by Nora's family so that Redmond would leave and Nora would be free to marry Quin.

Redmond's regiment fights a small battle in the Seven Years' War, but Grogan is fatally wounded. Redmond is soured on the service and escapes the army by stealing the horse, uniform, and papers of an officer. Making his way to Holland, he stays for a time with a German girl, but then moves on. He runs into Captain Potzdorf of the Prussian army. Potzdorf knows Redmond is an impostor, and he gives Redmond a choice: go back to the British army (where he will likely be executed for desertion) or join the Prussian army. Redmond chooses the latter and serves under Potzdorf, saving his commander's life, earning both the man's trust and a commendation.

After the war, Potzdorf asks Redmond to work in conjunction with the Prussian police. Redmond is to work for (and spy on) the Chevalier de Balibari, who turns out to be Redmond's fellow countryman. Redmond reveals the ruse to Balibari, and the two decide to work together. Redmond pretends to spy for Potzdorf, but instead Redmond and Balibari hatch a plan to enable them to leave Prussia. After their departure, the two men run gambling games in the homes of the wealthy across Europe. Redmond duels with gamblers who owe money. At a spa in Belgium, Redmond meets Lady Lyndon, a beautiful, rich woman who is married to Sir Charles Lyndon. After Sir Charles' death, Redmond marries Lady Lyndon (taking the title Barry Lyndon) much to the chagrin of her son, Lord Bullingdon.

Lady Lyndon gives birth to Barry's son, Bryan. Barry, however, spends little time at home, preferring to be out with other women, gambling and spending Lady Lyndon's fortune. Barry's mother, who comes to live with them in England, encourages Barry to get a title in case anything should happen to Lady Lyndon. Barry spends a lot of money entertaining influential people in order to achieve this. Lord Bullingdon ruins Barry's plan when he interrupts a party and explains to all the important guests how little respect he has for his stepfather. Barry retaliates physically, and the guests are horrified. Bullingdon leaves home.

Barry's son Bryan, meanwhile, is treated very well. Barry buys him a horse for his ninth birthday. Disregarding his parents' warnings, Bryan sneaks out to ride alone. Thrown from the horse, Bryan is paralyzed. He dies a few days later. After Bryan's death, Barry drinks and Lady Lyndon turns to religion. Lady Lyndon unsuccessfully attempts suicide, and Graham, the Lyndons' accountant, finds Bullingdon. When Lord Bullingdon returns, he demands satisfaction from Barry in the form of a duel. Bullingdon gets to shoot first, but his pistol malfunctions. Barry fires his own shot into the ground, hoping that Bullingdon will be satisfied. Bullingdon, however, takes a shot at Barry, hitting him in the leg. Part of Barry's leg is amputated to save his life.

Lord Bullingdon, who is now in control of his mother's estate, offers Barry a deal: Barry will leave England forever and end his marriage to Lady Lyndon in exchange for an annuity. If he stays in England, creditors will place him in debtors' prison. Barry accepts the deal, leaving with his mother to return to Ireland. He never sees Lady Lyndon again.

## THE SHINING

Jack Torrance arrives at the Overlook Hotel in Colorado to interview for the job of winter caretaker. Warned that the previous caretaker (Grady) murdered his family and committed suicide, Jack nevertheless takes the job. He will live at the hotel during the winter months with his wife Wendy and son Danny. Danny begins to have disturbing visions about the hotel. Wendy's conversation with his pediatrician reveals that Jack has previously had trouble with alcohol and that Danny's "imaginary" friend Tony has been visiting since Danny started at nursery school.

At the Overlook, Danny and Wendy meet Dick Hallorann, who communicates telepathically with Danny with what he calls "the shining." He warns Danny to stay out of room 237. A month later, Jack tells Wendy he is happy at the Overlook, but he grows more agitated as time passes. Danny's visions get worse, and he begins to believe that Jack is going to hurt him and Wendy. Jack has a disturbing nightmare, and Danny appears with bruises on his neck. Believing that Jack is responsible, Wendy takes Danny back to the family's apartment.

Jack, who is angry at Wendy for suspecting him, goes to the Gold Room where he mysteriously finds a bartender who appears to know him and who offers him alcohol. Wendy arrives in the Gold Room to inform Jack that there might be someone else in the hotel in room 237. Going to the room to investigate, Jack finds a beautiful naked woman who becomes an old woman who appears to be decomposing.

Halloran senses that something has gone wrong at the Overlook and travels from his summer job in Miami back to the Overlook. Danny goes into a trance, and Jack returns to the Gold Room to find a party in full swing. There he meets Grady, the previous caretaker, who informs him that Danny has used the shining to call Halloran for help.

Wendy decides she must get Danny down to the nearest town, but Jack—whose insanity seems to be confirmed by his manuscript consisting of nothing but the line "All work and no play makes Jack a dull boy"— wants to prevent her from leaving. Menaced by Jack, she hits him with a baseball bat, and he falls down the stairs. Locking him in the pantry, she runs out to the Sno-cat but finds that it has been disabled.

Jack, who has left the pantry with the help of Grady, threatens Wendy and Danny with an ax. Danny is able to escape out a window, but Wendy cannot. Jack is distracted from his attack by the sound of Halloran arriving in a Sno-cat. Jack kills Halloran with an ax, Danny runs into the hotel's hedge maze, and Wendy begins to see very disturbing things as she runs through the hotel. Danny retraces his steps and leaves Jack lost in the maze. He follows his own footsteps out and is reunited with Wendy. The two of them take Halloran's Sno-cat to safety, and Jack freezes to death in the maze. He appears in a photograph hanging on the wall of the Overlook, one that depicts a Fourth of July party from 1921.

## EYES WIDE SHUT

Married couple Bill and Alice Harford attend a Christmas party at the home of Victor Ziegler, a wealthy friend and patient of Bill. At the party, Bill meets up with old friend Nick Nightingale, who plays piano in the band. Bill makes plans to see Nick perform at the Sonata Café. While

Bill and Alice are apart, they flirt with other people, Alice with the older Sander Szavost and Bill with two young women, Gayle and Nuala. Bill is called away by Ziegler's associate to help with a young naked woman who has overdosed in Ziegler's bathroom. While Bill tries to revive Mandy, Alice and Sandor continue dancing. Mandy eventually wakes up, and Sandor tries to make plans to see Alice again. Later, back at the Harfords' apartment, Bill and Alice begin kissing in front of their bedroom mirror.

The next day, Bill goes to his office and sees patients while Alice takes care of the Harfords' daughter, Helena. That evening, Bill and Alice smoke pot and talk about Ziegler's party. In the course of this conversation Bill claims that women don't think about cheating, but Alice confesses that on vacation the previous year she was tempted by a handsome naval officer. A phone call interrupts their conversation and Bill leaves to go the house of a patient who has just died. The patient's daughter, Marion, professes love for Bill, but their conversation is interrupted by the arrival of her fiancé. Bill leaves and meets Domino, a prostitute who invites Bill to her apartment. Their first kiss is interrupted by a call from Alice, who is wondering when Bill is coming home. He tells her it'll be a while, but leaves Domino's apartment anyway. Arriving at the Sonata Café, Bill meets up with Nick who is just finishing his last set of the night. Mentioning another gig in a mysterious location, Nick tells Bill he can't bring him along. Bill knows the password, but Nick tells him he would also need a costume and mask.

Bill arrives at Rainbow Fashions and convinces the proprietor, Mr. Millich, to rent him a tuxedo, a cloak, and a mask. While they are looking for an appropriate outfit, Millich finds his teenaged daughter fooling around with two older Japanese men. Outraged, he threatens to call the police and locks the men in a room. After a long drive, Bill arrives at Somerton mansion in a taxicab. Once inside, he dons his mask and cloak and observes a ritual set to Nick's music. At the end of the ritual, nearly naked women choose partners from the masked partygoers. One seems to know Bill, and she urges him to leave. Bill walks around the party, observing couples and threesomes engaging in sex acts, although he does not join in. Again the woman appears and urges Bill to leave, but before he can, a man leads him back to the main room where the original ritual took place. The partygoers have assembled there for a trial of sorts where Bill is unmasked and then asked to undress. Bill tries to refuse, but the tribunal insists. The mysterious woman intercedes on his behalf and Bill is allowed to leave.

Bill returns home and finds Alice having a nightmare. When he wakes her, she tells him about the dream, in which she had sex with the naval officer and many other men and laughed at Bill as he watched them. The next day Bill attempts, unsuccessfully, to find Nick. The hotel clerk informs him that a frightened Nick was taken away by two large men early in the morning. Bill returns the cloak and tuxedo to Mr. Millich, but finds the mask is missing. Mr. Millich, who kindly says goodbye to the Japanese men from the previous night who are just now leaving, makes it clear that his young daughter is also available for rent. Bill drives out to the mansion again, but is given a typed letter asking him to leave off his inquiries. Returning to the city, Bill briefly stops at home but returns to the office in the evening. He tries to call Marion, but hangs up when her fiancé answers. Stopping by Domino's apartment, he finds she is not there. The woman in the apartment tells Bill Domino might not be coming back since she is HIV positive.

Bill walks the streets of Greenwich Village but notices he is being followed. Facing down the man, Bill ducks into a café. He reads a story in the newspaper about Amanda Curran, an ex–beauty queen who overdosed and is in critical condition. Thinking she is the woman who offered herself in his place at the orgy, Bill goes to the hospital and poses as her doctor. Informed by the receptionist that Amanda Curran died that afternoon, Bill is taken to the morgue to see the body. As he's leaving, he receives a call asking him to come to Ziegler's house. There, Ziegler explains that he was at the orgy and that the ad hoc trial was staged to get him to leave. He also tells Bill that the woman who interceded on his behalf was in fact Mandy from Ziegler's Christmas party. Ziegler assures Bill that she left the party safely and that her death really was a drug overdose.

Bill returns home to find the mask on the pillow next to Alice. He breaks down crying and wants to confess everything to her. The next morning, they take their daughter Christmas shopping at F.A.O. Schwarz. While Helena looks at toys, the Harfords decide that the events of the last few days—and even the last few years—do not tell the full story, but they should be grateful to have survived their adventures. Alice adds that they should "fuck" as soon as possible.

# Appendix C

───────────────◯───────────────

# Soundtracks and
# Track Lists

*Note: Wherever possible, tracks are listed as they are appear on album or CD covers, even when the information is erroneous. If the information originated from a vinyl record album, side listings (A and B or 1st and 2nd) have been retained.*

### COMMERCIAL AVAILABILITY OF SOUNDTRACKS

THE SOUNDTRACKS TO KUBRICK'S FIRST FEATURE FILMS—*Fear and Desire, Killer's Kiss, The Killing,* and *Paths of Glory*—were not released to the public. The first Kubrick film to have a commercially available soundtrack was *Spartacus*. The album—which featured only some of the cues in the film—was released in 1960 on the Decca label. The *Lolita* soundtrack followed in 1962. In addition to an album of music, there was also a pop single released on 45. For *Dr. Strangelove*, Kubrick released a 45 rpm single; side A was the Laurie Johnson Orchestra playing the *Theme from Dr. Strangelove*, and the B side featured a song called "Love That Bomb."[1] The film also re-popularized the World War II–era tune made famous by English singer Vera Lynn, "We'll Meet Again."

The initial soundtrack offering from MGM for the film *2001: A Space Odyssey* featured the preexistent classical excerpts that Kubrick used in the film, omitting Ligeti's *Aventures*, including a longer cue from his *Lux Aeterna*, and substituting a different version of *Also Sprach Zarathustra* than was heard in the film. It received many favorable reviews including four stars from *Billboard* magazine.[2] It was commercially successful, certified platinum (selling over one million units), and it introduced many people to the works of Richard Strauss and Györgi Ligeti. *Film Score Monthly* said of the soundtrack: "Its legacy in pop culture is nearly incalculable."[3] For the week ending 19 April 1969, the top two albums on the Billboard Classical LP list were Wendy Carlos's *Switched on Bach* at number one (twenty-one weeks on the chart), and the soundtrack to *2001: A Space Odyssey* in the second position (thirty-six weeks on the chart). At number seventeen on the same list was *Selections from 2001: A Space Odyssey*, which was a compilation of music from the Philadelphia Orchestra and the New York Philharmonic (thirty-five weeks on the chart).[4] The latter album was produced to capitalize on the great commercial success of the *2001* soundtrack.

In a 1996 re-release of the score (TCM/Rhino), the version of *Also Sprach Zarathustra* used by Kubrick (conducted by von Karajan) was included, as was Ligeti's *Aventures*, which had been altered for the film. There are also four supplemental tracks on the re-release: the version of *Zarathustra* on the original soundtrack album, *Lux Aeterna* in its entirety (as it appeared on the original MGM release), the unaltered version of *Aventures*, and Douglas Rain's performance of HAL's dialogue (see complete track list below).

The score to *A Clockwork Orange* featured the work of Wendy Carlos, whose previous album *Switched on Bach* went platinum and won three Grammy Awards in 1970. The *Clockwork Orange* soundtrack was also very popular, going gold and reaching number two on the Billboard Classical LP chart on 1 July 1972. It was ninety-seven on the Top LPs list the same week.[5] In March of 1972, both the score for *A Clockwork Orange* and *2001: A Space Odyssey* charted together, with *2001* in the fourth position and *A Clockwork Orange* at eighteen.[6] The soundtrack's highest position on the Billboard Top 100 was at number thirty-four.

The *A Clockwork Orange* soundtrack presents both the synthesized cues that Carlos created—Henry Purcell's *Funeral Music for Queen Mary* and Beethoven's Ninth Symphony—and traditional orchestral versions of other classical cues. There are also a few songs that are heard in the film, and there is an excerpt from Carlos's original composition, *Timesteps*. The success of the soundtrack to *A Clockwork Orange*, which spent thirty-one weeks on the Billboard Top 100,[7] inspired Wendy Carlos to revisit the material; three months after the soundtrack to *A Clockwork Orange* debuted, Carlos released *Walter Carlos' Clockwork Orange*, a collection of music that was intended for the film but which was not finished or had not been used by Kubrick. This album spent nine weeks on the Billboard chart.[8] Carlos issued a re-mastered edition of this album, now called *A Clockwork Orange: Wendy Carlos's Complete Original Score,* in 1998.

The soundtracks to the later films that featured preexistent music, *Barry Lyndon*, *The Shining*, *Full Metal Jacket*, and *Eyes Wide Shut*, were all commercially available, although none of them experienced the same kind of success as the scores for *2001* and *A Clockwork Orange*. The soundtrack to *The Shining* was commercially available only for a very short time; the album was pulled soon after its release over copyright problems and has not been available since 1980.

In recent years, there have been two compilation soundtracks commercially available featuring music from Kubrick's films, including cues from *Day of the Fight*, *Fear and Desire*, *Killer's Kiss*, *The Killing*, and *Paths of Glory*. The first of these compilations was called *Dr. Strangelove: Music from the Films of Stanley Kubrick*. It was recorded by the Prague Philharmonic Orchestra and released in May of 1999 by Silva America, a couple of months before *Eyes Wide Shut* premiered (and a couple of months after the death of Stanley Kubrick). This is the track list from that compilation:

### *Dr. Strangelove: Music from the Films of Stanley Kubrick* (1999, Silva America)

1. Also Sprach Zarathustra (Richard Strauss)—*2001: A Space Odyssey*
2. Main Title (Alex North)—*Spartacus*
3. Ode to Joy (Ludwig van Beethoven)—*A Clockwork Orange*
4. Women of Ireland (Traditional)—*Barry Lyndon*
5. Sarabande (G. F. Handel)—*Barry Lyndon*
6. Themes (Abigail Mead)—*Full Metal Jacket*
7. Surfin' Bird (Frazier, White, Harris, Wilson)—*Full Metal Jacket*
8. Main Title/The Robbery (Gerald Fried)—*The Killing*
9. Murder 'Mongst the Mannikins (Gerald Fried)—*Killer's Kiss*
10. A Meditation on War (Gerald Fried)—*Fear and Desire*
11. Madness (Gerald Fried)—*Fear and Desire*
12. The Patrol (Gerald Fried)—*Paths of Glory*
13. March of the Gloved Gladiators (Gerald Fried)—*Day of the Fight*
14. Main Theme (Wendy Carlos, Rachel Elkind)—*The Shining*
15. Midnight, the Stars and You (Campbell, Connelly, Woods)—*The Shining*
16. Love Theme (Bob Harris, arr. Grau)—*Lolita*
17. On the Beautiful Blue Danube (Johann Strauss)—*2001: A Space Odyssey*
18. The Bomb Run (Laurie Johnson)—*Dr. Strangelove*
19. We'll Meet Again (Charles and Parker)—*Dr. Strangelove*

There was also another compilation released at the end of 1999 called *Eyes Wide Shut: Music from Stanley Kubrick Movies*. It was recorded by and released by Golden Stars Holland. This album omits any tracks from Gerald Fried and instead includes, among other things, extra cues for *Eyes Wide Shut*, a different clip from Beethoven's Ninth, and Elgar's *Pomp and Circumstance* (both from *A Clockwork Orange*).

### *Eyes Wide Shut: Music from Stanley Kubrick Movies* (1999, Golden Stars Holland)

1. When I Fall in Love (Young/Heyman), The Hollywood Star Orchestra—*Eyes Wide Shut*
2. The Second Waltz from "Jazz Suite" (Shostakovich), Amsterdam Studio Orchestra—*Eyes Wide Shut*
3. Strangers in the Night (Kaempfert/Singleton/Snyder), The Hollywood Star Orchestra—*Eyes Wide Shut*
4. 2nd Movement from Symphony No. 9 (Beethoven), Prager Festival Orchestra—*A Clockwork Orange*
5. Pomp and Circumstance March, Op. 39 (Elgar), Radio Symphony Orchestra Bratislava—*A Clockwork Orange*
6. Tain't What You Do (It's the Way That Cha Do It) (Young/Oliver), Ella Fitzgerald—*Lolita*
7. Introduction from "Also Sprach Zarathustra" (R. Strauss), Slovenian Symphony Orchestra—*2001: A Space Odyssey*
8. Adagio from "Gayane" (Khachaturian), Sofia Symphony Orchestra—*The Killing*
9. Theme from Spartacus (Alex North), The Hollywood Star Orchestra—*Spartacus*
10. Sarabande (Handel), [no orchestra listed]—*Barry Lyndon*
11. German Dance No. 1 (Schubert), Slovenian Symphony Orchestra—*Barry Lyndon*
12. Third Movement from "Cello Concerto" (Vivaldi), Musici di San Marco—*Barry Lyndon*
13. Main Title from "The Shining" (Wendy Carlos, Rachel Elkind), The Hollywood Star Orchestra—*The Shining*
14. "Chapel of Love" (Spector/Greenwich/Barry), The Dixie Cups—*Full Metal Jacket*
15. We'll Meet Again (Charles/Parker), Vera Lynn—*Dr. Strangelove*

In 2005, Silva issued a second compilation of Kubrick's music, this time including the Shostakovich Waltz from *Eyes Wide Shut* and

Alex North's "Love Theme" from *Spartacus*. This album omits "Surfin' Bird," "Midnight, the Stars, and You," and "We'll Meet Again." Silva also changed the name of the compilation to *2001: Music from the Films of Stanley Kubrick*. The track list differs slightly from the original compilation:

### *2001: Music from the Films of Stanley Kubrick*
### (2005, Silva America)

1. Also Sprach Zarathustra (Richard Strauss)—*2001: A Space Odyssey*
2. Main Title (Alex North)—*Spartacus*
3. Love Theme (Alex North)—*Spartacus*
4. Women of Ireland (Traditional)—*Barry Lyndon*
5. Sarabande (G. F. Handel)—*Barry Lyndon*
6. Ode to Joy (Ludwig van Beethoven)—*A Clockwork Orange*
7. Themes (Abigail Mead)—*Full Metal Jacket*
8. Main Theme (Wendy Carlos, Rachel Elkind)—*The Shining*
9. Waltz from Jazz Suite No. 2 (Dmitri Shostakovich)—*Eyes Wide Shut*
10. Main Title/ The Robbery (Gerald Fried)—*The Killing*
11. Murder 'Mongst the Mannikins (Gerald Fried)—*Killer's Kiss*
12. A Meditation on War (Gerald Fried)—*Fear and Desire*
13. Madness (Gerald Fried)—*Fear and Desire*
14. The Patrol (Gerald Fried)—*Paths of Glory*
15. March of the Gloved Gladiators (Gerald Fried)—*Day of the Fight*
16. Love Theme (Bob Harris, arr. Grau)—*Lolita*
17. The Bomb Run (Laurie Johnson)—*Dr. Strangelove*
18. On the Beautiful Blue Danube (Johann Strauss)—*2001: A Space Odyssey*

### CHAPTER 2: COMPLETE TRACK LISTS

### *Spartacus: Original Motion Picture Soundtrack* (1960, MCA )

1. Main Title
2. Spartacus Love Theme
3. Gladiators Fight to the Death
4. Blue Shadows and Purple Hills
5. Homeward Bound (a: On to the Sea / b: Beside the Pool)
6. Hopeful Preparations—Vesuvius Camp
7. Prelude to Battle (a: Quiet Interlude / b: The Final Conflict)

8. Oysters and Snails—Festival
9. Headed for Freedom
10. Goodbye My Life, My Love—End Title

### *Lolita: The Original Soundtrack Recording* (1962, MGM)

1. Main Title (Bob Harris)
2. Quilty
3. Quilty As Charged, featuring James Mason and Peter Sellers
4. Ramsdale
5. Cherry Pies, featuring Shelley Winters and James Mason
6. Lolita Ya-Ya
7. Hula Hoop, featuring Sue Lyon and Shelley Winters
8. There's No You, Music and Lyrics by Tom Adair and Hal Hopper
9. Quilty's Caper
10. A Lovely, Lyrical, Lilting Name, featuring Peter Sellers and Shelley Winters
11. Put Your Dreams Away (For Another Day), Music by Paul Mann and Stephan Weiss, Lyrics by Ruth Lowe
12. Shelley Winters Cha Cha
13. Music to Eat By
14. Love Theme from *Lolita*, Music by Bob Harris
15. Diary Entry, featuring James Mason
16. The Last Martini
17. Charlotte Is Dead
18. Instant Music
19. Don't Smudge Your Toenails, featuring James Mason and Sue Lyon
20. The Strange Call
21. Mrs. Schiller
22. Twenty-Five Paces, featuring James Mason and Sue Lyon
23. End Title—Love Theme from *Lolita*

### *Stanley Kubrick's Dr. Strangelove or: How I Learned to Stop Worrying and Love the Bomb and Other Great Movie Themes* (1954, Colpix)

1. Dr. Strangelove: Theme, Laurie Johnson, The Laurie Johnson Orchestra

2. The Victors: Theme (My Special Dream), Sol Kaplan, Sol Kaplan and Orchestra
3. Bridge on the River Kwai: Colonel Bogey March, Malcolm Arnold, Morris Stoloff and Orchestra
4. Picnic: Moonglow, Morris Stoloff and Orchestra
5. From Here to Eternity: Theme, Morris Stoloff and Orchestra
6. Diamond Head: Theme, Johnny Williams Conducting the Columbia Pictures Studio Orchestra
7. Damn the Defiant!: Theme, Orchestra Conducted by Muir Mathieson
8. Lawrence of Arabia: Theme, Orchestra Conducted by Maurice Jarre
9. Psyche '59: Theme, Orchestra Conducted by K.V. Jones
10. In the French Style: Theme, Norman Percival and his Orchestra
11. Barrabas: Theme, Orchestra Conducted by Mario Nascimbene
12. Song Without End: The Rakoczy March, Orchestra Conducted by Morris Stoloff
13. The Interns: Theme (Toss Me a Scalpel), Leith Stevens and Orchestra

## *Full Metal Jacket Original Motion Picture Soundtrack* (1987, Warner Bros.)

1. Full Metal Jacket, Abigail Mead and Nigel Goulding
2. Hello Vietnam, Johnny Wright
3. Chapel of Love, The Dixie Cups
4. Wooly Bully, Sam the Sham and the Pharaohs
5. I Like it Like That, Chris Kenner
6. These Boots Are Made for Walking, Nancy Sinatra
7. Surfin' Bird, The Trashmen
8. The Marine's Hymn, The Goldman Band
9. Transition, Abigail Mead
10. Parris Island, Abigail Mead
11. Ruins, Abigail Mead
12. Leonard, Abigail Mead
13. Attack, Abigail Mead
14. Time Suspended, Abigail Mead
15. Sniper, Abigail Mead

## CHAPTER 3: COMPLETE TRACK LISTS
## FROM *2001: A SPACE ODYSSEY*

### *2001: A Space Odyssey Original Motion Picture Soundtrack* (1968, MGM)

Side 1

1. Also Sprach Zarathustra, Richard Strauss, Berlin Philharmonic Orchestra, conducted by Karl Böhm
2. Requiem for Soprano, Mezzo-Soprano, 2 Mixed Choirs and Orchestra, Ligeti, Bavarian Radio Orchestra, conducted by Francis Travis
3. Lux Aeterna, Ligeti, Stuttgart Schola Cantorum, conducted by Clytus Gottwald
4. The Blue Danube, Berlin Philharmonic Orchestra, Herbert von Karajan

Side 2

1. Gayane Ballet Suite (Adagio), Khachaturian, Leningrad Philharmonic Orchestra, conducted by Gennadi Rozhdestvensky
2. Atmospheres, Ligeti, Sudwestfunk Orchestra, conducted by Ernest Bour
3. The Blue Danube, Berlin Philharmonic Orchestra, Herbert von Karajan
4. Also Sprach Zarathustra, Berlin Philharmonic Orchestra, conducted by Karl Böhm

### *Music Inspired by MGM's Presentation of the Stanley Kubrick Production 2001: A Space Odyssey* (1970, MGM)

Side 1

1. Also Sprach Zarathustra, Richard Strauss, Berlin Philharmonic Orchestra, conducted by Karl Böhm
2. Coppelia, Leo Delibes, Berlin Philharmonic Orchestra, Herbert von Karajan
3. Lontano, György Ligeti, Sudwestfunk Orchestra, conducted by Ernest Bour
4. Entflieht Auf Leichten Kahnen, Anton Webern, Clytus Gottwald and the Stuttgart Schola Cantorum
5. Waltzes from Der Rosenkavalier, Richard Strauss, Berlin Philharmonic Orchestra, conducted by Karl Böhm

Side 2

1. Also Sprach Zarathustra Part 2, Richard Strauss, Berlin Philharmonic Orchestra, conducted by Karl Böhm
2. Volumina, Ligeti, Karl-Erik Welin, Organ
3. "Berceuse" from Gayane Suite, Khachaturian, Leningrad Philharmonic Orchestra, conducted by Gennadi Rozhdestvensky
4. Requiem [another part], Ligeti, Hessian Symphony Orchestra, conducted by Michael Gielen
5. Margarethe, Charles Gounod, Radio-Symphony Orchestra of Berlin, conducted by Ferenc Fricsay

### 2001: *A Space Odyssey Original Motion Picture Soundtrack* (1996 Digital Remaster, Word Entertainment)

1. Overture: Atmospheres, Ligeti, Sudwestfunk Orchestra, conducted by Ernest Bour
2. Main Title: Also Sprach Zarathustra, Richard Strauss, Vienna Philharmonic Orchestra, conducted by Herbert von Karajan
3. Requiem for Soprano, Mezzo Soprano, Two Mixed Choirs and Orchestra, Ligeti, Bavarian Radio Orchestra, conducted by Francis Travis
4. The Blue Danube, Johann Strauss, Berlin Philharmonic Orchestra, conducted by Herbert von Karajan
5. Lux Aeterna, Ligeti, Clytus Gottwald and the Stuttgart Schola Cantorum
6. Gayane Ballet Suite (Adagio), Leningrad Philharmonic Orchestra, conducted by Gennadi Rozhdestvensky
7. Jupiter and Beyond, all pieces by Ligeti: (a) Requiem for Soprano, Mezzo Soprano, Two Mixed Choirs and Orchestra, Bavarian Radio Orchestra, conducted by Francis Travis; (b) Atmospheres, Sudwestfunk Orchestra, conducted by Ernest Bour; (c) Adventures (altered for film), Internationale Musikinstitut Darmstadt, conducted by Ligeti
8. Also Sprach Zarathustra, Vienna Philharmonic Orchestra, conducted by Herbert von Karajan
9. The Blue Danube (Reprise), Berlin Philharmonic Orchestra, conducted by Herbert von Karajan

Supplemental Material

1. Also Sprach Zarathustra, Richard Strauss, Sudwestfunk Orchestra, conducted by Ernest Bour

2. Lux Aeterna, Clytus Gottwald and the Stuttgart Schola Cantorum
3. Adventures (unaltered), Internationale Musikinstitut Darmstadt, conducted by Ligeti
4. HAL 9000, featuring Douglas Rain

### *2001: A Space Odyssey—The Original Score* [by Alex North] (1993, Intrada)

1. Main Title
2. The Foraging
3. Eat Meat and the Kill
4. The Bluff
5. Night Terrors
6. The Dawn of Man
7. Space Station Docking
8. Trip to the Moon
9. Moon Rocket Bus
10. Space Talk
11. Interior Orion
12. Main Theme

### *Music for 2001: A Space Odyssey: The Original Score* (2007, Intrada Special Collection)

1. The Foraging
2. The Bluff
3. Night Terrors
4. Bones
5. Eat Meat and Kill
6. Space Station Docking
7. Space Talk
8. Trip to Moon
9. Moon Rocket Bus
10. The Foraging (alternate version AKA Dawn of Man)
11. Bonus Tracks
12. Eat Meat and Kill (Take 7—Wild)
13. Space Station (Take 4—Docking)
14. Docking (Take 2)

## CHAPTER 4: COMPLETE TRACK LISTS FROM
## *A CLOCKWORK ORANGE*

### *Stanley Kubrick's A Clockwork Orange* (1972, Warner Bros.)

Side A

1. Title Music from A Clockwork Orange (from Henry Purcell's Music for the Funeral of Queen Mary), Composer: [Wendy] Carlos and Rachel Elkind, Tempi Music BMI, Performed by [Wendy] Carlos 2:21
2. The Thieving Magpie (Abridged), Composer: Gioacchino Rossini, Performance: A Deutsche Grammophon recording 5:57
3. Theme from A Clockwork Orange (Beethoviana), Composer: [Wendy] Carlos and Rachel Elkind, Tempi Music BMI, Performed by [Wendy] Carlos 1:44
4. Ninth Symphony, Second Movement—Abridged, Composer: Ludwig van Beethoven, Performance: A Deutsche Grammophon Recording 3:48
5. March from A Clockwork Orange (Ninth Symphony, Fourth Movement—Abridged), Composer: Ludwig van Beethoven, Arr. [Wendy] Carlos, Tempi Music BMI, Performed by [Wendy] Carlos, Articulations by Rachel Elkind 7:00
6. William Tell Overture—Abridged, Composer: Gioacchino Rossini, Performed by [Wendy] Carlos 1:17

Side B

1. Pomp and Circumstance March No. I, Composer: Sir Edward Elgar 4:28
2. Pomp and Circumstance March No. IV—Abridged, Composer: Sir Edward Elgar 1:33
3. Timesteps (Excerpt), Composer: [Wendy] Carlos, Tempi Music BMI, Performed by [Wendy] Carlos 4:13
4. Overture to the Sun, Composer: Terry Tucker, Mills Music ASCAP 1:40
5. I Want to Marry a Lighthouse Keeper, Composer: Erika Eigen, Mills Music ASCAP, Performed by Erika Eigen [no timing]
6. William Tell Overture—Abridged, Composer: Gioacchino Rossini, Performance: A Deutsche Grammophon Recording 2:58

7. Suicide Scherzo (Ninth Symphony, Second Movement—Abridged), Composer: Ludwig van Beethoven, Arr. [Wendy] Carlos, Tempi Music BMI, Performed by [Wendy] Carlos 3:07
8. Ninth Symphony, Fourth Movement—Abridged, Composer: Ludwig van Beethoven, Performance: A Deutsche Grammophon Recording 1:34
9. Singin' in the Rain, Composed by: Arthur Freed, Nacio Herb Brown, Robbins Music ASCAP, Performed by Gene Kelly, an MGM Recording 2:36

### [Wendy] Carlos' A Clockwork Orange (1972, RCA Victor)

Side 1

1. Timesteps, [Wendy] Carlos (BMI, 13:50)
2. March from A Clockwork Orange (BMI, 7:00) (Beethoven: Ninth Symphony: Fourth Movement, Abridged), Articulations by Rachel Elkind, Arr. [Wendy] Carlos

Side 2

1. Title Music from A Clockwork Orange (BMI, 2:21) (from Purcell's "Music for the Funeral of Queen Mary"), [Wendy] Carlos and Rachel Elkind
2. La Gazza Ladra (P.D. 5:50) (The Thieving Magpie, Abridged), Gioacchino Rossini
3. Theme from A Clockwork Orange (BMI, 1:44) (Beethoviana), [Wendy] Carlos and Rachel Elkind
4. Ninth Symphony: Second Movement (P.D., 4:52), Ludwig van Beethoven
5. William Tell Overture, Abridged (P.D., 1:17), Gioacchino Rossini
6. Country Lane (BMI, 4:43), [Wendy] Carlos and Rachel Elkind

A recent re-issue includes the following tracks that were written for the film but unused. They were omitted from the LP because of time constraints:

Orange Minuet, written and performed by Wendy Carlos
Country Lane, written and performed by Wendy Carlos

## Chapter 5: Complete Track Lists
### from *Barry Lyndon*

### *Barry Lyndon: Original Soundtrack Album*
### (1975, Warner Bros.)

Side A

1. Sarabande—Main Title, Handel, National Philharmonic Orchestra, Leonard Rosenman, arr. and cond.
2. Women of Ireland, Sean Ó Riada; Chieftans
3. Piper's Maggot Jig, Traditional; Waterford Glass Band
4. The Sea-Maiden, Traditional; Chieftans
5. Tin Whistles, Sean Ó Riada; Paddy Moloney and Sean Potts
6. British Grenadiers, Traditional; Fifes and Drums, Rosenman, arr. and cond.
7. Hohenfriedberger March, Frederick the Great [attrib.]; Leonard Rosenman, cond.
8. Lilliburlero, Traditional; Fifes and Drums, Rosenman, arr. and cond.
9. Women of Ireland, Sean Ó Riada; Derek Bell, harp
10. March from *Idomeneo*, Mozart; EMI Records
11. Sarabande—Duel, Handel; National Philharmonic Orchestra, Rosenman, arr. and cond.

Side B

1. Lilliburlero, Traditional; Leslie Pearson, arr. and cond.
2. German Dance No. 1 in C Major, Schubert; National Philharmonic Orchestra, Rosenman, arr. and cond
3. Sarabande—Duel, Handel; National Philharmonic Orchestra, Rosenman, arr. and cond
4. Film Adaptation of the Cavatina from *Il Barbiere di Siviglia*, Paisiello; National Philharmonic Orchestra, Rosenman, arr. and cond
5. Cello concerto in E-minor (third movement), Vivaldi; Pierre Fournier, Cello, Festival Strings, Lucerne, Ralph Baumgartner, cond. Deutsche Grammophon
6. Adagio from Concerto for 2 Harpsichords and Orchestra in C minor, J. S. Bach; Karl Richter and Hedwig Bilgram, harpsichords, and the Munich Bach-Orchestra, Deutsche Grammophon

7. Film adaptation of Piano Trio in E-flat op. 100 (second movement), Schubert; Ralph Holmes, Violin; Moray Welsh, Cello; Anthony Goldstone, Piano; Rosenman, arr.
8. Sarabande—End-Title, Handel; National Philharmonic Orchestra, Rosenman, arr. and cond.

## CHAPTER 6: COMPLETE TRACK LISTS FROM *THE SHINING*

### *The Shining Original Soundtrack* (1980, Warner Bros.)

1. The Shining (Main Title) (3:27), Wendy Carlos and Rachel Elkind
2. Rocky Mountains (3:01), Wendy Carlos and Rachel Elkind
3. Lontano (10:11), Gyorgy Ligeti, Sinfonie-Orchestra des Sudwestfunks, Conducted by Ernest Bour
4. Music for Strings Percussion and Celesta (8:07), Bela Bartok, Berlin Philharmonic Orchestra, Conducted by Herbert von Karajan
5. Utrenja (Excerpt) (3:33), Krzysztof Penderecki, Symphony Orchestra of the National Philharmonic, Warsaw, Conducted by Andrzej Markowski
6. The Awakening of Jakob (7:55), Krzysztof Penderecki, Polish Radio National Symphony Orchestra, Conducted by Krzysztof Penderecki
7. De Natura Sonoris, No. 2 (8:56), Krzysztof Penderecki, Polish Radio National Symphony Orchestra, Conducted by Krzysztof Penderecki
8. Home (3:09), Henry Hall and the Gleneagles Hotel Band

### Scoring Options for *The Shining* by Wendy Carlos and Rachel Elkind

Archived at the University of the Arts London

### *The Shining:*—Album, Music by W. Carlos and R. Elkind

Side A

1. Title Music
2. High-Low
3. Danny Bells
4. Heartbeat Passage #1
5. Heartbeat Passage #2
6. Danny

Side B

1. Thought Clusters, Danny's 1st Esp (VerA)
2. Thought Clusters, Danny's 1st Esp (VerB)
3. Food Larder ESP
4. Psychic Shout Up Into Room 237 & Out
5. Psychic Shout & Room 237-While Seq.
6. Danny At Dart Board
7. Danny & Grady Twins
8. Single Loud Scream-Efx

## Disc 2: *The Shining,* music by Wendy Carlos and Rachel Elkind

Side A

1. Thought Transfers
2. Low And High
3. Low And High-Rich
4. Rich & High ESP
5. DC-10 @ 8 AM

Side B

1. The Shining—Title Music (New Mix)
2. The Shining—Title Music (Version of 7)
3. Winter Maze
4. Dream Man
5. Keepin' Out of Mischief Now

## Disc 3

1. Soft and slow Metaphor on "Dies Irae"
2. Vocal glissandi
3. Vocal "Dzzrrhr"'s
4. Whisperings
5. Low groaning moans
6. Small high shrieks
7. Low breath and growl sounds
8. Tapping of teeth or bone-rattlings
9. Piano—solo perform

Side B

1. Autoharp—solo perform
2. Vocal part of opening music
3. Glissing metal-rod on autoharp of opening music
4. Heartbeat—in clear
5. Slow upward portamento delay echo cluster
6. Gentle bells—"snow-like"
7. Winter's Efx of bell sounds

## Two Track #2 "Loops"

1. "Rocky Mountains" swaying 4ths, 5ths, and Am9ths in Brassy tones—rich (med. long cue)
2. "Low moanings" rich, a bit brassy and bassy—somber
3. More menacing low moans, rich, episodic—much bass (fairly loud)
4. Clustry, watery, soprano-like "ghosties"—ends in a high soft scream (short cue)
5. Medium watery "ghosties", slow build up in pitch, then "cluster" goes loud and nasty, more and more (good cue)
6. "Ghosties", solos, soprano and alto, sighs, siren-songs, music and very vocal-like, moves in waves (longish cue)
7. Moaning "Ghosties", alto and soprano, very high and end (med.)
8. Richer solo moaning "Ghosties", alto and tenor, soprano at end, moves up and in slow waves to scream
9. Duet—"Ghosties", vocal efx, small moans collect and move slowly up into cresc., slow gliss down as engine (longish, good cue)
10. Am9th low chord slowly moves up after low pulsating start, up to very high chord (med. Cue) (good sound)

## Two Track #5 "Wind and Textures"

1. Long wind—first low then "Stifled," then full with soft "moaning"
2. Shorter, outdoor, nastier version, with shimmer
3. Indoor brooding wind-atmosphere
4. Outdoor shimmery wind and efx
5. "The Snow"—wind with low Dies Irae
6. Danny and Wendy play in snow—wind and glassy and melancholy
7. Long bed—very wind-like and neutral
8. Long bed—softly shifting and complex

9. Long bed—neutral and shifting
10. Five chromatic cluster 16-voiced polyphonic performances (sample mixes only) (very good sounds built to suit given scenes)

**Two Track #6 "Piano and Autoharp efx and synth"**

Side A

1. fairly long, wide spaces very scary squeals and squeaks—ghosts
2. Three fat "swoops" as on "Ballroom" cues
3. Two large heavy crashes
4. High pitched shining/shimmer efx
5. Polymoog "Blood Bath" Grady twins bursts

Side B

1. Many Polymoog and synthesizer passages on "Dies Irae and miscel. Colors......(demo material) (for pos. extension)
2. 4 piano-renderings of "Dies Irae"

**Wendy Carlos: *Rediscovering Lost Scores, Volume I* (2005, East Side Digital)**

1. Colorado—'The Shining'
2. The Rocky Mountains—'The Shining'
3. Chase Music—'The Shining'
4. Nocturnal Valse Triste—'The Shining'
5. Greetings Ghosties—'The Shining'
6. Horror Show—'The Shining'
7. A Haunted Waltz—'The Shining'
8. Psychic Shout #237—'The Shining'
9. Danny—'The Shining'
10. Heartbeats And Worry—'The Shining'
11. Subliminal Ballroom—'The Shining'
12. Thought Clusters—'The Shining'
13. A Ghost Piano—'The Shining'
14. Visitors—'The Shining'
15. Dark Winds and Rustles—'The Shining'
16. Bumps in the Wind—'The Shining'
17. Setting with Medea—'The Shining'

18. Two Polymoog Improvisations—'The Shining'
19. Fanfare and Drunken 'Dies'—'The Shining'
20. Clockworks (Bloody Elevators)—'The Shining'
21. Danny Bells Ascending—'The Shining'
22. Postlude—'The Shining'
23. Stately Purcell—'Clockwork Orange'
24. Pop Purcell—'Clockwork Orange'
25. Trumpet Voluntary—'The Shining'
26. The Children of Peru—'UNICEF Films'
27. Shanty Town and Farewell—'UNICEF Films'
28. Daycare and the Colonel—'UNICEF Films'
29. Two Distant Walks—'UNICEF Films'
30. Ethiopian Life—'UNICEF Films'
31. Tanzanian Scenes—'UNICEF Films'
32. Three Hopeful Places—'UNICEF Films'

**Wendy Carlos: *Rediscovering Lost Scores, Volume II* (2005, East Side Digital)**

1. Shining Title Music—'The Shining'
2. Paraphrase for 'Cello—'The Shining'
3. Where's Jack?—'The Shining'
4. The Overlook—'The Shining'
5. Psychic—'The Shining'
6. Day of Wrath—'The Shining'
7. Paraphrase For Brass—'The Shining'
8. Title Music 'Dies'—'The Shining'
9. Clockworks 'Dies'—'The Shining'
10. Creation of Tron Vol. I—'Tron'
11. Creation of Tron Vol. II—'Tron'
12. Lightcycle Games—'Tron'
13. Anthem (Studio Version)—'Tron'
14. Little Interludes—'Tron'
15. Trinitron—'Tron'
16. Visit to a Morgue—'Split Second'
17. Return to the Morgue—'Split Second'
18. Woundings Title Music—'Woundings'
19. Angela's Walk—'Woundings'
20. Jimmy—'Woundings'
21. Louise—'Woundings'

22. Doug Does Angela—'Woundings'
23. Scattering Ashes—'Woundings'
24. Angela's Aftermath—'Woundings'
25. Jimmy Kills Louise—'Woundings'
26. In a Cemetery—'Woundings'
27. Fly Away and End—'Woundings'
28. Jiffy Test: Bee Dee Bei Mir—From Two Dolby Demos
29. Listen: Tannhauser—From Two Dolby Demos

## CHAPTER 7: COMPLETE TRACK LISTS FROM *EYES WIDE SHUT*

### Music from the Motion Picture Eyes Wide Shut (1999, Reprise)

1. Musica Ricercata, II (Mesto, rigido e cerimoniale), György Ligeti; Dominic Harlan
2. Waltz 2 From Jazz Suite [sic], Dmitri Shostakovich, The Royal Concertgebouw Orchestra, Conducted by Riccardo Chailly
3. Baby Did a Bad, Bad Thing, Chris Isaak
4. When I Fall in Love, Victor Young and Edward Heyman, The Victor Silvester Orchestra
5. I Got it Bad (and That Ain't Good), Duke Ellington and Paul Francis Webster; The Oscar Peterson Trio
6. Naval Officer, Jocelyn Pook; Jocelyn Pook, Conducted by Harvey Brough
7. The Dream, Jocelyn Pook; Jocelyn Pook, Conducted by Harvey Brough
8. Masked Ball, Jocelyn Pook
9. Migrations, Jocelyn Pook; Jocelyn Pook and the Jocelyn Pook Ensemble with Manickam Yogeswaran, Kelsey Michael and Harvey Brough
10. If I Had You, Shapiro, Campbell, and Connelly; Roy Gerson
11. Strangers in the Night, Snyder, Singleton, and Kaempfert, The Peter Hughes Orchestra
12. Blame It on My Youth, Oscar Levant and Edward Heyman; Brad Mehldau
13. Grey Clouds [Nuages Gris], Franz Liszt; Dominic Harlan
14. Musica Ricercata, II (Mesto, rigido e cerimoniale) [Reprise], György Ligeti; Dominic Harlan

## NOTES

1. The writers of this song are listed as Carter and Dewitt. On promotional versions of the release, the artist is listed as "Dr. Strangelove and the Fallouts."

2. *Billboard* 22 June 1968, 48.

3. Joe Sikoryak, "Great Film Scores," *Film Score Monthly* 5, no. 9 (November/December 2000): 36.

4. *Billboard* 19 April 1969, 35.

5. *Billboard* 1 July 1972, 21.

6. *Billboard* 4 March 1972, 41.

7. The album peaked at position thirty-four. Joel Whitburn, *Billboard: Top Albums 1955–2001* (Menomonee Falls, WI: Record Research, Inc., 2001), 1002.

8. *Walter Carlos' Clockwork Orange* peaked at 146 on the Billboard chart. Joel Whitburn, *Billboard: Top Albums 1955–2001* (Menomonee Falls, WI: Record Research, Inc., 2001),134.

# Bibliography

Adorno, Theodor, and Hans Eisler. *Composing for the Films*. London: Athelone Press, 1994.

Agel, Jerome, ed. *The Making of Kubrick's 2001*. New York: Signet, 1970.

Applegate, Celia, and Pamela Potter. "Germans as the 'People of Music': Genealogy of an Identity." In *Music and German National Identity*, ed. Celia Applegate and Pamela Potter, 1–35. Chicago: University of Chicago Press, 2002.

Arnold, Ben. "Piano Music: 1861–1886." In *The Liszt Companion*, ed. Ben Arnold, 139–177. Westport, CT: Greenwood Press, 2002, 140.

Barham, Jeremy. "Incorporating Monsters: Music as Context, Character and Construction in Kubrick's *The Shining*." In *Terror Tracks: Music, Sound and Horror Cinema*, ed. Philip Hayward, 137–161. London: Oakville, 2009.

Baxter, John. *Stanley Kubrick: A Biography*. New York: Carroll and Graf, 1997.

Bellettini, Lorenzo. "Freud's Contribution to Arthur Schnitzler's Prose Style." *Rocky Mountain E-Review of Language and Literature* 61, no. 2. Accessed 3 June 2012. http://rmmla.wsu.edu/ereview/61.2/articles/bellettini.asp.

Bender, John. "Farewell to the Master." *Film Score Monthly* 4, no. 8 (September/October 1999): 24–27, 48.

Berges, Marshal. Interview with Leonard Rosenman. "Home Q&A with Marshal Berges." *Los Angeles Times Home Magazine*, 37–40.

Berlioz, Hector, and Richard Strauss. *Treatise on Instrumentation*. Translated by Theodore Front. New York: Dover Publications, 1991.

Blakemore, William. "Kubrick's *Shining* Secret: Film's Hidden Horror Is the Murder of the Indian." *Washington Post,* July 12, 1987. Accessed 12 April 2012. http://williamblakemore.com/Blakemore-%20Kubrick%20Shining.pdf.

Bodde, Gerrit. *Musik in den Filmen von Stanley Kubrick*. Osnabruck: Der Andere Verlag, 2002.

Bond, Jeff. "A Clockwork Composer: Wendy Carlos." *Film Score Monthly* 4, no. 3 (March 1999): 18–23.
———. "Once in a Lifetime." *Film Score Monthly* 4, no. 8 (September/October 1999): 24–25.
Brantley, Ben. Review of *Blue Room*, Cort Theater, New York. *New York Times*, December 14, 1998. Accessed 7 June 2012. http://theater.nytimes.com/mem/theater/treview.html?html_title=&tols_title=BLUE+ROOM,+THE+(PLAY)&pdate=19981214&byline=By+BEN+BRANTLEY&id=1077011432284.
Brown, Garrett. "The Steadicam and *The Shining*." *American Cinematographer* 61, no. 8 (August 1980): 786–789.
Brown, Royal S. "Film and Classical Music." In *Film and the Arts in Symbiosis: A Resource Guide*, ed. Gary R. Edgerton, 165–215. New York: Greenwood Press, 1988.
———. *Overtones and Undertones: Reading Film Music*. Berkeley: University of California Press, 1994.
Buch, Esteban. *Beethoven's Ninth: A Political History*. Translated by Richard Miller. Chicago: University of Chicago Press, 1999.
Burgess, Anthony. *A Clockwork Orange*. New York: Ballantine Books, 1962; reprint, New York: Norton, 1986.
———. "On the Hopelessness of Turning Good Books into Films." *New York Times* April 20, 1975, 2, 15.
———. *This Man and Music*. New York: McGraw-Hill, 1982.
Caldwell, John, and Malcolm Boyd. "Dies Irae." In *The New Grove Dictionary of Music and Musicians*, ed. Stanley Sadie, 332–333. London: Macmillan, 2001.
Chase, Robert. *Dies Irae: A Guide to Requiem Music*. Lanham, MD: Scarecrow Press, 2003.
Chion, Michel. *Eyes Wide Shut*. Translated by Trista Selous. London: British Film Institute, 2002.
———. *Kubrick's Cinema Odyssey*. Translated by Claudia Gorbman. London: BFI Publishing, 2001.
Ciment, Michel. *Kubrick: The Definitive Edition*. Translated by Gilbert Adair. New York: Faber and Faber, 1999.
Clarke, Arthur C. *2001: A Space Odyssey*. New York: Penguin, 1993.
———. *The Lost Worlds of 2001*. New York: Signet Classics, 1972.
Clarke, Jim. "'Homesick for Sin': Why Burgess Revisited *A Clockwork Orange*." In *Portraits of the Artist in* A Clockwork Orange: *Papers and Music from the Anthony Burgess Centre's International Symposium 'The Avatars of* A Clockwork Orange' December 7–8, 2001, ed. Emmanuel Vernadakis and Graham Woodroffe, 69–78. Angers, France: Presses de l'Université d'Angers, 2003.
Clarke, Roger. "Putting the Knife into Stanley." *The Independent* August 2, 1999. Accessed 7 June 2012. http://www.independent.co.uk/arts-entertainment/monday-books-putting-the-knife-into-stanley-1110183.html.
Cloud, David, and Leslie Zador. "Alex North Interview: The Missing Score to *2001*." *Los Angeles Free Press*, November 12, 1970, 42, 39.

Cohen, Richard. "A Practical Guide to Re-Hearing *2001*." *New York Review of Science Fiction* 12, no. 7 (2000): 10–14.

Cocks, Geoffrey. "Death by Typewriter: Stanley Kubrick, the Holocaust, and *The Shining*." In *Depth of Field: Stanley Kubrick, Film, and the Uses of History*, ed. Geoffrey Cocks, James Diedrick, and Glenn Perusek, 185–217. Madison: University of Wisconsin Press, 2006.

———. *The Wolf at the Door: Stanley Kubrick, History, and the Holocaust.* New York: Peter Lang, 2004.

Code, David. "Rehearing *The Shining*: Musical Undercurrents in the Overlook Hotel." In *Music in the Horror Film: Listening to Fear*, ed. Neil William Lerner, 133–150. New York: Routledge, 2010.

Cook, David A. "American Horror: *The Shining*." *Film Literature Quarterly* 12, no.1 (1984): 2–4.

———. *A History of Narrative Film.* 3rd ed. New York: W. W. Norton, 1981.

Cook, Nicholas. *Beethoven: Symphony No. 9.* Cambridge: Cambridge University Press, 1993.

Cooke, Mervyn. *A History of Film Music.* New York: Cambridge University Press, 2005.

Cosgrove, Peter. "The Cinema of Attractions and the Novel in *Barry Lyndon* and *Tom Jones*." In *Eighteenth-Century Fiction on Screen*, ed. Robert Mayer, 16–34. Cambridge: Cambridge University Press, 2002.

Crilly, Ciarán. "The Bigger Picture: Ligeti's Music and the Films of Stanley Kubrick." In *György Ligeti: Of Foreign Lands and Strange Sounds*, ed. Louise Duschesneau and Wolfgang Marx, 245–254. Woodbridge: Bydell Press, 2011.

Crocker, Richard L., John Caldwell, and Alejandro E. Planchart. "Sequence." In *The New Grove Dictionary of Music and Musicians*, ed. Stanley Sadie, 91–107. London: Macmillan, 2001.

Crone, Rainer. *Stanley Kubrick: Drama and Shadows: Photographs 1945–1950.* London: Phaidon, 2005.

Davis, Victor. "Film Boost for Chieftans." *Daily Express* (London), September 30, 1975.

Dawson, Jan. "A Clockwork Orange." *British Film Institute Monthly Film Bulletin* 39, 457 (February 1972): 28–29.

Del Mar, Norman. *Richard Strauss: A Critical Commentary of His Life and Work, Vol I.* Ithaca, NY: Cornell University Press, 1986.

Dennis, David B. *Beethoven in German Politics 1870–1989.* New Haven, CT: Yale University Press, 1996.

———. "'Honor Your German Masters': The Use and Abuse of 'Classical' Composers in Nazi Propaganda." *Journal of Political and Military Sociology* 30, 2 (Winter 2002): 273–295.

DeVries, Daniel. *The Films of Stanley Kubrick.* Grand Rapids, MI: Eerdmans, 1973.

Donnelly, K. J. *The Spectre of Sound: Music in Film and Television*. London: BFI, 2005.

Dorfman, Ariel. *Death and the Maiden*. New York: Penguin, 1992.

Ebsworth, J[oseph] Woodfall, ed. *Choyce Drollery: Songs and Sonnets*: To which are added the extra songs of *Merry Drollery*, 1661, and *An Antidote Against Melancholy*, 1661. Boston, Lincolnshire: Printed by Robert Roberts, Strait Bar-Gate. 1886. From the Ebook and Texts Archive from the University of Toronto Robarts Library. Accessed 20 January 2012. www.archive.org/details/choycedrolleryso00ebswuoft.

Fay, Laurel E. *Shostakovich: A Life*. New York: Oxford University Press, 2000.

Ferrara, Serena. *Steadicam: Techniques and Aesthetics*. Oxford: Focal Press, 2000.

Fielding, Raymond. *The March of Time: 1935–1951*. New York: Oxford University Press, 1978.

Flinn, Caryl. *Strains of Utopia: Gender, Nostalgia, and Hollywood Film Music*. Princeton, NJ: Princeton University Press, 1992.

Foreman, Lewis. "The Winnowing-Fan: British Music in Wartime." In *Oh, My Horses! Elgar and the Great War,* ed. Lewis Foreman, 89–131. Rickmansworth: Elgar Enterprises, 2001.

Geduld, Carolyn. *Film Guide to 2001: A Space Odyssey*. Bloomington: Indiana University Press, 1973.

Gengaro, Christine. "It Was Lovely Music That Came to My Aid: Music's Contribution to the Narrative of the Novel, Film and Play *A Clockwork Orange*." Ph.D. Dissertation, University of Southern California, 2005.

Gorbman, Claudia, "Ears Wide Open: Kubrick's Music." In *Changing Tunes: The Use of Pre-Existing Music in Film*, ed. Phil Powrie and Robynn Stilwell, 3–18. Burlington, VT: Ashgate, 2006.

———. *Unheard Melodies: Narrative Film Music*. Bloomington: Indiana University Press, 1987.

Grant, Barry Keith. "Of Men and Monoliths: Science Fiction, Gender, and *2001: A Space Odyssey*." In *2001: A Space Odyssey: New Essays*, ed. Robert Kolker, 69–86. New York: Oxford University Press, 2006.

Griffiths, Paul. "György Ligeti." In *The New Grove Dictionary of Music and Musicians*, ed. Stanley Sadie, 690–696. London: Macmillan, 2001.

Gross, Larry. "Too Late the Hero." *Sight and Sound* 9, no. 9 (September 23, 1999): 20–23.

Gumenik, Arthur. "*A Clockwork Orange*: Novel into Film." *Film Heritage* 7, no. 4 (Summer 1972): 7–18.

Harris, Thomas. *The Silence of the Lambs*. New York: St. Martin's Press, 1988.

Heimerdinger, Julia. "'I have been compromised. I am now fighting against it.': Ligeti vs. Kubrick and the Music for *2001: A Space Odyssey*." *Journal of Film Music* 3, no. 2 (2011): 127–143.

Helm, Eugene, and Derek McCullough. "Frederick II." In *The New Grove Dictionary of Music and Musicians*, ed. Stanley Sadie, 218–219. London: Macmillan, 2001.

Henderson, Sonya Shoilevska. *Alex North, Film Composer*. Jefferson, NC: McFarland, 1993.

Hickman, Roger. *Reel Music: Exploring 100 Years of Film Music*. New York: Norton, 2006.

Hoile, Christopher. "The Uncanny and the Fairy Tale in Kubrick's *The Shining*." *Literature Film Quarterly* 12, no. 1 (1984): 5–12.

Howard, James. *Stanley Kubrick Companion*. London: B.T. Batsford, 1999.

Hughes, David. *The Complete Kubrick*. London: Virgin Publishing, 2000.

Hughes, Robert. "The Décor of Tomorrow's Hell." *Time Magazine*, December 27, 1971, reprinted in Mario Falsetto, ed. *Perspectives on Stanley Kubrick*, 185–186. New York: G.K. Hall, 1996.

Ito, Robert. "Cracking the Code in 'Heeere's Johnny!'" *New York Times*, January 29, 2012. Accessed 12 February 2012. http://www.nytimes.com/2012/01/29/movies/room-237-documentary-with-theories-about-the-shining.html.

Jackson, Neil. "Stanley Kubrick." In *Contemporary North American Film Directors: A Wallflower Critical Guide*, ed. Yoram Allon, Del Cullen, and Hannah Patterson, 263–265. London: Wallflower, 2000.

James, Nick. "At Home with the Kubricks." *Sight and Sound* 9, no. 9 (September 1999): 12–18.

Johnson, Sam. "'What's It Going to Be Then, Eh?' Deciphering Adolescent Violence and Adult Corruption in *A Clockwork Orange*." In *Portraits of the Artist in A Clockwork Orange Papers and Music from the Anthony Burgess Centre's International Symposium 'The Avatars of A Clockwork Orange,'* ed. Emmanuel Vernadakis and Graham Woodroffe, 27–40. Angers, France: Presses de l'Universite d'Angers, 2003.

Jordan, Randolph. "The Mask That Conceals Nothing: On the Concepts of Marital Fidelity and the Lo-Fi Soundscape in *Eyes Wide Shut*." In *Stanley Kubrick: Essays on His Films and Legacy*, ed. Gary D. Rhodes, 157–169. Jefferson, NC: McFarland, 2008.

Kael, Pauline. *Deeper into Movies*. Boston: Little, Brown, 1973.

———. *Going Steady*. Boston: Little, Brown, 1968.

Kagan, Norman. *The Cinema of Stanley Kubrick*. New York: Holt, Rinehart and Winston, 1972.

Kinderman, William. *Beethoven*. Oxford: Oxford University Press, 1995.

King, Stephen. *The Shining*. New York: Pocket Books, 1977.

Kracauer, Siegfried, *Theory of Film: The Redemption of Physical Reality*. New York: Oxford University Press, 1960.

Lehmann, Hans-Thies. "Film/Theatre: Masks/Identities in *Eyes Wide Shut*." In *Stanley Kubrick Catalogue*, 2nd ed., 234–243. Frankfurt am Main: Deutsches Filmmuseum, 2007.

Levinson, Peter J. *September in the Rain: The Life of Nelson Riddle*. New York: Billboard Books, 2001.

Levy, David. *Beethoven: The Ninth Symphony*. Rev. ed., Yale Music Masterworks Series. New Haven, CT: Yale University Press, 2003.

Ligeti, György. *Lontano*. Mainz: B. Schott's Söhne, 1967.

Lightman, Herb. Interview with John Alcott. "Photographing Stanley Kubrick's *The Shining*." *American Cinematographer* 61, no. 8 (August 1980): 780–785, 840–845.

Lionnet, Leonard. "Mysteries of the Overlook: Unraveling Stanley Kubrick's Soundtrack to *The Shining*." *Film Score Monthly* 9, no. 1 (January 2004): 44–47.

LoBrutto, Vincent. *Stanley Kubrick: A Biography*. New York: Da Capo Press, 1997.

Losseff, Nicky. "The Piano Concerto and Sonata for Two Pianos and Percussion." In *The Cambridge Companion to Bartók*, ed. Amanda Bayley, 118–132. Cambridge: Cambridge University Press, 2001.

MacDonald, Ian. *The New Shostakovich*. New edition, updated by Raymond Clarke. London: Pimlico, 2006.

Mainar, Luis M. Garcia. *Narrative and Stylistic Patterns in the Films of Stanley Kubrick*. Rochester, NY: Camden House, 1999.

McCarten, John. Review of *Fear and Desire*. *New Yorker*, April 11, 1953. Accessed 27 June 2011. http://archives.newyorker.com/?i=1953–04–11#folio=128.

McClary, Susan. *Feminine Endings*. Minneapolis: University of Minnesota Press, 1991.

McQuiston, Katherine. "An Effort to Decide": More Research into Kubrick's Music Choices for *2001: A Space Odyssey*." *Journal of Film Music* 3, no. 2 (2011): 145–154.

Merkley, Paul A. "'Stanley Hates This but I Like It!' North vs. Kubrick on the Music for *2001: A Space Odyssey*." *Journal of Film Music* 2, no. 1 (Fall 2007): 1–34.

Nabokov, Vladimir. *Lolita*. New York: Vintage International, 1989.

———. *Lolita: A Screenplay*. New York: McGraw-Hill, 1974.

Naremore, James. *On Kubrick*. London: British Film Institute, 2007.

Nelson, Chris. Liner notes to *Walter Carlos' A Clockwork Orange*. Rachel Elkind, producer. Columbia KC 31480, 1972.

Nelson, Thomas Allen. *Kubrick: Inside a Film Artist's Maze*. Bloomington: Indiana University Press, 1982.

Nettl, Bruno. *Heartland Excursions*. Chicago: University of Chicago Press, 1995.

Newman, Ernest. *The Life of Richard Wagner, Volume II: 1848–1860*. Cambridge: Cambridge University Press, 1933.

———. *The Wagner Operas*. Princeton, NJ: Princeton University Press, 1949.

Nobel, Robin. "Killers, Kisses . . . and *Lolita*." *Films and Filming* 7, no. 3 (December 1960): n.p.

Osborne, Richard. "La Gazza Ladra." In *New Grove Opera*, ed. Stanley Sadie, 366–367. New York: Macmillan Press, 1992.

Osbourne, Charles. *The Complete Operas of Mozart*. New York: Da Capo Press, 1978.

Phillips, Gene. *Stanley Kubrick: A Film Odyssey*. New York: Popular Library, 1975.

———, ed. *Stanley Kubrick Interviews*. Jackson: University Press of Mississippi, 2001.

Phillips, Gene D., and Rodney Hill. *Encyclopedia of Stanley Kubrick*. New York: Checkmark Books, 2002.

Phillips, Paul. "Alex in Eden: Prologue and Music to Burgess's Dramatization of *A Clockwork Orange*." In *Portraits of the Artist in* A Clockwork Orange *Papers and Music from the Anthony Burgess Centre's International Symposium 'The Avatars of* A Clockwork Orange' December 7–8, 2001, ed. Emmanuel Vernadakis and Graham Woodroffe, 113–129. Angers, France: Presses de l'Université d'Angers, 2003.

Pinch, Trevor, and Frank Trocco. *Analog Days: The Invention and Impact of the Moog Synthesizer*. Cambridge: Harvard University Press, 2002.

———. "The Social Construction of the Early Electronic Music Synthesizer." In *Music and Technology in the Twentieth Century*, ed. Hans-Joachim Braun, 67–83. Baltimore: Johns Hopkins University Press, 2000.

Prendergast, Mark. *The Ambient Century: From Mahler to Trance—The Evolution of Sound in the Electronic Age*. New York: Bloomsbury, 2000.

Pryor, Thomas M. Hollywood Dossier. *New York Times,* February 22, 1951.

Rabinowitz, Peter J. "A Bird of Like Rarest Spun Heavenmetal: Music in *A Clockwork Orange*." In *Stanley Kubrick's* A Clockwork Orange, ed. Stuart Y. McDougal, 109–130. New York: Cambridge University Press, 2003.

Rapée, Erno. *Motion Picture Moods for Pianists and Organists*. New York, 1924; reprint edition. New York: Arno, 1974.

Raphael, Frederic. *Eyes Wide Open: A Memoir of Stanley Kubrick*. New York: Ballantine Books, 1999.

Rasmussen, Randy. *Stanley Kubrick: Seven Films Analyzed*. Jefferson, NC: McFarland, 2001.

Ratner, Leonard. *Romantic Music: Sound and Syntax*. New York: Schirmer, 1992.

Reed, John. *Schubert: The Final Years*. New York: St. Martin's Press, 1972.

Robey, Tim. "Kubrick's Neglected Masterpiece." *The Telegraph,* February 5, 2009. Accessed 21 January 2012. http://www.telegraph.co.uk/culture/4524037/Barry-Lyndon-Kubricks-neglected-masterpiece.html.

Robinson, Michael F. "Giovanni Paisiello." In *The New Grove Dictionary of Music and Musicians*, ed. Stanley Sadie, 906=914. London: Macmillan, 2001.

Roche, Jerome. "Sarrusophone." In *The New Grove Dictionary of Music and Musicians*, ed. Stanley Sadie, 296–298. London: Macmillan, 2001.

Rosar, William. "The *Dies Irae* in *Citizen Kane*: Musical Hermeneutics Applied to Film Music." In *Film Music: Critical Approaches*, ed. K. J. Donnelly, 103–116. New York: Continuum, 2001.

Rosenbaum, Jonathan. "In Dream Begin Responsibilities" in *Depth of Field: Stanley Kubrick, Film and the Uses of History*, ed. Geoffrey Cocks, James Diedrick, and Glenn Perusek, 245–254. Madison: University of Wisconsin Press, 2006.

Roth, Ellen Shamis. "The Rhetoric of First Person Point of View in the Novel and Film Forms: A Study of Anthony Burgess' *A Clockwork Orange* and Henry James' *A Turn of the Screw* and Their Film Adaptations." Ph.D. Dissertation, New York University, 1978.

Schnitzler, Arthur. *Night Games and Other Stories and Novellas*. Translated by Margaret Schaefer. Chicago: Ivan R. Dee, 2002.

Schultheis, Bernd. "Expanse of Possibilities: Stanley Kubrick's Soundtracks in Notes." In *Stanley Kubrick Catalogue*, 2nd ed., 266–279. Frankfurt am Main: Deutsches Filmmuseum, 2007.

Searby, Michael D. *Ligeti's Stylistic Crisis: Transformation in His Musical Style 1974–1985*. Lanham, MD: Scarecrow Press, 2010.

Shakespeare, William. *The Complete Works*. New York: Dorset Press, 1988.

Shirakawa, Sam H. *The Devil's Music Master*. Oxford: Oxford University Press, 1992.

Sikoryak, Joe, ed. "Great Film Scores." *Film Score Monthly* 5, no. 9 (November/ December 2000): 26–44.

Singer, Samuel L. "24-Year-Old Is 'Factotum' of New Film." *Philadelphia Inquirer*, July 26, 1953, Sunday Morning Edition.

Smith, Steve C. *A Heart at Fire's Center: The Life and Music of Bernard Herrmann*. Berkeley: University of California Press, 1991.

Sobol, Louis. "New York Cavalcade." *Journal-American*, June 29, 1962.

Southern, Terry. *Blue Movie*. New York: Grove Press, 1970.

Stagg, Mildred. "Quiz Kid." *The Camera*, December 6, 1949.

Steinitz, Richard. *György Ligeti: Music of the Imagination*. Boston: Northeastern University Press, 2003.

Strick, Philip, and Penelope Houston. Interview with Stanley Kubrick from 1972. In *Stanley Kubrick Interviews*, ed. Gene D. Phillips, 126–139. Jackson: University Press of Mississippi, 2001.

Studwell, William E. *The National and Religious Song Reader: Patriotic, Traditional, and Sacred Songs from Around the World*. New York: Haworth Press, 1996.

Thackeray, William Makepeace. *The Memoirs of Barry Lyndon, Esq.*, ed. Andrew Sanders. Oxford: Oxford University Press, 2008.

Thirer, Irene. "Screenview." *New York Post*, March 27, 1953, 58.

Thomas, Adrian. "Penderecki." In *The New Grove Dictionary of Music and Musicians*, ed. Stanley Sadie, 305–309. London: Macmillan, 2001.

Thomas, Tony. *Film Score: The View from the Podium*. South Brunswick: A.S. Barnes, 1979.

Timberg, Scott "Halt, or I'll Play Vivaldi!" *Los Angeles Times*, February 13, 2005, sec. E, 35 and 40.

———. "Is Bach Playing? Look Out!" *Los Angeles Times*, August 24, 2003, sec. E, 34–35.

Von Gunden, Kenneth, and Stuart H. Stock. *Twenty All-Time Great Science Fiction Films*. New York: Arlington House, 1982.

Walker, Alexander. *Stanley Kubrick Directs*, expanded ed. New York: Harcourt Brace Jovanovich, 1972.

Walker, Alan. *Franz Liszt, Volume Three: The Final Years, 1861–1886*. New York: Alfred A. Knopf, 1996.

Webster, Patrick. *Love and Death in Kubrick: A Critical Study of the Films from Lolita through Eyes Wide Shut*. Jefferson, NC: McFarland, 2011.

Whitburn, Joel. *Billboard: Top Albums 1955–2001*. Menomenee Falls, WI: Record Research, 2001.

White, Susan B. *The Cinema of Max Ophuls: Magisterial Vision and the Figure of Woman*. New York: Columbia University Press, 1995.

Wilson, Earl. "It Happened Last Night." *New York Post,* May 14, 1962.

Yuzefovich, Victor. *Aram Khachaturian*. Translated by Nicholas Kournokoff and Vladimir Bobrov. New York: Sphinx Press, 1985.

Zaslaw, Neal. "Leclair." In *The New Grove Dictionary of Music and Musicians*, ed. Stanley Sadie, 444–448. London: Macmillan, 2001.

Zinman, David. *Fifty Grand Films of the Sixties and Seventies*. New York: Crown, 1986.

Zwerin, Mike. "Kubrick's Approval Sets Seal on Classical Crossover Success: Pook's Unique Musical Mix." *New York Times,* October 27, 1999. Accessed 27 April 2012. http://www.nytimes.com/1999/10/27/style/27iht-pook.t.html.

## WEBSITES

The Academy of Motion Picture Arts and Science. "Official Academy Awards Database." http://awardsdatabase.oscars.org/ampas_awards/BasicSearchInput.jsp.

AMC Filmsite. http://www.filmsite.org/aa75.html.

The American Catholic. "Lilliburlero." http://the-american-catholic.com/2011/04/09/lilliburlero/.

Archive of American Television. Interview with Gerald Fried. http://emmytv legends.org/interviews/people/gerald-fried.

BBC World Service. http://www.bbc.co.uk/worldservice/institutional/2009/03/000000_ws_sig_tune.shtml.

First Foot Guards. http://footguards.tripod.com/06ARTICLES/ART27_BritGren .htm.

Franciscan Archive. "Dies Irae [translation]." http://www.franciscan-archive.org/de_celano/opera/diesirae.html.

Gordon Stainforth (official website). http://www.gordonstainforth.co.uk/.

Granular Synthesis. http://www.granularsynthesis.com/hthesis/gabor2.html.

Internet Movie Database. "This Is America: They Fly with the Fleet." http://www .imdb.com/title/tt0346020/.

Jack Hylton: The Official Jack Hylton Website. http://www.jackhylton.com/.

Library of Congress. http://lcweb2.loc.gov/diglib/ihas/loc.natlib.ihas.200000024/default.html.

LVBeethoven. "Meet Beethoven at Heiligenstadt." http://www.lvbeethoven.com/MeetLvB/AustriaHeiligenstadtStatueHanlein.html.

Nelson Riddle: The Official Website. http://www.nelsonriddlemusic.com/nr_tv.htm.

Schott Music. "Krzysztof Penderecki." http://www.schott-music.com/shop/persons/
    featured/krzysztof-penderecki/index.html.
Soundtrack: Cinemascore and Soundtrack Archives. "Jocelyn Pook on *Eyes Wide
    Shut.*" (Interview with Jocelyn Pook by Rudy Koppl.) http://www.runmovies.eu/
    index.php?option=com_content&task=view&id=311&Itemid=57.
United States Coast Guard. http://www.uscg.mil/history/img/Sailors_All_Poster
    .jpg.
Visual Memory: Stanley Kubrik. "The Kubrik FAQ." (Frequently asked questions
    on *The Shining.*) http://www.visual-memory.co.uk/faq/html/shining/shining
    .html.
Wendy Carlos (official website). http://wendycarlos.com.

# Index

*2001: A Space Odyssey* (film), 33,
60, 69, 75, 105, 116, 159, 179,
183, 196, 214, 220, 226, 252,
259–260; adaptation of the novel,
72–73; Alex North's score to,
77–86; *Also Sprach Zarathustra* (R.
Strauss), 75, 78, 80, 82, 85, 87–89,
95; *Antarctica Suite* (Vaughn
Williams), 73 ; *The Blue Danube*
(J. Strauss), 77, 83, 84, 85, 87,
89–91, 109–110; "Daisy Bell,"
70, 98; *Gayane* (Khachaturian)
87, 94, 95–97; Ligeti's music in,
91–95; *Lux Aeterna* (Ligeti), 197,
198; *Midsummer Night's Dream*
(Mendelssohn), 73; soundtrack, 69,
74, 86–87, 134
*2001: A Space Odyssey* (novel), 72–73,
98; musical references in, 70–71

Academy Awards, 79, 131, 149, 152,
174, 181
Adorno, Theodor, 37–38
*Africa*, 79, 80
Agel, Jerome, 77
*A.I. Artificial Intelligence*, 219–220,
250, 251–252

Aldiss, Brian, 219
*Alexander Nevsky*, viii–ix, 35, 193
American Hindus against Defamation,
225, 227
anti-Semitism, 223, 253n35
*Apocalypse Now*, 189
Aragno, Riccardo, 149–150
Arbus, Diane, 215n13
*Aryan Papers*, 183, 219, 250
Asher, Rodney, 181

Bach, Carl Philipp Emanuel, 165, 170
Bach, Johann Sebastian, 71, 131,
138, 155; Concerto for Two
Harpsichords and Orchestra,
169–170
Baroque period (in music), 111, 133,
155, 170, 243
*Barry Lyndon*, 33, 76, 99, 147, 179,
184, 191, 192, 214, 222, 224, 229,
262–263; "The British Grenadiers,"
151, 161–162; candlelight filming
of, 175, 180, 222; Cello Concerto
in E minor (Vivaldi), 168–169;
choosing music for, 148–152;
Concerto for Two Harpsichords
(Bach), 169–170; differences

with source material, 147–148,
173–174; German Dance No. 1
C major (Schubert), 166–167;
Hohenfriedberger March, 163–
165; *Idomeneo* (Mozart), 154,
165–166; *Il Barbere di Siviglia*
(Paisiello), 167–168; Impromptu,
Op. 90 (Schubert), 172–173;
"Lilliburlero," 151, 154, 162–163;
Piano Trio in E-flat, Op. 100
(Schubert), 170–172; "Piper's
Maggot Jig," 159; Rosenman,
Leonard, 151–152, 156, 174–175;
Sarabande (Handel), 152, 154,
155–157; "Sea-Maiden," 154,
160; soundtrack album, 152–153;
"Tin Whistles," 160; "Women of
Ireland," 157–159
Bartók, Béla, 214; *Music for Strings,
Percussion, and Celesta*, 179, 191–
192, 198–201
Beethoven, Ludwig van, 29, 104, 108,
120, 122, 130, 132, 133, 138,
151, 228, 260–262; *Fidelio*, 230,
242, 244; Fifth Symphony, 114,
122, 123; Ninth Symphony, 109,
113, 117, 119, 120, 123–129, 132,
138–139; *Pastoral* Symphony, 71,
87; Third Symphony, 123; Violin
Concerto, 115
Begley, Louis, 183, 219
Bergman, Ingmar, 225
Berlioz, Hector, 31n27, 37, 71, 193
Bernstein, Leonard, 87, 133
Bhagavad Gita, 227, 238
Bible, 118, 202, 206
*Billboard*, 52, 134, 267, 268, 269
Biswell, Andrew, 105
Blakemore, Bill, 182
*Blue Movie*, 225
*Blue Room*, 221
Bodde, Gerrit, ix, 28, 55
Bowlly, Al, 211
Brando, Marlon, 33, 34, 57

Brant, Henry, 78, 82, 86
Brown, Garrett, 180–181
Brown, Royal S., 71
Burgess, Anthony, 103–104, 132, 133,
138–139; *A Clockwork Orange: A
Play with Music*, 106, 124, 132.
*See also A Clockwork Orange*
(novel)
Burlingame, Jon, 80, 81, 82, 84

Carlos, Wendy, 133–134, 141, 179;
*A Clockwork Orange* and, 86,
110–111, 116, 117, 122, 128, 129,
134, 137, 140, 147; *The Shining*
and, 86, 179, 186–190, 193–196,
228; *Switched on Bach*, 133–134,
139, 268
Cartier, Walter, 1, 4, 5, 15
*Casablanca*, 14
Ceoltóirí Cualann, 158–159
Chaplin, Charlie, 225
Chasan, Will, 7
Chieftans, 159, 161
Chion, Michel, 222, 232, 235, 245,
250
Chopin, Frédéric, 51, 199
Christian, Susanne, 27. *See also*
Kubrick, Christiane
Ciment, Michel, viii, 34, 60, 85, 86,
123, 148, 149, 184, 240
Clar, Arden, 15
Clarke, Arthur C., 70, 71–73, 98, 219.
*See also 2001: A Space Odyssey*
(novel)
classical music in film, 29, 74–75,
129–132
*Clean Break*, 18
Clift, Montgomery, 1, 2
*Clockwork Orange, A* (film), 33,
60, 67n75, 70, 75, 77, 99, 105,
131, 133, 147, 148, 179, 192,
214, 225, 260–262; adaptation,
104–105; Beethoven's music in,
104, 109, 114, 115, 122–128,

129; controversy surrounding, 225; differences with source material, 106–108; *Funeral Music for Queen Mary* (Purcell), 61, 106, 110–111, 140, 194; *Guillaume Tell* (Rossini), 116–117; "I Want to Marry a Lighthouse Keeper," 121; Ludovico treatment, 107, 109, 111, 117, 119, 121–123, 126, 127, 137, 139, 140; "Overture to the Sun," 121, 137; *Pomp and Circumstance* (Elgar), 112–113; *Scheherazade* (Rimsky-Korsakov), 118, 137, 140; "Singin' in the Rain," 67n75, 118–121, 130, 134; soundtracks for the film, 134–137; *The Thieving Magpie* (Rossini), 113–116, 132, 134; *Timesteps* (Carlos), 122, 134

*A Clockwork Orange* (novel), 103, 105, 106–108, 115, 125, 139; further adaptations of, 106, 132; music in, 104, 113, 115–117, 122, 128, 132, 138; Nadsat in, 105, 129, 138, 141n1; twenty-first chapter of, 107–108

Cocks, Geoffrey, 182–183, 201
Colpix, 59–60
Cook, David A., 182
Council of Trent, 193
Cowell, Henry, 189
Crone, Rainer, 18
Cruise, Tom, 222, 223, 249, 250
Crumb, George, 194
*The Curse of Frankenstein*, 52

D'Alessandro, Emilio, 224
*Dark Side of the Moon*, 183
*Day of the Fight*, 2, 6, 10, 14–15, 16; score, 2–5
De Rochemont, Richard, 7
*Death and the Maiden*, 131, 144n54
Debussy, Claude, 3, 247
Decca, 121, 211, 213
Delibes, Leo, 74, 87

the Delvets, 238–239
Demme, Jonathan, 131
Devries, Daniel, 83
Di Giulio, Ed, 180–181
*Dies Irae*, 61, 110–111, 134, 179, 188–190, 193–195, 196, 216n42, 246
Donnelly, K. J., 190, 191, 192, 194
Donnen, Stanley, 119
Dorfman, Ariel, 131
Douglas, Kirk, 46, 56, 65n34; *Paths of Glory*, 24, 90; *Spartacus*, 34, 36
*Dr. Strangelove*, 33, 57, 60, 69, 72, 225; score, 57–60
*Dr. Strangelove and the Fallouts*, 60
*Dragonslayer*, 79

Edwards, Douglas, 2, 6
Eigen, Erika, 121
Eisenstein, Sergei, viii–ix, xn2
Eisler, Hans, 37–38
Elgar, Edward, 112–113
Elkind, Rachel, 133, 134, 137, 186–190, 195
Ermey, R. Lee, 61, 63
*The Exorcist*, 86
*Eyes Wide Shut*, 33, 93, 196, 219–220, 223–225, 232, 264–266; "Baby Did a Bad, Bad Thing," 226, 233, 241; big band tunes, 240; choosing music for, 226; controversy surrounding, 225–226, 227; critical reception, 249–250; differences with source material, 222–223, 230, 248, 249; "I Want a Boy for Christmas," 238–239; jazz tunes, 241–242; "Jingle Bells," 249; *Musica Ricercata* (Ligeti), 226, 230, 238, 242–245; *Nuages gris* (Liszt), 226, 234, 247–248; Pook's music for, 226, 227, 230, 231, 233–238; "Rex Tremendae" (Mozart), 226, 246–247; Schnitzler, Arthur, 220–223, 230, 248; sound design,

248–249; soundtrack, 226–227; "Strangers in the Night," 231, 238, 240; Suite for Variety Orchestra (Shostakovich), 226, 231–233

Fairlight Series III synthesizer, 63
*Family Guy*, 181
*Fear and Desire*, 7–8, 14, 15, 25, 224; score, 8–13
Fellini, Federico, 149, 225
Ferrara, Serena, 180–181
*The Firm*, 222
Fleischer, Nathaniel, 3, 30n12
*The Flying Padre*, 5; score, 6
Frederick the Great, 163, 165
Frescobaldi, Girolamo, 243
Freud, Sigmund, 220–221, 223
Fried, Gerald, 2, 7, 76, 152, 176n7, 251; collaboration with Kubrick, 28–29; *Day of the Fight*, 3–5; *Fear and Desire*, 7–13; *Full Metal Jacket*, 33, 60, 182, 219, 222; *Killer's Kiss*, 14–18, 49; *Paths of Glory*, 24–29, 76; score and soundtrack, 61–63; *The Killing*, 19–24
Friedkin, William, 86

Geduld, Caroline, 90
George, Peter, 57
Gimbel, Norman, 15, 18
*The Gladiators*, 34
Gluck, Christoph Willibald, 103, 151
Goldsmith, Jerry, 76–77, 79–80
Gorbman, Claudia, 108
Gould, Glenn, 133
Grant, Barry Keith, 93
Grieg, Edvard, 74, 130

Hall, Henry, 213
Handel, George Frederick, 122, 151, 152; Sarabande, 155–157
"Happy Birthday," 61, 70, 97
Hare, David, 221
Harlan, Dominic, 229

Harlan, Jan, 75, 76, 83, 89, 92, 93, 97, 149, 150, 154, 185, 186, 187, 225, 228–230, 245, 250, 252
Harris, Bob, 48, 49, 50, 51, 52, 56, 66n47
Harris, James, 33, 49, 50
Harris, Thomas, 131
Hasford, Gustav, 60
Hayden, Sterling, 18, 57, 59
Haydn, 87, 122, 151, 167, 170
Henderson, Sanya, 35, 36, 40
Herr, Michael, 60
Herrmann, Bernard, 49, 66n48, 71
Hitchcock, Alfred, 66n48, 86
Hite, Bob, 6
Hitler, Adolph, 123, 130, 254n35
Hobbs, Katharina Kubrick, 224
Hollenback, Don, 7
Hölliger-North, Anna, 78
Hollywood blacklist, 46, 65n34
Houston, Penelope, 109
Hylton, Jack, 210–211

Industrial Light and Magic, 219
Intrada Records, 80, 85
Isaak, Chris, 226, 233

Jagger, Mick, 104
Jarre, Maurice, 60
jazz, viii, 16, 191; in *Killer's Kiss*, 16, 19; in *The Killing*, 19, 20, 21, 22, 23
Jesus Christ, 61, 118, 125, 201–202
"Johnny I Hardly Knew Ye," 58
Johnson, Laurie, 57–58, 59, 60
Jones, Quincy, 29
*Jurassic Park*, 219

Kael, Pauline, 69
Kagan, Norman, 36, 43
Karel, William, 183
Kazan, Elia, 35, 152
Kelly, Gene, 119–120
Keitel, Harvey, 222

Khachaturian, Aram, 87, 93; *Gayane*, 94, 95–97
Kidman, Nicole, 221, 222, 223, 224, 226, 249, 250, 253n14
*Killer's Kiss*, 2, 14, 19, 49, 224; score, 14–18
*The Killing*, 2, 18, 57; score, 19–24
King, Stephen, 179, 182, 183, 185, 187, 188, 212
Kodaly, Zoltan, 199
Korngold, Erich Wolfgang, 37
Kracauer, Siegfried, 121–122
Krushchev, Nikita, 201
Kubrick, Christiane, 27, 92, 115, 137, 183, 220, 223–224
Kubrick, Jacques (Jacob), viii
Kubrick, Stanley: Carlos, collaboration with, 70, 86, 133–134, 138, 147, 186–190, 228; choreographic use of music, 99, 109–110, 114, 129, 214, 237; Clarke, collaboration with, 70, 72–73; compilation album of film themes, 25–26; dissatisfaction with *Fear and Desire*, 13–14; dissatisfaction with *Spartacus*, 34; early years, vii–ix; editing film to music, ix, 76, 111, 125, 128, 129, 193, 197, 200–201, 214, 237; Fried, collaboration with, 2, 24, 28–29, 251; independence in filmmaking, 7, 13, 47, 70; musical sensibilities of, vii, 234, 250–251; Napoleon project, 47, 219; North, collaboration with, 47, 70, 78–79, 192; playing music on-set, 36, 56, 73–74, 217n63; Pook, collaboration with, 226, 228, 233–234; Raphael, collaboration with, 220, 222, 223, 230; Riddle, collaboration with, 49; Rosenman, collaboration with, 151–152, 156, 174–175; scoring techniques of, 49, 69, 234, 251; Stainforth, collaboration with, 192–193, 197, 200, 202; temp track,

use of, 73, 74, 76, 137; visual art, influence, 175, 223, 237
Kubrick, Vivian: *2001: A Space Odyssey*, 84; *Full Metal Jacket*, 60–63, 86; *The Shining*, 217–218n63

Lang, Fritz, 130
*Lawrence of Arabia*, 60
Lawson, Tony, 154
LeClair, Jean-Marie, 172
Lehmann, Hans-Thies, 220
leitmotifs, 36–38, 45
Levinson, Peter, 49, 51
*The Life and Death of Colonel Blimp*, 130–131
Ligeti, György, 82, 86, 91–95, 179, 189, 191, 192, 196–198, 201, 229, 230, 242–245, 246; *2001: A Space Odyssey*, 245; *Atmospheres*, 87, 91, 94, 95; *Aventures*, 92, 93, 95; *Eyes Wide Shut*, 196, 226, 229; *Kyrie (Requiem)*, 86, 91, 92, 94, 95, 201; *Lontano*, 86, 179, 196–198; *Lux Aeterna*, 87, 92, 197, 198, 201; *Musica Ricercata*, 226, 229–230, 238, 242–245, 246; *The Shining*, 196–198, 245; *Volumina*, 86
Liszt, Franz, 87, 155, 194, 247–248; *Nuages Gris*, 226, 234
Litvinoff, Si, 104
LoBrutto, Vincent, 2, 49, 89
*Lolita* (film), 28, 33, 47, 57, 60, 69, 104, 115, 222, 225; score, 49–57
*Lolita* (novel), 33, 47, 49, 52, 56, 104
*Lolita* (screenplay), 47–48, 53
*Look* magazine, 1, 2, 4, 18, 215n13
Lovejoy, Ray, 192
Levy, David, 123
Louis XIV, 155, 163
*The Luck of Barry Lyndon*, 147, 173–174
Lully, Jean-Baptiste, 155
Lynn, Vera, 58, 60
Lyon, Sue, 51–52, 56

*M*, 130, 131
*Mad* magazine, 106
Mahler, Gustav, 71, 151
Mainar, Luis M. Garcia, 58, 190
Mann, Anthony, 34
*The March of Time*, 1, 2, 3, 7
*Marooned*, 134
McCarten, John, 8
McClary, Susan, 124
McDowell, Malcolm, 106–107, 119, 120, 130
Mead, Abigail. *See* Vivian Kubrick
*The Memoirs of Barry Lyndon, Esq. See The Luck of Barry Lyndon*
Mendelssohn, Felix, 73, 83, 87, 131
MGM, 69, 73, 77, 86, 95, 197
Moloney, Paddy, 161
Monteverdi, Claudio, 103, 150
Moog, Bob, 133
Moog synthesizer, 110–111, 116, 117, 126–127, 133–134, 137, 138, 139, 140, 141
Motion Picture Association of America, 225
Mozart, Wolfgang, 29, 71, 87, 122, 129, 138, 150, 151, 165–166, 167, 170, 194, 228, 246; *Idomeneo*, 154, 165–166; "Rex Tremendae" (*Requiem*), 226, 246–247

Nabokov, Dmitri, 48–49
Nabokov, Vera, 48
Nabokov, Vladimir, 33, 47–48, 50, 52, 53, 105
Naremore, James, 34, 191, 222, 223
NASA, 183
Nazi party, 93, 123, 127, 130, 131, 139, 202, 231
*Network*, 184
Nietzsche, Friedrich, 88
*A Night to Remember*, 90
Noble, Ray, 211–212
North, Alex: *2001: A Space Odyssey*, 71, 77–86, 150; *Dragonslayer*, 79;

*The Shoes of the Fisherman*, 79; *Spartacus*, 34–36, 38–47, 76, 192

Ó Dornín, Peader, 158
Ó Riada, Sean, 157–159, 160
*One-Eyed Jacks*, 34, 57
*One Million Years B.C.*, 125
Ophüls, Max, 221
Orff, Karl, 71
Oscars. *See* Academy Awards

Paisiello, Giovanni, 151, 167–168
*Paths of Glory*, 13, 24, 33, 34, 45, 47, 63, 75, 84, 90, 181, 222, 252; score, 24–29, 31n40
Penderecki, Krzysztof, 179, 191, 192, 201–202, 203–204, 214, 245; *Awakening of Jacob*, 196, 202, 205, 206–207, 208; *De Natura Sonoris No.1*, 205, 207–209; *De Natura Sonoris No. 2*, 205, 206, 207–208; *Dies Irae*, 217n46; *Kanon for Orchestra and Tape*, 205, 209–210; *Polymorphia*, 205, 207–209; *St. Luke's Passion*, 201, 209; *Threnody to the Victims of Hiroshima*, 201, 208; *Utrenja*, 202, 205, 206, 209–210
Peri, Jacopo, 103
Perveler, Martin, 7
Pickens, Slim, 57
Pietrzak, Alexander, 7
Pollack, Sydney, 222
*Poltergeist*, 182
Polymoog, 189, 216n25
Pook, Jocelyn, 86, 226, 230, 233–238, 249
Potts, Sean, 161
pre-existent music in film, 29, 57, 70, 74–77, 98, 133, 138, 147, 175, 214, 251
Previn, André, 149
Prokofiev, Sergei, viii–ix, xn3, 35, 193

Purcell, Henry, 151, 162; *Funeral Music for Queen Mary,* 61, 106, 110–111, 140, 194

Rachmaninoff, Sergei, 50, 155, 194
Rapée, Erno, 74
Raphael, Frederic, 222, 223, 225, 230; *Eyes Wide Open: A Memoir of Stanley Kubrick,* 220
*Red Alert,* 57
Redman, Nick, 80
Rich, Adrienne, 124
Riddle, Nelson, 48, 49–50, 51–54
Rimsky-Korsakov, Nikolai, *Scheherazade,* 118, 137, 140
*The Road Runner Show,* 214
Rolling Stones, 63, 104–105
Roman Catholic Church, 79; Requiem Mass, 111, 193, 246
*Roots,* 29
Rosar, William H., 194
Rosenman, Leonard, 151–152, 156, 174–175
Rossini, Gioacchino, 168; *Guillaume Tell,* 116–117; *The Thieving Magpie,* 113–116, 132, 134
Rósza, Miklós, 46
Rota, Nino, 149

Sackler, Howard O., 13
Schenker, Heinrich, 124
Schiller, Friedrich, 123
*Schindler's List,* 131, 219
Schnitzler, Arthur, 220–221, 223, 248, 249
Schoenberg, Arnold, 88, 151
Schubert, Franz, 74, 131, 191, 229; German Dance No. 1 in C major, 166–167; Impromptu, Op. 90, 172–173; Piano Trio in E-flat, Op. 100, 156, 170–172
Schultheis, Bernd, ix, 14, 19, 24, 38–39, 54
*The Seafarers,* 6–7

Searby, Michael D., 197
Sellers, Peter: *Lolita,* 50; *Dr. Strangelove,* 57
Seven Years' War, 151, 158, 165, 262
Shakespeare, William, 13, 31n25
Shilkret, Nathaniel, 5, 6
Shostakovich, Dmitri, Suite for Variety Orchestra, 226, 231–233
*The Shining* (film), 33, 56, 60, 61, 70, 86, 93, 99, 175, 179, 203–204, 220, 222, 229, 245, 263–264; Carlos, Wendy and Rachel Elkind, 134, 186–190, 193–196, 228; choosing music for, 184–186; *Dies Irae,* 111, 179, 188–190, 193–195, 196, 246; differences with source material, 182, 184, 212; "It's All Forgotten Now," 212–213; Lontano (Ligeti), 179, 196–198; "Masquerade" (Hylton), 210–211; "Midnight, the Stars, and You," 211–212, 213; *Music for Strings, Percussion, and Celesta* (Bartók), 179, 191, 192, 198–201; Penderecki's music in, 196, 201–202, 205–210; "Rocky Mountains" (Carlos), 190, 195–196; "The Shining" (Carlos), 194–195; "Shining/Heartbeat" (Carlos), 190, 196, 198, 205, 207; *Valse Trieste* (Sibelius), 186; various theories of meaning of, 182–184, 191 201–202
*The Shining* (novel), 179, 182, 183, 185, 187, 212
*Shoes of the Fisherman,* 79
Sibelius, Jean, 71, 186
*The Silence of the Lambs,* 131
*The Simpsons,* 106, 181
Singer, Alex, viii, 1–2, 5
Sinatra, Frank, 49–50, 56
Snaith, Yolande, 233, 236
soundtracks to Kubrick's films: commercial availability, 267–269;

track lists, 134–137, 187–188,
152–153, 269–286
Southern, Terry, 57, 225
*Spartacus*, 28, 33, 34, 50, 56, 57, 69,
76, 77; score, 36, 38–47, 64n20,
64n21
Spielberg, Steven, 219–220, 251. *See
also A.I. Artificial Intelligence*
Stadtmueller, Fred, 5–6
Stainforth, Gordon, 192–193, 197,
200, 201, 202, 205, 207, 214
Stalin, Joseph, 201, 243, 244
*Stanley Kubrick: A Life in Pictures*, 89,
93, 187, 244
*Star Trek*, 29, 32n47, 176n7
Steadicam, 180–181, 185, 195
Steiner, Max, 37
Strauss, Johann, Jr., 93, 159; *The Blue
Danube*, 83–84, 85, 87, 89–91,
109–110; *Künsterleben* waltz, 26, 90
Strauss, Richard, 31n27, 93, 159; *Also
Sprach Zarathustra*, 75, 78, 80, 82,
85, 87–89, 95; *Der Rosenkavalier*,
87, 251–252
Stravinsky, Igor, 56, 217–218n63
Sunforest, 121
Süssmayr, Franz Xavier, 246

Thackeray, William Makepeace, 147,
148, 173
Timberline Lodge, 215n16
Tomasulo, Frank, 7
*Torn Curtain*, 66n48, 86
Tucker, Terry, 121, 137

Van Doren, Mark, 8
Varèse, Edgard, 189
Vaughn Williams, Ralph, 73
Verdi, Giuseppe, 71, 150, 194
Victor Sylvester Orchestra, 240
Visconti, Luigi, 149
Vitali, Leon, 224
Vivaldi, Antonio, 151, 155; Cello
Concerto in E Minor, 168–169
vocoder, 98, 127

Wagner, Richard, 37, 123, 124,
228–229, 253n35; *Ring Cycle*, 37,
229; *Tristan und Isolde*, 228–229;
Wesendonck Lieder, 228–230
waltz, ix, 10, 26, 28, 83–84, 89–91,
109–110, 211, 221, 231–233,
251–252
Warner Bros., 13, 105, 149, 185, 213,
219, 225, 227, 232, 250
*Wartime Lies*, 183, 219
Weidner, Jay, 183–184
Wesendonck, Mathilde, 228–229
White, Lionel, 18
Williams, John: *A.I. Artificial
Intelligence*, 251–252; leitmotifs
and, 38
Willingham, Calder, 47
World War I, 24, 112, 131, 201–202
World War II, 58, 92, 93, 131

Yogeswaran, Manickam, 238

Zeiss lenses, 175

# About the Author

**Christine Lee Gengaro** is associate professor of music at Los Angeles City College where she teaches voice, music theory, and music education. She is a graduate of the PhD program in historical musicology at the University of Southern California and has presented and published papers about classical music and popular culture in the United States and abroad. She spent her early musical life as a singer and instrumentalist, turning to musicology in graduate school. While there, she was fortunate enough to act as assistant to the editor of the *Journal of the American Musicological Society* and to serve as executive editor of the online interdisciplinary music journal *Resonance*. In addition to teaching, she is an avid writer. She is the current program annotator for the Los Angeles Chamber Orchestra, but has also written program notes for the *Mozartwoche* concert series in Vienna, the Ford Theatre Foundation, the St. Paul Chamber Orchestra, and Camerata Pacifica. She resides in Los Angeles and spends her free time writing fiction and playing music with two local bands.